Abstracts
from the
Northern Standard
and the
Red River District [Texas]

Volume 1
August 20, 1842–August 19, 1848

Richard B. Marrin and Lorna Geer Sheppard

HERITAGE BOOKS
2011

HERITAGE BOOKS
AN IMPRINT OF HERITAGE BOOKS, INC.

Books, CDs, and more—Worldwide

For our listing of thousands of titles see our website
at
www.HeritageBooks.com

Published 2011 by
HERITAGE BOOKS, INC.
Publishing Division
100 Railroad Ave. #104
Westminster, Maryland 21157

Copyright © 2006 Richard B. Marrin
and Lorna Geer Sheppard

Cover photograph courtesy of Institute of Texan Cultures

All rights reserved. No part of this book may be reproduced or transmitted in any form or by any means, electronic or mechanical, including photocopying, recording or by any information storage and retrieval system without written permission from the author, except for the inclusion of brief quotations in a review.

International Standard Book Numbers
Paperbound: 978-0-7884-3567-6
Clothbound: 978-0-7884-8970-9

Table of Contents

Introduction............................. v

A Sketch of Clarksville, the
Red River District and Northern Texas
in the 1840's............................ 1

Abstracts............................... 15

Endnotes............................... 259

Personal Name Index...................... 273

Introduction

The Northern Standard was a weekly newspaper published in Clarksville, a small town in Red River County, in the northeastern corner of Texas. The paper had been founded in 1842, three years before the independent Republic of Texas annexed itself to the United States as its twenty-eighth state. Its founder, owner and publisher was Major Charles De Morse. He would continue in those roles for nearly fifty years. Massachusetts born, Connecticut educated, the twenty-six-year-old De Morse had been a New York City lawyer, with offices on Wall Street, before coming to Texas to fight in its War of Independence from Mexico.

After independence, De Morse resumed the practice of law, not in New York but in Matagorda, Texas, a settlement of 1,650 transplanted New Englanders at the mouth of the Colorado River as it emptied into the Gulf of Mexico. He also began dabbling in newspapers, becoming a journalist for the *Daily Bulletin* in Austin, reporting on the activities of the Texas legislature.

Convinced by the leading citizens of the Red River District of the need for a newspaper for their vast region and its increasing population, De Morse founded *The Northern Standard*. He would continue to edit, publish and own it for forty-six years and the paper would grow to become the second largest in circulation in Texas. De Morse earned the dual accolades of the *Father of Texas Journalism* and *Father of the Democratic Press in Texas*. During the Civil War, he served as colonel in the Confederate Calvary and was nominated to run for governor of the state in 1873 and 1886.

For almost half a century, *The Standard*, as it came to be called, captured, in contemporaneous accounts, pictures of a developing Texas. De Morse reported firsthand on the activities of Clarksville, Red River County and the other counties of Northeastern Texas. These articles mention marriages and deaths, celebrations of their holy days and holidays, the progress of the crops, the different weather conditions, what the merchants in the square had to sell, and a hundred other threads that, woven together, present us with a tapestry of the day-to-day life of the Texas settler/pioneer from 1842 to 1848.

For the genealogist, the pages of *The Standard* are untapped resources to find ancestors who were crossing the continent in search of the American dream. Available only on microfilm, sometimes unreadable, the paper published thousands of advertisements, public and legal notices, announcements of weddings and deaths, lists of letters waiting at the post office and scores of other items, identifying citizens of the region.

This work is intended to dig out and index those identities, buried for 150 years. Because of the difficulty in reading some water damaged issues of *The Standard*-a small percentage of the material-best efforts have been made at spelling and middle initials. Names may be spelled differently in different issues so the reader must look closely at near spellings. Sometimes initials are given, sometimes the first name. Is James J. Ward (whose name appears thirteen times) the same person as J. Ward, J. J. Ward or Jas. J. Ward, each of whom is mentioned once? And what about Jas. J. Ward Sr. or Jas J. Ward Jr.? At other times, it is difficult to read an initial and variants are provided. Also, there are instances where an individual's name may appear in more than one place in a particular issue, although the index will not indicate it.

The authors apologize for these imperfections. We have done the best we can.

A SKETCH OF CLARKSVILLE, RED RIVER COUNTY AND NORTHERN TEXAS IN THE 1840s

It might be helpful for the reader, who finds an ancestor in the pages of *The Standard,* to learn more about the society in which his kin lived. Items from *The Standard* may be given some flesh, if we begin with a brief overview of Charles De Morse, Clarksville and Red River County during the period 1842 through 1848.[1]

Red River County was huge in those days. It was the mother county, in whole or part, to thirty-nine present-day Texas counties. When Texas completed its annexation to the United States, Clarksville was still a hamlet, not much more than a dozen years old. It stood at the edge of the pine forests of East Texas and the lightly wooded and highly fertile blackland prairie that stretched westward, seemingly forever. It was an outgrowth of the first permanent American settlement in Texas at Pecan Point in 1815 on the Red River. Before that, it had been the home of the Caddo Indians[2] and the roaming grounds of the elk, buffalo, mustang and numerous other wild animals.

The town had been named after its founder, James Clark, a Tennessee-born adventurer of Scotch ancestry, and his wife Isabella.[3] He convinced an immigrating family—that of Isaac Smathers—to stop and settle there. As an inducement, he gave Smathers a choice lot and enlisted the efforts of neighbors to erect, in a single day, a log house for him. The next day, they built a house for Clark as well and the Town of Clarksville was off and running.

Who were the people of Clarksville and the other villages beginning to pop up around Texas? What were they like? From where had they come? Were they self-reliant? Good neighbors? Lawless or lawful? Healthy or ailing? These are a few of but scores of questions about the people who settled Clarksville and towns like it across northern Texas.[4]

More questions include, What did small western towns look like 150 years ago? How were they laid out? Where were the stores and blacksmith shops, the churches and saloons, the homes of its citizens? Was there crime—gun fights in the street, as in the movies? Was there fun? Were the woods really full of wild animals and Indians? What did farmers raise and what did they do with it when they raised it? What holidays did the people celebrate? Did the children go to school? These are all aspects of daily life that rarely make the history books.

Let's look at the town of Clarksville, as preserved by *The Standard*, to answer some of these questions.

Clarksville claimed to have a population of 750, but it may have exaggerated a bit so as to boast itself a town. The 1848 census showed just 633 persons in town: 422 white and 204 slaves and 5 not described, which probably indicated freed slaves. The county seat, Clarksville, had a sixth of the total population of the entire county of Red River. The county had a white population of 2,316, a slave population of 1,456 and nineteen freed slaves. Compare this to Texas as a whole, which had a population of 100,508 whites, 35,038 slaves and 229 free blacks.[5] However, as impressive as was the growth of the nation's twenty-eighth state, it had still but a tiny fraction, less than one percent, of the United States' population of 23,298,000.

The core of Texas population had been Anglos and Mexicans; descendants of pioneers who had settled in Texas a generation earlier, while it was a state of Mexico. They fought successfully for their independence in 1835. After that, new settlers came in waves to northern Texas from all the states of the Union. More were from the South than the North, and the southern planters brought with them their African-American slaves, without whom growing cotton would have been physically and economically impossible. Emigrants from foreign lands came too, many from Germany and France, but from all of Western Europe. Some Native Americans were peaceful, like the Choctaw, Caddos and Delaware in the north and east. Others were wild and warlike, Comanches and Apaches among them, in central, south and west Texas.

The citizens of Clarksville had their social and religious sides and often the two merged.

Clarksville has been called the Cradle of Protestantism[6] in Texas, because it was the site of the first Protestant preaching in Texas, then a state of Catholic Mexico.[7] Benjamin Clark, a veteran of the American Revolution,[8] was the father of James Clark, who founded Clarksville. Another son of his, Gilbert, also a Methodist preacher, settled in Clarksville and brought Methodism to the village as did the Reverend John Witherspoon Pettigrew McKenzie.[9] The still flourishing First Presbyterian Church of Clarksville had as its predecessor a congregation organized in June 1833 by the Rev. Milton Estill.[10] Arguably, Protestantism had its beginnings in Texas with these early churches.

Associated loosely with the churches were fraternal organizations: the Masons, the Sons of Temperance,[11] the Knights Templar and the Odd Fellows, to name several. They espoused what today we would call small-town values, including being a good neighbor and fellow citizen.

Red River County also enjoyed a plentiful supply of timber that stood nearby. A neighboring forest was crucial. Without a ready supply of good timber, houses and commercial buildings could not be erected and farms could not be fenced.[12] When timber became scarce with more and more immigrants, brick became an alternative.[13] Fresh water was also ample, maybe inexhaustible; nothing less than the prior winter's rainfall, which in Clarksville is usually copious. It was also a healthy climate as De Morse frequently bragged, free from the cholera and yellow fever epidemics that periodically inflicted the rest of Texas.

Groceries, cotton gins, and lumber and grain mills, serving the farmers, became centers of tiny settlements scattered throughout the countryside. However, clustered in larger towns like Clarksville, were the merchants, professional men, "mechanics" and artisans of different sorts: tinners, carpenters, and smiths, among them. They gathered about the public square, which in Clarksville, like most Texas county seats, was smack in the middle of the town. A courthouse anchored the square, drawing the citizens of the county to town on a regular basis. The original courthouse in Clarksville was a double log cabin that had been built about 1834. Court was in session twice a year, for at least a two-week period each time, sometimes longer. This activity brought to town a flock of lawyers from other counties, as well as the participants in the lawsuits: the plaintiffs and defendants, the witnesses, the jurors and the curious. Politicians, railroad promoters and pedlars of patent medicines and other products took advantage of the large crowds to ply their goods. Often, there was entertainment during these court weeks: balls, horse races and traveling shows. Clarksville was a bustling town during court week. To capture this traffic, businesses bought up the lots on the square, which led to more traffic and more commercial interests, thereby increasing the value of the surrounding acreage. That was how Clarksville had started.[14]

None of the first edition structures on Clarksville's square remain, due to major fires in 1851 and 1856, and the normal ravages of time, hurried along by man's desire to always build bigger and better. The brick buildings that stand today on parts of the square did not follow the second fire by much. Visit the square today and imagine dirt streets crowded with wagons, not cars; with elevated boardwalks instead of sidewalks; and the image of old Clarksville reappears.

Clarksville was on a major route into Texas for the immigrants who crossed at Jonesboro. It had a thriving hotel business on the square: Mrs. Donoho's Hotel, Thompson's, and the Star Hotel.

Many of these businesses advertised in *The Standard*, identified themselves to readers as being "on the Square." Sometimes, they revealed the actual side of the square, north, south, east or west, where they were. Even a partial list, taken from the advertising sections of *The Standard*, reveals how varied the Clarksville's businesses community was. For example, if a visitor to town wanted to purchase clothes, he or she had a choice. Alexander's, a ladies dress shop, bragged as having the "tastiest articles in the way of Ladies Dresses that has ever been in Clarksville--laces, fringes, ribbons, and scarfs etc." J. P. and C. C. Dale, called themselves "merchant tailors" and advertised "ready made clothing of all kinds and qualities." Oliver & Chatfield, proudly displaying a cowboy boot as its logo, offered "Ladies' Fine Gaitesets" and men's and children's shoes, as well as hats "of the latest style." W. P. Dickson & Co, located on the East Side of the Public Square, carried "general merchandise" and James Gordon advertised "spring and summer goods." There was a "mattress manufactory" on Main Street, one door above Raines Blacksmith shop that sold both "cotton shuck" and "spring mattresses." There appeared to be enough business to keep two jewelers competitive.

If food were the object of the visit to the Square, Gilbert Ragin had a "food shop: fruits, confections and eatables of various sorts." Mrs. Lee's confectionary with candies and cakes was next to Thomson's Hotel. Mr. John Farret, also a confectioner, had "some choice apples and edibles of various kinds at [his] neat establishment on Main Street."

Physicians clustered about the square. Drs. Barry & Moore, for example, had their "medicine & surgery offices" at Mrs. Donoho's Hotel. A surgeon dentist was next door. Wholesale and resale druggists could be found at the southeastern corner of the Square. All but a very few lawyers, had their offices in one of the county seats, usually near the Courthouse: "on the south west side of the Public Square" or "next door the District Clerk's" or "next to store of John Gordon" or even "upstairs in the Courthouse."

The equivalent to today's gas stations and garages were livery stables and Clarksville did not lack them. Messrs. Thompson had a "fine large commodious and well stocked livery stable on Mulberry Street between the Masonic Hall and Church Street," a little south of the square. F. M. Sims was a "Wagon Maker and carriage repairer" and blacksmith. Mr. West's black smith's shop was nearby as was Shanahan's and Brim's Cabinet Shop and Chair Manufactory. Shanahan also made coffins and took care of funeral arrangements.

The public square served other purposes than as a market. Clarksville was only ten miles from the Red River. Toward the end of winter or in early spring, when the Red River rose sufficiently to let the steamers from Shreveport and New Orleans up as far as the Clarksville landing, the town became hectic again. Wagons full of cotton passed through it, on their way to deposit their season's harvest at dockside for the expected steamboats. These steamboats had not arrived empty. Their cargos up river were merchandise for the storekeepers on the square to sell.

There was a surprising number of private boarding schools in and around Clarksville, which had become the major educational center of northern Texas from the first days[15] through the Civil War. Affluent planters would send their children, male and female alike,[16] to these schools. The students and staffs of the several schools were a vital part of the community. Upwards of fifty percent of the town's white population of five hundred were students from different parts of Texas and Arkansas!

The academic year consisted of two sessions of five months each. The first started usually toward the end of January, the second around August, with a month back home for the students in between sessions. At the end of the terms, just before the students returned home, there were the dreaded "examinations." Unlike today, where students display what they have learned in tests taken on paper and privately graded by the teacher, the examinations of the 1840s were more public, with family and townspeople in attendance. After they were completed, there would be celebrations, usually dances at one of Clarksville's hotels on the square.

Three miles out of town to the southwest was McKenzie College, higher in the level of the education than the academies and institutions. Named after its founder and president, a Methodist minister, it began in 1841. Its first school building was a log cabin, sixteen by eighteen feet, with a log left out on one side to provide ventilation for the students crowded within. There were two dormitories, one for women and one for men. They were named Graft and Duke after the two carpenters who had constructed them. Later, it expanded to four large buildings on nine hundred acres. According to De Morse, "the number of students in this institute [was] greater than any other private school in Texas or perhaps in the Southwest. It is attended by scholars from all parts of Texas."[17]

And, of course, there was always activity when those four-horse stages would pull in several times a week from Little Rock, Waco, Austin or Shreveport,[18] loaded with visitors and the mail.[19]

What was there to do for fun in Clarksville and its Red River countryside, a century and a half ago? There were no Dairy Queens, movie houses, or malls, save the public square, for folks to congregate and visit. Yet, as *The Standard* bears witness, the citizens had a full, wholesome social life.

Weddings were then, as now, times to celebrate. Increasingly, more of the fairer sex, homegrown or from the thousands immigrating to Texas from other parts of the United States and Europe, made weddings the most common social activity. *The Standard* often published something endearing about the newlyweds, especially if the couple had observed the custom then of sending a piece of the wedding cake (and sometimes wine) to the editor of the paper.

Clarksville entertainment ranged from the intellectual to the sedate, from the boring to almost "devil may care" conduct. On the least exciting end of the spectrum were the church sermons, the talks on temperance, political oratory and the occasional visiting professor who lectured on the new sciences of biology and psychology. Musical entertainment was big in Clarksville. There were plenty of willing musicians of different performance levels: students, accomplished amateurs and professionals. Clarksville's two girls schools, the Clarksville Female Academy and the Clarksville Female Institute, regularly held concerts for parents and friends to show off the their students' progress. The public was always invited.

On occasion, professional talent came through town and put on shows, especially as the town became more settled: traveling circuses, troupes of performers like Johnson's Southern Minstrels, juggling and dancing.

The ladies of the Methodist Church in town had a concert and *"tableaux"* to raise money. A *tableau vivant*, French for "living picture," was the representation of a picture or scene by people properly costumed and posed.

Dancing was also big in Clarksville a century and a half ago. The town had its own instructor and "balls" were popular among the young and adults. Usually, they were associated with holidays and were held in one of the hotels in town and cost about $2.50 to $3.00 per person.

The Texans of the 1840s and 1850s celebrated holidays as well, chief among them the Fourth of July.[20] The citizens of Clarksville took very seriously their duty to commemorate the nation's founding. The senior men of the community sat in formal session to plan the day's events. It was quite special and dear to them. In many cases, their grandfathers had fought in the American Revolution. Some of the citizens themselves had been in the Texas Revolution against Mexico in 1835, which had been patterned on the American Revolution. They knew well the sacrifices made and the peril encountered by their forebears and they were careful that Independence Day was properly observed.

Clarksville had about 750 residents in 1846, many of whom would join the townspeople in the center of the town for the festivities. Often the day began with, or featured, a parade or procession[21] that would start or end in the public square.

A reading of the Declaration of Independence was delivered by the best speakers in the area. The "Grand Barbecue" that followed the speeches and singing was "made up of choice materials with enough to spare." There was no lack of food in Red River County and the cooks "did things up brown" so that the public dinner was as generous and tasty as imagination can picture. After dinner, the townspeople danced!

While the Fourth of July was the most intensely celebrated holiday, it was not the only one. Texas, of course, had its own Day of Independence, March 2, commemorating that day in 1835 when Texas declared her independence from Mexico. For the first-generation Texans like De Morse, who had participated in the war and who had been citizens of the Republic of Texas for the decade of her existence, there was a deeper feeling for the day than newcomers could appreciate. The day was observed in much the same way that the Fourth of July was with speeches, parades and dinners. De Morse urged that the holiday be regularly celebrated.

May 1, May Day, is an ancient holiday, once celebrated with dancing around ribboned Maypoles and the crowning of "Queens of the May" to preside over the festivities. It might not have been how May Day had been celebrated on the village green in Merry Old England some centuries before, but there were some telltale similarities. Maidens still figured prominently in the celebration. They were provided by the two well-reputed girls' schools in town. The sponsor changed from year to year.[22]

Thanksgiving, of course, can be traced back to the Pilgrims in 1621 and has been celebrated regularly since then.[23] The people of Clarksville did as well. The week between Christmas and New Year's was one long holiday. "The Christmas holidays come but once a year and there is a general disposition in this land (where necessity does not drive men like beasts of prey) to enjoy them." De Morse wrote, calling it "the annual week of leisure and recreation." He would shut down *The Standard* for the last week of December to give himself and his staff a week of rest. Instead of work, the townspeople, "especially the juvenile portion," would enjoy public balls and private social gatherings.

Holiday celebrations, like July Fourth, brought people from the country into town. So did the immigrant wagons that had crossed the Red River at Jonesboro from Arkansas and points east. They needed to resupply themselves in Clarksville for the rest of their trip west to the Texas frontier.

Often our pictures of a frontier town are of windy, dusty streets, primitive structures, a sheriff's office, a place to get a drink and the like. Clarksville does not prove to the point, however. If anything, the contrary was true. According to *The Standard* and De Morse, Clarksville was a neat, prosperous community. The citizens encouraged each other to keep their town attractive to these newcomers, especially to the immigrants, who were looking for a place to settle. De Morse urged that a portion of the square be made into a park, that attractive trees be planted around town, that commercial signs be set out to help direct the traveler in his shopping, but that they be appropriate.

It is difficult for us today to imagine a Texas without highways and airports, connecting and making manageable the enormity of the state's geography. A century ago, it was the railroad that was the modern wonder. It and the telegraph wires that ran alongside the track would revolutionize communications and travel within Texas and to the outside world. However, totally forgotten is the time, a generation before the railroad, when internal transportation depended on the rivers of Texas.[24]

The Red River is 1,360 miles long, the second longest in Texas. It stretches from the Mississippi and the Gulf of Mexico on one end, north to Arkansas, west across the entire state of Texas and then into the mountains of New Mexico. A key to the success of Clarksville and the settlement of the towns of the Red River Valley and North Texas was the landing or docks along the Red River. It permitted Texas to hook into the river commerce. One landing was just ten miles north of Clarksville. It had some stores, warehouses, and its own name, Roland.[25] At Roland and other river ports in winter and springtime as the "navigation" of the river permitted, the planters of North Texas would send their cotton by steamboat or flatboat down the Red River to Shreveport, where the Red River joined the Mississippi. From Shreveport, the market in New Orleans was only two days away by steamer. After the cotton was sold in New Orleans, it would be transported on sailing ships to the cotton and textile mills of either New England or London, where thousands upon thousands of workers waited to turn nature's fiber into fabrics of fashion.[26]

The prairie of northern Texas drew the interest of early settlers. It was certainly fertile. The Caddo Indians had cultivated corn, beans and squash there with agricultural methods no more sophisticated than burning the ground cover, punching the soil with a pointed stick and dropping in a seed.

The land was inexpensive, even compared to other places in Texas. For example, in central Texas, around Austin, farmland in the immediate vicinity of the town—that is, from one to ten miles outside—cost ten to twenty-five dollars an acre. In the Red River Valley it could be had for two dollars an acre or less. Compared to other parts of the United States, buying land in Texas was a smart choice. People from the East could sell their worn-out lands at high prices—there being a demand for land in the populated East—and use the proceeds to buy a much larger tract of fertile virgin soil. It was why many came west.

In the 1840s, cotton was king: the U.S. crop was worth sixty-five million dollars. The economies of England and New England were as dependent upon it as were the South and Texas.[27] De Morse reported in *The Standard* of December 10, 1842 that Alexander Mabane, living upon the River in Lamar county, had picked 24,000 pounds of seed cotton from six acres of land. His whole field of forty-five acres had averaged 3,300 pounds per acre.

While De Morse knew that cotton needed to be the principal crop of northern Texas, he nevertheless advocated that more wheat be grown. It made sense. There was a strong local market, a number of military posts to be supplied, many hungry immigrants arriving in the state and, when the wheat was milled into flour, it could be exported to New Orleans by river.[28]

A variety of "table vegetables" and fruits were also grown in North Texas on both the larger plantations and in the small gardens of the townspeople. De Morse ran contests for the largest fruits and vegetables from the North Texas region. A year's subscription to *The Standard* was usually the prize.[29] There was also a wide variety of fruit for sale, often in wagons in the streets of the towns: watermelons, apples, plums and pears.

The farmers of North Texas grew a lot of corn as well. At first, corn had been grown for domestic consumption or for export to neighboring counties.[30] Corn could also be sold to the immigrants who needed it to carry them through winter until they could plant their own crops.

The Standard reported on a variety of other crops besides cotton, wheat, corn and traditional fruits and vegetables, such as pecans, "mast" (a product of the pine forest, such as needles and acorns, that made excellent feed for hogs), even tobacco, and, later, Chinese sugar cane.[31]

In the 1840s and 1850s Texas was not yet known for its cattle or cowboys. That would come after the Civil War. However, the early planters did raise livestock. For example, *The Standard* reported on a three-and-a-half-year-old hog, fattened for only four months, which weighed 402 pounds.[32] De Morse also tried to convince northern Texans to adopt sheep raising and thereby substitute wool for cotton as its principal crop. Cattle were beginning to play an important role. In 1844, the annual consumption of cattle in Texas would be about 24,000 head. De Morse predicted that would increase at the rate of thirty percent annually.

Climate can be either a blessing or a bane and, often, the line between "enough" and "too much" of a good thing is very thin. Today, Clarksville's climate is relatively mild, with sufficient precipitation to permit large scale agriculture. Winters are moderate with only occasional cold waves, while the summers are typically long and warm. The average mean temperature is 64 degrees Fahrenheit. The mean temperature in January is 44 and, for July, 83. The average rainfall is 43.5 inches. It is not normally a stormy place, except during the tornado season, and then it sometimes is a very stormy place.

Was the climate the same a century and a half ago? Regular weather records do not appear to have been taken in Texas until the 1870s. *The Standard,* however, goes back to August 1842, and each issue usually provided some inkling of the weather outside, sometimes as separate items, other times associated with reports on the progress of the river or the prospects for the crops. Aberrations in the weather patterns were duly noted.

For example, *The Standard's* first report on extraordinary weather was in its January 28, 1843 issue. Huge winter "freshets"—the surges from rivers and creeks, fed by torrents of rain and swollen beyond their banks—swept away everything in their path, including the town of Jonesboro on the Red River. The overflow had been "greater and more destructive than is within the recollection of the oldest settlers in this section of country, a period of 23 or 24 years. It is, at this time, probably fourteen feet higher than has ever before been known."

The winter of 1843 that began with this destructive freshet was an extraordinarily cold one across Texas. In mid-March, several inches of snow fell in Clarksville and the cold was described as "intense."[33] Sometimes the precipitation and cold coincided. A late November ice storm in 1848 "came in the form of sleet which covered everything exposed. The smallest twigs of the trees were covered in ice, in the quantity of ten times their own bulk, while the larger limbs and fences and house tops, showed a regularly increased surface of an inch thickness."[34] Perhaps with some hyperbole, De Morse claimed in the December 8, 1848 paper that "a look out upon the prairie gave to the sight a look of utter desolation, an appearance worthy of the Russian wild in the dead of winter, except, perhaps, in that there would be more snow, while this was all ice."

The next summer, 1844, unusually high temperatures predominated with heat for a two- or three-week period "more oppressive than we have ever before felt it, during our residence in the Republic." The thermometer had been at 90 in the shade and 141 in the sun, according to *The Standard* of August 7, 1844. The heat was accompanied by drought, and the people, livestock and crops of the region all suffered mightily.[35]

On the other hand, most years, rain in northern Texas is by no means a rarity. The Red River Valley can be a rainy place, but that is not necessarily a curse to an agricultural region. Some years, however, it can be *very* rainy. In fact, for years, Clarksville held the Texas record for annual rainfall, 109.38 inches in 1873, more than two and a half time its normal. The average in Texas is about twenty-seven inches.

The year 1849 must have been a wet whopper as well. No detailed records were kept, but a year long litany in *The Standard* is proof enough that it was severe. Sleet and very cold rains—sometimes just drizzle—lasted all winter, so much so that De Morse complained that it was the worst he had seen in his thirteen years in Texas. A few weeks later, the editor *pro tem*, who filled in for De Morse and had lived in Texas for twelve years, concurred. Sleet and very cold rains, sometimes hard, sometimes just drizzling, were to last all winter.

Spring brought hail storms. One day in May, there were three of them with hail the size of which ranged "from small rifle balls to small hens eggs." There was rain, rain and more rain, which greatly affected planting and the growth of crops.[36] It almost rained out the Fourth of July celebration, caused flooding which washed out two of Clarksville's bridges over the Delaware Creek, and brought De Morse to his breaking point. He reached into the Bible for the only comparison he had left: "The Floods—One of the Olden Times and the One Present."

There are some surprises, however. Red River Valley is known today as Tornado Alley, yet in the eighteen years of *The Standard* from 1842 to 1858, only two such storms were reported, both in the 1850's.[37] One was in Cooke County, west of Gainesville, in 1854 where six lives and much property were lost. It knocked down houses, killed cattle, and carried fences out of sight, sparing only those who hid in cellars and the bottoms of dry creek beds. The other tornado was reported near Dallas and wiped out a small settlement. Why so few?

Anyway, if the reader finds an ancestor within, this may give an idea of how she or he lived. In some ways, it was not unlike today. In other ways, it was a time of grit, hard work and values that may never come again.

ABTRACTS FROM *THE NORTHERN STANDARD*

From The Northern Standard, August 20, 1842

married
on August 4, 1842 by the Reverend Samuel Corley, Mr. William McAdams to Miss Sarah Turner, both of Red River County

on August 4, 1842 by the Reverend Samuel Corley, Mr. Isaac Matthews to Miss Mary Turner, both of Red River County

on August 7, 1842 by [Thomas] Williams, Esq., Mr. James Clark to Miss Nancy Kenner, both of Red River County

on August 9, 1842 by the Reverend Samuel Corley, Mr. Colin Aims to Miss Harriet Potter, both of Red River County

on August 11, 1842 by the Reverend Samuel Corley, Mr. Mont Vaughn to Miss Roseanne Lawes, both of Red River County

on August 11, 1842 by the Reverend Samuel Corley, Mr. Abner McKenzie to Mrs. Mary Denton, both of Red River County

political and election news[38]
the following have announced their candidacy for public office
Colonel W. Sims, Candidate for County Surveyor
Sam Huffer, Candidate for County Surveyor

W. B Stout, Chief Justice of Red River County, announces the election for the representative from Red River County to the Congress of the Republic of Texas. Voting to take place at the following polling locations with presiding officers as indicated.

Poll location	Presiding officer
at Andrew Titus'	James Atkinson
at John Stiles'	John Stiles

at Ulysses Auglier's	Thos. F. Bayarly
at Clarksville	John T. Clark
at Clarksville	Wm. Donoho
at William Gregg's	A.H. McKinzie
at Wm. Humphries'	Isaac Wilson
at John Robbins'	Jas. W. Green
at Travis G. Wright's	Wm. Mayo
at Jonesborough	Gideon Mims
at Ripleys'	H.H. Clifton
at Fort Sherman	Jno. Brewer
at Uriah Moons'	Jesse Janes
at Daingerfield	W. J. Hamilton
at Daniel Bancroft's	K.A. Wellborn
at Meyers'	Wm. Merrill
at Smithland	Charles Janes

commercial announcements
Joseph Harrison and Wm. M. Harrison, partners in Joseph Harrison & Co. will continue in the sale of goods in their store in Clarksville.

Wright & Montgomery advertises its store in Clarksville

Charles W. Russell advertises his services for bricklaying

lost head right certificate[39]
notice by John B. Carter that he has lost or mislaid his Head Right certificates, and those of James Berry, Wm. Y. Lacey and William McCown and that, if not found, he will apply for new ones

strays[40]
notice by C.S. Young, four miles east of Clarksville, that his horse has strayed or been stolen

notice by Charles W. Russell that his horse has strayed or been stolen

administration of estates [41]
notice that Henrietta Basin has been appointed executrix of the Estate of George Basin, deceased

notice that George Gordon and Charles Aims have been appointed executors of the estate of Robert Potter

professional cards
Dr. J. Herrick
Dr. George Gordon
Dr. Parks
Dr. S. Kinzey (Office at residence of James W. Sims

B. H. Martin
Attorney and Counselor at Law, Clarksville "Will attend to various courts of the 7th Judicial District"

Eben'r Allen, Attorney at Law --Clarksville

E. H. Tarrant, Attorney at Law --Boston, Bowie County

John H. Craig, Attorney at Law -- Clarksville

Wm. C. Young, Attorney at Law --Clarksville, Red River County

H. R. Latimer, Attorney at Law -- Clarksville

Charles De Morse, Attorney and Counselor at Clarksville, "will practice only in Criminal Cases and the collection of Foreign Debts"
****

From The Northern Standard, August 27, 1842

court news
article complimenting Hon. John T. Mills, Justice of the 7th Judicial District.

married
on Thursday evening, [August 25, 1842] by Ulysses Auglier, Esq., Thos. F. Bayarly to Mrs. Minerva Ann Oliver, both of Red River County

on August 21, 1842 by the Reverend Samuel Corley, Mr. Andrew Vaugey to Miss Louisa Willow, both of Lamar County

lawsuits filed [42]
notice of filing of divorce action in the County of Lamar by Edward Stuart against Polly Stuart, *aka* Polly Brown, given by A.G. Kimbell, Clerk of Lamar County by John R. Craddock, Deputy Clerk

notice of filing of divorce action in the County of Lamar by Salina Davit against Samuel K. Davit, given by A.G. Kimbell, Clerk of Lamar County by John R. Craddock, Deputy Clerk

notice of filing of divorce action in the County of Lamar by John J. Nicholson against Elizabeth Nicholson, given by A.G. Kimbell, Clerk of Lamar County by John R. Craddock, Deputy Clerk

notice of filing of divorce action in the County of Lamar by William Bledsoe against Adalina Bledsoe, given by A.G. Kimbell, Clerk of Lamar County by John R. Craddock, Deputy Clerk

administration of estates
R.W. Lee appointed Administrator of Estate of Daniel R. Jackson of Fannin County

lost head right certificate
notice by Elinor Langsford, Clarksville, for lost certificate
****

From The Northern Standard, September 3, 1842

court news
The Grand Jurors for the County of Lamar thank the Hon. John T. Mills, Presiding Judge and the District attorney, John Benton Jr for their assistance in the most recent session of the Grand Jury. The Grand Jury consisted of:

C.B. Bonner, Foreman	J. B. Hill
John O. Clark	Alex'r Benner
Robert Ragsdale	Jon. B. S. Ewing
Charles Logan	J. H. Mabane
W. Barren	J. W. Riley
Z. Birdwell	D. K. Pace
Daniel T. Alexander	
W. M. Berris	

Thomas Jackson, Bailiff
A.G. Kimbell, Clerk
John R. Craddock, Deputy Clerk

administration of estates
John Jackson and Rachael Jackson appointed administrators of the Estate of Bushred W. Osburn.

Charles Aimes and George Gordon appointed administrators of the Estate of Robert Potter.
****

From The Northern Standard, September 10, 1842

Texas wildlife
seen at the residence of John Robbins in Goez Prarie, a buffalo Calf, which was brought from the headwaters of the Sabine, about 50 miles from town and was part of a herd which numbered at least 500 heads

entertainment news
To appear in Clarksville, E. L. Harvey and display his talent of ventriloquism and mimicry; tickets, fifty cents each, may be had

at the grocery of Mr. Regin or at the door in the evening.

Mr. C. W. Russel informs citizens of Clarksville hat he will give a series of dramatic presentations, and singing and dancing

school news
advertisement for Mrs. Weathered's Pine Creek Female Institute, James H. Johnston, President

married
on September 4, 1842, by the Reverend Samuel Corley, Alfred Aikins to Mary Anne Roup

administration of estates
Edward Wideman, administrator of the Estate of Joseph Dick has filed his accounting of same and will be discharged; by order issued of Wm. B. Stout, Chief Justice and *ex officio* Judge of Probate for Red River County and J. C. Hart, Clerk for, and *ex officio* Clerk of, Probate for Red River County

John Emberson, appointed administrator of the Estate of John Emberson has filed his accounting of same and will be discharged; by orders of Wm. B. Stout, and J. C. Hart.

Samuel Fulton, administrator of the Estate of Andrew Lee, has filed his accounting of same and will be discharged; by orders of Wm. B. Stout and J. C. Hart, Clerk for, and *ex officio* Clerk of, Probate for Red River County

William C. Harrison, administrator of the Estate of J. G. Mahlin, has filed his accounting of same and will be discharged by orders of Wm. B. Stout and J. C. Hart

James G Wright, administrator of the Estate of Lewis T. King, has filed his accounting of same and will be discharged by orders of Wm. B. Stout and J. C. Hart.
****

From the Northern Standard, September 17, 1842

agricultural news
Mr. R. G. Miller of Lamar county writes that he raised 30 bushels of wheat to the acre.

Gilbert Clark advertises sheep for sale at his premises near Clarksville

newspaper business
William T. Montgomery, Esq. will attend to the *Standard* during De Morse absence

married
on September 15, 1842 by the Reverend Samuel Corley, W. C. Ingram to Miss Sarah Pope

professional card
Brad C. Fowler, attorney
****

From The Northern Standard, September 24, 1842

commercial announcement
Chas. W. Russels. merchant, advertises STAR CANDY for sale at his store in Clarksville during the Court weeks

miscellaneous
thank you to Mr Donohe from a "Traveler" who stayed at the Clarksville House

runaway slaves
notice by Lemuel Blanton regarding two runaway slaves, Isaac and Harriet, taken up and belonging to James Avery, living in Louisiana, Caddo Parish

land for sale
advertisement by James H. Johnson as to tracts of land for sale, situated on Red River, in what is known as Jonesboro Prairie

administration of estates
D. Rowett appointed administrator of the Estate of Jacob Black.

Mary F. Morgan appointed administrator of the Estate of Peter Morgan

Priscilla Stephens appointed administrator of the Estate of John Stevens

lawsuit filed
notice by Clerk of Court to Urias Pace that he has been sued in trespass by John G. Jewett

lost head right certificate
lost head right certificate, advertised by Joseph Cox
****

From The Northern Standard, October 1, 1842

agricultural news
L. Hopkins, near Clarksville, had two "boys" who picked 607 pounds of clean merchantable cotton in one day between them

a "yellow" boy, named Isaac, belonging to Mr. Besky picked 340 lbs.

public notice
all claims against Red River County should be filed with J. C. Hart, as per order of W. B. Stout

stop payment[43]
stop payment of note given by Isaiah H Lawton to John Meek because underlying purchase of slave did not comport with bill of sale
****

The Northern Standard, October 8, 1842 issue was not published
****

From The Northern Standard, October 15, 1842

commercial announcements
J. R. Tanner advertises his stoneware "manufactory" at Marshall, in Harrison County

William Selfe advises the residents of Clarksville that he provides instructions in Music, upon the Violin, Flute, Flagcol and Key Bugle

local references for New Orleans commission broker McMahon, Trotter and Pearsell includes William M. Harrison of Clarksville, Major James E. Browning of Dekalb and Col. Charles Lewis of Bowie.

R. M. Hopkins has opened the grocery formerly owned by B. W. Osburn in Clarksville

political and election news
M. W. Matthews, the Representative from Red River County to the Congress of the Republic of Texas, will be in Clarksville to receive from his constituents any instructions they may want to give him.

letters left at post office [44]
list of letters in Clarksville post office from May 31, 1842 through September 21, 1842. If not picked up by December 31, 1842, they will be sent to the GPO as dead letters:

Beird, William
Baly, C. C.
Box, James
Bowers, William
Bundress, Isaac
Bledsoe, George B.
Cowen, Thomas
Crew, Enoch
Corper, Alfred
English, James C.
Fowler, Elizabeth

Frasels, Robert
Ferguson, Richard
Hooker, Samuel
Hampton, John
Hammock, J.
James, Henry
Jackson, Edmund
Legwood, Thomas Y.
Morgan, Joseph
McClure, W.C.
Milligan or Latimer

McKnight, William
Morrell, Amos
Pry, Peter or D. Gallaway
Rogers, Mary Jane
Reviere, William K.
Smith, E.M.
Smith, Robert B.
Silkwood, Mrs. P.
Stanley, Fermay

South, Charles
Thompson, Wiley
Worthington, Christy
Walker, Benjamin
Ragweed, Thomas
Wait, Pator

John Morton, Post Master

lost property
L. J. Pollock has lost notes signed by Wm. Sparks in favor of Christopher Jones

lost discharge in favor of William Cole, assigned to John R. Carter

lost head right certificate
lost or mislaid Francis Smith's head right certificate

stop payment
Caution: L .J. Pollock has put into the hands of Robert C. Graves for collection notes of Livingston Skinner, Allen Urquhart, William Hughs, J. V. Cherry and David Bouton, the proceeds of which has not been remitted to him

stop payment on note given by John R. Carter to George F. Lawton

stop payment of note made by Isaiah Lawson payable to John Meek

administration of estates
Mark Roberts appointed administrator of the Estate of Joseph Lowell.

Daniel Montaque, who is the administrator of the Estates of Jesse Wallace, Alfred Clark and H. Bryant has filed his accountings of same and will be discharged by orders of James O'Neal, Chief Justice of Fannin County and Judge of Probate Court for Fannin and R.W. Lee, Clerk of same.

Benjamin Kendell, administrator of the Estate of Joseph Kendell has filed his accounting of same and will be discharged; by orders issued by Wm. B. Stout, Chief Justice and *ex officio* Judge of Probate for Red River County and J. C. Hart, Clerk for, and ex officio Clerk of Probate of, Red River County
****

From the Northern Standard, October 22, 1842

public notice
those subscribers who have not paid up for the building of the County jail for Red River should pay Major West by order of W. W. Lewis and William Comb

administration of estates
Martin Poor appointed by Bowie Probate court administrator of the Estate of John R. Roger.
****

From The Northern Standard, October 29, 1842

agricultural news
Dr. Kinzie, has a sweet potato grown on the plantation of Mr. John Bourland, Esq. 18 inches in circumference, 12 inches long and weighing 7 pounds.

T. G. Wright, Esq. of Pine Creek has a sweet potato that weights 8 3/4 pounds, is 19 3/4 inches in circumference and 22 inches in length.

newspaper business
Travis G. Wright, P.M., Pine Creek
Samuel M. Fulton, P.M., Franklin, Lamar County
William Brown, Paris, Lamar County
John B. Craddock, Paris, Lamar County
J. W.O. Stanfield, P.M., Harrison County

Jesse Shelton, Fort Shelton, Lamar County
J. A. Caldwell, Warren, Fannin County
Bailey English, P.M., Fort English, Fannin County
D. Rowlett, P.M., Lexington, Fannin, County
J. G. Jewett, P.M., Raleigh Fannin County
J. J. Williams P.M., Dekalb, Bowie, County
Gen. E. H. Tarrant, Bowie County
Hon. James Grimes, Montgomery County
A. Sterne, P.M., Nacogdoches
Travis G. Brooks. P.M., St Augustine
C. K. Andrews, Harrison County
Col. James Love, Galveston
James Shaw, Esq., Houston
Col. G. T. Wood, Liberty
John W, Harrison, Lagrange
E.M. Johnson, Washington
Samuel E. Boufnan, Matagorda

lost head right certificate
lost or mislaid head right certificate in Lamar County of Nehimiah Scott

lost or mislaid certificates of John Davis and John Morton

lost or mislaid certificate of Joseph Cox in Red River County

administration of estates
Jane Holloway appointed *administratix* of the Estate of Barnes Holloway of Bowie County.

professional card
Ambrose Spencer, Jr., Esq.
****

From The Northern Standard, November 5, 1842

public notices
R. M Hopkins revokes all powers of attorney previously given.

stop payment
on note given by John L. Lovejoy to James Bird as the property underlying the transaction failed to be sound

administration of estates
Bartholemew Figuers, administrator of the Estate of Robert Borland, has filed his accounting of same and will be discharged; order issued by Wm. B. Stout, Chief Justice and *ex officio* Judge of Probate for Red River County and J. C. Hart, Clerk for, and *ex officio* Clerk of, Probate for Red River County

Daniel Morris appointed administrator of the Estate of John Ball of Bowie County.

J. W. Dabbs appointed administrator of the Estate of Johnson Paxton of Bowie County.
****
The Northern Standard issues of November 12 and 19, 1842 were not published
****

From *The Northern Standard*, November 26, 1842

hostilities with Mexico
Letter from B. H. Martin of Clarksville extorting citizens to help to defend western region of the Republic from Mexico

temperance meeting
to be held in Fort Shelton; speeches by B. H. Martin and Rev. McKenzie; officers of movement are Jesse Shelton and A. J. Fowler

married
in Red River County, on November 23, 1842 by Rev J. M. Sampson, Napoleon Patton and Miss Lucinda Proctor

in Lamar County, in September by N. Maddox Esq., Ephraim Williams to Miss Americe Jackson

in Lamar County, November 20, 1842 by J. H. Crook Esq., Henry

Trimble to Miss Jane Graham

in Lamar County, by N. Maddox, Esq., on September 8, 1842, John T Bryant to Martha Weatherspoon

in Lamar County, before John A. Dillingham, Esq., William McConal of Fannin County to Miss Martha Ann Smith

commercial announcement
advertisement for brick making and laying in Red River County by Z. M. Paul

stray
horse strayed or stolen from Thomas Willison and E.M. Smith

stop payment
stop payment of note from William Wellborn to James W. Warehoof on grounds of fraud

administration of estates
B. D. Moore appointed administrator of the Estate of Josiah P. Wheat of Red River County.
****

From *The Northern Standard*, December 3, 1842

administration of estates
Elizabeth Gray appointed *administratix* of the Estate of Thomas Gray of Harrison County

land for sale
Advertisement for Land Agency, engaged in buying and selling Texas property. Contact:
C.R. Johns, Dekalb, Bowie County
H. D. Mason, Boston, Bowie County
Levi M Rice, Boston, Bowie County
****

From *The Northern Standard*, December 10, 1842

agricultural news
Alexander Mabane, living upon the Red River in Lamar County picked from six acres of land 24,000 pounds of seed cotton and his whole field of 45 acres averaged 3,300 pounds.

Richard G Miller of Lamar County raised 65 bushels of corn to the acre upon prairie lands.

school news
advertisement for the Clarksville Academy, under management of the Rev. James Sampoon and the following Trustees:

James Latimer	George Gordon
Gilbert Clark	John Ware
R. H. Martin	Eben'r Allen
John Morton	William Ritchie
W. H. Vining	

church news
The Rev. J. W. P. McKinzie will preach at Fort Shelton on Christmas Day.
Jesse Shelton, President
J. A. Fowler, Vice Pres't

fraternal organizations news
The Members of the Masonic fraternity are reminded that an Oration will be delivered at the Church in Clarksville by Brother J. W. P. McKinzie of Friendship Lodge, No. 16
George H. Bagby, Secretary

river news
advertisement that new Texas built Steamboat, *Red River Planter*, is at Berlin and ready to receive freight at the commencement of the fall business.
John Dryer, Berlin

commercial announcement
Steam engine and grist mill to be built within 4 or 5 miles of Clarksville by Messrs Latimer and Bagby and other others of our enterprising citizens. With the bricks available from Mr. Tomilson, this will improve the image of the Town, causing the removal of unsightly buildings now upon our streets and the erection of others more creditable to the taste and conducive to the comfort of our citizens

crime news
A difference occurred in San Augustine a few days since between Gen J.P. Henderson and a Mr Napoleon Garner, which resulted in the death of the latter

married
by the Rev. Samuel Corley, Dudley Gillum and Miss Patsy Mason, both of Red River County

lost head right certificate
lost or mislaid certificates of Thomas C. Baker in Red River County, as well as one in Bowie County

lost or mislaid certificate of Andrew Thomas in Fannin County

lost or mislaid certificate of C. R. Johns in Red River County, advertised by J. H. Darnall

administration of estates
Mark Roberts appointed administrator of the Estate of Joseph Sewell of Fannin County

William E. Wiley appointed administrator of the Estate of Nathaniel T. Journey of Fannin County

land for sale
for sale town lots in new town of Burleson, the new county seat of Fannin County, near Fort English. Announcement made by James R. O'Neal, Chief Justice of Fannin County

announcement made by Commissioners W. R. D. Ward, H. B.

Kelsey and John Lott For of town lots for sale in town of Marshall, Harrison County

professional card
John R. Bedford, Esq.

****

From *The Northern Standard*, December 17, 1842

agricultural news
Richard G. Miller of Lamar County, has grown a gourd which measures in circumference 5 foot, 9 inches and holds more than five buckets of water.

obituary
on November 4, 1842, in Lamar County, Mrs. Jane Allen, wife of William Allen, aged 33

administration of estates
John Morton appointed administrator of the Estate of Joseph Farris of Red River County

lawsuit filed
Notice of filing of divorce action by Mary Murphy against James Murphy of Red River County, published by W. H. Vining, Clerk of District Court of Red River County

****

From *The Northern Standard*, December 24, 1842

public notices
Thomas C. Forbes calls in all obligations owed him

Latimer & Johnson call in all obligations owed it

commercial announcement
T.G. Wright advertises that he has received for sale a supply of coffee, farm implements, school books and stationery

administration of estates
Silas A. Colville appointed administrator of the Estate of James A. Caldwell.

James Burkham appointed administrator of the Estate of Richard Rhodes

lost head right certificate
lost or mislaid certificate given John Crane regarding land in Shelby County

lost or mislaid certificate of Jonathan W. Lupton of Red River County
****

From *The Northern Standard*, December 31, 1842

land for sale
William M Williams has 10,000 acres of land to sell in Lamar and Fannin Counties

lawsuit filed
filed in the Republic of Texas, County of Lamar, Justice Court, Beat No. 5 by Thomas Dowdy against John Morgan and Joshua Morgan action for trespass; order issued by J. P Dillingham, Justice of the Peace

lost discharge
lost or mislaid Discharge from 1st Regiment of regular infantry of the Army of Texas, dated December 1839 or January 1840 by James Ferr

stop payment
on note given by Sanford G. Slayton to William K. Rievere

professional card
William W. Williams, Esq.

1843

From *The Northern Standard*, January 14, 1843

local news
report on the fire at the gin and grist mill of W.H. Vining Esq.,of Clarksville, which burned to the ground

Clarksville Ordinance No. II forbids cutting down trees in any of the public streets without an express permission in writing from the Mayor or the Board of Aldermen, under penalty of twenty dollars and cost of court for every tree so cut. The offender to be tried before the mayor upon complaint of any citizen of the town, and in case there is sufficient evidence to convict him, summary execution to issue, returnable as soon as practical.

Clarksville Ordinance No. III. All persons forbidden to discharge weapons, within town limits of the corporation, either by day or by night, under the penalty of five dollars for every such offence, or, in default of payment, confinement for 12 hours: Nothing contained in this Ordinance shall be construed to prevent any person from shooting on any town lot, any hogs, cattle or other animals intended for food.
                    Charles DeMorse, Mayor
                    Hugh F. Young, Sec'y

married
on the 1st of December in Lamar County, by A.N. Hopkins Esq., Mr. Merrett Brandon to Miss Elizabeth E Finley

on the 1 st of December in Lamar County, by A.N. Hopkins Esq., Mr. James Rodgers, late of the state of Alabama to Miss Mary Birdwell

stop payment
on note given by G. W. Wright and T. G. Wright to William C Hamilton and Jeremiah Adams because it was fraudulently induced

public notice
Gilbert Ragin, having sold out his entire stock of groceries, wishes to settle up old bills of those indebted to him. As times are hard and much complained of, he will not demand cotton, corn, pork or potatoes but will receive cash or its passing values. B.H. Martin Esq., of Clarksville is his authorized agent of the undersigned for payment

Thomas C. Forbes calls upon everyone to pay any debts owed him

Wright, Montgomery calls everyone to pay all debts owed

administration of estates
Rhoda Watson appointed administrator of the Estate of James Watson in Bowie County. Notice given by attorney E. H. Tarrant

Edward West appointed administrator of the Estate of James McClish of Red River County.

lost land certificate
lost or mislaid a certificate for 1280 acres of land granted E. H. Tarrant as Guardian of the heirs of Simon Gillam

letters left at Post Office
list of letters in Clarksville post office from September 30, 1842 to the 31st of December:

Allen, Ebenezer
Alexander, Miss Electra
Cox, William B
Crutcher, Thomas
Davis, John
Daniels, William C.
Daring, A.P.
Fleming, William
Glover, William.
Gregg, William
Giddien, Richard
Hawkins, William B..
Hamilton, W. E.
Hart, Dr.
King, Mrs. Elizabeth
Kincaide, George N.
Lawrence, William
Moore, James
Moore, Abel
Madden, Robert
Paterson, John
Pincham, Peter
Rutherford, J. W.
Spencer, Oliver
Sharp, Anthony
Sullivan, Adam

Smith, Mrs Mary E
Stuart, Charles
Scott, Solomon
Townsley, R.
Williams, William M.

Ware, Dr.
Wright, James G.
Wing, Carrol

Morton P.M.
****

From *The Northern Standard*, January 14, 1843

newspaper business
announcement of a new paper being published in Marshall, Harrison County, called *Marshall Review* and edited by a Mr. Shelton

public notices
E.D. Barnet tells all those persons indebted to him to pay their obligations

announcement by Dr. John Ware that he is leaving the practice of medicine and wanting people to pay up whatever they owe him

W. F. T. Hart, drug store proprietor, asks everyone to pay his bill

stop payment
Robert Weatherred warns not to accept his note to William Mays because it has already been paid

land for sale
sale of property by Martin Guest, administrator of the Estate of Joseph Guest

notice by Administrator Thomas Farmer of sale of land certificate for 640 acres, the head right of Roger McCown, deceased, to highest bidder, pursuant to order of Red River County Probate Court.

strays
Hugh B. Lilley has taken up horse appraised by Joel Hughes

and J.C. Gamigaw to be worth $20; notice by W. J. Hamilton, Justice of the Peace

William Morse has taken up horse appraised by A. L. Hinston and William Edmondson to be worth $20; notice by W M.. Mays, Justice of the Peace

administration of estates
Eben'r Allen and Elizabeth Parks appointed as administrators to the Estate of Charles W. Parks of Red River County

Samuel Erwin appointed as administrator of the Estate of Jonathan T. Hobbs of Fannin County

A.H. Latimer appointed as administrator of the Estate of James W. Dickson of Red River County.

William Davis appointed as administrator of the Estate of John Davis of Lamar County. Make claims and payments to William M. Williams, Attorney.

Keziah Martin appointed as administrator of the Estate of Thomas T. Martin of Lamar County. Make claims and payments to William M. Williams, Attorney.

Matilda Harman appointed as administrator of the Estate of Henry J. Harman of Lamar County. Make claims and payments to William M. Williams, Attorney.

Peter Viser appointed as administrator of the Estate of Thomas Brumly of Lamar County

married
on the 13th of January, by James B. Wooten Esq., Mr. Simeon Wagley to Mrs. Malvina Wiley, both of Red River County

obituary
on January 6, 1843, Fanny M. Russell, consort of Charles W. Russell, aged 37

professional card
E. H . Tarrant & S. M. Peters
Attorneys at Law. Boston Bowie County –will attend all the District Courts in the eastern portion of the Republic and the Supreme Court

****

From *The Northern Standard, January 21, 1843*

married
on Thursday evening last [Jan.19,1843] by the Rev. J. W. P. McKenzie, Mr. Richard Tomlinson to Miss Sarah Eliza Dickson, both of Red River County

professional card
The undersigned will receive any legal business from clients of William R. Scurry or persons wishing to engage his services at the next District Court
            Charles De Morse, Agent of Wm. R. Scurry

administration of estates
John D. Thomas appointed as administrator of the Estate of Richard Thomas of Lamar County .

S. K. Woodrow appointed as administrator of the Estate of Nancy K. Woodward of Fannin County .

****

From *The Northern Standard*, January 28, 1843

personals

TO THE LADIES OF THE NEW ENGLAND STATES
The undersigned, having formed themselves into a society called "The Matrimonial Club", now offer themselves as candidates for matrimony to the fair sex; any lady, under the age of forty and over the age of fifteen, who feels desirous of becoming a member of the Society, will please forward her name to Pine Creek or Jonesboro, Texas and it will be thankfully received by:

P. B. Johnson T.B. Mullins
B.F. Corke E. Young
James Kiney Wm. Scurlock
Henry Ashbrooks W. H. Beard
Benjamin Gooch Benj. Parkinson
J.E. Browning R.R. Watkins
F.G. Fitzpatrick W. W. Wren
Lafayette Fogg J. R. Ludlow
Gideon Mims, Pres't
J.P. Williamson, Sec'y

married
on Tuesday evening last, by the Rev. Mr. Duke, Mr. John Cameron of Lamar County to Miss Lynette Dern of Red River County

school news
examination at Mrs. Weatherred's Female Institute at Pine Creek is to take place February 9 and 10. General attendance is invited

land for sale
notice of Trustee's sale by Amos Morrill, on behalf of John H. Fowler, of one half a league of land in Lamar County. It adjoins the land of Mr. Green Orr; also about 1,100 acres from the headright of John Patterson and adjoining the land of Griffin Onstot; also land from the headright of Adam Hampton and adjoining the land of M. Click

administration of estates
Martin Guest appointed as administrator of the Estate of Joseph Guest of Red River County.

T. J. Ward appointed as administrator of the Estate of Samuel Rogers of Red River County.

lawsuit filed
order issued by E. W. Lee, Clerk of the District Court, Fannin County in lawsuit entitled *W.C. Young, assignee of Frank S. Holcomb, against Thomas Smith and Frank S. Holcomb,* permitting service of the complaint in action for debt

notice of mortgage foreclosure action, *John R. Craddock against Curtis Jernegan* issued by A.G. Kimbell, Clerk of the District Court of Lamar County by J. R. Craddock, Deputy Clerk

Suit in equity action, *Benjamin F Bourland against James Johnson* issued by A.G. Kimbell, Clerk of the District Court of Lamar County by J. R. Craddock, Deputy Clerk

Suit in equity, *James Ward against Isaac M Reed* issued by A.G. Kimbell, Clerk of the District Court of Lamar County by J. R. Craddock, Deputy Clerk

Suit in equity, *J. G. Jouett against J. S. Johnson* issued by A.G. Kimbell, Clerk of the District Court of Lamar County by J. R. Craddock, Deputy Clerk

Suit in suit in equity, *W. M. Burris against Peter Harper* issued by A.G. Kimbell, Clerk of the District Court of Lamar County by J. R. Craddock, Deputy Clerk

professional card
William G. Crump
Attorney and Counselor at Law
Clarksville, Red River County
****

From The Northern Standard, February 4, 1843

personals
   TO THE LADIES OF THE WORLD

The undersigned are members of the Pin Hook Bachelor Club Society and desirous of changing the same at the altar. Therefore, if any of the fair sex whose sympathies could be raised on our behalf, from fourteen to seventy five years of age, would drop us a line, directed at Pin Hook, it will meet with quite a cordial reception by

J. R. Craddock	W. M. Fulton
J. O. Clark	A. J. Clark
Robert Price	C. W. Sadler

N. R. Harlin   A. J. Buts
J. A. Dillingham
B.C. Fowler

Isaac Caldwell, President
W.G. Garvin, Sec'y

stop payment
notice by D. K. Jamison not to take note he gave S.T. Allen because Allen now owes him more than that.

administration of estates
notice by W.B. Stout of a special session of the Red River County Probate Court to issue letters testamentary to Robert Smith in connection with the estate of Hon. Robert Porter.

T.G. Wright , administrator of the Estate of Gabriel N. Martin , is selling off slaves owned by the Estate.

Richard H. Sowell and Louisa Sowell, appointed successor administrators to Mark Roberts of the Estate of Joseph Sowell of Fannin County

weather news
article describing the flooding caused by rushing, swollen rivers that escaped their banks and did extensive damage, including erasing Jonesborough from the map. The items include a letter from Capt. T.G. Wright, which mentioned the names of some of citizens affected by the flooding, including James Ward and Messrs King, Mim, Revere, Mabane, Denson, Riker, Scurlock, and Peake, as well a Major Tinnan, Col. Johnson, Dr. Boyce and Gen. Dyer.

commercial announcement
T. J. Cornelius advertises for sale sugar, coffee and salt at the store of Joseph Harrison & Co.

Professional cards
T.F. Smith
Attorney and counselor at Law

Burleson, County Seat of Fannin County
will attend to any legal business entrusted to his care

R.& W.R. Scurry
Attorneys and counselors at law
    Address
W.R. Scurry .... Clarksville
R. Scurry........... San Augustine
****

From The Northern Standard, February 16, 1843

Indian news
Mr. Parker of Montgomery County passed through Clarksville with his nephew and grandson who were captured by the Comanches but purchased by friendly Delawares who arranged for their freedom. The grandson is the son of a Mrs. Plummer, who herself had been a captive as well.
****

From The Northern Standard, February 23, 1843

crime news
Mark W. Doss confined in Red River County jail, upon the charge of murdering Benjamin Blanton, escaped on Monday night last. The jailbreak also resulted in the escape of a prisoner, named Payne, confined for horse stealing

court news
Judge Mills has arrived in town

election news
election returns from Lamar County
for Sheriff
William R. Brown ... 243
Elbert Early ... 162

for Coroner
J. S. Lovejoy... 30
G. Russell. ... 16
D. Meyers. ... 32
J.R. Hager 39

for County Surveyor
J. T. Harman... 205
Williams... 19

letters left in Post Office
letters remaining in the office of *The Standard* for which postage must be paid

John R. Jones	Harvey White
O.B. Reed	Allen Urquhart
John Rattan	Edward Wideman
John G. Jouett	Adam Sheeks
Col. Jas. H. Carnes	Thomas Jouett
Jason Whitney	James Benton
R.T. Bryarly	James Gillet
B.C. Rabb	A.G. Gromber
John H. McCarty	

public notice
notice by H. F. Young, Sec'y, that sealed bids will be received by the Mayor of Clarksville for repairing of bridge

land for sale
notice by E. H. Tarrant, Trustee, of sale of property, deeded by James Hamilton for the use and benefit of Amos Dry

administration of estates
Kezziah Fowler appointed administrator of the Estate of Wm. Fowler of Bowie County

commercial announcement
Richard Miller of Bowie County advertises the stud service of his stallion *Lygurgus*

professional card
W.B. Stout,
Attorney at law, Clarksville
will attend the district courts of Lamar and Red River and also execute deeds, bonds etc
****

From The Northern Standard, March 2, 1843

professional card
        Dr. R. R. Rogers
Will attend to the practice of Medicine in all its branches and can be found at his residence on the West end of the Town, unless professionally engaged.

letters left in Post Office
additional letters remaining in the office of the Standard Mail

Mrs. Kezziah Fowler	Newman McGee
Edward Irby	Mrs. Louisa K Harrison
Dr. John H. Davis	George Cruger
B.S. Sloan	Jas, Brasham
Gen. James Carter	Alfred Slack
Martin Johnson	Geo H. & B.C. Bagby
Dr. John S. Peters	John G. Jouett
A.B. Manion	James Carter
V. B. Reed	Jas. W. Green
Alex. W. Hodge	John Watson
Richard Lock	Jackson Taggle
Dr. L. E. Griffith	James Gillam
A. B. McClure	
Roswell W. Lee	

commercial announcement
J. S. Mayfield has declined going West until the movements of our enemy, or the policy of our country, shall again call the citizens to arms; in the interim, he will devote himself to his profession. He solicits the support of his friends and former patrons. He will devote his attention particularly to the investigation of land titles
Address: Nacogdoches
****

From The Northern Standard, March 9, 1843

professional cards
        Dr. George Gordon
still continues the practice of Medicine and may be found at all times, when not professionally engaged, at his residence in Clarksville.

E. S. Look M.D. respectfully informs the citizens of Clarksville and the surrounding neighborhood that he has located at this place. Dr. Look is a regular graduate of the Cincinnati Medical College and has had twelve years of practice, eight of which have been in the Southern Country and part as Surgeon in the United States Army. He gives particular attention to Surgical and Obstetrical cases and diseases in general of women and children.

Dr. I. Herrick tends to his services to the Citizens of Clarksville and surrounding neighborhood in the Practice of Physic, Surgery and Obstetrics. He may be found at all times at his office on Broad Street, near Wm. Donoho's Hotel, unless professionally engaged.
****

From The Northern Standard, March 16, 1843

land for sale
John B Craig, executor of the Estate of John B Denton, selling land of the estate including acreage from the headrights of Robert Price, James Sadler and James McCoy

administration of estates
Martin Glover appointed administrator of the Estate of V. M. Subrett of Red River County

notice given by W.B. Stout, Chief Justice Judge of Probate of Red River County and by J.C. Hart, Clerk of the County and the Probate Court, that Ephraim D. Moore, administrator of the Estate of David Wardlaw, had filed an accounting regrading the Estate

notice given by W.B. Stout, Chief Justice Judge of Probate of Red River County and by J.C. Hart, Clerk of the County and the Probate Court, that James Burkham, administrator of the Estate of Charles Burkham, had filed an accounting regrading the Estate.
****

From The Northern Standard, March 23, 1843

court news
invitation to the Hon John T. Mills by William C. Young, W.R. Scurry and B. H. Martin, on behalf of the Jurists Association of the Seventh Judicial District, to deliver an address "upon the

character of [the legal] profession and the Duties of Attorneys" and his acceptance of the invitation

stray
advertisement by John R. Woolridge for a lost hound, last seen some 8 miles outside of town

runaway
says his name is Bill and was taken up by Ebenezer Fraizer. He had been brought to this County by a man named Timmins and had belonged to a man by the name of Graham in Pickins District, South Carolina. Notice given by Martin Glover, Sheriff of Bowie County

administration of estates
William W. Brotherton appointed administrator of the Estate of Scott Smith of Fannin County.

Elizabeth Wafer, *administratix* of the Estate of Wesley Tollett of Red River County, has filed an accounting on Estate

Letters Testamentry issued to James Hefflefinger as administrator of Estate of Fleming George of Red River County

John D. Pettijohn appointed administrator of the Estate of B.D. Alexander of Lamar County.

letters left in Post Office
additional letters remaining in the office of the Standard

Lewis Nolin	William Finley
Ambrose Spencer, Jr.	John Griffin
Charles T. McPherson	Adam T. Poe
John Nidever	Messrs Williamson and
William McK. Ball	Bowerman
B.H. Martin	

agricultural news
Agricultural Society formed in Lamar County with officers: Hon Wm. Crisp, President; A. J. Fowler, Esq., Vice President, Dr. E. L. Grififths, Secretary and Claiborne Chisum, Esq., Treasurer
****

From The Northern Standard, April 6, 1843

local news
temperance meeting to be held in Clarksville in commemoration of the Battle of San Jacinto. Rev. James Sampson will deliver a temperance address and H.R. Latimer, Esq. will also speak

court news
Judge Mills of the District Court for Red River County disposed of more than one hundred cases, after a session of two weeks and retains the high estimations our citizens awarded him, at the first circuit he made in this District. He dispatches business with a rapidity seldom surpassed.

married
in Lamar County on the 5th of March, by the Rev. William Brackteen, Mr. Live Goins and Mrs. Margaret Whorton

in Lamar County on the 7th of March, by the Rev. Ramsey Potts, Mr. John McMinn to Miss Eveline S. Majors

in Lamar County on the 14th of March, by A.N. Hopkins, Esq., Mr. Greenberry Walding to Miss Sarah Harvick

letters left in Post Office
remaining at the Post Office in Clarksville, on the 1st Day of April,

Bowers, Thomas	Jones, Henry
Bransom, Charles	Moore, Wm. H.
Brown, John	Needham, Lewis
Burnes, Thomas L.	Pearson, John T.
Cox, William B.	Rhodes, William N.
Galloway, Daniel.	Smith, Thomas F.
Halm, Rob't S.	Stephens, Isham
Hill, Bernard	Watson, John M.
Henderson, Col. L .D.	Wright, G. W.
Hounskell, Joseph	Ward, James
Jones, Henry W.	

H.R. Latimer P.M.

strays
taken up by John W. Ellet in Bowie County, a brown mule, no

brand perceivable, and valued to be worth forty two dollars and fifty cents.
                    John A. McKinney, J.P.

administration of estates
notice by W.B. Stout, Chief Justice Judge of Probate of Red River County, and by J. C. Hart, Clerk of the County and the Probate Court, that C.R. Johns, administrator of the estate of William Donohoe, has filed an accounting

notice by W.B. Stout, Chief Justice Judge of Probate of Red River County and by J. C. Hart, Clerk of the County and the Probate Court, that C.R. Johns, administrator of the estate of Anderson Taylor, has filed an accounting.

George Gordon and D. N. Alley have been appointed administrators of the Estate of A. D. Duncan.

John A Talbott has been appointed administrator of the Estate of William McFarlin.

Henry Stoneham and James Stoneham appointed administrators of the Estate of William Stoneham.

Mr. Hefflefinger of Bowie County, on behalf of Estate of Fleming George, is selling such perishables as sheep cattle, corn, and wool
****

From The Northern Standard, April 13, 1843

commercial announcement
Grocery ad by Gilbert Ragin

public notice
Stephen Kinzey wants everyone to pay him what he is owed and unpaid obligations will be put into the hands of Sheriff West for collection

stop payment
Charles Stewart stops payment on note from him to Joseph H. Gordon because it was obtained in fraud and the consideration given for the note failed

bankruptcy filing
Berkley J Fuller will apply on the first Saturday in May next, for a discharge in Bankruptcy before the Chief Judge of Fannin County

professional card
Amos Morrill in Clarksville

****

From The Northern Standard, April 20, 1843

court news
Chief Justice Hemphill, Major Reily and Judge Mills arrived in town on Monday evening last.

crime news
Col. James R. Cook of Washington County was shot in the back by a man named Atkins.

Reward offered for return of stolen horse by R.M. Jones

stray
stray horse taken up by James J Ward, appraised at $30 and brought before acting Justice of the Peace, J. W. Green, County of Red River, Beat no. 6.

land for sale
sale of land by for George Gordon and D. N. Alley, administrators of the Estate of A.D. Duncan, including acreage originally within the headrights given John Kiterel, and, in Paschal County, acreage in the headrights of Robert B. Fowler, Bradford C. Fowler, Wm Davis, (near E. N. Frazier's) and L. W. Perry.

****

From The Northern Standard, April 27, 1843

election news
advertisement suggesting that Hon. A H. Latimer should run for Senator in the next Congress of the Republic.

public notice
C. Vernoy requests that he be paid by all those owing him

administration of estates
Notice by W.B. Stout, Chief Justice Judge of Probate of Red River County and by J. C. Hart, Clerk of the County and the Probate Court, appointing James Riley, administrator of the Estate of John Eastwood

****

From *The Northern Standard*, May 4, 1843

crime news
warning to be on the lookout for a swindler named Rhinehart who in Fannin County pretended to be an agent of a rich German man in Jonesboro.

lawsuit filed
notice by Thomas Crutcher, Clerk of the District Court for Bowie County, in action brought by John N Stuart against David P Key and attaching some of defendant's property for an outstanding debt.

letters left at Post Office
additional letters remaining in the office of *The Standard*

John P. Campbell	Charles Logan
H. M. Allen	Mills Whitley
Thomas Skinner	John Little
Martha Smith	Jason Whitney
A.G. Cromber	

****

From *The Northern Standard*, May 11, 1843

agricultural news
rise in the river and Captain Wright summoned to Pine Hills to take care of his cotton

election news
public meeting of the citizens of Red River County, held at the courthouse in Clarksville, to discuss nomination of candidates for the next session of the Congress of Texas. Col. C. English was called to be chairman and H.R. Latimer, secretary. Charles De Morse addressed the group and the following were appointed to serve on a nominating committee:

Wm. B. Stout
A.W. King
John Ware
William C. Young
Philip Duty
E.M. Smith
Gilbert Clark
Jas. H. Johnson
Wm. Ritchey
Wm. Skurlock
Jas. W. Sims
James J. Ward
Wm. T. Montgomery
John Robbins

Thos. Willison
John Stiles
Edward West
O. H. King
Wm. M. Harrison
Wm. J Hamilton
Ballard Bagby
A.G. Melton
B. F. Linn
J. C Hale
George Gordon
Wm. Humphries
James Aktinson

****

From The Northern Standard, May 18, 1843

crime news
the trial of Rose for the murder of Robert Potter continues

administration of estates
Sarah Dean appointed administrator of the Estate of Edward M. Dean of Red River County.

stray
notice, published by D. M. Chisholm, Justice of the Peace of Bowie County regarding stray horse taken up by R. C. Harris

Jno. M. Bourland and B.C Bagby appointed administrators of Estate of George Millhin.

letters left at Post Office
additional letters remaining in the office of *The Standard*
Mrs. Salina Barnet
Robert Weatherred
Wm C.Young
****

From The Northern Standard, **May 25, 1843**

crime news
Reward offered by R. M. Jones for the return of two horses stolen six miles above the mouth of the Bois d'Arc, on the Choctaw side, near Mr. Bush's Ferry. One had been run in Fannin County against a horse owned by the Harts

runaway
ran away from the residence of Levi Jordan, four miles south of Daingerfield, on Sunday, the 30th of April last, a Negro man belonging to the undersigned. Said Negro is 27 years old, 5 foot 2 inches high, will weight between 160 and 170 pounds, and is of a dark copper color. Said Negro is named Lewis and formerly belonged to Vade Hughes. He had on when he went away a shirt and pantaloons. I will give a liberal reward upon his apprehension and delivery to me, at my residence near Daingerfield or to Miles Reed, three miles northwest of Clarksville.
      David Bruton

stop payment
on forged note given to C.B. Johns by Joseph P. Campbell of Bowie County who was the assignee of another. Note is now in the hands of Major Campbell
****

From The Northern Standard, **June 8, 1843**

public notice
Wm. B. Stout is Charles De Morse's agent, during his absences from town

commercial announcement
A. M. Crocks and Charles C. Dale announce they have opened up a tailor's shop in Clarksville directly east of the Court house, in the room most recently occupied by Capt. Vining as Clerk of the Court

election news
report on meeting in Bowie County which nominated James N. Smith as a suitable candidate to represent the county at the next session of the Congress of the Republic of Texas. Gen. E. H.

Tarrant was nominated as a suitable candidate for Senator; John
S. Peters was Chairman of the Nominating Committee and Jesse
Benton Jr., Secretary

fraternal organizations news
notice given by George H. Bagby, Secretary, to members of the
Masonic Friendship Lodge No. 16 and to the public in general
that an Oration will be delivered in the Church in Clarksville on
Saturday, June 21, the anniversary of John the Baptist

land for sale
public sale of town lots in the town of Mount Vernon, the County
seat of Lamar County
Commissioners: George Wilson, Joel Wafer and Jesse Shelton

runaway
notice by Sheriff Edward West, Sheriff of Red River County, that
a runaway slave had been captured, who says his name is Eli, that
he belongs to Terrence Lee of Liberty County, and that he had
been brought to Texas from South Carolina

administration of estates
notice given by W.B. Stout, Chief Justice Judge of Probate of
Red River County and by J. C. Hart, Clerk of the County and the
Probate Court, that James H. Johnson and Bradford C. Fowler
have been appointed administrators of an estate
****

Report from *The Northern Standard*, June 15, 1843

Indian news
four hundred and fifty dollars has been subscribed in Red River
County for the protection of the southwestern frontier. A..J.
Titus holds the subscription paper and has raised a company of
men, all volunteers

lawsuit filed
commencement of a suit in equity in the District Court of Bowie
County, Spring term, entitled *Benj. J. Bourland vs James
Johnson.* The suit involves ownership in land which was
variously owned by James Craft, John Welch and John L.
Lovejoy. Notice was issued by A.G. Kimbell, Clerk of Court and
his Deputy, D.O. Norton

commencement of a suit in equity in the District Court of Bowie
County, Spring term, entitled *Wm. M Burris vs Peter Harper and
Benjamin Gooch*. The suit involves land ownership issues;
notice was issued by A.G. Kimbell, Clerk of Court and his
Deputy, D.O. Norton

stray
notice given by Massack H. Janes, acting Justice of the Peace of
Bowie County that a stray horse has been taken up by Jarret
James

sale of land
W. S. McClure, administrator of Estate of Wm. Johnson of Red
River, will offer for sale one third of a league of land

administration of estates
W. S. McClure appointed Administrator of the Estate of Thomas
Sattathite of Red River County.

W. S. McClure appointed Administrator of the Estate of William
Johnson of Red River County.

****

From *The Northern Standard*, June 22, 1843

school news
Report on the examination of students of Clarksville Academy,
Rev. James Sampson, Preceptor, which ended with a debate
between Master Wooldridge and Master Latimer

Report on the examination of students of Mrs. Weatherford's
school

election news
notice by Geo. W. Wright, candidate for the Red River Senatorial
District as to locations where he was speaking, including at H.H.
Griffin's residence in Bowie County and at Dr. Wm. M. Burris, in
Lamar County

commercial announcements
Jas. Thos. Lee has opened a "CHEAP CASH STORE" and has
for sale an assortment of merchandise among which are "fancy
and staple dry goods", including silks, chalets, shawls,

handkerchiefs, calicoes, hats, boots, shoes, silk and palm leaf hats, straw and gingham bonnets, as well as groceries, hardware, farming utensils and books

D.H. Dyer has for sale 300 bales of spun yarn. Apply to Ira S. Poor, near Clarksville or to D.H. Dyer at his residence in Mount Hope, Bowie County.

****

From The Northern Standard, **June 29, 1843**

lawsuit filed
notice, given by W. H. Vining, Clerk of the District Court for Red River County, of commencement of action for divorce filed by Thomas J. Cornelius against Sarah T. Cornelius

notice, given by W. H. Vining, Clerk of the District Court for Red River County, of commencement of action for divorce filed by Abia Dyer against William Dyer

election news
letter from A.H. Latimer urging that the Capital of the Republic be returned to Austin

school news
report, signed Visitor, on final examinations at Mrs Weatherred's school

lost headright certificate
notice by Archibald Goodman that he has lost his head right certificate, No. 562, third class, for 320 acres of land granted by the Board of Land Commissioners of Red River County

notice by Samuel Burke has lost his head right certificate, No. 714, for a third of a league of land granted him by the Board of Land Commissioners of Red River County

administration of estates
W. S. McClure appointed administrator of the Estate of Barnet Hicklin of Red River County

sports news
Elbert Early and his horse *Tennessean* challenge the owners of

Reindeer to a race anywhere in Bowie, Red River, Lamar, or Fannin Counties, stakes to be $1,000 or more

****

From The Northern Standard, **July 6, 1843**

letters left at Post Office
list of letters left in the Post Office in Clarksville

Aimes, Charles 2
Allen, Ebenezer 2
Ballard, Bartley
Bell, Davis
Bird, Isaac
Birphen, Rev.
Bowers, W. P.
Brown, John
Buress, Jas. E.
Burnes, Thomas L.
Burnett, Ishan
Bush, Evan
Clape, David
Corley, Samuel C.
Cornelius, Thomas J.
Cox, Mrs. Aner
Craig & Norris
Craig, J. B. Esquire
Crownover, Benj.
Crump, Mr.
Crump, W. G. Esq.
Crutcher, Thomas 2
Dean, Levi D.
Derdon, John
Dillingham, Miss Nancy
Doron, Thom. Esq
Doss, Mark K.
Doss, Thomas J.
Drenon, David
Dyer, Gen. John H.
Easter, Jas. or Burnett, A.G.
Ellis, Peter
Fulton, Sam'l N.
Gordon Jas. H.
Graham R.H.

Gray, W. M.
Green, James W. Esq.
Greenwell, W. H.
Guest, Isaac
Hamilton, R.W.
Hammock, A. J.
Hartknapp, Chas.
Hill, Mrs. Sarah E.
Hopkins, Iss. E.
Houston, Marmakuke T.
Hudson A.B.
Hughs, Robert
Jackson, Slocomb
Jones, Henry W.
Keeth, Gabriel
King, Jas.
Kinnar, Miss Nancy
Kinzie, Steven
Langlord, Eli
Lanier, Archer B.
Latimer, A.H.
Lynn, B. F.
Martin, Col. B. H.
Matthews, Mansel W. 4
McCall, David
McCarrinack, Hardy
McCrackin, Ovid
McKenzie, Sam'l B.
McSpadin, W.B. 2
Meadows, J. J.
Morgan, J. F.
Murphy, Mrs. Mary
Oliver, J.
Oneal, W. P.
Orton, B.B.

Parker, Westly
Patrick, Jas. W.
Peck, Samuel
Pettyjohn, Jas. G.
Ragsdale, Robert
Reed, Joseph
Revere, W. K.
Rice, Z. R.
Scott, Sol J.
Shannon, Jefferson
Simons, Miss Jones
Simons, E.C.
Sims, Wm.
Sinclair, Sam'l M.
Slayton, Miss Lucy
Smith, E.M.
Smith, S.C.
Stallions, Abraham

Sterling, James A.
Stewart, Byrns   2
Stors, Augustus 2
Sulles, John B.
Thom, D. K.
Vining, W. H.
Ward, Mrs. Levion
Ward, Jas.
Ward, J. J.
Ward, John
Ware, Andrew
Ware, Dr. John
West, Mr.
White, Sam'l D.
Williams, W. M.
Wilson, Jas.
Wooten, James B.
Wright, G. W.

E.M. Smith, P.M.

administration of estates
Charles Jackson appointed administrator of the Estate of James Keatherly, John Stephens, Jun., and William Allen .

Levi M. Rick appointed administrator of the Estate of George Collard of Bowie County.

Katharine Collum appointed administrator of the Estate of Charles Collum of Bowie County .

William J Hayes appointed administrator of the Estate of Allen Bryzzul of Bowie County

professional card
W. S. Todd
Attorney at Law
has located himself at Boston, Bowie County and will practice his profession in all the Courts of the Seventh Judicial District
****

From The Northern Standard, **July 13, 1843**

public notice
W.B. Hawkins has appointed W.R. Scurry as his agent/attorney in fact during Hawkins absence in the United States.

S. Mittower has appointed Capt. Joshua Bowerman as his agent/attorney in fact during his absence in the United States.

sports news
Martin Glover and his horse *Dolly* challenge the owners of the foals of *Reindeer* to a race over the best course in the District, wherever that may be, for a thousand dollars, cotton or cash
****

From The Northern Standard, **July 20, 1843**

election news
E. H. Tarrant is a candidate for Major General of the Militia of the Republic of Texas

Col. B. H. Martin is a candidate for Brigadier General of the Fourth Brigade of Militia of the Republic of Texas

In connection with the September 4th election in Red River County to elect one Senator and one Representative to the Congress of the Republic, the following are the voting locations and the presiding officers for said election as ordered by W.B. Stout, Chief Justice of Red River County

Precinct No. 1 at W.S. Mitchells   J.B. Wooten J.P.
Precinct No. 2 at John Stiles   John McCurly J.P
Precinct No. 3 at Ulysses Aiguer's   Ulysses Aiguer J.P.
Precinct No. 4 at Clarksville   John T. Clark
Precinct No. 6 at W. Humphries   Isaac Wilson J.P.
Precinct No. 7 at John Robbins   Lovel Coffman J.P
Precinct No. 8 at T.G. Wright's   A.S, Johnston J.P.
Precinct No. 9 at Clifton's Springs   H.H. Clifton J.P.
Precinct No. 15 at Henry W. Jones   Alex Nevill, J.P
At Jas, F. Box's   Robert E. Matthews

lost headright certificate
of David Sample, No. 145 of 650 acres in Red River County;

notice given by Hiram Baker and Caroline Baker

****

From The Northern Standard, July 27, 1843

election news
W.B. Stout announces that he is not a candidate for the office of Brigadier General of the Fourth Brigade of the Texas Militia

Wm. R. Scurry will be a candidate for the Representative of Red River County in the coming Congress

married
on the 24th of July, 1843 by Thom. Willison, Esq., Mr. William Brown to Mrs Elizabeth McAnier, both of Red River County

on July 26th, 1843 by Thom. Willison, Esq., Mr. Francis L. Blanton to Miss Mary McAnier, both of Red River County

crime news
$100 reward by Ordera Watson, Sheriff of Milam County, for the capture of Littleberry B. Franks and Lucius Johnson, wanted for the murder of Henry Castledine

runaways
notice by Edward West, Sheriff of Red River County of runaway taken up, who says his name is Tom and that he belongs to Capt. Thomas Hudly, formerly of Mississippi who has moved to Texas

notice by W.D. Browning, agent for John P. Campbell regarding two runaways Negro boys, Joe and Carter

stray
stray recovered by Louis Holcomb in Bowie County; notice given by E. Frazier, J.P.

****

There were no issues of From *The Northern Standard* in August or the first week of September, 1843 because of lack of paper due to the Red River's not being navigable

****

From The Northern Standard, **September 14, 1843**

election news
for Representatives to the Congress of the Republic of Texas, Ward is elected by a six vote majority in Bowie County. Wm H. Bourland, who was unopposed, won in Lamar County. Dr. Rowlett was elected by a ten vote majority in Fannin and G. W. Wright is elected Senator for the District

obituary
Miss Rebecca Ann Lamar, amiable and accomplished daughter of our ex-President Lamar, aged 16.

****

From The Northern Standard, **September 21, 1843**

crime news
report on altercation in Austin between John Nolan and Capt. Mark B. Lewis, where Nolan was killed. Opposite the nine pin alley of Mr. McKean, Col. L.P. Cook and George Barret attempted to kill Lewis. Alexander Peyton shot at Barret missed him and Barret then shot Peyton down. Arrest warrant issued by Judge Baylor, charged Cook with murder of Capt. Lewis

local news
rejection of letter from Lamar County, signed "Ben Long" which is not sufficiently interesting for publication

sports news
The fall horse racing season over the Clarksville course, will include:
R. Tonalisson' bay filly, *Texana*, sire *Leviathan*
John Loring's sorrel horse *Red River*, sire *Ben Franklin*
William Donaho's brown filly *Comanche*, sire *Sir Archy*
William Hart's bay horse, *James Polk*, sire *Pete Whetstone*
William B. Hughes, *Joe Jackson*, sire *Imported Lapdog*
R. W. Russel's filly, *Queen*, sire *Experiment*
J. E. Hopkins sorrel mare, *Wild Cat*, sire not known

commercial announcements
advertisement by A. Dodd of his general store in Mount Vernon, then seat of Lamar County

advertisement by Samuel Baker, a Commission Merchant from

New Orleans who gives R. M. Hopkins of Clarksville and Major
S.M. Peters of Boston, Bowie County, as references

runaway
advertisement by Thomas A. Bagley, Sheriff of Fannin County,
of the capture of a runaway slave by Andrew Manson. The
runaway says he belongs to Frank Henderson of Rapides Parish,
Louisiana.
****

From *The Northern Standard*, September 28, 1843

agricultural news
Wm. S. Johnson advises that he had picked 371 pounds of cotton
by one hand and 323 by another on the place of Col. L. D.
Header, near Clarksville

court news
The District Court, Hon. John T. Mills presiding, adjourned. A
large number of cases have been disposed of.

election news
Col. B. H. Martin announces his candidacy for Brigadier General
of the Fourth Brigade of the Texas Militia.

administration of estates
notice by J.C. Hart, Clerk County Court and ex officio of Probate
Court for Red River County, that Matthew Dillard, administrator
of the Estate of James Stephenson, has filed his accounting

notice by J. C. Hart, Clerk County Court and ex officio of
Probate Court for Red River County, that James J. Ward,
administrator of the Estate of Abraham Ogden, has filed his
accounting.
****

From *The Northern Standard*, October 7, 1843

local news
report that Captain John Robbins will leave Clarksville for the
purpose of cutting a road from this place to Kinsborough, on the
Trinity.

runaway
reward offered by Joseph Scott , from Caddo Parish, 4 miles from Greenwood, Louisiana, for the return of his runaway slave, Lewis, who had been captured while swimming across the Red River, was lodged in the Clarksville jail, but who escaped. It is thought he is aiming to make his way to the Creek Nation

reward offered by William Martin of Bossiere Parish, Louisiana, for the return of his runaway slave, Bob, who has a rifle gun with him

administration of estates
Bailey Inglish has been appointed administrator of the Estate of Asa Hartfield in Fannin County.

letters left at Post Office
list of letter at Clarksville Post office, on October 1, 1843,

Abbot, William O.	Long, Jacob
Anderson, R.G.	Martin, Guest
Baily, Claibourne C.	Mash, Seaving
Bateman, James W.	Matthews, Joseph
Beat, William	McDonall, Dan'l Esq.
Bell, W. H.	Nantz, Drury
Benge, William B.	Neely, Samuel
Bourland, James	Nevil, Alexander
Bowie, Daniel (2)	Newbourn, T .J. or.
Cameron, John	Brogden, Mr.
Corley, Samuel C.	Park, W. A.
Cox, George W.	Perry, Josiah D.
Davison, Wm. or Israel	Ray, John
Dickson, J. A.	Shrewsbury, Charles
Donald, Dan. Esq.	Simmons, James
Dragoo, John	Simms, C.H.
Duncan, Rob't	Sims, Mat. F.
Duncan, George	South, Charles or Wm.
Guest, Martin	Spencer, Oliver
Hamilton, Ebenezer R. (2)	Stalcup, Joseph or Rhesa
Hardkins, G. W.	Waits, James
Harmon, Joseph	Wilkins, John O.
Keith, Wm. S.L.	Wright, Thomas
Lee, James	

E.M. Smith P.M.
****

From The Northern Standard, October 14, 1843

crime news
reward offered for the apprehension of Mark W. Doss, who stole wagon and later killed Jacob Blanton

court news
notice by Hugh F. Young that, upon motion made by Ebenezer Allen and upon the consent of the members of that Bar, that he has been appointed Commissioner to take depositions of all the cases pending in the several counties of the Judicial District and the order of appointment has been certified by Wade H. Vining, Clerk, District Court Red River County

bankruptcy filings
notice that J. E. Chism will seek a discharge in bankruptcy from the Chief Judge of Bowie County

notice that Elizabeth R. Chism will seek a discharge in bankruptcy from the Chief Judge of Bowie County

notice that Marshall W. Northington will seek a discharge in bankruptcy from the Chief Judge of Bowie County

land for sale
Notice by W. S. McClure, administrator of the Estate of Wm. Johnson of Red River County that the Estate will sell one third of a league of land, the headright of B.W. Osbourne, lying on the waters of Black Cypress on the Trammel Trace, Bowie County

administration of estates
John Paxton has been appointed administrator of the Estate of M.D.G. Godley in Bowie County

lost property
notice by Wm. Young that he has lost a certificate, which had been issued to him as administrator of the Estate of Richard Hazelwood, for 640 acres in Bowie County, Number 8, dated May 3, 1841
****

From The Northern Standard, October 21, 1843

sports news
Report on race won by Wm. Hart's Colt *Pete Whetstone*

public notices
notice by W.B. Stout, Chief Justice of Red River County, that the Board of Land Commissioners for the County will meet for the purposes of issuing Land Certificates on the first Monday in each month

notice by W.B. Stout, Chief Justice of Red River County that all Justices of the Peace of the County to attend the court house on November 13 for the purpose of transacting the business of the County.

administration of estates
Richard G. Miller has been appointed administrator of the Estate of Samuel Peck of Lamar County
****

From The Northern Standard, October 28, 1843

obituary
Mrs. Sarah Whitaker of Bowie County, consort of Willis Whitaker, Esq. in the 33rd year of her life

commercial announcement
notice that the tailoring partnership Crooks & Dale has been dissolved by mutual consent but that Charles O. Dale will carry on the business at the shop in Clarksville formerly occupied by Mr. Simons and lately as the offices of Dr. Hart

public notices
notice by Henry Stout that William B. Stout is his agent during his absence

runaway
advertisement by Thomas A. Bagley, Sheriff of Fannin County, of the capture of a runaway slave by Henry Banin. The runaway says he belongs to William Martin living near Shreveport, Louisiana.

letters left at Post Office
list of letter left at Boston Post office in Bowie County

Blyth, William	Robinson, Charles
Brackney, John or	Sandlin, A. K.
Bacon, James A.	Sheriff of Bowie County
District Clerk, Bowie	Watson, Colman
Lary, Henry J.	Woolerton, William
Myers, Gibson Dr.	Young, Charles
Peebles, Ephraim	

John A. McKinney P.M
****

From The Northern Standard, November 4, 1843

married
on November 2, 1843, by the Rev. James Samson, Amos Morrill, a native of Salisbury, Massachusetts to Miss Miranda A. Dickson of Red River County

land for rent
advertisement by W.B. Stout to rent 60 acres of land, under good fence, dwelling house, and lots.

stray
notice of strayed horse of I. D. Lawson

administration of estates
Susanah Dean has been appointed administrator of the Estate of Asa Dean of Red River County

Henry W. Jones has been appointed administrator of the Estate of Jesse Jones of Red River County

Cynthia Morton and Rufus Morton have been appointed administrators of the Estate of John Morton of Red River County
****

From The Northern Standard, November 11, 1843

public notice
Thomas Forbes gives notice that he requires immediate payment by those who are indebted to him or else he will put the obligations up for collection

stray
John Stiles, Justice of the Peace, advises that James Chute and David Thomas have appraised the runaway shown to them by Morris Ward to be worth $27.50.

A.S. Johnson, Justice of the Peace, advises that Elisha Clampitt, Samuel L. Lakin and James H. King have appraised the runaway shown to them John Audrey to be worth $25.

A.S. Johnson, Justice of the Peace, advises that Elisha Clampitt and James H. King have appraised the runaway shown to them William H. Moran to be worth $50.
****

From The Northern Standard, November 18 , 1843

public notices
Wright, Montgomery & Co gives notice that it needs all indebted to it to pay their obligations or else collection efforts will follow

stray
J. C. Hart, Clerk, County Court, Red River County, advises that N. Brewer and F. Stanley have appraised the runaway shown to them by Davidson Colville and brought before Thomas Williams Justice of the Peace, to be worth $27.50.
****

From The Northern Standard, November 25, 1843

obituary
died at his residence at Savannah, 12 miles below town, on Thursday, the 21st instant, Col. James Titus, the late senator from this District, aged 68 years. He had been born in Virginia on December 10,1775, moved, when young, to Tennessee near Nashville and from there to Alabama where he was several times a member of the legislature, then to Shelby county, Tennessee and then to Texas

stray
John R. Craddock, Clerk, County Court, Lamar County, advises that E. Brune and M.T. Sharp have appraised the runaway taken up by Greenberry W. Dorsey, at his residence on Sulfur Fork and brought before Jason Wilson, Justice of the Peace, to be worth $15.00.

John R. Craddock, Clerk, County Court, Lamar County, advises that Zachariah Birdwell and Nathan Petty have appraised the stray, taken up by James Wallen at his residence on Sulfur Fork and brought before Jason Wilson, Justice of the Peace, to be worth $23.00
****

From The Northern Standard, December 2, 1843

married
in Lamar County, on November 1, 1843, by the Rev. J. W. P. McKenzie, Dr. C. C. Cooper to Miss Catherine E. Harmon

in Lamar County, on November 5, 1843, by A.N. Hopkins, Esq., Col. Lindley Johnson to Miss Everly[n] C. Merrill

in Lamar County, on November 9, 1843, by the Rev. Samuel Corly, Mr. J. W. Tomilson of Red River County to Miss Pamela Jane Gibbons

administration of estates
notice by J. C. Hart, Clerk County Court and ex officio of Probate Court for Red River County, that Isaac Moore and L. V. Moore, administrators of the Estate of Joshua Moore, have filed their accounting with the Court

notice that Joseph Hammerick has been appointed administrator of the Estate of Jesse Kelly of Bowie County.

Notice that Wm. W. Davis has been appointed administrator of the Estate of John H. Davis of Red River County
****

From The Northern Standard, December 9, 1843

agricultural news
Jacob McFarlane has returned from Washington, Texas and reports excessive rain throughout the interior that has prevented cotton picking and that large quantities of corn destroyed because it could not be gathered

fraternal organizations news
Notice by E.M. Smith, Sec'y, that the Members of Friendship Lodge No. 16 of the Free and Accepted Masons will have a

public procession in Clarksville on December 27 in
commemoration of St. John the Evangelist

commercial announcement
advertisement by James Thomas Lee that he just received for sale
a shipment of whiskey, apples, bagging and rope

public notice
notice by Gilbert Ragin that he has given to Thomas Willison
Esq. for collection all notes due him

stop payment
notice given by Hardy McCormack not to trade for notes given
by given him by G. W. Wright and T. G. Wright as they have
been stolen from his possession
****

From The Northern Standard, December 16, 1843

commercial announcement
Editor takes notice of new advertiser, Mr. L. D. VanDyke who
deals in silks, satins, hoisery; Mr. VanDyke lives next door to
Messrs. Lawton and Shelton

administration of estates
notice by James Hefflefinger, administrator, by virtue of an
order of a Probate Court of Red River County, that he will hire
out to the highest bidder, for the term of one year, a Negro man
named Tom, belonging to the succession of Fleming George,
deceased.

I. Herrick has been appointed administrator of the Estate of Peter
Crigger of Red River County
****

1844

From The Northern Standard, January 13, 1844

commercial announcements
Notice by L. D. Dyke of the continuation of his auction sale of
the remainder of the stock of his store.

Advertisement by M'Mahon, Trotter & Pearsall, New Orleans Commission Merchants which lists as references William M. Harrison, Esq. of Clarksville; Mayor James E. Browning of De Kalb and Col. Charles Lewis of Bowie County

advertisement by Look & Hall for drugs, medicines, paints and oils

advertisement by William M. Harrison regarding "new goods" he has for sale at his store in Clarksville

notice by James M. Sharp that he will publish a newspaper in Clarksville under the name *Witness*

lost headright certificate
notice by Jesse Adams for 320 acres in the County of Bastrop given him by the Republic of Texas

public notice
J. Shelton & Co. requests all persons indebted to it to pay up

administration of estates
Amos Morrill has been appointed administrator of the Estate of Elisha .C. Simons of Red River County

Elizabeth Fitzgerald has been appointed administrator of the Estate of Jabaz Fitzgerald in Fannin County

bankruptcy filing
notice by John M. Dyer that he is applying for a discharge in bankruptcy

school news
Notice that the Pedee Academy has engaged the services of the Rev. David K. Thom, who comes well recommended as a teacher. The notice was signed by Alexander Mabane, William Tinnan, W.C. Harrison; A.M. Hodge, and L. W. Tinnan

land for sale
notice by John S. Peters, as Executor of the Estate of L. Peters, of the sale of the land known as the Myrtle Spring tract in Bowie County, about 4,000 acres on the Red River, about 6 miles below Spanish Buffs

election news
election notices, given by W.B. Stout, Chief Justice of Red River County, for the offices of Coroner, Sheriff, Justices of the Peace, and Constables and establishing the following voting precincts or beats and the presiding officer at each:

Beat No. 1 at Wm. S. Mitchell's by J. B. Wooten
Beat No. 2 at John Stiles' by Jn. McCurly
Beat No. 3 at Ulysses Aiguier's by U. Aiguier
Beat No. 4 at Clarksville north side by J. T. Clark
Beat No. 5 at Clarksville Courthouse by Wm. Donho
Beat No. 6 at Wm. Humpries by Isaac Wilson
Beat No. 7 at John Robbins by L. Coffman
Beat No. 8 at T.G. Wright's by Gideon Mims
Beat No. 9 at W. Gregg's old place by G. Clark
Beat No. 10 at Clifton's Springs by H.H. Clifton
Beat No. 11 at H. W. Jones by Alex. Nevill
Beat No. 12 at Thos. F. Box by W. J. Hamilton

letters left at Post Office
list of letters in the Clarksville Post Office

Barry, Mrs. Margaret M.
Bell, Daniel
Beny, Mrs. Elenor
Brown, Stephen
Clement, Simeon
Clement, E. N.
Cornelius, Thomas Jefferson
Dawson, Israel
Dearing, Allen J.
Harmon, Col. John T.
Kingsbury, Rev. Cyrus
Martin, Col. B. H.
McClure,. W. S.
McKenni, Mrs. M.
Moore, Joseph P.
Patrick, James W.
Price, John

Patton, Samuel B.
Rhodes Jr., Capt. Wm. N.
Robinson, J. J.
Rogers, A. L.
Scurry, R.R.
Sims, Mat. F. Esq.
Spencer, Oliver H.
Tumey, John R.
Waits, James
Wilson, George
Wright, Thomas
Wright, G. W.
Wyckum, Samuel
Yarmouth, Mitchell
Young, Hugh F.

E.M. Smith P.M.

professional card
Advertisement by E. S. Look M.D. of his medical services and

that he was a graduate of the Cincinnati Medical College
****

The January 20, 1844 issue of *The Standard* is missing and the January 27, 1844 issue was not printed
****

From The Northern Standard, February 3, 1844

married
on January 22, 1844 by Thomas Willison, Esq., Mr. Joseph Cartwright to Sarah C. Wilkins, both of Red River County

on January 7, 1844, by John Dillingham, Esq., Mr. Nelson Staits to Nancy W. Dillingham of Lamar County

election news
Thom Willison, Esq. announces his candidacy for Justice of the Peace, Beat 5

A.M. Crooks announces his candidacy for Justice of the Peace, Beat 6

lawsuit filed
notice issued by Isaac Banta, Justice of the Peace to defendant Lawrence W. Fern in an action commenced against him by Samuel Erwin that an order of attachment had been executed upon defendant's property including a horse, a gun and six volumes of the English or Common laws

administration of estates
John W. Wever been appointed administrator of the Estate of Samuel K. Blythe in Bowie County

E. H. Tarrant been appointed administrator of the Estate of Simon P. Hughes Fitzgerald in Bowie County

E. H. Tarrant been appointed administrator of the Estate of James Alford in Bowie County

H. D. Mason been appointed administrator of the Estate of George Cullum in Bowie County
****

From The Northern Standard, February 10, 1844

settlements and immigration news
Major F. B. Ely of Louisville, the agent of the Trinity Company, arrived in town on Wednesday, on his way to the Colony. He is performing the arrangements necessary to ensure compliance with the contract --250 families resident there, and 250 houses erected on as many sections of land, by June 1, 1845. Maj. Ely also advises on mineral finds including potting clay, lead ore, and anthracite coal.
****

From The Northern Standard, February 17, 1844

commercial announcements
Wm. M. Harrison has garden seeds for sale

notice by Jas. Thos. Lee that he has for sale 14 barrels whiskey; 15 barrels green apples, 50 pieces bagging; 25 coils rope

notice by D.H. Dyer, for John Evans, telling those paying for notes in cotton should deliver it to James Latimer's Gin

school news
advertisement for Mrs. Weatherred's Clarksville Female Academy

professional card
B. H. Martin & S.D. White
Attorneys at law
Clarksville
Will attend the various courts of the 7th Judicial District
****

From The Northern Standard, February 24, 1844

court news
Wm. C Young has been appointed District Attorney for this District. "The appointment is, we think, a good one and will be generally acceptable to the people of the District"

public notice
notice by J. Shelton and Doak & Time of the dissolution of J. Shelton & Co.. Geo. F. Lawton is agent to make collections

From The Northern Standard, March 2, 1844

church news
Rev. Mr. Levi Chack will deliver a lecture in Clarksville

administration of estates
Wm. Scurlock has been appointed administrator of the Estate of Elisha Simmons in Red River County

L. D. Bryant appointed administrator of the Estate of Matthew Dillard in Red River County

public notice
notice given by Wm. M. Williams, Jason Wilsonn and John Yearry regarding laying out of Central National Road
****

From The Northern Standard, March 9, 1844

settlements and immigration news
advertisement by F.B. Ely, Agent of the Colonizing Co. Texas. Bonham, Fannin Co. to emigrants to settle in Trinity Colony that all families who proceed to the Colony, make their selections, build their cabins, and occupy the same, on or before the June 1, 1844, will be awarded 640 acres, or one section of land. Young men over 17 years, half a section, or 320 acres. Mere visit and selection without improvement will secure no rights. Actual settlement and improvement is indispensable.

church news
The Rev. Mr. Chack will deliver a Lecture in Clarksville on the third Sabbath of March instant.
Topic: Matthew 16th Chapter and 28th Verse: "And fear not them which kill the body, but are not able to kill the soul -- but rather fear him which is able to destroy both soul and body in hell."

married
in February by Joseph Lyday, Esq., Dr H. . McDonald to Mrs. Sarah Turner

professional card
advertisement of Dr W. F. T. Hart that he still continue the practice of medicine

bankruptcy filing
John H. Dyer notifies his creditors that he will appear before the Chief Justice for the county of Red River for a discharge in bankruptcy.

administration of estates
Samuel B. Hervey appointed administrator of the estate of Elbert Mathews of Red River County.

Notice by W.R. Stout that all sales by administrators which were not advertised will be disallowed

A. J. Titus and T.F. Titus appointed administrators of the estate of James Titus of Red River County.

lawsuit filed
legal action by James Stoneham and his wife Polly Stoneham against the heirs of James Burnham why Wm. W. Williams, John Emberson, Joshua Bowerman, Samuel M. Fulton and W.C. Harrison should not be appointed commissioners to divide and distribute the land; ordered by W.B. Stout and notice given by J. C. Hart, Clerk

notice, ordered by W.B. Stout and executed by J. C. Hart, Chief Justice an Clerk of Red River County that a legal action has been brought by Isaac Moore against the heirs of Joshua Moore to notify R. P. Moore; Anne Settle and her husband Marcus G. Settle, who all live outside the Republic; Mary Moore, widow of the deceased, I. V. Moore; Larena Williams and her husband H.L. Williams; Whitfield Moore; Caroline Edmonson and her husband William Edmonson;. West Moore; and Mary Jane Moore, by her guardian Wm. Edmonson, all of whom are within the Republic, why John T. Harmon, Geo. W. Wright and R. G. Miller should not divide and distribute the estate.
****

From The Northern Standard, March 16, 1844.

married
on Sunday evening, March 10, 1844, by the Rev. Samuel Corly, Mr. Hugh F. Young to Miss Angeline Alexander, both of Red River County

From The Northern Standard, March 20, 1844

school news
Jas. Sampson principal of the Clarksville Academy, advises the public that he has associated with Mr. R.W. Maddin, as an assistant at the school.

Notice by S.B. Johnn, Secretary to the Board of Trustees, that the preparatory department of DeKalb College is now ready for the services of Mr. Alexander J. Russell as teacher.

land for sale
H.H. Clifton will sell to arriving emigrants livestock (cattle, sheep and hogs) and a tract of 400 acres of land lying on the south side of White Oak Creek, where the road South forks to Shreveport and Nacogdoches. The place is part timbered and part prairie, and includes some very superior bottom land. He also has for sale a tract of 640 acres upon the waters of Big Cypress, lying across the road to Nacogdoches

Geo. Gordon is offering Clarksville town lots for sale

the Commissioners appointed by law will attend in Paris, the seat of Justice for Lamar county on Friday and Saturday, the 5th and 6th of April next, for the purpose of selling the lots in town. The terms will be liberal and made known the day of the sale and perhaps the building of a court house may be let at the same time. Paris is situated in the middle of the county, in a beautifully healthy place and is now, no doubt permanently established as the seat of justice for Lamar county.
By order of the Commissioners: C. Chisom; G.W. Still; H.L. Williams; J. Emberson J.; Griffin,

public notice
Notice by S.W. Sims, County Surveyor of Red River County has dismissed John Mathews and no surveys from him will be received

commercial announcements
advertisement by Wm. H. Newland and M. Byers that "BODOC", will stand as stud at Dr. Gordon's stable in Clarksville, and at Col. R. Hamilton's, six miles north east of Clarksville

notice: L. W. Tinnan offers to purchase young Negroes from twelve to twenty years of age.

Auction: J. Shelton & Co., by Geo. F. Lawton, plans to sell at public auction all its stock of goods on hand at its store in Clarksville

runaway
notice placed by T.G. Wright, on behalf of Amelia Bell on Pine Creek in Red River County, that a slave, Bob, ran away

lost headright certificate
notice by Lemuel Bracken for 640 acres in Red River County

local news
Undersigned commissioners, appointed by Congress to view, mark and lay out the Central National Road from Trinity to Red River, have named the other commissioners, viz: R.W. Box of Houston County, and James Bradshaw of Nacogdoches County. All will meet at Dallas on the Trinity River on the 13th day of April, 1844 next to consider operations.
Wm.M. Williams, Jason Wilson and John Yearey

****

From The Northern Standard, March 27, 1844

settlements and immigration news
Mr. J. Eliot, an agent of the Trinity Colony Company, informed us that everything was progressing well, and that there was no difficulty with Indians. The Colonists have organized themselves into two militia companies, to act in case there should be need, and a third company will be organized. He repeats the assurances previously made by Major Ely, that the Company will comply with their contract, and that there will be no forfeiture of the grant.

****

From The Northern Standard, April 3, 1844

commercial announcement
A small salt manufactory has recently been erected by Mr. P. Lockhart, near a small pond about twelve miles west of Gonzales town. Mr. Lockhart has made during the last year about 100 bushels of salt similar in texture to the salt found in the lakes

near Corpus Christi

letters left at Post Office
list of letters in the Post office at Fort Towson for citizens of
Texas

Sam'l Browning –Forks of the Trinity	Josephus M---------Fannin Stirling E. Williams –Lamar
Wm. Fitzgerald – Fannin	John L. Farquhart
Isaac J. Baily –Texas	Washington County
Wm. Lenon –Fannin	

list of letters in Clarksville Post office

Alexander, James M.	Langford, Miss Rosette
Beard, Andrew	Millikin, Mrs. Sarah
Booth, James	Mays, John Esq.
Byers, A.M.	Morris, Joseph
Barton, John B.	Main, John
Basham, Wm. C.	Olgesby, Mr.
Black, John D.	Perry, Josiah D.
Bryant, Solomon	Perkinson, B. H
Craig & Norris	Poor, Ira J.
Campbell, J. P.	Reed, W.
Chisum, Claiborn	Revere, Wm. K.
Cox, Wm. B.	Standerfer, Jesse M.
Dodd, A. Esq.	Stevenson, Elizabeth
Dearing, A.D.	Stroud, A.
Dagley, Wm. or Thos.	Sheriff of Red River County
Evens, Jesse	Sheldon, Mr.
Fowler, Col J. H.	Shearer, Spencer
Fraley, David W.	Spain, L. D.
Garrouth, John R.	Turner, John
Holeman, Cyrus	Tarrant, E. H.
Hefner, Alfred	Waits, James
Halbrook, Mr.	Wither, John W.
Henderson, Mrs. Malinda	Wilkinson, John O.
Hancock, Joseph	Wills, Maj.
Kimble, John Esq.	Woods, J. W.
Kinsey, S.	Young, Wm. C.
Kuster, Washington	
Linn, B.F.	

lost head right certificate
Notice by Holland Coffee for a third of a league of land in Fannin County

bankruptcy filing
Notice by Thos L Cowan will apply for a discharge in bankruptcy
****

From The Northern Standard, April 10, 1844

school news
Mrs. Eliza Todd advertises her new school for girls in Boston

public notice
T. J. Cornelius is compelled to collect from all those who owe him and the collection will be left in the hands of E.M. Smith

stray
notice given by J. Loring that a gray colt has strayed from Philip Duty, Esq.

Administration of estates
E. D. Hughart has been appointed administrator of the Estate of William Slingsand in Red River County

E. D. Hughart has been appointed administrator of the Estate of Joseph Atkinson in Red River County

land for sale
D. Morris, administrator of the Estate of John Ball will sell one third a league of land next to Mason and Rice near Boston, Bowie County
****

From The Northern Standard, April 17, 1844

election news
MEETING OF THE CITIZENS OF THE SOUTHERN DIVISION OF RED RIVER
The meeting having been called to order, Isaac Hughes was called to the chair and B.W. Gray appointed Clerk. Dr. Mathews addressed the chair relative to the importance of nominating some gentleman as a candidate for Congress, whose qualifications, integrity, and respectability were known.

qualifications, integrity, and respectability were known.
A motion was made and seconded, that Wm. R. Scurry Esq. be nominated as a candidate for Congress, which was unanimously assented to.
On motion, it was resolved, that a committee of three be appointed to wait upon Mr. Scurry and inform him of the nomination; and the following gentlemen were appointed: M. W. Mathews, O. H. King, and W. J. Hamilton, who returned in a short time, attended by Mr. Scurry.
Lastly, it was moved and seconded that the minutes of this meeting be forwarded to *The Northern Standard*, for publication; and that the thanks of the meeting be rendered to Maj. De Morse for his courtesy in publishing the same.
    Isaac Hughes, President
    B. W. Gray, Secretary

Lamar County election results, reported by J. R. Craddock selection of county seat: Paris 219, Somerville 4

For Sheriff: E. Early defeated J. D. Thomas and Geo. Mabane
For Coroner: D. Myers defeated G. W. Russell and L. J. Lovejoy
For Colonel: A.N. Hopkins defeated T.B. Edmonson
For Lt. Colonel: Z.B. Miller defeated G. Richardson and H. Stiles
For Major: A. J. Clark beat D. K. Pace, J. J. Jeffers and N. Anderson

obituaries
at his father's residence, near Clarksville, on April 11, 1844, John Jones Vining, aged 24. He was Deputy Clerk of the District Court Red River County, his father being Chief Clerk

professional card
W.R. Scurry & M. W. Mathews
Attorneys and Counselors at Law have formed a special co-partnership for practice in Southern District of Red River
W. R. Scurry -- Clarksville
& M. W. Mathews -- Daingerfield

sports news
L. W. Perry and W.O. Richards, owners of the horse *Tennessean* challenge the owner of *Reindeer* to a race, which is followed by an acceptance by *Reindeer's* owner –D. Doak

lost property
notice by Samuel Hughes of lost certificate for land in Red River County

notice by Henry Banta of lost certificate for 220 acres of land in Fannin County

administration of estates
Pamela Brooks has been appointed administrator of the Estate of Bevin Brooks in Red River County

Eldridge Hopkins has been appointed administrator of the Estate of Henry Hopkins in Red River County

river and shipping news
Meeting of the citizens of the Southern Division of Red River, in the town of Dangerfield, on April 6, 1844 to devise a plan to clear the Cypress to allow navigation from Smithland to Jefferson. The purpose of the meeting was given by Dr. M. W. Matthews, Col. B. H. Martin, and Dr. Tabor. Isaac Hughes, Esq. was called to the Chair and B. W. Gray appointed clerk.
After the organization of the meeting, the following persons were appointed to a committee which should devise the best and most expeditious plan for accomplishing the purpose of the meeting: Isaac Hughes; M.W. Matthews; E.G. Rogers; J.D. Crawford; B. Gooch; Allen Urquhart; B. W. Gray; W. Peacock; and Mr. Wilson.

Capt. Booth of Bowie County has just taken out his second load of cotton from Stevenson's Ferry and is well satisfied as to the navigable qualities of the Sulphur.
****

From The Northern Standard, April 24, 1844

court news
The sickness of Judge Mills, who is still indisposed, prevented the session of the Court in Harrison County. It is unfortunate for the peace and good name of the Republic, the collection of the Revenue, and the profile of the grave and venerable District Attorney, who had a fine field before him in that little rotten borough, that the Court was not held. We understand that, had there been a Court, the criminal docket would have been graced with some twenty beautiful little cases for murder, besides other

graceful and popular employments in that region; such as
defrauding the Government of its tax revenues.

employment
good blacksmith could get constant employment at Boston,
Bowie County. I will furnish a shop, tools, and give good wages
to such a workman.
        S. H. Ellis

stray
dark bay horse has strayed from Thos. F. Smith and should be
returned to Wm. Donoho Esq

bankruptcy notice
Edward Hughart, George W. McCurley and William Foreman are
trustees to sell assets of John H. Dyer whom the court has
declared bankrupt

Information wanted by Green W. Whitfield about Wright W.
Whitfield, a youth, who in 1837 left Limestone County, Alabama
for Texas, and was only heard once by his friends since and is
supposed to be dead. If any gentleman acquainted with said
Whitfield, will forward any information concerning him to the
subscriber living in the United States, Alabama, Limestone
County, at Athens, he will surely confer an obligation on the
friends and relations of the delinquent.
****

From The Northern Standard, May 1, 1844

bankruptcy notice
Hugh F. Young, S.D. White and Charles De Morse are appointed
receivers to sell the property of Thomas A. Cowan, adjudged a
bankrupt

lawsuit filed
notice by W. H. Vining, Clerk for the District Court of Red River
County in the action for debt, entitled *William B. Johnson
against James Nall* that defendant is non resident of the Republic
and ordering service of process by publication of this notice in
The Standard for a period of three months

A notice by W. H. Vining, Clerk for the District Court of Red
River County in the action for debt, entitled *Matthew T Logan*

against Debtor James Fagan, who is a non resident of the Republic

administration of estates
Notice by J. C. Hart, Clerk of the County Court of Red River County that James J. Ward, has been appointed administrator of the Estate of Jeffrey Brown

notice that Letters Testamentary have been issued in Red River County to Amelia Bell and T.G. Wright as administrators of the Estate of Daniel Bell

commercial announcements
advertisement for the stud services of the horse *Reindeer* by Musgrove & Vernoy

advertisement s for the stud services of the horse *John Bell* at James J. Ward's, ten miles west of Clarksville; advertised by W.F. Cock
****

From The Northern Standard, May 8, 1844

married
on the 14th day of April, 1844, at Jordan's Mills by, W.L. Hamilton Esq., Mr. W. H. Benton, recently from Tennessee, to Miss Ellennor Jordan, daughter of Levi Jordan, Esq.

on the 14th day of April, 1844, at Jordan's Mills, by W.L. Hamilton Esq., Mr. John Millstead to Miss Susan Starkes, daughter of Mr. Aaron Starkes

administration of estates
Henry Trimble has been appointed by Lamar County Probate Court as administrator of the Estate of Loyd M. Garrison

notice by W.B. Stout, Probate Judge, that all persons holding claims against deceased persons estates are required by law as soon as they are acknowledged by an administrator, to file them with the Probate Court. Compliance with this will be found advantageous to the claimant

Sarah Riley has been appointed by Lamar County Probate Court as administrator of the Estate of James Riley

Nancy Stephens has been appointed by Lamar County Probate Court as administrator of the Estate of Jno. Stephens

Sarah Newburn and Thomas J. Newburn have been appointed by Lamar County Probate Court as administrators of the Estate of Jas. G. Wright

Wm. R. Brown has been appointed by Lamar County Probate Court as administrator of the Estate of August J. Butts

commercial announcements
George Gordon advertises that he has 156 bushels of corn for sale

Latimer, Bagby & Co advertise their steam mill for sawing lumber.

sporting news
Wm. F. T. Hart announces sweepstakes race for stallions only to be held in Clarksville on third Friday in October next
****

From *The Northern Standard*, May 15, 1844

commercial announcements
W. M. Harrison announces that he just received assorted gingham umbrellas, summer shoes, drab, cashmere and Palmeto hats,

James H. Johnson has two new copper stills for sale at cost. Carriage horses or cattle will be received in payment

lawsuit filed
notice by J. Long, Clerk District Court of Lamar County in the case in equity brought by George W. Wright against William C. Hamilton, Jeremiah Adams, Gilbert Combs, Joseph Hamilton and Martha P. Hamilton that, since defendants Adams and Joseph Hamilton

notice by J. Long, Clerk District Court of Lamar County in the case in equity brought by *Wm. M. Burris against Peter Harper and Benjamin Gooch*

runaway
notice of a runaway slave from Alfred Bailes, residing in the

Southern Division of Red River County. His name is Tom and he was once the property of Capt. Richard Finn of Lost Prairie, Arkansas. He was caught last year when he ran away from George Wilson Esq. of Blossom Prairie. If caught, he should be delivered to Dr. Hart, near Clarksville

lost property
Notice by Samuel Blagg, administrator of the Estate of James Blagg that James Blagg's certificate, no. 48, for one third a league of land in Fannin County has been lost

administration of estates
John A. Throckmorton and Malinda Throckmorton have been appointed by Fannin County Probate Court as administrators of the Estate of W. E. Throckmorton

John P. Simons and Catherine Simons have been appointed by Lamar County Probate Court as administrators of the Estate of Benjamin Simons
****
The Northern Standard, May 22, 1844 was not legible
****

From The Northern Standard, May 29, 1844

married
on Thursday evening the 23d *inst.*, by the Rev. J. W. P. McKenzie, Mr. L. D. Van Dyke of Bowie County to Miss Adelia F. West, daughter of Major Edward West of this county, at his residence near town.

by A.N. Hopkins, Esq on the 18th day of March, 1844, Mr. D.O. Norton to Miss Lydia A. Crabtree

by A.N. Hoke Esq. on March 19,1844, David R. Ween to Mary Hobbs

by J. H. Crook, Esq., on March 2, 1844, Mr. E. Thompson to Rhoda Payne

by J. H. Crook, Esq., on the 19th of April, Mr. John Croce to Lucretia Thompson

by L. V. Moore, Esq., on the 7th of April, Mr. Henry Robertson to Miss Nancy Blankenship

by J. H. Crook, Esq., on the 22nd April, Mr. L. Ratton to Miss Elita Cooper, all of Lamar County

by Lovell Coffman, Esq., on the 16th *inst.* Mr. Thomas Speaks, to Miss Jane Raney, all of Red River County.

by Lovell Coffman, Esq., on the 28th *inst.*, Mr. James Pairam to Miss Amena Clampet, all of Pine Creek.

Letters left at Post Office
lList of Letters remaining at the Post office at Fort Towson, Choctaw Nation,

Asby, M.J.
Aleen, Ebenezer
Bell, David G.
Bell, P.
Bell, David
Babb, David
Beal, R.R.
Barney, Lucien or Henry
Browning, Samuel
Cameron, John
Cornelius, John
Conrad, Rudolf
Cocke, B.F.
Cocksan, L. M.
Clay, Bartley
Carson, Charles
Carson, John
McCullen, Theodotia M.
Dail, William
Dillard, Matthew
Dagicy, H. Miss
Duncan, James
Dulaney, William
Estimauville, Sohia Mrs.
Fenly, Jas. D.
Field, William
Foye, James
Golding, James
Gossert, Presly (2)
Glass, John C.

Glen, George
Glover, Wm.
Graham, L.
Griggs, D. P.
Herrington, John or
Bailey, Isaac (2)
Hall, P.F. c/o
Hundenwick, W.
Homer, Robert
Hodge, A.M.
Howard, David or Wm. C.
Horn, Benny
Harrison, J. W.
Hancock, Jos.
James, Wm.
Ingraham, Wm. C.
Jackson, D.C. or
Morgan, Sam
Jackson, Charles
Kear, James
Kendrix, Martha
Leach, Marcus
Lucky, Hugh
Lenox, Wm.
Loving, James
Loving, Oliver
Mitchell, J. G.
Morgan, Samuel
McFarlane, B.C.
McFarlane, A.W.

Miller, Wm. G.
Marler, H.
Merreal, C.
Magry, R. P.
Mainor, J.
McCarty, J. H.
Maran, Wm. H.
Miles, A.
Mittower, A.
Mylor, Chas.
Martin, B. H.
Martin, Wm. G.
Montiew, S.
Monk, J.
Moore, John
Nickerson, John J.
Nott, J.
Seawright, John and Wm. M.
Scott, N. or Sarah A.
Smith, T.F.
Smith, F.
South, S. or Wm.
Stuart, W. P.
Sawyer, Horace
Steinson, John
Stephens, John
Sanford, D.

Saunders, S.
Stores, J.
Standerfer, J. M.
Truesdale, J. N.
Thomas, J. F.
Thomas, D. K.
Turner, Wm.
Tinnen, L. W.
Wood, D. R.
Walden, J.
Ware, J.
Walker, R.
Witin, R. M..
Williams, S. E.
Williams, A.G.
Wideman, E and T.
Worcester, N. and S.
Wortham, Thomas
Worthington, C.
Wagan, D.A.
Wilson, H. W.
Wilson, Jason
Wilson, J.
Wards, W.
Young, Elijah
Zagan, James

local news
notice by Jason Wilson, John Yeary, Mat. F. Sims and A.B. Manion, Commissioners, that contract for the bridging of a section of the Central National Road, will be let at John Loring's place in Fannin County on July 1, 1844. The section will extend from Dallas on the Trinity River to the crossing of the North Sulphur to the Red River.

public notices
notice by George W. Lawton, as agent, collecting the debt owed to J. Shelton & Co. He also has notes for collection due the firm by the firm Doak & Titus

stray
notice from J. C. Hart, County Clerk of Red River County that stray was taken up by Isaac Guest and estrayed before Lowell Coffman and appraised by W. Q. Richards and Elisha Ball

administration of estates
notice that John P. Craig has been appointed by Red River County Probate Court as executor of the Estate of Jno. B. Denton

John N. King and Nathaniel King have been appointed by Red River County Probate Court as executors of the Estate of Robert F. Floyd

Allen Urquhart and Nancy Johnson have been appointed by Red River County Probate Court the administrators of the Estate of Isaac H. Johnson

H.L. Williams has been appointed by Lamar County Probate Court as Executor of the Estate of Warren C. Williams

Susan Eskridge has been appointed administrator by Southern District Red River County Probate Court of the Estate of H. F. Eskridge

Daniel Jones has been appointed administrator by Southern District Red River County Probate Court of the Estate of Andrew Jones

Thomas J. White has been appointed administrator by Southern District Red River County Probate Court of the Estate of George Calmes
****

From The Northern Standard, June 5, 1844

court news
Hon. P.C. Jack, Judge of the 6th Judicial District, has been nominated as a candidate for Vice president of the Republic upon the ticket with General Burleson

school news
notice that Mrs. Weatherred's school in Clarksville will resume sessions on June 17

sporting news
Challenge by J. J. Muskgrove to race his horse, *Reindeer* against *Tennessean*

commercial announcement
James B. Shanahan announces that he has opened a shop on Main Street in Clarksville, near the Bridge, where he intends to manufacture cabinet furniture

administration of estates
Alfred Chandler has been appointed administrator by Lamar County Probate Court of the Estate of Noah Reeder

notice by J.C. Hart, Clerk of the Red River County Probate Court, that John H. McAnear has filed his accounting as administrator of the Estate of Jesse A. Smith
****
The Northern Standard, June 12, 1844 was not legible
****

From The Northern Standard, June 15, 1844

crime news
news report on of trial in Gonzalez County of Edward D. Davis, charged with the murder of William Polk, Hon. William E. Jones presiding. After twenty minutes of deliberating, the jury returned a verdict of guilty. The Court pronounced the sentence of death upon Davis, which was to take place on Friday 31st inst, but the prisoner has since made his escape.

settlements and immigration news
news report that Major Ely, the agent for the Trinity Colony assures that there will be more than enough families within the bounds of the Colony to comply with the contact, some 2,000 families
****

From The Northern Standard, June 19, 1844

agricultural news
I. H. Fishback has full blooded Saxony and Leicester Sheep for sale

stop payment
R. C. Harris cautions not to accept a note given by him to Cross and Willard of Bowie County, in the amount of $1,200 on the ground that it has already been paid.

public notice
notice by Joab Lynch that he was no long responsible for the debts of his wife Rebecca Lynch who has left his bed and board

stray
notice from J. C. Hart, County Clerk of Red River County of stray which was taken up by Daniel Sinclair and estrayed before S. W. Hillis and appraised by John M. Ritchey and D. R. Korn

notice from J. C. Hart, County Clerk of Red River County which was taken up by Phillip Shaffer and estrayed before L. Coffman J.P. and appraised by James B. Vaden and A. Colby

bankruptcy filing
notice by Joseph Nall to his creditors that he was going to apply the Chief Justice of the County of Red River County for a discharge in bankruptcy

lost property
notice by A.G. Kimbell that he has lost his land certificate for 640 acres of land, granted him by the Board of Land Commissioners of Red River County

land for sale
advertisement by James H. Johnston of Jonesboro for the sale of 8,196 acres of land, with improvements thereon for $8,000 in cash

From The Northern Standard, June 26, 1844

obituary
in Trinity Colony, on June 21, 1844, Samuel Browning, formerly of Louisville, Ky. and the City of Austin, aged 43. He was an original contractor for the Trinity Colony, under the Grant of 1841. He settled in it when it was a wilderness.

married
on the 23rd of June, 1844 by Thos. Willison, Esq., Mr. James Heath to Miss Rosetta Langford

on Thursday last, June 24, 1844, by the Hon. Wm. B. Stout, Mr. Wm. M. B. Fullerton to Miss Martha Gum

election news
announcement of Wm. R. Scurry, Esq. as candidate to be Representative of Red River County to the Congress of the Republic

lost property
notice by James H. Johnson that he has lost the bounty land warrant, issued to him as assignee of Mitchel Keller, for 320 acres of land

public notice
Wright & Montgomery having expired, creditors are to make payments either to W. T. Montgomery or T.G. Wright

bankruptcy filing
Notice by D.H. Dyer to his creditors that he was going to apply the Chief Justice of the County of Bowie for a discharge in bankruptcy

reward offered
$50 reward offered by John P. Simpson of Bonham, for the return of his horse and the thief, $25 for either

church news
a meeting of the Board of Managers of the Texas Bible Society to be held in Austin to celebrate the Seventh anniversary of the Society and to devise measures to promote its great prosperity.
Chauncy Richardson
First Vice President of the Texas Bible Society
****

From The Northern Standard, July 3, 1844

letters left at Post Office
letters left in Clarksville Post Office, as of the first day of July,

Allen, Ebenezer
Allen, Jesse
Blair, Andrew J.
Bateman, James W.(2)
Barker, William
Binion, John
Bowerman, Joshua
Bruton, Joseph R.
Billingsby, Jesse
Baskins, John
Baley, Claborn
Cave, W. J.
Clement, William H.
Cock, William F.
Crump, P.
Drennon, E.
Dickson, P.
Douglass, W.
Fowler, Rebecca
Fishback, Isaac H.
Fitzhugh, Lucas F.
Forman, W. W.
Ferguson, P.M.
Gragg, John
Gray, B. W.
Grimm, J. W.
Harris, Nath.
Hall, William
Hammock, Jackson
Harmon, John T.
Hayden, Moses
Halsabrook
Hancock, Joseph
Kinsey, Dr. S.
King, L.S.
Lawrance, McD.
Lynn, Benj. F.
Lernay, D.
Johnson, E.M.
Jones, A. E.
Jordan, John
Inglish, Campbell, Esq.
Monkhouse, J. M.
Mitchell, E. H. (2)
McCullough, Sam
Morton, Rufus
Martin, Hardy
Manley, Moore G. or
Manley, Mrs. S.F.
McCurley, Geo.
Morris, Jonathan
Nugent, John
Nall, Wm.
Parvis, John T.

Park, Wm. A.
Reed, Joseph
Rutherford, Right
Riker, N.M.
Ritchey, John
Richardson, Elizabeth
Smith, Mitchell
Smith& Darnell
Smith, C.M. (2)
Spencer, Oliver (2)
Sheck, A.
Stallings, Ab
Shearer, Spencer (2)
Tomilson, Wm.

VanDyke, Mrs. Delia F.
Walker, J. H.
Wright, T.G. (2)
Willborn, Wm.
Ward, Morris
Wheat, Wm.
Wells, Maj.
Warhop, J.
Walts, James
Young, R.
Young H.P.

administration of estates
notice by J. C. Hart, Probate Court, Red River County, that W. S. McClure, administrator of the Estate of Abner Lee has filed his accounting of the Estate

notice by J. C. Hart, Probate Court, Red River County, that W. S. McClure, administrator of the Estate of E. Johnson, has filed his accounting of the Estate.

Notice by J. C. Hart, Probate Court, Red River County, that W.S. McClure, administrator of the Estate of David Russell, has filed his accounting of the Estate

J.C. Parrish has been appointed Administrator on the Estate of James M. Garner and Bashaell Garner in Fannin County, Eastern Division

W. N. Vining has been appointed administrator by Red River County Probate Court of the Estate of John J. Vining

W.S. McClure has been appointed administrator by Lamar County Probate Court of the Estate of Abner Lee

Order from J. C. Hart, Probate Clerk of Red River County, requiring Ephraim D. Moore, administrator of the Estate of Joshua Wheat, to publish a notice to creditors for four weeks in *The Standard*.

stray
notice from J. C. Hart, County Clerk of Red River, of a stray taken up by Levi Dean and estrayed before John Stiles J.P. and appraised by S. Hemphill and John Tuomy

river and shipping news
notice that a public ferry is being established a mile below the public landing (or Brummitt's ferry) on Red River by J. W. Dircks, Cedar Bluff
****

From The Northern Standard, July 10, 1844

election news
announcement of Col. J. C. English as a candidate for Representative for Red River County, to the Congress of the Republic of Texas

announcement of Robert S. Hamilton of the 1st regiment as a candidate for Brigadier General of this Brigade

administration of estates
Thomas Dennis has been appointed administrator by Lamar County Probate Court of the Estate of James Dennis

W. S. McClure has been appointed administrator by Lamar County Probate Court of the Estate of W. Johnson
****

From The Northern Standard, July 17, 1844

election news
announcement of Isaac M. Brewer as a candidate for Colonel of the First Regiment, 4th Brigade, Texas Militia

From The Northern Standard, July 24, 1844

election news
political announcement from Samuel Huffer, who wishes to be elected County Surveyor, for which office Col. Sims is also a candidate. Huffer cites his accomplishments such as mapping the Sulphur Fork, although he gives credit to Judge Clark, Mr. Donoho and T.G. Wright

school news
advertisement, by Mrs. Eliza A. Todd for her Ringwood Female Seminary in Bowie County. She lists as her references: Judge James N. Smith, Judge Richard Ellis, Col. Charles Lewis, Col. Heatherly, Dr. J. W. Fort, Mr. James Browning and Col. Charles Moores

law suit filed
notice by H. Bayliss, Clerk District Court of Bowie County in the action for debt brought by Wright & Montgomery against Grant Lincicum, a non resident of the Republic.

Notice by H. Bayliss, Clerk District Court of Bowie County in the case arising out of an attachment brought by S.B. Johns against Benjamin Crawford, a non resident of the Republic .

notice by H. Bayliss, Clerk District Court of Bowie County in the action for debt brought by James Younger against Grant Lincicum that defendant, a non resident of the Republic

bankruptcy filing
notice by David O. Norton to his creditors that he is going to apply the Chief Justice of Lamar County for a discharge in bankruptcy

runaway
runaway from George Gordon, the Negro woman, Peg, formerly owned by Mrs. Smith (then Mrs. Wilson) of Pine Creek

From The Northern Standard, July 31, 1844

crime news
news report of the hanging of some repeat felons who had robbed and murdered some friendly Caddo Indians on the south side of South Sulphur, in Fannin county, about two miles from the line between Fannin and Lamar. They were: Andrew Jones, Harvey White, L. Wray and Mitchell, all lately from Missouri. Two other men, Ireland and Harris, were arrested but convicted of nothing more than theft, were made too hang the others.

election news

Poll location	Presiding officer
at W.S. Mitchell's	James B. Wooten, J.P.
at John Stiles	John Stiles, J.P.
at Ulysses Aguiere	Eliot Branden, J.P.
at Clarksville	John T. Clark, J.P.
at William Greggs	W.W. Foreman, J.P.
at Wm. Humphries	Benj. Crownover, J.P.
at John Robbins	Thomas J. Shannon, J.P.
at Travis G. Wright's store	Wm. Mays
at Clifton Springs	Thom. L. Burns
at H. W. Jones	Alexander Nevill
at Daingerfield	E.G. Rogers
at James F. Box's	Green H. Crowder
at Cannons	Wm. V. Hughes
at Smithland	Geo. W. Smith
at Stephen Peters	Stephen Peters
at J.C. Chawans	J. Baily
at Jos. Hammaracks	Benj. Merrill

set by the order of W.B. Stout, Chief Justice of Red River County

commercial announcement
advertisement for groceries and hardware of all varieties by Ragin & Deen

****

From The Northern Standard, August 7, 1844

court news
Judge Mills arrived in town

election news
Col. Anderson returned home from a visit to Lamar County and then left for Boston in Bowie County where he will address the citizens

response by S.W. Sims, current County Surveyor, to advertisement by rival Samuel Huffer

agricultural news
muskmelon, raised by Maj. Jas. W. Sims, measured thirty three inches in length

crime news
The notorious John A. Murrell is a few miles above Robbin's Ferry on the Trinity

settlements and immigration news
Judge Toler, who has been at Bonham in Fannin County, reports the arrival of many families from Illinois and Missouri who are encamped there on their way to the upper Trinity

land for sale
notice of sale by W. M. McClure, administrator of the Estate of Solomon Watson, 320 acres of land in Fannin County

Notice of sale by W.M. McClure, administrator of the Estate of Wm. Johnson, 1/3 a league of land in Red River County on the waters of Black Cypress
****

From The Northern Standard, August 14, 1844

stop payment
notice by Isaac Guest not to accept promissory note in the

amount of $183 which he gave to James M. Shell, said note having been obtained by one James A. Dickson, because it has already been paid

runaway
runaway slave, named Robert, from G. C. Johnston from Shreveport

professional card
S. H. Morgan & R. K. Clark
Partners in the practice of law, Seventh Judicial District , will attend to all business that may be referred to them with punctuality and fidelity
S. H. Morgan at Clarksville
R. K. Clark at Paris
****

From The Northern Standard, August 21, 1844

settlements and immigration news
Letter to Charles De Morse from Charles Fenton Mercer where he explains and answers complaints about his colony on the Trinity

obituary
news report that R.D. Sebring, Editor of the *Evening News* in Galveston, was one of 15 to 20 victims a day there, dying from an unrecognized disease that was said not to be Yellow Fever

Col. Wm. Pettus of Austin County, one of the old settlers and a regular attendant at the Seat of Government died on July 27, 1844

died of Gastrotitis at his plantation in the Southern District of Red River, Noah Lilly in the 74th year; born in 1771 in Martin County in North Carolina and came to Texas in 1837

election news
Paid advertisement by B. Gooch in opposition to claims of

Samuel Huffer

land for sale
notice by Martin Glover, administrator to the Estate of
Valentine M. Sublett of the sale of 20,000 acres lying of the
west side of the Trinity River, in Robertson County

stray
Notice from L. Coffman, Justice of the Peace of Red River
County that two mares taken by Elisha Clampett of Pine Creek
were appraised by W. H. Marrow and Isaac Moore

administration of estates
John L. Moore has been appointed administrator by Lamar
County Probate Court of the Estate of Gardner Reed

John L. Moore has been appointed administrator by Lamar
County Probate Court of the Estate of John Castleberry

local news
news item on "Splendid" Barbeque on July, 16th, the day set
aside by General James Smith of the County of Rusk to be
celebrated in commemoration of the eventful 16th of July,
1839, it being the day that the brave heroic and patriotic
Generals Rusk and Smith, whipped and drove from that
delightful and beautiful county that savage nation of people
known as the Cherokee Indians
****

From The Northern Standard, August 28, 1844

reward
notice by John Hill and James Logan, Agent for the Creeks, of
$1,500 Reward, for the apprehension of James L. Dawson and
John R. Baylor for the murder of Seaborn Hill, in the Creek
Nation.

election news
additional statement by Samuel Huffer in contest for County
Surveyor in response to Benjamin Gooch comments

professional card
Dr. I Herrick tends his services to the Citizens of Clarksville

and surrounding neighborhood in the practice of Physic,
Surgery, and Obsterics. He may be found at all times at his
office on Broad Street, near Wm. Donoho's Hotel

commercial announcement
Look & Hall advertises its "drugs, medicines, paints and oils"
just received from Philadelphia
****

From The Northern Standard, September 4, 1844

medicinal springs
item that the waters of Dalby's Springs, owned by a gentleman
named Dalby and situated in Bowie County, has medicinal
virtues, peculiar color etc and is becoming quite a place of
fashionable resort.

obituary
In Bowie County, on August 22, 1844, Alfred Harris, after a
very short illness, aged about 12 years, the son of R. C. Harris,
Esq.
****

From The Northern Standard, September 11, 1844

stray
notice from J. C. Hart, County Clerk of Red River, of stray
taken up by Elias F. Walker and estrayed before James B.
Wootten, J.P. and appraised by Charles C. Wellborn and Lewis
Autry

administration of estates
notice from J. C. Hart, Probate Court, Red River County, that
Amos Morrill, administrator of the Estate of John Tweedy, has
filed his accounting of the Estate

lost property
notice by E. H. Tarrant that he has lost a land warrant for 300
acres of land, issued to M. W. Matthews for three months
military service under Capt. Wm. Becknell from July to
October, 1836

Notice by Jeremiah Henson that he has lost his headright

certificate for 640 acres of land in Paschal County

obituary
Hon. Wm. H. Jack died at the residence of Gov. Runnels, on the Brazos, on Wednesday. He was on his way home from Houston where he had hurried too late to visit the dying bed of his brother.

commercial announcement
notice by S.S. Turner has 20 Negroes for sale
****
The Northern Standard was not published on September 18, 1844
****

From The Northern Standard, September 25, 1844

administration of estates
Henry S. Janes has been appointed administrator by Bowie County Probate Court of the Estate of M. H. Janes

commercial announcement
T.. Cornelius announces that he intends "to reduce goods" and will sell his inventory "for cotton or cash"
****

From The Northern Standard, October 2, 1844

Texas minerals
report on mineral wealth of the Upper Trinity, in lead and coal, if not gold and silver. Major Barksdale, agent for the Louisville Company, is collecting ore samples, including sulphur, which can be found in large quantities and very pure. There is also anthracite coal in immense quantities

married
on December 7, 1843 by J. T. Harmon, Mr. L. J. Cook to Mrs. Matilda Marmuth in Lamar County

on March 18, 1844 by A.N. Hopkins, Mr. D.O. Norton to Miss Lydia Crabtree in Lamar County

on the 13th of June, 1844 by A.N. Hopkins, David R. Ween

and Miss Mary Hobbs

on March 2, 1844 by J. H. Crook, Mr. Edward Thompson to Miss Rhoda Page in Lamar County

on the 11th day of July 1844 by L. V. Moore, Joseph Smith, Esq. to Mrs L.F. Workman in Lamar County

on July 1, 1844 by J A. Dillingham, Mr. Greenville Davis to Miss Nancy Taylor in Lamar County

on July 31, 1844 by the Rev. W. Brackson, Reuben Williams to Polly Barnett in Lamar County

on June 2, 1844 by Joel Wafer, Esq., Mr. J. Suly to Miss Sarah Clark in Lamar County

on July 7, 1844 by Joel Wafer, Esq., Mr. Mr E. H. Ayres to Miss E. L.Palew in Lamar County

on August 8, 1844 by G. S. Bonner Esq., Mr. China M. Robinson to Miss Malinda Lawden in Lamar County

on the 29th of August 1844, by the Rev. J. H.. Shook, Mr Young Borger to Miss A.H.Bell in Lamar County

by Lucian Barney , Esq., Mr. John Davis to Elizabeth Brumly, in Lamar County (specific date in 1844 not provided)

on August 21, 1844 by Lucian Barney, Esq., Mr. Jas. Ledbetter to Miss Mary Atkinson in Lamar County

on September 1, 1844 by I.. J. Nowell, Esq., Mr Cyrus Johnson to Miss Ann Prince in Lamar County

on the 15th day of July, 1844, by Geo. Wilson, Esq., Mr. John Nall to Miss Polly A. Cardel in Lamar County

on September 17th, 1844 by A.N. Hopkins, Mr. Benjamin Green to Miss Mary Beekam in Lamar County

on the 29th of August, 1844 by the Rev. J. H. Shook, Mr. Eli Cox to Miss May Murray in Lamar County on August 26, 1844, by G. S. Bonner, Mr. A. N. Graham to Miss Mary J. Shidmore in Lamar County

obituary
Enoch Crow, Esq. at his residence four miles east of Paris, Lamar County, of congestive fever

bankruptcy notice
George F. Lawton, Daniel Draper, and Thomas J. Newbern, Trustees of the estate of Joseph Nall, a bankrupt, will sell his assets at the next Sheriff's Sale

administration of estates
Charles Jackson has been appointed executor by the Fannin County Probate Court of the Estate of Silas C. Colville of Shawneetown in Fannin All those indebted to the estate should make payments to James M. Randolph, also of Shawneetown

reward
$150 Reward for the return of runaway Negro Boy Adam, offered by master M. Watson

commercial announcement
Notice by T. J. Cornelius that he will reduce inventory for cash or cotton
****

From The Northern Standard, October 9, 1844

agricultural news
Robert Mills, Esq. of Brazoria, will probably make 600 bales of cotton this year.

crime news
The trial of Wm. Matthews, indicted for the murder of Pleasant M. Gwinn, in Clarksville eight months earlier, was held in the last term of the District Court in Red River County and resulted in his conviction for manslaughter.

Administration of estates
James N. Smith has been appointed executor by the Lamar County Probate Court of the Estate of John T. Smith.

letters at Post Office
list of Letters remaining at Clarksville Post office as of Oct. 1, 1844.

Anderson, Andy 2	Kimball, John
Barker, William 3	Turgle, Jackson
Binnion, John	Lyday, A.
Brylarly, Thomas F.	Lupton, Joseph L
Boots, William	Langford, E.N.
Cook, Elijah	Musgrove, J.J.
Clement, John C.	McPeters, Jonathan
Clark, Wiley	McFarland, Robert
Cherry, James	Morrill, Amos
Candle, Mrs. M. Linda	Patterson, J.H.
Daniel, Lewis W. 2	Rogers, E.G.
Duncan, Charles R.	White, Joseph
Duncan, H.S.	Wingate, Truit
Davis, William H.	Ewing, Clayton
Dean, Thomas	Sandler, William
Evans, William	Smith, Caleb
Elliot, W.A.	Simons, E.C.
Fugate, Rubin M.2	Towney, John R.
Fowler, J.S.	Wilkins, John O.
Fullerton, William	Webb, Alexander W.
Fullerton, J.M.	Woods, Thomas
Finley, William L.	Williamson & Bowerman
Huffer, Samuel	Wall, Lenard
Hudson, William	Waits, James
Hall, A.	
Jordan, Thomas	

Post Master,
A.M. Crooks

commercial announcement
notice to Planters from James T. Lee that he has rigging and coils of rope for sale at his store in Clarksville
****

From The Northern Standard, October 16, 1844

crime news
account of two men, named Flynt and Mullens, who were arrested in Clarksville, upon suspicion of Negro stealing and

dealing in counterfeit coins. Their Negro accomplice had made an appointment with a Negro of Mr. William Donoho, to meet him at night and Mr. Donoho's Negro suspected and advised the authorities.

professional card
John R. Craddock, Notary Public in Paris, Lamar County will execute deeds, bonds and other instruments of writing

land for sale
D. N. Alley "will sell low, part cash and part on time, seven hundred and one acres of land, situated two miles south of Clarksville, adjoining John Butler on the south, with between two and three hundred acres of excellent prairie, the remainder of the tract well timbered, and rich arable land. This land, from its contiguity to Town, its fine supply of water and wood, and its situation in one of the most dense settlements in the Republic, is very desirable for any immigrant who wishes to have the advantages and convenience of a well settled country, with rich land at a low price.
The tract will be sold in lots to suit purchasers.
Apply to W.B. Stout, or Wm. Donoho, Clarksville, or to D. N. Alley near Daingerfield.

administration of estates
Christopher Elmore and Lucinda Fry have been appointed administrators by the Lamar County Probate Court of the Estate of Benjamin J. Fry.
****

From The Northern Standard, October 30, 1844

married
on the 16th of October, 1844 by Hon. W.B. Stout, Mr James M. Sharp to Miss Mary Dean

obituary
George W. Mabane of consumption at his father's residence in Lamar County on October 18, 1844

commercial announcement
Wm. G. Kerley from the Saline Salt Works in Sevier County Arkansas has salt to sell

announcement by W.B. Stout that on December 1, 1844 that he was traveling to Austin and, in exchange for reasonable compensation would attend to anyone's business there, such as land patents

school news
James Sampson announces that the Clarksville Academy will hold examinations on the first Monday of November

runaway
advertisement for the return of Negro boy Bob, placed by Wm. G. Kerley from the Saline Salt Works in Sevier County Arkansas

lawsuit filed
notice by John A. Rutherford, Justice of the Peace in Lamar County in the action to recover $63 and interest brought by John R. Craddock against Abram Mittower

lost property
notice by James H. Johnson of lost land warrant assigned to him by Mitchell Keller

notice by R.W. Milholland of lost or stolen horse in Lamar County
****

From The Northern Standard, October 23, 1844

election news
announcement that Isaac N. Brewer is a candidate for Colonel of the First Regiment, 4th Brigade, Texas Militia

settlements and immigration news
description of lands in cultivation in the Northern and Southern Divisions of Red River County, provided by Edward Huggart, Assessor of Red River County

sports news
challenges by Hart & Co on behalf of its horse *Albert Gallantin*
****

From The Northern Standard, November 6, 1844

employment
advertisement by Beard & Cochran for four good house carpenters of sober habit; also a first rate cabinet workman can find a good situation

lost headright certificate
notice by James Ball that he has lost the head right certificate given to John Bouler in Fannin County for 320 acres

stray
notice from J. C. Hart of Red River County that Sam W. Hillis, Justice of the Peace estrayed two mares taken up by Robert C. Fleming. They were appraised by Willaim R. M. Duncan and John N. Ritchey

sports news
challenge by C.E. Hilburn to horse *Albert Gallatin*
****

From The Northern Standard, November 13, 1844

sports news
report on the match race for $600 between Martin Glover's *Premium* and Dr. Hart's horse,*Albert Gallatin*, four mile heats.
****

From The Northern Standard, November 20, 1844

court news
Ebenezer Allen, Esq. of Clarksville is appointed Attorney General of the Republic. There is not a man in the country whose acquirements and capacity would do more credit to the nation. He will leave many here who appreciate highly his talents, his virtues, and his amiability of deportment

church news
Rev. Dr. McCloskky of the Christian Baptist denomination will preach at the courthouse in Clarksville next Sunday

obituary
Hon. Isaac Van Zandt, late representative from this

Government to the United States died at Coffeeville, Alabama on his way home

crime news
The case of Amanda Moore, who was charged with conspiring in the murder of her father, was taken up last Thursday, Messrs Clark, Martin and Hill appearing for the accused and Messrs Scurry, Jennings and Burke on the part of the state. The trial created considerable interest, and, after a protracted continuance of four days, the jury, after a few minutes deliberations, returned with a verdict of Not Guilty, when the prisoner was released.

Harrison County -- From Marshall, we learn that the District Court has adjourned after a session of five weeks and the accomplishment of much business. An attempt was made by a fellow named Neal to shoot Judge Ochiltree. Gen'l Henderson overheard his threats, stopped him at the door and told him he would shoot him if he moved any closer to the Judge, whereupon Neal walked off.
Twenty two indictments for murder were found and forty odd for aggravated cases of assault with intent to kill, showing pretty clearly that there was a need for a Court.

Mrs. Van Dyke and her Negro woman were charged, in collusion with the daughter, in the murder of old Mr. Van Dyke in Rusk County and sent to Harrison for trial, was remanded to Rusk.

runaways
runaway, from James H. King, a Negro woman named Frances. A reward of $30 will be paid to anyone who will deliver the woman to Wm. Donoho in Clarksville

runaway from R.W. Hamilton, living on Red River, a Negro man named Jeff

public notice
J. H. Shelton & Co calls for those indebted to pay their bills

administration of estates
Elizabeth Crow appointed executrix by the Lamar County Probate Court of the Estate of Enoch Crow

From The Northern Standard, November 27, 1844

commercial announcement
Stearn Flour Mill has been purchased by Dr. Boyce in Bowie, and he will have here this winter the machinery for a regular manufacturing mill

professional card
copartnership existing between Ebenezer Allen and Wm. S. Todd will continue as heretobefore. All papers and documents connected with pending matters are in the hands of W. M . Todd, to whom clients are refereed. Mr Allen expects to attend all the Courts in the District as usual

public notice
notice by Edward West that people indebted to L. D. Van Dyke should pay their bills

administration of estates
Benjamin South has been appointed administrator of the Estate of John M. Nelson.

Notice by Sarah Newbern and Thomas J. Newbern, as administrators of property near that of James G. Wright, deceased
****

From The Northern Standard, December 4, 1844

crime news
Broke Jail -- On Sunday night last, John Chapman, who was charged with the murder of a man by the name of Barkly and who was confined in the [Harrison] county jail for appearance at the next term of the District Court

married
on the 3rd November, 1844, by L. Coffman, Esq., Mr. James Henderson to Mrs. Sarah Kuykendall, all of this County.

church news
Rev. Nathan Skook will preach at the Methodist Church in Clarksville on Sunday next, at 11 o'clock A.M.

professional card
E. S. Look and A. M. Hall announce the dissolution of their partnership and Dr. Look will keep the stock of medicine "at the old stand"

bankruptcy filing
George A. Brown will apply for a discharge in bankruptcy before the Chief Judge of Red River County

lawsuits filed
notice by W. H. Vining, Clerk of the District Court of Red River County, of a chancery action entitled James W. Wauhop against John Selveter

notice by W. H. Vining, Clerk of the District Court of Red River County, of an action for debt entitled *Samuel Taylor against Levi Jourdan*
****

From The Northern Standard, December 12, 1844

sports news
race over the Dayton Grove Track -- A match race for $1,000 a side between Alfred Bailes' horse and James Bourland's horse, *Berkshire Boar*, will come off at the Dayton Grove Track, one mile and a half from town on Friday

for sale or rent
notice by Henry S. Jeanes, as administrator of estate of Massack H. Jeanes, of the sale of personal property, corn, cattle, horses; also 15 or 16 Negroes for hire --all on a credit of 12 months

notice by Geo. W. Wright, as guardian of the minor heirs of Gabriel N. Martin, for the hire of his Negroes for 12 months

land for sale
notice by E. H. Tarrant, administrator of the Estate of J. H. Hall 3000 acres of land, in Bowie County, fronting for two miles on the Red River, on credit terms of 1,2,3,4,5 years --equal payments-- as well as a 1/3 of a league of land, J. H. Hall's headright, lying adjoining the town of Boston and near the property of James G. Wright, deceased

bankruptcy filing
John L. Clark will apply for a discharge in bankruptcy before the Chief Judge of Red River County

administration of estates
notice by George Cordon and D. N. Alley, administrators of Estate of A.D. Duncan, that they will terminate business of estate in one final sale
****

From *The Northern Standard*, December 19, 1844

crime news
Nancy Van Dyke and the Negro Nancy, who were kept several months in Harrison county as State's prisoners, were convicted a few days since in the District Court of Nacagdoches, for the murder of John Vandike, which was committed in Rusk county about eighteen months ago

public notice
notice by Edward Hughart, Assessor of Red River County, that all those in the Sheriff's Tax book can pay half the tax now and the other half in 30 days
****

From *The Northern Standard*, December 26, 1844

crime news
President Houston has pardoned Mrs. Van Dyke and the Negro, Nancy, convicted of the murder of Mr. Van Dyke at the last session of the District Court for Nacogdoches County.

sports news
The quarter race between the *Barkshire Boar* and *Rackamaroleon*, for $1,000 a side, came off on Saturday last. *Rackamaroleon* kept the lead for about two hundred yards, when the *Boar* came up and passed him with great ease, and passed the judges' stand some 30 or 40 feet ahead, under a tight rein. We understand that Mr. Bailes, the loser of the race, has since purchased the Boar

challenge by John Loring to the owners of the horse *Pete Whetstone* to a race

election news
notice by W.B. Stout, Chief Justice of Red River County of general election of town of Clarksville officials, to be conducted by E.M. Smith

letter to Chas. De Morse from W.R. Scurry, Red River County representative in Austin reporting that Ebenezer Allen of our place is appointed Attorney General. Ochiltree has been appointed Secretary of the Treasury

the following are appointed poll monitors: H. J. Turner; L. M. Coe; T. A. Anderson; G. W. Bowles; J. H. Savegh; J. C. Rogers; J. H. Thomas; D. M. Currin; J. C. Galla; L. C. Haynes; T. Ewells

fraternal organizations news
Members of the Masonic Fraternity celebrated the anniversary of St. John the Evangelist on December 27 with a procession, a band playing music and an oration by the reverend brother Samuel Corley in the church in Clarksville and a dinner at the hotel of Doctor Ward

wanted to purchase
E. P. Parris advertises to purchase slave boy

strays
notice by John T. Mills of lost or stolen horse

public notice
notice by T. J. Cornelius that those owing him money had 20 days to pay or else he was putting their accounts into the hands of E.M. Smith of Clarksville for collection

administration of estates
advertisement by D. Rowlett that he has finished the administration of Estate of Carter H. Clifft in Fannin County

lawsuit filed
notice issued by Thomas C Bean, Clerk of the District Court for Fannin County, in the lawsuit styled *Simeon K. Woodrow, administrator of the estate of Nancy K. Woodrow against the heirs of Jacob Black, John Hoyman* and his brother (first name not known) to foreclose mortgage

professional card
J. H. Harvey, attorney and counselor at law, will practice in the courts of the Fifth, Sixth and Seventh Judicial Districts and the Supreme Court of the Republic. Office in Marshall, Harrison County

land for sale
advertisement for farm for sale three miles west of Clarksville. Inquire of J. W. P. McKenzie

notice by Amos Morrill, agent of sale of a block of 8 lots in town, known a Block three and containing the personal residence of Charles De Morse

commercial announcements
advertisement for hauling services by Thos. D. Lee

advertisement for the sale of fancy and other dry goods by Thos. D. Lee

advertisement for sale by A. W. King of fruit trees

advertisement for sale by M. Looney and A.W. Richardson of lime
****

1845

From The Northern Standard, January 16, 1845

school news
advertisement by Eliza A. Todd on behalf of the Ringwood Female Academy. Her references in Bowie county are Judge James N. Smith, Judge Richard Ellis, Col. Charles Lewis, Col. Heatherly, Mr. James Browning, and Col. Charles

commercial announcement
advertisement by Thom. D Lee to buy oats and to trade Beeswax, Honey, Peltry, Hides and Tallow for Merchandise

public notice
George Gordon warns people not to take wood from his lands

newspaper business
notice that Col. Bryan, at Dallas, will act as *The Standard's* agent there

professional card
notice of law partnership between E. H. Tarrant and E.M. Peters. E. H. Tarrant will continue to practice in the courts of the Seventh District and in the Supreme Court of the District and will keep his office in Boston, Bowie County

election news
Col. B. H. Martin elected Mayor of Clarksville and Amos H. Rounssville, Town Constable

obituaries
in Sevier county, Arkansas, while on his way to Texas, Major John Starkey, late of St Clair County, Illinois, age 52

in Clarksville, on January 6th, 1845, Mrs. Electa Angelina Young, wife of Hugh F. Young, aged 22 years.
****

From The Northern Standard, January 23, 1845

list of letters at Clarksville Post Office as of January 1, 1845, published by A.M. Crooks P.M.

Anderson, Andy
Brotherton, John 2
Baker, Col. J. Y.
Badgman, James W.
Bailes, A.
Bailes, Alfred
James, W.
Baird, Andrew S.
Bishop, William N.
Billey, Wesley
Cocks, Benjamin F. Esq.
Clerk of the County Court
Childers, Levi
Crenshaw, Lewis A.D.
Cooper, Benjamin
Clapp, David, Esq.
Crump, William G.

Dirkson, James A. 2
Dragon, John
Davison, Josiah
Davis, H.E.
Faris, John
Fishback, Isaac H.
Fort, Joseph M.
Grand, Stephen
Green, James W.
Gray, W. J.
Greaves, Jon S.
Griggs, Andrew
Glass, Robert
Horg, E. H.
Hale, Abedage 2
Heatherly, Thomas Col.
Henderson, Archibald

Henderman, M.C.
Harris, Virgil K.
Hill, Elizabeth Mrs.
Hogan, G.M.
Johnson, James H.
Johnson, Riley
Kline, Chas. F.
Lydny, Joseph
Lamar, Edmund
Lawrence, D.H.
Lawrence, O. W.
McClure, W. S.
Mmoore, John L.
McDonald, Alex
Marler, W.S.
Mather, Jas.

Mather & Stats
Parlien, Wm. Maj.
Parish, Leam
Slean, Thom.E.
Seawright, John
Seed, Campbell
Smith, Samuel C.
Sims, E. A Mrs.
South C.
South, Wm.
Wright, Thomas C.
West, Edward
Wilson, M.G.
Woods, Thomas
Wren, Nicholas

commercial announcement
notice by *The Northern Standard* that legal forms could be purchased in Clarksville and, from John R. Craddock, *The Standard's* Agent in Paris, Lamar County

lawsuit filed
notice from W. H. Vining, Red River County District Court Clerk to William B Hawkins that he and Robert Hamilton have been sued by Willie C. Thompson for $600 for fees owed him as an overseer in Hickman's Prairie, Bowie County

public notices
notice of dissolution of partnership of Matthieson & Coles, given by U. Matthieson and W. L. F Coles in Paris, Lamar County

notice that those owing fees to Justice of the Peace Thom. Willson, can save further charges by paying him at his office at the Post Office which is across the street from the Hotel of Dr. Wood

stray
notice by L. M. Rick, Clerk of the County Court of Bowie County, that Gatewood Glover has taken up a stray horse and brought him to David M. Chisolm, Esq

land for sale
notice by B.F. Lynn of 500 acre farm, 8 miles north of Clarksville, is for sale. It is 90 acres of prairie and the rest is rich bottom land
****

From The Northern Standard, January 30, 1845

administration of estates
notice that W. S. McClure, administrator of the Estate of Isaac Gideon of Red River County, will sell as much of the Estate as is necessary to pay debts of the Estate

sporting news
response by N. Doak, to challenge issued by John Loring regarding horse race
****

From The Northern Standard, February 6, 1845

commercial announcements
William Donoho offers the stud services of his steed *Duke Luzborough* at his stable in Clarksville

advertisement by Dr. E. S. Look of medicines for sale

Latimer, Bagley & Co advertises its new steam mill

Thoms D. Lee advertises *Peter Whetstone* for sale from Washita Quarry

notice by J. Swanson that at William Donoho stable in Clarksville that horse *Duke Luzbororough* will act as a stud

Texas history
news item that Jesse Walker, Esq just returned from the Trinity and discovered, on Sister Grove Fork of the Trinity, the bones of a man and a horse. It was about 10 miles north of the Throckmorton Settlement. There were military buttons and tin cup which had the name P. Jefferson. Item speculated that the man had been dead three or four years and had been left there by Col. Cooke's command when they ran the Military Road

runaway
runaway from R.M. Hopkins, a Negro man: named George

bankrupt estate
S. H. Ellis, C.R. Johns and A.A. Williams have been appointed trustees of the estate of bankrupt D. H. Dyer

public notice
notice from Amos Morrill that he has the books of the J. Shelton & Co. and is collecting funds owed it

lawsuit filed
notice from A. Long, Clerk of the District Court of Lamar County of order permitting service by publication against defendant Millican in the action for debt brought by *Curtis Moore against James S. Johnson, Elijah Millican and John R. Craddock*

notice by J. Long, Clerk, in lawsuit styled *William C. Young against Thomas J. Newbern, Samuel E Powers and Jacob Long*, pending in Lamar County District Court

notice by J. Long, Clerk, in lawsuit in divorce action for abandonment brought by *William T.P. Coles against Latitia B Coles*, pending in Lamar County District Court

notice by J. Long, Clerk, in lawsuit styled *William C. Young against Thomas J. Newbern and Ebenezer Allen* for $200 debt, pending in Lamar County District Court

notice by W. H. Vining, clerk of Red River District Court, to Stephen Kinney that he has been sued by William C. Denton for $350

administration of estates
Samuel S. Smith appointed administrator of the Estate of James Holloway in Red River County

Joel Halbert appointed administrator of the Estate of Jon Halbert of Bowie County

Wm. M. Williams has been appointed administrator of Estate of Joshua Bowerman and agent for Abram Mittower and Isaac

C. Williamson and on behalf of Bowerman & Mittower and Williamson & Bowerman

W. S. McClure, has been appointed administrator of the Estate of Isaac Gideon of Red River County

land for sale
George Gordon and D. N. Alley advertise the sale of six town lots in Clarksville belonging to the estate of A.D. Duncan in order to settle debt of $400 owed by estate
****

From The Northern Standard, February 13, 1845

sporting news
report on race between Nelson Doak's horse *James K Polk* and L. W. Perry & Co's horse *Tennessean*

election news
returns from Lamar County election: for Chief Justice, W. M. Crisp defeated I.A. Rutherford, and I. S. Gillett; for Sheriff, Red Russell defeated J. H. Crook and I.F. Crawford and E. R. Miller ; for County Surveyor, J. T. Harmon defeated W. Evans; for District Clerk, J. Long was the only candidate; for County Clerk, J. R. Craddock defeated T. R.H. Potteets and for Coroner D. Meyers was unopposed.

commercial announcement
J. C. Hart and Geo. W. Hart advertise the stud services of their horse *Albert Gallatin*

public notice
Wm. M. Harrison warns those indebted to pay up

professional card
Doctor W. F. T. Hart advises that he has sold his stock of blooded horses and has returned to the practice of medicine in Clarksville

administration of estates
Samuel S. Smith appointed administrator of Estate of Cannon Smith in Red River County

Samuel S. Smith appointed administrator of Estate of Henry M. Canaday in Red River County

lawsuit filed
notice by W. H. Vining, Clerk of District Court of Red River County in action styled *Wm. B. Stout against Daniel McKinney, Guardian of the Minor Heirs of Wm. Collom, deceased and James N. Smith and Pharough Kitchens*, to whom he unfaithfully diverted the property belonging to the wards

lost property
I.W. Fishback lost discharge of Wm. King, which called for the payment of 330 acres and the payment of three months services in the Texas army in 1836 in the company of Capt. John Becknell
****

FromThe Northern Standard, February 20, 1845

bankruptcy filing
Wm. Gragg will apply to the Chief Justice of Red River County for a discharge in bankruptcy

Thomas Y. Logwood will apply to the Chief Justice of Bowie County for a discharge in bankruptcy

public notice
notice by S. H. Ellis that the firm of Ellis & Van Dyke has been dissolved by mutual consent and Mr. Ellis recommends his friends to L. D. Van Dyke who will continue to sell merchandise in Boston, Bowie County

John J Duncan of Washburn Prairie in Missouri seeks information on Richard H. Toler of Bowie County

notice by Henry Worthman that his wife Rossanna Worthman has left with James C. Warren

runaway
notice by M. Glover sheriff of Red River County that a Negro, calling himself Isaac has been taken in Bowie county. He says he belongs to William Kinchelo of Mississippi

stop payment
Public cautioned not to purchase a note by Preston H. Hall to George W. Nutt for $310 as it was obtained in fraud and without consideration

stray
notice by Charles De Morse as to horse that strayed from residence of J. S. Sharkey on White Oak prairie

land for rent
Samuel Fulton advertise farm for rent, which has 30 acres of cultivated fields, houses and corn cribs about 10 miles northeast of Clarksville. Inquiries to be made to John McCurly, Esq., residing on the premises or to Amos Morrill of Clarksville
****

From The Northern Standard, February 27, 1845

commercial announcement
advertisement by Wm. Ward of Star Hotel in Clarksville

administration of estates
notice that Ann Smith has been appointed administratrix of Estate of Philip Smith in Fannin County

stray
notice by James T. Lee of horse strayed or stolen horse from Blossom Prairie

public notice
notice by Thom. Lee that all those indebted to the late house of James T. Lee should pay what they owe
****

FromThe Northern Standard, March 6, 1845

newspaper business
Editor acknowledges Mr. Reed of Fort Towson who provided him a copy of the *Madisonian* of February 7. 1845

commercial announcements
J. C. Hart and G. W. Hart offers the stud services of their horse

Albert Gallatin, at their farm one mile and a quarter South West from Clarksville.

Thos. D. Lee offers for sale "to the Patrons of the Turf" the fine blooded race horse *WOODPECKER*,

Cash or its equivalent will be paid for Corn, Fodder and Hay by Thos. D. Lee

Wm. Ward respectfully "informs his friends and the traveling public that he has opened the Star Hotel in Clarksville," a two story, "spacious establishment, for the accommodation of visitors, . eligibly situated on the public square of the Town. . . and has attached to it a very large stable, which will be kept well supplied with provender."

just received and for sale a lot of whetstones from the celebrated Washom Quarry, by Thos. D. Lee.

first rate Spinning Machine, new and of a good quality. Enquire of W.B. Stout.

lime for sale at the brick yard of M. Looney and J. A. Richardson, half a mile east of town.

Wanted, a few bushels for seed. Apply to Thos. D. Lee

advertisement by H. W. Shelton for the lease of four slaves for a two or three year term.

administration of estates
John Ballew has been appointed administrator of the Estate of Robert Ballew of Bowie County

strays
notice by appraisers A.G. .Melton and James Matthews of their report, sworn to before Ulysses Aiguer, Justice of the Peace of Red River County , of horse taken up by Leven and Karber had a value of $25

Notice by W.B. Stout of strayed horse

Notice that James Wilson of Clarksville borrowed a mare from

H.S. Slayton for the purpose of riding 30 miles on urgent business and has not returned.

strayed or stolen from the residence of J. S. Starkey on White Oak prairie, a chestnut sorrel horse. Any information thankfully received by Starkey, or by Charles De Morse.
****

From The Northern Standard, March 13, 1845

Indian news
news items that, according to the Hon. S. F. Smith of Fannin County, that Congress has made arrangements for a ranging company of 15 men to protect the Fannin frontier; a party of hostile Indians chased two slaves belonging to Mr. McIntyre of Warren

settlement and immigration news
letter to Charles De Morse from D. Rowlett, agent for C.F. Mercer in Lamar County that grant is in tact

professional cards
P. J. Pillans, attorney and counselor at law
will attend the courts of the 7th District; office in Bonham, Fannin County

John Taylor, attorney at law; will attend the courts of Fannin, Lamar, Red River, Bowie and Harrison Counties
residence at Marshall, Harrison County

lost property
notice by James Shannon of lost land certificate, belonging to Spencer Asbury, for 320 acres in Fannin County

administration of estates
M. H. Dixon has been appointed administrator o f the Estate of Calvin Fielden of Fannin County

M. H. Dixon has been appointed the administrator of the Estate of James Davenport of Fannin County

William S. Sadler has been appointed executor of the Estate of C..W. Sadler of Lamar County

strays
notice by James Wilson that H.S. Slayton had lied, for he had returned as soon as it was in his power, to do so, owing to high water

strayed or stolen from the lower edge of Blossom Prairie, a brown mare mule. A suitable reward will be given for her delivery to Isaac Smothers or James T. Lee.

commercial announcements
notice by C. Vernoot that his horse *Reindeer* will stand for services at Clarksville and ten miles west of town at James J. Ward's

D. Lee that his horse *Woodpecker,* will stand for stud services 10 miles east of Clarksville at John Stiles's place and ten miles west of town at John Robbins'

E. S. Look has garden seeds for sale

advertisement by Wm. M. Williams of groceries for sale

S.M. Peters advertises his law books for sale -1/3 cash and balance due next October
****

From The Northern Standard, May 13, 1845

local news
news item about soldier from Fort Towson, named Johnson, who had been in Clarksville on a visit, was drowned in Pine Creek on his return. He had been in service nearly eight years, and his time of enlistment would have expired in about three months. He had acquired some money while in service, and had purchased land a few miles from Town, on which he intended settling, when discharged.

annexation news
report on the public meeting held among the citizens of Bowie County regarding the subject of annexation. Upon the motion of the Hon. James N. Smith, Collin McKinney, Esq. was called to the Chair and Dr. John S. Peters was appointed Secretary. The object of the meeting was explained by Gen.

Thomas J. Rusk and a committee was formed to draft resolutions to express the sentiment of the citizens. The Committee included Gen. E. H. Tarrant, Judge Jas. N. Smith, David M. Chisholm Esq., Dr J. W. Fort, Isaac Hughes Esq., Capt. W. P. Rose, John W. Scott, Col. Charles Lewis, C.R. Johns Esq., Wm. C. Young Esq., S.B. Morgan Esq.,and John Speak. The Hon. John T. Mills addressed the gathering

letters left at Letters left in Bowie Post office.

Battle, C. W. Esq
Bennet, J., Clerk of District Court
Daken, Jacob
Ellis, William B.
Graham, R .B.
Glover, Mrs. Mary Ann
Hendrick, Sol. B Esq.
Jackson, Charles
Loop, John
Lunn, William
Lamar, Samuel 2

Walton, General Charles
McFarland, Dr. James M.
Kinney, James
Nevill, A.
Powell, Matthew N.
Rogers, Simeon
Russel, James W.
Searey, Merit
Searey, L.C.
Smith, Mrs. Polina
Streme, John
Ward, Mathias

Post Master L. D. VanDyke

public notices
notice to Public that Joel Halbert and his son John Halbert made a false oath before John A. McKinney, Cross& Willard, Henry Carbow and H.M. Derrybery that they had stolen a Negro named Riall , despite their having issued a bill of sale for him. Joel Halbert has fled to Missouri; John Halbert has fled to the western portion of te Republic

notice by E. H. Tarrant to all not to cut any wood on his land on Pecan Bayou as he has an agent grant to cut timber there

administration of estates
Chas. F.M. Gudrian has been appointed administrator of the Estate of Jeremiah Moncey of Fannin County

Dorothy Harty has been appointed administratix of the Estate of Dennis Harty of Red River County

C.R. Johns has been appointed administrator of the Estates of James W. Russell and J. G. Johns Moncey of Bowie County

runaway
Martin Glover, Sheriff of Bowie County, has taken up a runaway slave, Bob, who says he belongs to Geo. Brown, living at White Oak

stray
notice by Fannin County Clerk, R.W. Lee, that appraisers J.D. Cowan and W. S. McClure of horses shown to them by George H. Bagby and have sworn thus to Samuel Ervin, Justice of the Peace of Fannin County

commercial announcements
advertisement by Darnall & Dickson for linens, cloths, clothes and hardware
****

From The Northern Standard, May 20, 1845

stray
running at large, somewhere on or near Gregg's Creek, a red cow, with white spots on the body, that formerly belonged to Mr. Kincaid.

annexation news
item regarding meeting in Fannin County on the issue of annexation. George M. Smith was called to the chair and Dr. John H. Wilson was appointed Secretary and resolutions were drafted, calling for annexation. G.A. Everts spoke in favor of the resolutions. Dr. D. Rowlett and Major P. J. Pillans made speeches opposing annexation. Capt Cowall conducted a vote and the vote was 2-1 in favor of the annexation

professional cards
Henry D. Woodsworth,
attorney and counselor at law
Paris, Lamar County

James S. Gillet
attorney and counselor at law
Paris, Lamar County

commercial announcements
Cornelius & Smith have salt, sugar etc. for sale at their store in Clarksville

notice by Edward West of stud services for his horse *Tennessean* at his stable in the Town of Clarksville
****

From The Northern Standard, May 30, 1845

annexation news
notices that Col. Wm. C. Young, A.H. Latimer, Esq., John T. Mills, Ballard C. Bagby, Col. James Gilliam and Charles De Morse are all candidate to be Red River County representatives to the Convention in Austin on Annexation to the U.S.

election news
notice by W.B. Stout, Chief Justice of Red River County for the election of the three delegates to Convention on Annexation and designating polling places and presiding officers at each poll

Precinct No. 1 at Mitchell's -Henry C. Hocker
Precinct No. 2 at Stiles - John Stiles
Precinct No. 3 at Ulysses Aguler's - Ulysses Aguler J.P.
Precincts No. 4 & 5 at Clarksville -John Clark
Precinct No.6 at William Humphries - Benjamin Crownever.
Precinct No. 7 at John Robbins - Lovell Coffman J.P.
Precinct No. 8 at T.G. Wright's store - I. H. Dircks J.P.
Precinct No. 9 at William Gregg's -W. W . Foreman J.P.
Precinct No. 10 at Stephen Keith's- T.L. Burns J.P.
            at Norris' Rufus Morton
Precinct No. 11 at Henry W. Jones - Alex. Nevill
Precinct No. 12 at James F. Box's - Benjamin Gooch

lost property
David Bruton advertises that he lost his discharge that entitled him to 1/3 of a league of land in Red River County and that he would apply for a replacement

public notice
notice by Thomas William Ward, Commissioner of the General Land Office regarding payment of dues and returning of field

notes
****

From The Northern Standard, May 31, 1845

annexation news
Charles De Morse, a candidate for member of the Convention, hopes to meet more voters

public notices
Notice to the Public that Joel Halbert and John, his son, swore a false oath before John A. McKinney Esq. that Cross and Willard and Henry Carbow had robbed him of a certain Negro boy named Riall, by taking said Negro from his farm. Since that time, said Halberts have left this section of Country to avoid prosecution for perjury, Joel Halbert having gone to Missouri, and John Halbert to the western portion of this Republic. The object of this notice is to warn all persons against the said Joel and John Halbert, wherever they may be, as base, perjured and dishonest, of which the records of this County are witness

if Richard H. Toler, who, when last heard from, was residing in Bowie County, Texas, will address a letter to John J. Duncan at Washburn's Prairie, State of Missouri, he will hear of something to his advantage

notice by Commissioners Jason Wilson, John Yeary, Matt. F. Sims, A.B. Manion that the contract for the opening and bridging "The Central National Road" of the Republic of Texas, beginning at Dallas, on the Trinity River, to the crossing on North Sulphur, to Red River, will be let at John Loring's, in Fannin County.

lawsuit filed
notice to Joseph Claiborne by Wade H. Vining, Clerk of District Court of Red River County, in action brought against him by William W. Davis in the amount of $400 for his neglect of duty as a common crier, while captain of the steamer *John H. Bills*

notice by George Wilson of the filing of an attachment upon Negro woman Sarah and her child for $50 sought in the lawsuit entitled Jacob Chism by his agent J. C. Chism against Thomas Newbern and Sarah Newbern

obituary
the funeral sermon of the late Miss Nancy Ann Ward will be preached on the 5th Sabbath in June at the residence of her father James J. Ward, by the Rev. Samuel Corley.
****

From The Northern Standard, June 7, 1845

crime news
at Marshall, on Friday last, at the execution of the Negroes who were convicted at their last District Court for the murder of their master, Mr. Wilson, a young man-- the son of Major John Maulding of that place-- unfortunately met with his death by the accidental discharge of this own gun. He was one of the guard which was attending the execution.

annexation news
Red River County results
Col. Wm. C Young, 444
A.H. Latimer, 321
John T. Mills, 251
Ballard C. Bagby, 240
Charles De Morse, 231
Col. James Gilliam, 167
Wright, 148

Lamar County results
H.R. Latimer, 276
Gen. W. Wright, 198
Wm. M. Williams, 171
C.A. Warfield, 153
Jas. S. Gillet, 156

Fannin County results
Judge Everts and Col. Evans elected

Bowie County results
General Tarrant, Ennis Ury and Dr. Chambers were elected to be members of the Convention on Annexation

commercial announcements
advertisement for "Cheap Cash Store" run by George C. Gooding, "at his old stand in Fort Towson" who has linens, clothes, boots , groceries etc. for sale

James Chute advertises white and black smithing, gun smithing, cabinet work, wagon making at Ballard's, 6 miles east of Clarksville

strays
notice by I. H. Fishback that he has found two mares

notice by I. M. Rice, Chief Clerk of the County Court of Bowie County, that two horses were taken up and estrayed before R.E. Hines, Justice of the Peace in Bowie County, values being fixed by Henry Curbow and R. M. Richardson, appraisers

notice by I. M. Rice, Chief Clerk of the County Court of Bowie County, that a horse was taken up and estrayed before J. A. McKinney, Justice of the Peace in Bowie County, at the request of A.D. Watson, value being fixed by Henry Curbow and R. M. Richardson, appraisers

notice that a horse was taken up and estrayed before J.A. McKinney, Justice of the Peace in Bowie County, which had been taken up W. S. Todd value being fixed by Henry Curbow and J. W. Dabbs, appraisers
****

From The Northern Standard, June 14, 1845

crime news
news item that Richard Sowell was killed in Bonham on the day of the election by a Mr. Turner, first name unknown. Sowell had been threatening and pursuing Turner all over town. Turner cut Sowell in the abdomen with a Bowie knife. Turner was examined by a magistrate and discharged for acting in self defense

newspaper business
Alexander S. Johnson in Fannin County and John R. Craddock Esq. or Jacob Long in Lamar County will act as agents for *The Northern Standard*

strays
notice by D. M. Chisholm, Justice of the Peace of Bowie County, that a horse was estrayed before him, value being fixed by John M. Kimbell and John Pinkston, appraisers

notice that a horse was taken up by John Glover and estrayed before R.E. Hines, Justice of the Peace in Bowie County, value being fixed by Henry Curbow and N. B Patton, appraisers

notice that a horse was taken up by Thomas Y. Logwood, living ten miles southwest of Boston and estrayed before J. A. McKinney, Justice of the Peace in Bowie County, value being fixed by Jesse Daniels and John Russell, appraisers

notice that a horse was taken up by N. H. Patittie and estrayed before Benjamin Crownowner, Justice of the Peace in Red River County, value being fixed by Daniel Harris and John Harris, appraisers

public notice
notice by W.B. Stout , President of Land Board, requiring return of conditional certificates before any issuance of unconditional certificates.
****

From The Northern Standard, June 21, 1845

public notice
any one who owes J. C. Hart should make payment

any one who owes A.H. Goodin should make payment

lost property
notice by John B. Loving that he has lost a large powder horn with a wide red worsted girth and with strap attached to it. Some initials upon it, not recollected.

obituary
in Clarksville, on Sunday evening, June 15, 1845 of Cholera Morbus, Marinda, infant daughter of Dr. E. S. Look

professional card
Law Association
B.P. Smith and J. F. Johnson, having associated themselves in the practice of law, will attend to all the courts held in the 7th Judicial District. All business entrusted to their care, will be attended to promptly and faithfully; office in Clarksville, Texas

commercial announcements
advertisement by H. Little & Co of new store in Clarksville –"good goods, low prices and liberal terms"

Wm. M. Harrison advertises that he has received new goods which he offers for sale
****

The Northern Standard, June 28, 1845

commercial announcements
advertisement by Cornelius & Smith of "a general assortment of Merchandise, -- to wit -- 50 sacks salt, 23 bbl. Sugar, 50 sacks best Rio Coffee, domestics brown and bleached; a variety of prints and muslins, summer and winter clothing; saddlery, hats, boots and shoes "and other articles too tedious to mention."

Advertisement by Darnall & Dickson that they have just received from New Orleans an entire new and splendid stock of dry goods and groceries, which they offer for sale at the store formerly occupied by J. Shelton & Co.

lost headright certificate
lost land certificate by Harris Johnson– a league and a labor of land, issued to Samuel Jeffus in Red River County

stray
notice that a horse was taken up by John D. Stanley and estrayed before A.M. Crooks, Justice of the Peace in Red River County and Adam Ribble, values being fixed by Amos H. Rounsaville, appraiser

administration of estates
Notice by J .C. Hart, Clerk of the Probate Court of Red River County that Jas. J. Ward, Jr. administrator of the Estate of Jas.

J. Ward, Sr., that he is filing final settlement of estate

military news
notice from Sidney Sherman, Major General of the Texas Militia to Brid. Gen Lindlay Johnson to complete organization of his command

river and shipping news
advertisement by W.J. Bosworth " on board the Steamer *Hempstead,* lying at Smith's Landing and awaiting a rise in the tides" groceries of different types and ready made clothing

annexation news
Because John T. Mills has resigned his commission, a new notice by W.B. Stout, Chief Justice of Red River County to elect a replacement to attend the Convention on annexation: Designation of polling places and presiding officers at each poll
Precinct No.1 at Mitchell's -Henry C. Hocker
Precinct No. 2 at Stiles - John Stiles
Precinct No. 3 at Ulysses Agulier's - Ulysses Agulier J.P.
Precinct No. 4 & 5 at Clarksville -John Clark
Precinct No.6 at William Humphries - Benjamin Crownever.
Precinct No. 7 at John Robbins - Lovell Coffman J.P.
Precinct No. 8 at T.G. Wright's store - I.H. Dircks J.P.
Precinct No. 9 at William Gregg's - W.W. Foreman J.P.
Precinct No. 10 at Stephen Keith's- T.L. Burns J.P.
At Norris' –Rufus Morton
Precinct No. 11 at Henry W. Jones - Alex. Nevill
Precinct No. 12 at James F. Box's - Benjamin Gooch
****

From The Northern Standard, July 5, 1845

agricultural news
at the offices of *The Standard*, for examination, are two cotton bolls, one raised by Thomas Willison, Esq., on White Oak prairie and the other raised by Gabriel Ketchin on the timbered land contiguous to the prairie

local news
news item on improvements in the town of Clarksville gives mention to the new hotel of Dr. Ward and the new residence house of Dr. Look

annexation news
letters to Charles De Morse from W. H. Bourland and S.B. Johns describing pending matters in Austin at the Congress regarding issue of annexation

church news
announcement of meeting of the Methodist Episcopal Church will be held at the school house in Stephen Keith's neighborhood, near White Oak Prairie

commercial announcement
Advertisement that W. T .F. Cole has just arrived in Paris with a selection of dry goods and other merchandise to sell

public notice
Thom. D. Lee appoints J. T. Lee and Wm. F. Young as his agents while he is absent

stray
notice that a horse was taken up by H.S. Janes and estrayed before J. A. McKinney, Justice of the Peace in Bowie County, value being fixed by Henry B Curbow and Wm. J. Hays, appraisers
****

FromThe Northern Standard, July 12, 1845

commercial announcements
advertisement by W. J. Bosworth of flour, whiskey, corn, bacon, tobacco, coffee and ready made clothing, on board Steamer *Bampsted,* now lying at Smith's Landing

advertisement by Gilbert Ragin "to the lovers of good eating and others" for the whiskeys, wines and other alcoholic beverages, candies, tobaccos, spices etc. at his store in Clarksville.

Geo. W. Dyer has four slaves for sale

newspaper business
Editor thanks T.G. Wright and David S. Kaufman for sending him public documents

bankruptcy filing
Joel Halbert will apply to the Chief Justice of Bowie County for a discharge in bankruptcy

administration of estates
John Loring has been appointed administrator of the Estate of Clarke Saunders of Red River County

Wm. Tinnin, Alex Mabane and A.M. Hodge have been appointed executors of the Estate of L. W. Tinnin of Lamar County

stray
notice by J. C. Hart, County Clerk of Red River County, that a horse was taken up by Daniel Kings and estrayed before R. J. Holbrook, Justice of the Peace in Red River County, value being fixed by Wm. M Ewing and Jas. Rutherford, appraisers

lawsuit filed
notice from Thomas C Bean, Clerk of the District Court of Fannin County that William McCarty, defendant in a pending legal action, is being served by publication.
****
no newspaper for July 19, 1845 as there is a shortage of paper
****

From The Northern Standard, July 26, 1845

letters left at Post Office
Notice by A.M. Crooks Post Master of the Clarksville Post Office

Allin, William
Allen, Hugh
Alexander, Isaac
Alexander, Isaac W.
Aiguier, Ulysses
Bates, James
Brooks, Thomas
Clark, John T.
Chambers, John G.
Cooper, R.
Clark, Rev.
Dillon, H. K.
Doss, James W.

Estes, James
Flatt, William
Findley, D.C.
Hughes, Robert
Hopkins, R. M.
Harmon, M.
Hamilton, Col. Robert
Heath, Jas.
Heath, Richard
Jonakin, Malinda
Jackson, James
Jackson, T. H.
Julien, James

Johnson, John
Kinsey, Dr. S.
Linn, Judge
Murray, Richard S.
Monkhouse, J.
Morrow, Bethel
Neely, Samuel
Nelson, John E.
Nall, Robert
Overton, Richard
Param, Richard
Perria, William
Richey, William
Reay, Capt. John
Scurry, William R. 8
Smith, F. P.

Smith, James Reves
Smith, Mary E.
Scarborough, D.B.
Thompson, W.C.
Upton, Egbert
Vincent, Thomas
Williams, J. W.
Williamson, Matilda
Whitesides, John M.
Wilson, John
White, T. J.
Wright, Thomas
Waits, Jas.
Williams, Alex
Young, W. C. 2

lawsuits filed
Notice from Thomas C. Bean, Clerk of the District Court of Bowie County, that in the action styled *William S. Beaty against Henry S. Peters et al* for the sum of $740 that defendants Henry S. Peters, William S. Peters, Daniel J. Carroll, Alexander Mc Kee, Roland Gibson, Robert Espie, William M. Olerhlson, Daniel Spillman, Robert D. Stering, William C. Peters, John Peters, William Scott, Tomothy Grey and Samuel Browning are served by publication

notice from Thomas C. Bean, Clerk of the District Court of Bowie County, that, in the action styled *Katherine Cullum, adminisrtratix of the Estate of Charles Cullum (for the use of the succession of J. T. Hall) against William B. Hawkins et* al that defendant Hawkins is served by publication

lost headright certificate
notice by Mark R Roberts that he has lost his land certificate for a league and labor of land in Fannin County

stray
notice by Amos Morrill for a lost or stolen horse
****

From The Northern Standard, August 2, 1845

commercial announcement
Gilbert Ragin has for sale: Old Rye, Monogahels and Corn Whiskey, Champagne, Cogume, Peneh, American and French Brandy, Holland Gin, American, Jamaica and New England Rum, Port Madeira, Teperiffe, Claret, Muscat, Sweet and Dry Malaga Wines, Wine, Cherries, a superior article of old Port and Madeira, Brandy Cherries, Cordials and Syrups, Porter & Ale, Wine & Cider Vinegar, Pickled Lobsters, Sardines, Smoked and Pickled Herrings, Choice Pickles, Strawberry Preserves, Pilot Bread, French Biscuit, Sugar Crackers, Boston Crackers and Soda Crackers. Raisins, Rock and other Candies, Almonds, Sugar, Coffee, Tea, Chocolate, Molasses and Salt, Flour and Rice, Tobacco of various qualities, Cigars, Fine cut smoking Tobacco and Pipes, Spices, Leaf Sugar, Black & Cayenne Pepper, Mustard, Dye Stuffs of all kinds, Starch, Blacking, Sulphur, Shoe Thread, Percussion Caps, Castor Oil, Turpentine, Crockery Ware, Glass Ware, Wooden buckets, Tubs, Rope, Bed Cord & Plough Lines, Powder, Lead & Shot, Wax & Sperm Candles, Window Glass, Nails, Shaving Soap & Bar Soap, Fire Crackers, Foolscap & Letter Paper.

annexation news
Election notice issued by W. B. Stout, upon authorization of Anson Jones, President of the Republic, setting forth polling places and officers for September election of representatives to the Congress of the Republic

Beat No.1.	at Mitchell's, Jas. Gilliam, J.P.
Beat No.2	at Stiles, Solomon Bryant, J.P.
Beat No.3	at Ulysses Agulier's, Ulysses Agulier J.P.
Beats No.4 & 5	at Clarksville, Samuel Hillis, J.P.
Beat No.6	at William Humphries, Benjamin Crownever.
Beat No.7	at John Robbins, Lovell Coffman J.P.
Beat No. 8	at Pine Creek, I.H. Dircks J.P.
Beat No. 9	at William Gregg's, Lewis J. Berry, J.P.
Beat No.10	at Duly's, Wm. Becknell
	at Stephen Keith's, Thomas .L. Burns J.P.
	at Norris', Rufus Morton
Beat No.11	at Henry W. Jones, Alex. Nevill
Beat No. 12	at James F. Box's, R. J. Holbrook
Beat No. 13	at James Burkham's, Joseph Cartwright

****

From The Northern Standard, August 9, 1845

crime news
letter to Charles De Morse from S. W. Sims, County Surveyor for Red River County regarding some allegedly fraudulent land claims made by a Col. Ward

annexation news
various letters and reports to Charles De Morse by H.R. Latimer, A.H. Latimer and L. D. Evans regarding the Convention in Austin to consider annexation and other items of interest regarding Convention, including letters that referred to Bagby's arrival in Austin from Clarksville and Wm. R. Scurry's return to Clarksville

church news
announcement that Friends of Temperance will meet at the House of Rev. James Sampson and march in procession to the Methodist Church

strays
notice by L. M. Rice, County Clerk of Red River County, that a horse was taken up by H.S. Jones and brought before R.E. Hines, Justice of the Peace in Red River County, value being fixed by J. P. M. Ford and R. Booth, appraisers

notice by L. M. Rice, County Clerk of Red River County, that a horse was taken up by Isaac Bruton and brought before Lewis Needham, Justice of the Peace in Red River County, value being fixed by I. H. Reed and William V. Hughes, appraisers
****

From The Northern Standard, August 16, 1845

hostilities with Mexico
news item that the Hon. Wm. H Scurry arrived in town from Austin, who says there is a rumor that the Mexicans have captured Corpus Christi

agricultural news
notice that John W. West raised a muskmelon 28 inches round

election news
George Lawton has announced his candidacy for County Clerk of Red River County

obituary
died at the residence of her father in Red River County, Mrs Mary Ann S., youngest daughter of James and Ann Latimer

commercial announcement
J. P. Reilly advertises his grocery and dry goods store in Pine Bluffs
****
The issues of *The Standard* for August, all of September and October and most of November were not published because a lack of paper due to low water in the Red River
****
From The Northern Standard, November 23, 1845

court news
report on the meeting of the Clarksville Bar Association convened to commemorate the death of Rufus M. Clark, Esq. of Paris, Lamar County. J. W. Latimer proposed resolutions in the memory of the deceased. B. H. Martin is the Chairman and W.L. Sharp was the secretary

sporting news
report on the Clarksville races and horses entered by J. C. Hart, G. W. Hart and J. Ward

obituary
died of scarlet fever, 8 miles south of Clarksville, Sarah Isabella, infant daughter of W.B. and Matilda Stout, 1 year 11 months and fourteen days of age

election news
election notice issued by W. B. Stout, of election polls and their officials
at Mitchell's, Henry Hocker, J.P.
at Stiles, Solomon Bryant, J.P.
at Ulysses Agulier's, Ulysses Agulier J.P.
at Clarksville, Samuel Hillis, J.P.
at William Humphries, Benjamin Crownever.
at John Robbins, Lovell Coffman J.P.

at Pine Creek, I. H. Dircks J.P.
at Gregg's, Lewis L. D. Barry, J.P.
at James Burkam's, J. Batemen
at Henry Duty's, Wm. Becknell
at Stephen Keith's, Thomas L. Burns, J.P.
at Norris', Rufus Morton
at Henry W. Jones, Alex. Nevill
James F. Box's, R. L. Matthews

Notice from W.B. Stout that he will address the public at various locations including at H. W. Jones and Stephen Keith's

professional card
W.L. Sharp
Attorney and Counselor at law
Office: Paris, Lamar County

public notices
notice from Campbell English that he was no longer responsible for the debts of Elizabeth English, his wife, who has left his bed and board

Thos. Willison advertises that "those owing me fees will save the additional charge of an Execution by paying me within ten days." His office is at the Post Office, opposite the new Hotel of Dr. Ward.

lost property
notice that Jackson M'Farland has lost his land certificate in Red River County

land for sale
notice by B.F. Lynn to sell a farm, located 5 miles north east of Clarksville, of 300 acres, of which 90 acres are prairie and the remainder rich bottom land. The place has on it a comfortable dwelling and assorted out-houses, and 50 acres of the prairie are in a state of cultivation. Also, for sale, a tract of land, of 2,900 acres adjoining the Smith land Tract.
****

From The Northern Standard, December 3, 1845

commercial announcements
Gilbert & Co of Pine Creek advises that its Steam Saw Mill is now in operation and that they will deliver lumber at 25 dollars a thousand at Clarksville, Paris, or any other place within 30 miles of the mill. They will deliver lumber at the Pine Bluffs at twenty dollars a thousand, or they will sell at the mill which is within a mile and a half of Wright's old store at fifteen dollars a thousand.

E.M. Smith of Clarksville will offer at auction a quantity of Goods, Wares and Merchandise -- also a good lot of Groceries and a credit of 6 months.

election news
announcement of the candidacy of W.B. Stout as representative of Red River County to the legislature

announcement of the candidacy of James Gilliam as representative of Red River County to the legislature

announcement of the candidacy of Thom. Willson as representative of Red River County to the legislature

sporting news
report by J. C. Hart about his horse's performance at the recent Clarksville races

public notices
notice by J. C. Hart asking those indebted to him to pay

stop payment
W.B. Stout warns not to accept the note he executed to George S. Park because it was fraudulently induced

administration of estates
Mary W. Donoho appointed administratrix of the Estate of William Donoho in Red River County

A.S. Johnson appointed administrator of the Estate of N. K. Woodroe and Simeon K. Woodroe in Fannin County

Charles Ames appointed administrator of the Estate of Robert Potter in Bowie County

Martin G. Nall appointed administrator of the Estate of John Nall in Red River County

Nakcissa Jouett appointed executrix of the Estate of John G. Jouett in Fannin County
****

From The Northern Standard, December, 10, 1845

election news
notice by L. D. Henderson that he is a candidate for the legislature from Red River County

runaway
notice by R. M. Hopkins of a runaway slave, named Calvin.

school news
advertisement my Mrs. Weatherred for Clarksville Female Academy
****

From The Northern Standard, December, 17, 1845

agricultural news
Sampson Smith Esq, has given *The Standard* a specimen of his turnip patch; a couple of sprouts, one 26 inches around, weighing five pounds; the other 24 inches around, weighing 8 1/2 pounds.

election news
Wade H. Vining announces his candidacy for District Clerk of Red River County

F. Young announces his candidacy fo District Clerk of Red River County

A. J. Titus announces his candidacy for County Clerk of Red River County

school news
advertisement by E. A. Todd for Ringwood Female Seminary

lawsuit filed
notice of service by publication in divorce action styled *Ann Morlab Kendall against James Kendall* in Lamar County

stray
notice by J. C. Hart, Clerk of the County Court of Red River County, that a horse estrayed before James Benj. Wooten Justice of the Peace was appraised by Jesse Walker and George Fariss

lost property
notice regarding lost land certificate by Holland Coffee, Certificate originally issued to Samuel Stuart
****

From The Northern Standard, December, 24, 1845

election news
Samuel W. Sims is a candidate for County Clerk for Red River County

married
on December 23, 1845, by the Rev. Samuel Corley, Hon. Ballard C. Bagby, to Miss Amanda Bagby, daughter of Major John A. Bagby; all of Red River county this County

commercial announcement
Charles De Morse has house logs for sale, 48 first rate, hewed pine logs, 18 feet long

lost property
lost land certificate by William D. Davis 300 acres of land in Fannin County

public notice
announcement of Dissolution of partnership of T. J. Cornelius and E.M. Smith

settlement and immigration news
notice by John J. Smith, Willis Stewart, W.C. Peters, Trustees

of the Texas Emigration and Land company attaching statement of Henry Pirtle, James Guthrie, P.S. Loughborough, Garnet Duncan, all of Louisville Kentucky regarding validity of land ownership

notice that Darnall & Dickson are prepared to buy or make Cash advances on Cotton in hand.

stray
stray mare taken up W. W. Forreman, estrayed before L. D. Barry, J.P., in Red River County, valued by D. N. Barry and S. Grant

administration of estates
Catherine Gerdis appointed executrix of the Estate of E. Gerdis of Bowie County

lawsuit filed
notice by J. Long, Clerk of the District Court of Lamar County, of service by publication in action *Malinda Davis against Thomas Dennis, administrator of the Estate of John Dennis, Colby Dennis, Elizabeth Garret and her husband George Garret, Kitarah Garret and her husband William Garett*

notice by J. Long, Clerk of the District Court of Lamar County of service by publication in action for a debt of $840, styled *Alexander Mabane, William Tinnan and Alexander M. Hodge as executors of the Estate of L. W. Tinnnan against William N Porter, John B. Craig, Wm. C. Young, J. T. Harmon, James Bourland, M. W. Matthews, Albert G. Kimbell, George W. Wright and Travis G Wright*

notice by J. Long, Clerk of the District Court of Lamar County, of service by publication in action *styled Samuel M. Fulton against James Richey and Polly Richey*. Complaint states that plaintiff and Robert Cravens were partners purchased the head right of John C. Lamb in Bowie County, which he did not convey

Notice by J. Long, Clerk of the District Court of Lamar County, of service by publication in action styled *William M. Williams as agent for A. Mintower against Charles Graham* in connection with attachment of certain personal property belonging to defendant

fraternal organizations
notice by Samuel D. White, Secretary "to all Free and Accepted Masons that, at a Regular Meeting of Friendship Lodge No. 16, held in Clarksville Texas on the night of September 5, it was resolved by the Lodge unanimously that Samuel E. Powers, a M.M., who has been convicted by this Lodge of gross, unseasonable conduct be expelled forever from all the privileges of Masonry."
****

1846

From The Northern Standard, January 7, 1846

election news
announcement of the candidacy of Edward West for the office of Sheriff of Red River County

report that Alexander Russell, Esq. and Col. B. H. Durham were elected representatives from Bowie County

school news
E. A. Todd announces that examinations at Ringwood Female Seminary will take place on the last Friday and Saturday in January

commercial announcements
Wm. M. Harrison and Robert M. Graham have become co-partners in a mercantile establishment to be called Harrison & Graham

advertisement of Hamilton, M'Kinder & Co, Commission Merchants, of New Orleans listing T. J. Cornelius, R. M. Hopkins and Philip Duty of Clarksville and James Moseshouse of Roland as references

public notice
Look & Griffith announces the dissolution of its partnership

administration of estates
advertisement by Mary Donoho of sale by her as administrator of the Estate of William Donoho
****

From The Northern Standard, January 14, 1846

election news
announcement of the candidacy of David S. Kaufman, Esq. for the office of Representative to the United States Congress for the Eastern and Northern Districts of Texas

announcement of the candidacy of William R. Scurry for the office of Representative to the United States Congress for the Eastern and Northern Districts of Texas

announcement of the candidacy of Amos H. Rounnaville for the office of Constable of Beat No. Five in Red River County

annexation news
report on the meeting of the citizens of Clarksville on January 10, 1845, when it was learned the annexation of Texas to the United States had been finally consumated. Major John A. Bagby was elected chairman and John R. Bedford, Secretary of the meeting. On a motion by Col. Wm. C. Young, a committee was chosen to draft a resolution expressive of the sentiments of the meeting. The Committee consisted of Wm. C. Young, W.R. Scurry, J. A. Whittlesey, J. W. Latimer and Charles De Morse.
A second committee was appointed to find the appropriate persons to read the U.S. Constitution and to address the citizens on the subject of annexation. Dr. George Gordon, S.S. Turner and Thom. D. Lee were appointed to that committee

letters left at Post Office
list published by A.M. Crooks, Post Master, of letters at Clarksville Post Office

Alexander, A.
Andrews, William S.
Bryarly, Thomas F.
Bagwell, G. W.
Balls, William
Brown, Matthew

Becknell, Capt. William
Braten, John D.
Bonner, George S.
Blythe, William T.
Brooks, Thomas
Caldwell, Sam

Crain, John
Clark, Mr.
Casbeer, John
Cox, Hiram W.
Carter, J. C.
Clark, A. J.
Coner, Col. Benjamin
Colby, Anthony
Dawson, Israel
Davis, William W.
De Morse, Charles
Dickens, Townsend
Dean, Miss Irene
Estes, James
Edmonson, Turner B.
Fullerton, W. N.
Fowler, Col. John H.
Fish, Nathan S.
Fisher, Jesse
Goodall, James P.
Hardaway, H.
Hart, J. C.
Hammock, Andrew J.
Hubbard, Walter G.
Hamilton sr. , Robert
Hail, Stephen S.
Johnson, John
Jones, Gen. T. W.
Klein, Charles F. D.
Lockett, Richard R.
Lynch, Joab
Lucy, R.J.
Lee J.T.
Luckey, Hugh
McKenzie, Samuel B.
Mather, Joseph
Martin, William C.
Morris, Joseph
Merrell, David

Miller, Andrew
McClendon, Jackson
Mimms, Gideon
Orr, Rev. Green
Prior, John
Posey, Leaden
Price, R.E.
Parris, Thaddeus
Rhodes, Peter
Rippy, William P.
Roberts, Elijah
Robbins, Rebecca
Spencer, Oliver or Hamilton, M.
Skinner, James 3
Sloan, A.M.
Sampson, Rev. James 2
Smith, James
Shelton, E.J.
Stalcup, William
Sims, Samuel W.
St. Clair, Charles
Scarborrough, D.B.
Sloors, Joshua
Sharp, William L.
Tankersley, Richard
Tumey, John R.
Taylor, Joseph P.
Vining, Thomas. L.
Vincent, Thomas
Wood, James
Whiteside, W.N.
Weelsh, Wm.
Wright, Travis G.
Williams, W.S. H.
Ward, James
West, Major F. 2

lawsuit filed
notice by A.M. Crooks, Justice of the Peace of Beat No. 5 of

144

the Magistrate's Court that an order of attachment has issued in the action entitled *George H. Clifton against Henry H. Clifton*. Suit is for the repayment of a loan in the amount of $41. 89

public notice
notice by Eliza Poor to trespasser not to cut and remove wood from the lands of Ira S. Poor

school news
notice by E. A. Todd as to commencement of next term of Ringwood Female Seminary

stray
notice of stray horse by Adam Ribble

lost property
lost land certificate by Alfred Moore for certificate issued to Levin S. Sargeant for 1280 acres in Red River County

professional card
Samuel R. Campbell and Jas. S. Gillet have formed Campbell and Gillet, Attorneys and Counselors at Law, will practice in the counties of Fannin, Lamar, Red River, Bowie and Harrison. Office in Paris, Lamar County
****

From *The Northern Standard*, January 21, 1846

professional card
John R. Bedford
Attorney At Law will attend the courts of the counties of Fannin, Lamar, Red River, Bowie and Harrison. Professional business entrusted to his care will be promptly attended to. Offices at the Star Hotel, Clarksville Texas

stop payment
notice by John T. Mills not to accept notes given by him to A. McCardle

lawsuits filed
notice issued by Thomas C. Bean, Clerk of the District Court for Fannin County, in the lawsuit styled *Sandford and George Turner, against John N. Bryan* to recover a debt of $292

notice issued by Thomas C. Bean, Clerk of the District Court for Fannin County, in the lawsuit styled *Abram Black against James Rawson* to recover a debt of $135

notice issued by Thomas C. Bean, Clerk of the District Court for Fannin County, in the lawsuit styled *Catherine Towers against George W. Towers* for divorce

notice issued by Thomas C. Bean, Clerk of the District Court for Fannin County, in the lawsuit styled *Jonathan Allen against Alexander Zachary* in Chancery

notice issued by Thomas C. Bean, Clerk of the District Court, by R.W. Lee, his deputy, for Fannin County, in the lawsuit styled *John D. Black against Mary Black and John Hayman and the unknown heirs of Jacob Black* to establish ownership of certain land

notice issued by Thomas C. Bean, Clerk of the District Court for Fannin County, in the lawsuit styled *William Trimble against Hiel S. Allen* to recover a debt of $174

notice issued by H. Bayless, Clerk of the District Court for Bowie County in the action entitled *Katherine Collum, as Administratix of the Estate of Charles Collum against William R. Hawkins, Robert Hamilton, John Peters, T. J. Cornelius and E. Ury* to recover a debt of appeal bond

notice by W. H. Vining, Clerk of the District Court for Red River County Court, of service of process by publication in action for divorce entitled Samuel S. Turner against Mariah Turner. Mariah Turner had left plaintiff's bed and board

notice by W. H. Vining, Clerk of the District Court for Red River County Court, to Mary Sims, formerly Mary Wilson of Mississsippi of service of process by publication in action for divorce brought by her husband Reddick J. Sims.

letters left at Post Office
list published by L.D. VanDyke, Post Master, of letters at Boston Post Office

Allen, William K.	Booth, Benjamin
Bennet, Joshua	Clerk of the County Court 2

Dr. Chambers
Daniels, Jesse
Davis, William Esq.
Dalby, Col. J. C.
Clerk of the District Court
Ellet, J. W. Esq.
Glass J. C.
George, Mr.
Holloway, Mrs. June
Jones, William
Lewis, Col. Charles
Lindsay, Mrs. E.M.
Looney, William

Maudling, P. Esq.
McCloskey, J. J.
Pinter, Thomas
Paxton, W. J. 2
Passon, J. Esq.
Peacock, William
Rice, Francisco
Runnels, Gen Jackson
Smith, Mrs. Elizabeth
Turner, Jas.
Trigg, Jas.
Wooten, William W.

election news
election notice issued by W. B. Stout, of election polls and their officials
at Mitchell's , Henry Hocker, J.P.
at Burkam's, Jonathan Bateman
at Stiles, Solomon Bryant, J.P.
at Ulysses Agulier's, Ulysses Agulier J.P.
at Courthouse, Clarksville, A.M. Crooks
at Clarksville, Samuel Hillis, J.P.
at William Humphries, Benjamin Crownever
at John Robbins, Lovell Coffman J.P.
at Pine Creek, I. H. Dircks J.P.
at Gregg's, L.D. Barry, J.P.
at Henry Duty's, Wm. Becknell
at Stephen Keith's, Thomas L. Burns, J.P.
at Norris', Rufus Morton
at Henry W. Jones, Alex. Nevill
at James F. Box's, R. L. Matthews
****

From *The Northern Standard*, January 28, 1846

administration of estates
Wm. F. Hamilton has been appointed administrator of the Estate of Robert Hamilton

notice by J. C. Hart, Clerk of Red River County, that horse, taken up by William H. Taylor and brought before R.J. Holbrook, Justice of the Peace, was appraised by Thomas

McG. Rutherford and J. H. Rutherford at $12

commercial announcement
H. Little & Co announces opening of store in Clarksville
****

From The Northern Standard, February 4, 1846

agricultural news
Mr. Dircks sends letter to Charles De Morse regarding newspaper contests for largest potato

local news
dwelling house on the plantation of Hamilton and Rainey at Pecan Point was burnt. Fire began in dirt chimney and spread so rapidly that the property within could not be removed. Mr. Rainey lost $380 in money and the firm of Hamilton and Rainey lost a large amount of rope and bagging

election news
results
for Sheriff of Red River County Edward West beat Doak, 218 to 122
for District Clerk   Wade H. Vining 152; Foreman, 132; F. Young 62;
for County Clerk George Lawton 133; Hamilton 105; Samuel W. Sims 41; A. J. Titus 53 and Bailey 9

professional card
Drs. Gordon and Walker announce a partnership in the practice of medicine in Clarksville

land for sale
announcement of sale of lots in Albion, 16 miles north of Clarksville on the south bank of the Red River, at Park's Bluff. Developers are George S. Park, Edward West, Henry Little, W. M. Harrison, J. J. Montgomery, W. T. Montgomery and Bennet H. Martin

public notice
H. Little & Co calls for all to settle their accounts

stop payment
John Tyson cautions public from taking the note given by him to Sterling Smith as it was obtained through fraud and misrepresentation

lost property
Charles De Morse advertises for his lost land certificate for 1/3 a league of land in Matagorda County, which had been in the hands of John W. Hayden, surveyor, who has left the country. De Morse also would apply for another missing certificate for 2/3 of a league and a labor of land in same county which had been with Dr. Robert H. Wynne to locate the land, but who has nor responded to correspondence

Bartley Ballard is going to apply for a lost certificate, on a certificate originally given to Nicholas Maxwell by the Board of Land Commissioners of Red River County
****

From The Northern Standard, February 11, 1846

lawsuit filed
notice in lawsuit in Fannin County brought by Thomas Murphy and Hiram W. Rayburn

administration of estates
notice that Catherine Gordon has qualified as executrix of the Estate of E. Gordon of DeKalb, Bowie County

notice that William H. Boyce has been appointed administrator of the Estate of Isham J. Boyce of Dekalb, Bowie County

stray
notice by J. C. Hart, Clerk of the County of Red River, that a horse taken by William B. Taylor and brought before R.J. Holbrook, Justice of the peace of Red River County, has been valued at $38 by Thomas McG. Rutherford and A.M. Rutherford

runaway
notice by R.M Hopkins of a runaway slave

election news
announcement of candidacy of David S. Kaufman and Wm. R. Scurry for the office of Representative to the U.S. Congress for the Northern and Eastern Districts of Texas

sporting news
notice by Martin Glover of horse races to be held following spring at Clarksville Jockey Club
****

From The Northern Standard, February 18, 1846

public notice
notice by Joseph McCarty that he has appointed William Tinnan as his agent during his absence

commercial notice
advertisement by E.M. Tarrant of Chambers Creek, Robertson County, L. M. Rice of Bowie County and Wm. Henderson of Red River County that they will act as land agents
****

From The Northern Standard, February 25, 1846

public notices
notice by Lucy Ann Cullum, warning people not to trespass on her property
****

From The Northern Standard, March 11, 1846

agricultural news
letter from Jno. Dircks regarding the planting of potatoes

advertisement that Jesse Shelton has property livestock for sale and that George Lawton is authorized to sell it

election news
notice by Hon. William B. Ochiltree that he is running as representative from Northern and Eastern districts of Texas

administration of estates
George Smith has been s named administrator of the Estate of

John Woodley and will sell assets and horses

William F. Hamilton appointed executor of the Estate of Robert Hamilton

notice by L. M. Rice, Bowie County Clerk to the legatees of the Estate of George Cullum to file claims

notice of order by W.B. Stout, published by clerk, George F. Lawton, in Probate Court, that Marcus W. Caudle has filed accounting for Estate of John A. Caudle

stray
notice that a horse has been taken up by Samuel McCullough and brought before Thomas L. Burns, Justice of the Peace, and appraised by Rufus Morton and Thomas Wilson

notice by J. R. Craddock, Clerk of Lamar County, regarding stray horse taken up by Simon Derrick, brought before Hiram McMillan, Justice of the Peace, and appraised by John Roland and Amos Ridge

lost headright certificate
notice by Peter Miller of lost headright certificate, granted to James J. Ward for a league and labor of land in Red River County

land for sale
advertisement that Joseph C. Hart has various pieces of land for sale in the vicinity of Clarksville

professional card
notice by Dr George H. Wooten that he will practice medicine in Clarksville at office lately used by W. H. Vining, District Clerk
****

From The Northern Standard, March 18, 1846

election news
letter to Major De Morse from A. J. Russell regarding events in Austin

agricultural news
letter from A.W. King regarding remarks of John Henry Dircks on large sweet potato he grew; Mr. King wants a competition on watermelons, radishes, peaches, apples, plums, grapes and raspberries

runaway
notice of runaway from Alias Phillips at Blossom Prairie, two slave girls, Matilda and Nancy

administration of estates
Notice by R.W. Lee, Clerk, to the heirs of Wm. E. Throckmorton that the Fannin County Probate court has appointed William H. Pulliam, Joseph H. Wilcox and Thomas Ratan to divide and distribute his lands

commercial announcements
advertisement by N. R. Harland has opened a shop to do saddlery work

advertisement by Henry Smith that his horse, *Tom Marshall*, will stand stud at farm of E.M. Hopkins, 1 mile northeast of Clarksville

professional card
Brad C. Fowler Esq., Attorney at Law, Paris, Lamar County, will practice in all the counties of Northern Texas
****

From The Northern Standard,, March 25, 1846

election announcements
David S. Kaufman announces he is also running as representative from Northern and Eastern districts

William R. Scurry announces he is also running as representative from Northern and Eastern districts

river and steamboat news
communication from our correspondent, Mr. J. H. Dircks, living on Henry's Landing on the Red River, reporting "Red River is rising and very red, indicating a good stage for boats"

school news
notice by David K. Thom of his school 18 miles south of Paris, Lamar County.

runaway
notice by Isaac N. Jackson of runaway slave from Robert Hamilton in Arkansas

stray
notice by S. W. Sims of runaway horse
****
There was no issue of *The Standard* from March 25, 1846 until May 6, 1846
****

From *The Northern Standard*, May 6, 1846

sporting news
results of the Clarksville Jockey Club Race, Benjamin Johnson's horse beat Johnson & Aik's horse

public notices
notice by William M. Harrison that those indebted to him should pay up

administration of estates
notice by James J Ward, administrator of the Estate of Hugh Luckey, of probate sale

lost property
Notice by Vincent H. Tims of lost certificate of John Wagnon for land in Fannin County

professional announcements
professional card of S. K. McCowen, attorney at Law, Bonham, Fannin county
****

From *The Northern Standard, May 13, 1846*

commercial announcements
advertisement by R. Chatfield & Co of its new store in Clarksville

advertisement by H. Little & Co. of its store in Clarksville

advertisement by J. P. Reilly of his grocery store at Pine Bluffs

advertisement by Thomas Gregg of Clarksville of his dance school

school news
advertisement by Mrs. E. A. Todd of Ringwood Female Seminary

letters left at Post Office
notice by P.J. Pillans, Postmaster of List of Letters at Bonham

Allen, Jno. T.	Lee, Sussanah
Britton, Joseph	Mars, James F.
Butler, Reese	Morrison, Dr. A.
Bean, John	McLary, W.
Baker, Thomas C.	Madden, Robert W.
Black, John D.	Rowlett, Dr. Daniel
Clark, D.	Rattan, Thomas
Dooley, George W.	Stalcup, Thomas
Davis, Rev.	Schlinter, Joseph
Earley, Col. Gilbert	Taylor, R. H.
Fitzhugh, Gabriel	Taylor, J. Claxon
Homer, Dr.	Wall, Preston H.
Jackson, Charles	Williamson, John
Joy, George	Williams, Jon D.
Losson, Abey	Yeacum, Adam
Locke, John	
Lodge, Constantine	

stray
notice by R. R. Gilbert, acting Justice of the Peace in Red River County, that horse, taken up by William H. Taylor and brought before him, has been appraised by Nathaniel T. Sutherland and Allen G. Hardin at $25

lost headright certificate
notice by Tomisher Bowers of a lost head right certificate of Elijah D. Bowers in Galveston County

administration of estates
Notice that William G. Miller, administrator of the Estate of

Redin G. Crisp, for creditors to pay all moneys owed the Estate.

Gilbert Ragin has been appointed administrator of the Estate of Gary Ragin

land for sale
advertisement by D. N. Alley of lands for sale
****

From The Northern Standard, May 20, 1846

school news
advertisement by James Sampson for Clarksville Academy
****

From The Northern Standard, May 27, 1846

married
in Clarksville on May 21, 1846 by the Rev. Washington Fields, Mr. John Bradbury and Nancy G. Collins

professional card
Royston & Cocke, attorneys at law: G. D. Royston and J. W Cocke, office in Washington, Hempstead County, Arkansas

administration of estates
notice by R.T. Brylarly, administrator of the estates of John W. Davis II and William W. Davis in Red River County, advising creditors to make their claims either to him or in his absence to J. F. Johnson, Esq

lawsuit filed
attachment granted plaintiff by J. Morrisson, Justice of the Peace, Lamar County, in action entitled *John L. Dillingham versus William Anderson*
****

From The Northern Standard, June 3, 1846

hostilities with Mexico
In Fannin County, Capt. Evans has raised and left with 76 men, who were raised in three days. Col Montague left on the 30th

with 65 men and Col Charles E. Hensley will leave on the 7th with another company.

election announcements
James Jenkins announces his candidacy for Assessor and Collector for Red River County

Col. William C. Towne of Red River County announces his candidacy for Major General of the First Division of the Texas Militia, comprised of the counties of Fannin, Lamar, Red River and Bowie

F .F. Coles announces his candidacy for Brigadier General of the First Division of the Texas Militia, Assessor and Collector for Red River County

married
on the 26th of May, 1846 by the Rev. James Sampson, Mr John Carter to Mrs. Mary Anne Dinwiddle

commercial announcements
advertisement by C. C. Alexander of "another new store in Clarksville"

R. Chatfield & Co announce a new wholesale and retail store in Clarksville

H. Little & Co advertises the arrival of new goods at its store in Clarksville

Darnall & Dickson advertises the arrival of new goods at its store in Clarksville

advertisement for music, painting and drawing lessons by Mrs. Ann Ellet at Ringwood Female Seminary

public notices
notice by W.B. Stout, Chief Justice of Red River County, setting out the Justice Precincts in Red River

notice by W.B. Stout, Chief Justice of Red River County, appointing S. H. Morris, Joseph Mather and John Monkhower as Notaries in Red River

lost property
notice of lost land certificate by James Burkham for a league and a labor of land held by Charles A. Burkham, granted him in 1838 the Board of Land Commissioners of Red River County

strays
notice by George F. Lawton, Clerk, that Richard S. Gilbert, acting Justice of the Peace in Red River County, at a hearing regarding stray horse taken up by Peter B. Johnston, valued it at $40 based upon appraisals by Marcus Caudle and William Boots

notice by b George F. Lawton, Clerk, that Richard S. Gilbert, acting Justice of the Peace in Red River County, at a hearing regarding stray horse taken up by H. Brummitt, valued it at $30 based upon appraisals by Samuel Fulton and Thomas H. Roberts

notice by John R. Craddock that P. Lynch, Justice of the Peace in Lamar County, at a hearing regarding stray horse taken up by Josiah Davis, valued it at $15 based upon appraisals by W.C. Denton and W. H. Manze

notice by John R. Craddock that John A Dillingham, Justice of the Peace in Lamar County, at a hearing regarding stray horse taken up by Joel W. Howling, valued it at $15 based upon appraisals by Daniel W. Lee and W. H. Morrow

lawsuits filed
notice by George F. Lawton, Clerk, of an order by W.B. Stout, Judge of Probate in Red River County, in action entitled *James M. Sharp and his wife Mary M., vs. Sarah Dean, Joab A. Dean, Speer Dean, Thomas Dean Levi Dean, James Dean and George Dean*

notice by Wade H Vining, Clerk of Red River District Court, of Petition for divorce brought by Thomas M Dale against Matilda Dale

public notice
George Gordon of Clarksville warns anyone from taking any timber from his lands

administration of estates

notice by R.W. Lee, Clerk of the Probate Court of Fannin County, that Joseph A. Wilcox, Thomas Ratan and William H. Pulliam have been appointed commissioners of the real estate of William E. Throckmorton, deceased

****

From The Northern Standard, June 10, 1846

hostilities with Mexico
company of Bowie volunteers arrived in Clarksville and, on Sunday morning, they passed through, displaying their banner twice around the public square. A fine body of men, most of them young, are commanded by Capt Levi M. Rice, 1st Lieutenant Sam'l F. Mosley, 2d Lieut. B.M. Richardson.

Fourth of July Celebrations
public meeting was held of the Citizens of Clarksville near the courthouse, chaired by John A. Bagby and Amos Morrill, Secretary, where the resolution was offered and passed that John T. Mills be the Orator at the Fourth of July celebration

commercial announcement
Samuel Weaver and William Marshall announce they are in business together in the Wagon Making, and Plough Stocking business

*professional card*s
Henry D. Woodsworth, Attorney and Counselor at Law
will practice in the courts of the Seventh Judicial District
office in Paris, Lamar County

S. H Morgan, Attorney and Counselor at Law
will practice in all the Seventh Judicial District
will attend to all business which is entrusted to him with punctuality and fidelity; office in Clarksville

Law Association of B.P. Smith and J. F. Johnson
Having associated themselves together in the practice of law , will attend all courts held in of the Seventh Judicial District. All business entrusted to them will be attended to promptly and faithfully; office in Clarksville

P. J. Pillans
Attorney and Counselor at Law; will practice in all the Seventh
Judicial District; office in Bonham, Fannin County

J. R. Martin, Attorney and Counselor at Law; Fifth, Sixth and
the Seventh Judicial District; office in Marshall, Harrison
County

W. B. Stout; Attorney and Counselor at Law; office in
Clarksville will practice in the District Courts of Lamar and
Red River Counties
****

From The Northern Standard, June 17, 1846

commercial announcement
saddlery advertisement by N. R. Harland; his shop is next to
Donoho's Hotel in Clarksville

election announcements
Samuel W. Sims is a candidate for Brigadier General of the 2nd
Brigade, 2nd Division, Texas Militia

Charles C. Wellburn is a candidate for Colonel of the 2nd
Brigade, 2nd Division, Texas Militia

A. J. Titus is a candidate for Assessor and Collector, Red River
County

river and steamboat news
communication from Capt. T. G. Wright regarding removal of
raft in River will be in next week's paper

Fourth of July celebration
John T. Mills has accepted invitation to be the orator at Fourth
of July celebrations

hostilities with Mexico
Col. Wm. N. Porter, formerly of Bowie County, is in Memphis
Tennessee, raising a company for War against Mexico

report on the speech of Mrs. Todd and the reply of Lieutenant
Mosley at the presentation of a banner to the Bowie County

Volunteers for the War against Mexico

stray
notice by George F Lawton, Clerk, that Richard S. Gilbert, acting Justice of the Peace in Red River County, at a hearing regarding a stray horse taken up by Peter Johnston valued it at $40 based upon appraisals by Marcus Caudle and Wm. Boots

professional cards
advertisement by Drs. Gordon and Walker of their medical office in Clarksville

advertisement by Drs. Look and Peters of their medical office in Clarksville
****

From The Northern Standard, June 24, 1846

Fourth of July celebration
At Millville, on Pine Creek, a Fourth of July barbeque is planned. Sam Smith is the President and Dr. Sutherland, Vice President
****

From The Northern Standard, July 1, 1846

river and steamboat news
report from Capt. T. G. Wright regarding removal of raft in River

commercial announcement
S. H. Clark announces that he paints houses, signs and carriages in Clarksville

administration of estates
Wm. M. Burris has been appointed administrator of the Estate of Godfry Ethridge

land for sale
Elizabeth Moore, *administratix* of the Estate of Allison Moore, announces sale of 1200 acres of land on Red River

public notices
notice by John R. Bedford that clients having business with William C. Young and S. H. Morgan [who have gone off to the War against Mexico] should see him as he has their papers

notice by W.B. Stout of appointment of S. H. Morgan, Joseph Mather and John Monkhouse as Notaries for Red River County

lawsuits filed
notice by Lamar County District Court in action entitled *John L. Dillingham v. William Anderson* of process being served on him in connection which judgment owed by him to J. W. Tyson

notice from Bowie County District Court (H. Bayless, Clerk) in action styled *Isaac N. Jones against Presley S. George and Jesse H George* of pendency of action against them

stray
notice by John R. Craddock, Clerk, that P. Lynch, Justice of the Peace in Lamar County, at a hearing regarding stray horse taken up by Joseph Davis valued it at $15 based upon appraisals by W. C. Denton and W. H. Manze

school news
advertisement by E. A. Todd of Ringwood Female Academy

election announcements
letter from James Jenings to the voters regarding his bid to be elected Assessor and Collector

notice by W.B. Stout that the voting will take place in the Justice precincts at places of A. J. Titus, John Stiles, R.S. Gilbert's Steam Mill, and John Robbins

notice by W.B. Stout as to location of polling places and election officials at each location
Precinct 1 at A. J. Titus, James C. English
Precinct 2 at John Stiles, Ulysses Aguler
Precinct 3 at Clarksville, L. D. Barry
Precinct 4 at Pine Creek, M.S. Gilbert
Precinct 5 at John Robbin's, T. J. Shannon
Precinct 6 at Roland Nickle

In Titus County
Precinct 1 at Morton's, Joseph H. Gordon
Precinct 2 at M. Keith's, Thomas Williams
Precinct 3 at M. W. Jones, Charles Jones
Precinct 4 at Tankerely's old place, M. Stewart
Precinct 5 at Hallbrook's, J. R. Hallbrook
****

From The Northern Standard, July 8, 1846

election announcements
Col. James H. Rogers announces he is candidate for Brigadier General of the Second Brigade, First Division, Texas Militia

Gen. M. G. Wilson will not be a candidate for Brigadier General of the Second Brigade, First Division, Texas Militia

Capt. William Crenshaw announces he is candidate for Brigadier General of the Second Brigade, First Division, Texas Militia, Fannin and Lamar Counties

land for sale
Smith & Mitchell advertise lots for sale in the new town of Bezzetta on the west side of the Trinity River, fifty miles below Dallas

administration of estates
Martin A. Poer has been appointed administrator of the Estate of Solomon Poer of Bowie County

public notice
notice to all by F.X. Commson not to buy 36 cords of bois d'arc wood which he has purchased from D. G. Ball from Doaksville

Fourth of July celebrations
anniversary of our Independence was celebrated in Clarksville in really fine style. The oration of Judge Mills elicited general admiration. Following the oration was the execution, also in fine style, of the National Anthems, *Hail Columbia* and *The Star Spangled Banner*, which were sung by the choir of ladies and gentlemen, accompanied by instrumental music.

At Dangerfield on the Fourth of July, an excellent oration was delivered by Col. Jas. H Rogers, after which some 300 persons partook of a barbecue.
****

From The Northern Standard, July 15, 1846

letters left at Post Office
list of letters at the Post Office at Fort Towson, Choctaw Nation

Anderson, G. N.
Allen, David
Abbot, William Y.
Allen, Simon
Anderson, David
Alexander, C. C.
Allen, John
Allen, John T.
Armitage, Hon. K.
Anderson, E. F.
Ames, William F.
Acock, William P.
Armstrong, Robert
Burke, Wm. or T.
Ball, Elishai
Beams, Gilbert
Beller, John W.
Baugess, Franklin
Brown, William
Brashiers, Elmind
Burnett, John T.
Burney, R.A.
Bassford, Hezeklah
Bennet, Joshua
Bayless, Hezeklah
Barry, L. D. and D. N.
Bryant, L. D.
Bryant, William
Bishop, Oliver
Buttle, Susan G.
Bonner, George S.
Bryerly, Thomas F.

Blanton, Lemeuel
Babb, James L.
Billingsby, Jesse
Chapman, J. W.
Cochran, W. M.
Coffey, William
Chisum, Jacob G.
Crowdon, William N.
Cobb, Samuel or James Pickens
Cooper, Henry
Churdale, Mark
Compton, J. B.
Colbert, Margaret
Colbert, Robert
Cobb, Dr.
Colbert, James
Cawfield, Ruthy
Cowan, Thomas L.
Caudle, Millinda
Cobb, R.F.
Clark, John T.
Dudley, Warton K.
Duncan, John
Dodd, Jane
Dougherty, Nathe
Dickin, John S.
Dalion, Samuel, L.
Drummond, John W.
Davis, Mrs. Julia
Dowdle, Marion
Davis, Dr. John
Epperson, B. H.

163

Ewing, Salina
Fowler, John R. O.
Folsom, Lyman
Fulller, Calvin P.
Finely, John B.
Fletch, J. J. & A.&.W
Fort, Josiah
Fanning, N.S.
Fieldlin, James
Foster, James or J. H. Carr
Foster, J. W
Finley, Wayne
Folsom, Daniel
Folson, Sophia
Gibson, J.P.
Good, William C.
Givens, N.. James
Gooch,Jr., M. B.
Gay, William R.
Glen, John
Gibson, Ivey
Gibson, Joseph P.
Glass, John C.
Green, James W.
Gill, John
Glenn, Joseph B.
Grant, Jones
Grimes, Hiram A.
Harrison, Ann
Hunt, James
Hart, Hardin
Hood, Alex J.
Hall, Jefferson
Hasrman, Capt. Lewis
Henderson, W. F.
Hodge, A.M.
Hays, Marcus
Horn, Jeremiah
Harrison, Zada
Hall, Stephen S.
Harrison, William O.
Hiks, Harvey
Harkins, James

Hain, John
Hudson, Wiley
Hudson, Robert
Harrison, William H.
Harlins, Daniel
Hargis, Mahala
Harleson, Benj. C.
Hobbs, Isaac
Irvin, Addison M.
Ishcommore, Nelson
James, Chrisitiana
Jacobs, John H.
Jackson, Edman T.
Jeffries, James
Jackson, F.M.
Johnson, Enoch
Johnson, B.C.
Jones, Robert
Kissam, W. W.
Katherine, Robert
King, Thomas
Little & Co., Henry
Liday, Jacob
Lumley, Thomas
Lock, Leander
Labroom, Peyter
Lilley, Thomas B.
Larner, William
Linman, Jan C.
Lewin, Mary E.
McGlaughlin, Smith
Morgan, Joshua
McCray, Levi
Mebane, Temp A.
Montgomery, L.G.
Malocene, Benjamin
McGlaughlin, Miss S.
Morgan, James M.
Moore, Zacharia
McPhail, Robert
Mathews, Elbert
Mason, Daniel
Montague, Daniel

Maskins, John
McNeil, J. A.
McNeil, N.
Mann, William H.
Mosley, S. F.
Martin, Dr. M.M.
Moore, Mary J.
McFarland, Samuel
McMullen, Hiram
Norton, Pichney A.
Neil, E.M.
Osborn, George Thomas
Oliver, Leavin
Peters, Dr. Samuel
Peck, Adam G.
Prince, T.
Posey, L.
Potick, Thomas R.
Pattern, Robert
Peel, James E.
Porter, Jr., James B.
Richardson, George
Robinson, Lizzy
Ragin, Gilbert
Rogers, John H.
Ryburn, Col. H. W.
Riker, M.M.
Reeves, John G.
Rogers, E. W.
Stanlee, Elbert C.
Spence, Joseph P.
Sanders, J. T.
Stone, Solomon
Sims, F.M.
Stevenson, James
Sharp, William L.
Seildekum, Miss A.
Stone, Arthur T.
Spain, William K. D.
Smith, George W.
Smith, R. E. D.
Stephenson, John P.
Stacy, John F.

Shannon, Thomas J.
Skunkell, Willey
Snow, Ely
Spencer, Oliver
Simms, Nancy
Scot, Robert
Skunkell, Emery
Thomas, William
Terrel, James
Thompson, Eliza G.
Treaghber, William
Tomliman, John
Taylor, E.
Thom, John H.
Towet, Thomas J.
Trumbull, Robert
Taylor, E.
Thompson, William
Vallon, James H.
Vellon, Ludwick
Vanderver, Mrs. Eliza
Vine, Nathaniel
Wilson, Thomas
Womble, John
Williams, James M.
Williams, James
Willis, Thomas
Wilson, Dr. Harvey
Williamson, Isaac C.
Whistenburgh, M W.
White, Addison L.
Williams, A.M.
Wilson, H. W.
Williams, John D.
Ward, William
Wilson, John
Walkers, Mrs. E. H.
Whinney, A.H.
Weatherby, B.F.
Willis, James
Ward, Silas
Wilson, John B.
Wilson, Elisha T.

Walker, Lewis H.
Willhelms, T. & H.

Ward, M.

letters left in Clarksville Post Office
Alexander, C. C.
Alexander, Mrs. E.
Adams
Ake, Felix G.
Ashley, Alvin
Autry, L.
Andrews, William B.
Benton, Nathaniel G.
Benton, John
Baily, J. C.
Bailey, Isaac
Butler, J.
Blanlon, William
Brazelton, John

Barnes, William
Bredwell, Elijah M.
Blackwell, James A.
Clark, J. F.
Carver, Benjamin
Crisp, Duncan
Canada, Jesse
Clampett, L. D.
Campbell, Robert
Clevenger, Thomas
Campell, Attorney at law
Cox, Hiram or Washington
Carney, E. W.

obituary
in Red River County, on July 12, 1846, of consumption, L.T. Collins, son of Didamia Collins. If other son, John Collins were to see this notice, he should know his mother is in a strange land and need assistance.
****
The issues of *The Northern Standard* between July 16 and August 7, 1846 are missing
****

From The Northern Standard, August 8, 1846

election announcements
election returns in Lamar County: W. M. Crisp for Chief Judge, J.A. Rutherford in second place; for District Court Clerk, unopposed, J. Long; for County Clerk, J. R. Craddock is first, Wm. B. Brown, second and J. W. Smith, in third place; R. Russell for Sheriff, C. K. Hellman in second; for assessor and collector in first place was James Wilson, with Isaac J. Newell in second; Militia Officer, William C Young, W. T. F. Coles, in both Lamar and Hopkins

obituary
in Clarksville, on the 23 rd of July, John J. Montgomery,46 years of age, formerly of Giles County, Tennessee. He was an enthusiastic citizen and a strictly just man

letters left at Post Office
notice by Post Master   L. D. Van Dyke of Letters at Bowie Post Office

Brooks, Miss P.
Berry, Capt E.
Bayliss, H.
Ball, Dr. S, H.
Bird, Maj. Jonathan
Barcroft, Daniela
Cornelius, Abraham
Clawson, M & D
Daniel, Jesse
Epperson, Mark
Earle, Samuel
Guest, Joseph
Graham, John or Andrew
Bella
Henry, C.J.
Holloway, William
Haygood, O.S.
Hawkins, William
Holloway, Mrs. John
Hartell, William
Holcombs, A.F.
Harrison, Philip
Heatherely, Thompson
Irvine, M. A.
John, C.R.
Johnson, B. W.
Love, Thomas

McFarlan, S.M.
Mitchell, M.M.
McKay, Daniel B.
Mosley, S. F.
Mitchell, Mrs. Mary
Maylie, M. Saunders
Milner, Thomas W.
McCloskey, John
McKinney, William
Park, Thomas
Poor, Martin A.
Palmer, H.S.
Robertson, Charles
Rice, L. M.
Shults, John W,
Southland, Mary
Topp, William
Tarrant, Gen. E. H.
Vining, William W.
Walker, Miss Sarah
Wyatt, Col. P. S.
Walsh, C. M.
Wellborn, K.A.
White, Thomas J.
Wooten, William W.

election announcement
notice by James R. Wooten as to location of polling places and election officials at each location for election of Probate Judge and other positions in Red River County
Precinct 1 at A. J. Titus, Solomon Bryant
Precinct 2 at John Stiles, John Stiles
Precinct 3 at Clarksville, John A. Bagby

Precinct 4 at Pine Creek, N.T. Sutherland
Precinct 5 at John Robbin's, L. Coffman
Precinct 6 at Humphries's Spring, John Humphries

lawsuit filed
notice from William W. H. Vining Clerk of the Red River Court to Sarah Ann R. Oliver that her husband John R. Oliver was seeking a divorce from their marriage of March, 1837

stray
notice by George F. Lawton, Clerk of Red River County, of stray horse taken up by Isaac Guest and appraised by W. C. Richards and William Warner and hearing held before Lovell Coffman, acting Justice of the Peace

commercial announcement
Isaiah W. Wells advertises "New Cheap Store at Pine Bluffs, Texas
****

From The Northern Standard, August 15, 1846

election announcements
Lovell Coffman is a candidate for Colonel of the 1st Regiment, 2nd Brigade, 1st Division of the Texas Militia

Gilbert Clark is candidate for Probate Judge of Red River County

James Wooten is candidate for Probate Judge of Red River County

Charles C. Wellburn is a candidate for Colonel of the 1st Regiment, 2nd Brigade, 1st Division of the Texas Militia
****

From The Northern Standard, August 22, 1846

obituary
Charles De Morse, Jr. aged seven and son of publisher Charles De Morse, was killed when kicked by a horse on August 15, 1846
****

From The Northern Standard, August 29, 1846

commercial announcement
advertisement by R. Chatfield & Co in Clarksville of Dr. Hull's throat lozenges for sale

stop payment
Rhine & Kohn gives notice that the note it gave to Allen Urquhart for land purchases, the titles of which are not clear
****

From The Northern Standard, September 5, 1846

obituary
Laura Badger of Lamar County of bilbous fever, an infant,

land for sale
land for sale in Fannin County by William M Hunt of Bonham
****
The September 12, 19, 26, and October 3 and 10, 1846 issues of *The Northern Standard*, are illegible
****

From The Northern Standard, September 26, 1846

obituaries
died at Jonesborough, Red River County, on September 20, 1846, Mrs. Jane Chandler Gill, wife of William H. Gill

died on September 19, 1846, of congested chill, Harriet Sophronia Jane Bowers, wife of William M. Bowers, aged 15 years, eleven months and eleven days; leaves a son
****

From The Northern Standard, October 10, 1846

letters left at Post Office
list of letter at Clarksville Post office

Albright, William	Arnold, Bird
Abel, Green B.	Allen, Hugh
Allen, R. C.	Assessor and Collector,
Adams, Benjamin	Red River County

Arnold, Bird
Allen, Hugh
Assessor and Collector,
Red River County
Brettain, Bartlet
Bonner, George
Ballard, N.G.
Buel, Daniel G.
Benton, William H.
Bennet, E. H.
Barnett, Martin
Braddley, Thomas L.
Bowden, William M.
Bowers, Tomishes
Brooks, Z.
Britain, M. J.
Barker, William
Barnes, William
Bailey, Francis B.
Banon, Polly
Brown, Sarah M.
Bromley, Samuel
Barzell, Allen
Bell, H.L.
Bundren, Isaac
Campbell, Robert
Collins, Didenmed
Colville, Davidson or
James H. Garvin
Childress, Levi G.
Coffman, Lovel
Cain, Lucy A. R.
Charboutne, James
Corley, Samuel
Crisp, William M.
Clerk Circuit Court, Red
River County
Chaney, Garrison
Clapp, W.
Cooper, George
Cheatham, Cyrus
Casber, John
Dearing, Albion or
S.P. Greenman

Driver, John
Davidson, James L.
Doss, J. W
Devenport, James B.
Elliot, B. E.
Edwards, Thom C.
Ewing, William
Elliot, William
Eakridge, H. F. or
A.W. Webb
Fleming, Thom. B.
Frager, Enoch
Fuller, Joel C.
Fleming, J. J. M.
Fowler, R. O.
Fields, J. W.
Fanning, William
Fleming, W.
Fraley, C. L.
Fleming, R. C. or
Samuel W. Hills
Goodell, James P.
Gough, James H.
Gregg, Thomas
Green, James W.
Gilliland, Allen
Glenn, John
Harris, Virgil
Hopkins, Richard
Hickey, W. W.
Hardin, Sarah W. M.
Hemmingway, H.C.
Hamilton, R.W.
Hopkins, David
Harris, Newton
Harmon, William
Hensley, Charles S.
Henderson, William F.
Jordan, William
Johnson, Enoch S.
Jordan, William L.
Jacobs, Samuel
Kline, C. F.
Cline, Charles F or James

Blackwell
Langford, Eli
Longwish, Rubie
Langley, Samuel
Lawler, James E.
Lewelling, Thomas
Lowhon, Hugh M.
Leal, Charles
McRee, Nancy L.
Matthews, Richard H.
Moore, E.D.
Martin, Thomas
Monkhouse, John
Marshall, J. G.
Mason, Henry D.
Morgan, John F.
Montgomery, T.S.
Moore, G.B.
Matthews, M. W. or
George Goodman
McCowan, James
Mullins, B. W.
Morris, Thomas J.
Matthews, David R.
Murphy, Dubart
McDonald, V.
Overby, William
Ofspring, John
Otwell, John R.
Powel, John M.
Peters, Richard
Pollard, George
Potter, William
Parker, Rebecca H.
Patton, John
Parks, James
Price, William
Prince, Orestes

Perry, C.B.
Patrick, Sussannah
Priestly, Catherine W.
Roper, Thomas
Richardson, James A.
Robertson, William F.
Richard, William
Rose, Moron
Rind, Henry G.
Stroud, Allen
Stephens, George
Stephen, A.F.
Smith, R.E. D.
Sinlangh, John
Smith, Caleb
Scurlock, William
Sheriff, Red River County
Stewart, James
Turner, M.M.
Tweedy, Thompson
Urguhart, Allen
Vining, J.
Wagley, Joseph
Wallace, Andrew M.
West, Terrel
Williams, Robert
Walker, James
Webb, Alexander
White, Samuel W.
Ward, Jordan P.
Woods, John H.
Wills, J. W.
Webb, Samuel
Williams, William R.
Whiteman, David W.
Warson, Jane
Williams, V.

A.M. Crooks P.M.
****

From The Northern Standard, October 17, 1846

election announcements
announcement of candidacy of David S. Kaufman for the U.S. House of Representatives.

Announcement of candidacy of John A. Bagby for Chief Justice of Red River County

public notice
notice by A. J. Titus for Assessor and Collector of Red River County, of taxes due

land for sale
advertisement by William H. Hunt of Bonham, Fannin County of land to sell to "travelers, emigrants and others"

stop payment
notice by John Lovejoy of Paris dishonoring notes he had given

stray
notice by Thomas D. Lee of strayed horse

lost property
notice by R. C. Harris, Bowie County, of lost land certificate of Frances Godly of Red River County

letters left at Post Office
letters at post office at Fort Towson, Choctaw Nation

Armistead, L.A. U.S.A,
Allen, William
Allen, Thomas
Allen, A. D.
Burney, David F.
Burns, Uriah
Barker, Miss J.
Briarly, J. H.
Broocklin, Katherine
Barnes, Joseph
Benton, Jesse
Bobber, G. W.
Bryant, Wm.
Bean, John
Brookfield, E. H.
Carnell, W.G.
Cole, James
Cochran, Col. D.
Cochran, William M
Clampet, E. or William F. Bowers
Collins, Mrs C.
DeVille, Patrick
Duty, M.T.
Doolittle, Harrison
Elliot, E.G. USA
Ellis, John
Fowlken, E. K.
Furnace, Benjamin J.
Foster, G. W.

Fisher, Miss E.
Frazier, Sweeney
Fulton, G. H.
Fulton, C.T.
Hardway, Ainsworth
Hargrave, J. B.
Harrison, Mrs. Louise
Hendrix, John
Harrison, William C.
Hooker, William
Houston, W.B.
Hopkins, Eldridge
Hudson, Wiley
Hart, William T.
Harney, William R.
Hill, Aaron
Hodges, J. S.
Hemingway, R. C.
Hand, B.
Hemingway, M.C.
Harrison, James W.
Harrison, John
Hodge, Alex. M.
Jacobs, John D.
Jackson, E.T.
Johnston, Miss A.S.
Jeffries, James R.
Jeffers, James
Johnson, W. R.
Keys, William
Ludwig, J. F.
Lemmon, C.
Lee, Jacob
McMullen, James
Matlock, Gideon C.
McKinney, Edwin
McKay, M
Morris, John
Moore Mrs. E. B.
Majors, John P.
Merrill, D. M.
Moore, Miles
McKown, Robert P.
McIntosh, James

Otis, Peter
Oliver, John
Potts, Thomas
Porter, James M.
Polite, William
Pinkham, Melvin Miles
Phillips, A.
Potts, Joseph B.
Pickens, J & S. Cobb
Reddy, James
Rewlett, Dr.
Riley, James
Robson, George T.
Richards, Martin
Riley, Isaac
Rogers, A.
Reade, V. or J.
Roberts, O. E
Schillee, I.
Stele, John
Scott, Mrs. Sarah N.
Slaton, W.L.
Seward, R. B.
Sullivan, Michael
Spence, James P.
Stewart, William P.
Seabbrey, Mrs. W.
South, E.
Tallbot, Rev. N.M.
Tompson, William
Vickens, Eli
Taylor, R. M.
Tuns, Mrs. Rebecca or Isabella Edmonson
Thompson, Giles
Talbott, Mrs. Isabel
Taylor, E.
Terry, John S.
Thompson, J. Esq.
Teague, William
Telark, William
Wilson, Robert
Wall, D. W.

173

Worthington, C
Ware, John
Williams, M.G.
Watson, William A
Whitney, A.H.
Walker, Thomas
Wilson, David
Ware, Joseph
Wilson, M.G.
Whitney, A.H.
Washburn, Thomas S.

Walker, Thomas
Wilson, Davis
Ware, Joseph
Wicks, Jr. William P.
Woodard
Warrin, Abel
Wall, J. D. W.
Williams, Joseph M.
Young, Elijah

George C. Gooding, P.M.
****

From The Northern Standard, October 24, 1846

professional card
notice of law partnership between W.C. Young and S. H Morgan, Clarksville

land for sale
for sale by Charles De Morse *The Standard* Printing Office and the lot on which it stands

notice that Smith & Mitchell have lots for sale in the new town of Bezzetta on the Trinity River

notice seeking investors in the development of the Town of Albion on Red River made by George S. Park, Edward West, Henry Little, W. M. Harrison, J. J. Montgomery, W. T. Montgomery and Bennet H. Martin

election announcements
election Notice by John A. Bagby, Chief Justice of Red River County that the polling places for the November 3 election for U.S. Representative to Congress, will be
Precinct No.1 Soloman Bryant, J.P.
Precinct No.2 John Stiles, J.P.
Precinct No.3 A.M Crooks, J.P.
Precinct No.4 J.W Green, J.P.
Precinct No.5 Lovell Coffman, J.P.
Precinct No.6 Benjamin Croweaver, J.P.

Announcement of the candidacy of Lewis Coffman for position of colonel in Texas militia

newspaper business
Major P. J. Pillans is running the *Standard's* office in Bonham

school news
advertisement for Miss Russell's school

stop payment
notice by Jonas W. Williams dishonoring notes he had given

administration of estates
George Smith has been appointed administrator of the Estate of John Woodley

Mary N. Ryder has been appointed is the administrator of the Estate of John F. Reilly

strays
notice by Charles De Morse of his horse having strayed or been stolen

commercial announcement
notice by De Morse selling legal forms and noting that John R. Craddock was his agent in Paris, Lamar County
****

From The Northern Standard, November 7, 1846

agricultural news
Benjamin Croweaver brought the editor some specimens of Blossom Prairie radishes

election announcements
announcement of the candidacy of Charles C. Wellburn to be colonel of Texas militia

land for sale
notice by L. Goddard of the sale of lots in the town of Buffalo, county seat for Henderson County

lawsuit filed
notice of B. H. Doss in action entitled *Martin M. Ragsdale*

against William D. Ogden pending in Lamar County Court

lost property
notice of lost land certificate by R. Harris
****
No *Northern Standard*, for November 21, 1846
****

From The Northern Standard, November 28, 1846

military news
list of Major and Brigadier Generals in region
William C. Young, Major General -1st Division
W. T. F. Cole, Brig. General -1st Division, 1st Brigade
J. H. Rogers, Brig. General -1st Division, 2nd Brigade

crime news
in Grayson District court, Charles Galloway, who was charged in the murder of Col. Coffee, has been acquitted by public sentiment. There were several witnesses to the act and it was clearly a case of self defense in the last extremity

Execution. A Negro man belonging to William Grinder of Fannin County, found guilty at the term of the District Court of the murder of Morgan Marks, a white man in the employment of Mr Grinder, is to be hung on Friday next in Bonham

settlement and immigration news
Col. Ball of Kentucky is on his way to the Trinity Colony with a party of surveyors

agricultural news
Col. Epperson of Bowie has presented the editor with large red potato weighing 5 and three quarter pounds

commercial announcements
E.S. Look has glass jars and black varnish for saddlers available at his store in Clarksville

James S. Johnston advertises the Star Hotel in Clarksville

professional card
Wm. M. Harrison and R.H. Graham have taken B.O. Bagby into their partnership

lawsuit filed
notice from J. Long, Clerk of the District Court, sitting in Lamar, to Sarah A. Day advising her of commencement of action for divorce by her husband Samuel Day, witnessed by Reddin Russell, Lamar County sheriff

notice from V.H. Vining, Clerk of the Court of Red River, sworn to by Edward West, Sheriff, to Joseph Swigley that he been made a defendant in action commenced by Isaac H. Patterson, that Swigley and his partner, Richard S. Gilbert, doing business as Gilbert and Swigley, for breach of contract

stop payment
notice by Jonas W. Williams dishonoring note given to Nathaniel Vise
****

From The Northern Standard, December 5, 1846

obituary
on November 13, 1846 at Savannah, Red River County, Mrs. Rebecca Titus in the 59th year of her age, widow of James Titus; she was born in Davison County Tennessee, the daughter of Col. R. Edmonson

public notice
notice that those indebted to L. D. Van Dyke should pay up

for sale
Notice by Rev. J. W. P. McKensie that he will sell a Negro woman and one child, the property of William L. Robert and Colon D. McRae, all minors

lost property
notice by W. F. Hamilton of lost land certificate of Robert Hamilton, assignee of Joseph Black

commercial announcement
advertisement by Cynthia Caton that she has taken over the Clarksville Hotel, formerly owned by the late James Clark, then by Mr. Musgrove and then George F. Lawton, on Main Street in Clarksville
****

From The Northern Standard, December 12, 1846

land for sale
B. W. Gray, Clerk, by the Order of Alexander Neville, Chairman of the Committee to develop county seat for Titus County, advertises the sale of lots in Mount Pleasant.

sporting news
notice of horse race to be held in Paris, Lamar County in Spring term of District Court. Two entries to date are horse of John Loving of Fannin County and Col. Robert M. Jones of Lake West, Choctaw Nation

for lease
S.S. Turner announces he has Negroes to hire

school news
E. A. Todd announces her Ringwood Female Academy, at Ringwood, Bowie County

for sale
H. D. Mason will sell 70 Negroes as a part of the estate of Henry Smith, deceased of Red River County

commercial announcement
William Perry advertises his Soda Lake Hotel in the Town of Jefferson; the ladies department will be under the supervision of Mrs. Perry

advertisement by George W. Wright for Lamar Hotel in Paris
****

From The Northern Standard, December 19, 1846

crime news
Jesse, the Negro belonging to Mr. Grinder of Fannin County, who was sentenced to be hung for the murder of Morgan Marks, underwent the sentence of law at Bonham on the 27th ult. He died with fortitude

agricultural news
letter to Major De Morse from H. W. Ryburn that he has a bigger radish than that reported by Samson Smith

professional card
Dr. George H. Wooten will practice medicine in Clarksville at office lately used by W. H. Vining, District Clerk

stray
notice by George F. Lawton, Clerk that Thomas Morris and Anthony Colby, in a hearing before Lovell Coffman, Justice of the Peace, appraised a stray horse, found by Henry Riker at $20

administration of estates
notice by L. M. Rice, Bowie County clerk, to the legatees of the Estate of George Cullum to file claims

order by W.B. Stout, published by clerk George F. Lawton in Probate Court of Red River County that Marcus W . Candle has filed an accounting for Estate of John A. Candle

strays
notice by J. R. Craddock, Clerk, of stray taken up by Simon Derrick, brought before Hiram McMillan, Justice of Peace and appraised by John Roland and Amos Ridge

notice by George F. Lawton, Clerk, that Thomas Morris and Anthony Colby, at a hearing before Lovell Coffman, Justice of the Peace, appraised a stray horse, found by Henry Riker at $20
****

From The Northern Standard, December 24, 1846

obituary
Rebecca Dale, who died on December 19, aged 21. She left a husband and three small children and was a member of the Baptist Church of Clarksville

land for sale
Curtis Jordan advertising land for sale in Lamar County

administration of estates
George W. Cox, administrator of the estate of Evander Leech, of Lamar County, has filed an accounting on the Estate

stray
notice by George F. Lawton, Clerk, that Nathan G. Butler has found a stray in Red River County, that has been appraised by

Nicholas M. Maxwell and Jesse F. Hales at 30 dollars at hearing before John Stiles, Justice of the Peace

****

1847

From The Northern Standard for January 5, 1847

election news
Levi Coffman announces his candidacy for Colonel in the First Brigade

newspaper business
Editor gives his thanks to R. C. Hemmingway and Frank H. Clark for providing some of the newspapers referred to in this issue

obituaries
Samuel S. Smith of Clarksville died on December 31, 1846 at the age of 44

Judge Richard Ellis of Bowie County died on December 30, 1846. He had been born in Virginia and came to Texas in 1834

lost headright certificate
notice by Berry Merchant of lost headright certificate

lands for rent or sale
advertisement by Dr. George Gordon to rent his farm, 100 acres in cultivation, immediately adjoining Clarksville

notice of sale of town lots in Greenville, Hunt County by Commissioners Isaac Banta, J. W. Lane, James Homes and Jas. Booker

Jas. H. Johnston advertises land for sale in Jonesborough Prairie, Red River County

lawsuits filed
notice by A. Keith, constable in Titus County, to Christian Adams to appear before Thomas Willson, Justice of the Peace of Titus County, upon affidavit of John H. Balley.

Notice given by Thomas Willson in lawsuit by William Milligan against George B. Clinton

strays
notice by George F. Lawton that a stray was taken up by Peter Ringo in Red River County and appraised by James McCrorry and John McCrorry at $8 at hearing before Benjamin Crownover, Justice of the Peace

notice by George F. Lawton of a mule found by Nathan Butler and appraised at $30 by Nicholas Maxwell and Jesse Hales in hearing before John Stiles

administration of estates
notice by Thomas A. Bagley, Sheriff of Red River County that Simon E. Woodrow has been appointed administrator of the Estate of Nancy Woodrow

George W. Cox has been appointed administrator of Estate of Evander Leech of Lamar County

Charlotte Smith has been appointed administratrix of the Estate of John W. Smith of Lamar County

H. Mason has been appointed administrator of the Estate of Henry Smith of Red River County

runaway
reward offered by Thomas M. Rowland of runaway from the farm of John H. Hedge of Collin County, a slave man named Nathan

commercial advertisements
advertisement by S. H. Clark, "House, Sign and Carriage Painter" in Clarksville

S.S. Look advertises pharmaceuticals for sale

advertisement by Tilmon Patterson, Cotton Gin manufacturer, who directs would be purchases to see the gin he built for S.M. Hopkins in the vicinity of Clarksville

professional card
James M. Morphis

Attorney and Counselor at law; will practice in all the counties of the Eighth District and will attend to the solicitation of claims throughout the state; Office Paris, Lamar County

****

From *The Northern Standard* for January 15, 1847

professional card
Burrel P. Smith
Attorney and Counselor at Law, Clarksville; will practice in all courts of the Eight Judicial District

administration of estates
Hamlin has been appointed administrator of the Estate of Warner C. Williams in Lamar County

lawsuit filed
notice by H. Bayless, Clerk of the Court of Bowie County, that a summons has been issued by William J. Hays, Sheriff to William Crutcher

****

From *The Northern Standard* for January 23, 1847

agricultural news
superior cotton raised upon the plantation of Captain C. C. Herbert, on the Colorado, in the vicinity of Eagle Lake

obituaries
Col. James Johnson, died at his residence in Clarksville, at age of 41. He was from Bertie County, North Carolina

In Austin, Dr. John G. Chalmers, 46, from Halifax County, Va.

List of letters left at Post Office
partial list of Letters left at Bowie Post Office

Arnold, M.	Dwight, Jonathan E.
Bedford, Dr. R.	Dye, Kelsey
Burnett, E. D.	Dye, Jacob
Bell, John T.	Emerson, Margaret
Cobb, Richard T.	Farrington, Maj. R.
Carter, Colbert	Flack, M.C.
Cunningham, William	Graham, Ellen
Dooley, Wm.	Greer, B. H.

Gay, William
Gilbert, Michael
Kelly, Henry

Johnson, A. J.
Williams, John

partial list of letters left at Clarksville Post Office by John Loop, Post master

Williams, James
Watson, Thomas

White, Robert
Wilkins, John

professional card
J. F. Johnson
Attorney and Counselor at Law, Clarksville; will practice in all courts of the Eight Judicial District

public notice
notice by J. A. Bagby, Chief Judge of Red River County, that all holding claims against the county should come forward
****

From The Northern Standard for January 30, 1847

newspaper business
Editor thanks Mr. Read of Fort Towson who provided some newspapers for this issue

public notice
Mr. Tanner of the mail delivery reported he had made arrangements with Mr. Hunt in Bonham to open up new mail routes
****

From The Northern Standard for February 6, 1847

public notice
Jephtha Vining appoints W.B. Stout his agent during his absence

married
Dr. W. Anderson to Miss Sussanah Locks of Denton

administration of estates
William W. Fullerton is appointed administrator of the Estate of John M. Fullerton of Navarro County

H. Metherly is appointed the administrator of the Estate of Thomas Metherly of Lamar County

Hugh Cox has been appointed administrator of Estate of Archibald McKeller of Fannin County

Elizabeth Moores has been appointed administratix of the Estate of William Moores

Wesley Young has been appointed administrator of the Estate of Henry Young, Navarro County

Moses M. Hughes has been appointed administrator of the Estate of James Hughes of Navarro County

lawsuit filed
notice by Red River County Probate Court of action styled *Ephraim D. Moore, administrator of the Estate of David Wardlaw against Mary Moore, James Wardlaw and John Wardlaw, Ann Sharp, wife of John Sharp and Elizabeth Tankearsly, heirs*, to determine title to property formerly owned by James Gagahan in Titus; Judge was James Wooten, Probate, George Lawton, Clerk
****

From The Northern Standard for February 13, 1847

letters at Post Office
list by S.K. M'Gowen, P.M. of letter left at Bonham

Armitin, Thomas	Brady, Zephanish
Anderson, James	Bredon, W.W.
Allenon, Perry	Been, John
Allen, Dixon	Bryant, John
Arnspiger, M.D.	Ballard, Frederick F.
Adriance, Cornelius	Black, John D.
Armstrong, Septemus	Bishop, H.V.
Adams, Fitch	Brown, Squire
Ashlock, Meridith	Byrne, James
Bravell, Robert	Borbac, James

Baily, James
Booth, Thomas
Brummitt, John W.
Bager, Miss Mary Anne
Bird, Jonathan
Black, William
Bradly, Thomas C.
Butler, James
Bowerman, Joshua
Beeman, Mrs. Sarah Ann
Brown, John
Barron, S.D.
Chafflin, Charles
Campbell, Mr. Esq.
Glendenen, Matthew
Couch, George
Colton, Michael G.
Conant, S.D.
Clark, William A.
Cunningham, John
Cook, D.C.
Carroll, Jacob
Carr, John
Hardy, Martin
Carpenter, S. E.
Coffman, John
Cravens, Mrs. Zerelda
Dearmen, John
Dearmen, John A.
Dearmen, Taylor
Dearmen, G.
Degreffenraid, William B.
Donel, James
Dunnon, Hickman
Dillingham, J. E.
Dye, Jacob
Dickens, John S.
Denton, Parson
Evans, Wm. C.
Flattery, M.Y.
Apperson, Petty
Fitch, Richard A.
Ferrin, W. H.
Foreman, Solinda

Fitch, C. H.
Failing, Elizabeth
Roberts, Joseph
Gibson, Robert A.
Gooch, Benjamin
Gutherie, R.H.
Godsy, B.J.
Glenn, James B.
Gordon, Julian
Hitzbugh, William
Hause, Vardeman
Henry, James
Hobbs, Thomas
Hudric, H.G.
Howe, A. J.
Hart, Josiah
Harvey, Louisa J. T.
Henely, Daniel
Hodges, Mrs. Sally Ann
Henely, Henry
Hagood, Cephas
Haygood, S.G.
Hubbard, Thomas
Harris, William J.
Harbol, David
Holdery, G. W.
Harper, Elijah
Harrell, Richard
Herron, John M
Hoppes, M. Charles
Johnson, Nathan
Jones, Theodore
Jones, William M.
Jitt, William
Jennings, John
Jennings, James H.
Johnson, John S.
Jones, John H.B.
Johnson, William P.
Jones, John
Knoz, William
Kean, John
Keen, Miss
Keen, J. W.

185

King, Miss Margaret
King, James
King, William
Landrum, J.
Lewis, William C.
Laurence, Mrs. W.
Lee, John
Lee, Robert
Lee, Peter
Langford, M. H.
Lively, Anderson
Lucas, George F.
Lewis, Reuben
Lowe, Manson
Lloyd, Richard
Lady, Milton W.
Lyday, Andrew
Lane, David
Lock, John
Lee, Charles
Larrence, James
Leonard, Elizabeth
Lynch, James
Miller, Nicholas
McDonald, Charles
Mars, J. R.
Morrey, Daniel
McNealy, Friar
More, Edward
Morrow, Cicero
Mosley, Daniel
Merrick, James C.
Mars, James H.
Mechem, Joel
Morrison, D. M.
McKeller, Archibald
May, Joshua
Moore, Thomas
Mars, Samuel W.
McDuffie, John
Martin, John B.
Mills, Edward
McDonald, Thomas
Marrs, Jeremiah

Matthewson, Robert
May, A. J.
Mooney, Edward
Moses, Henry Philip
Nail, Mrs. Anne
Newton, Hervy
Oldham, H. F.
Ogle, David
Overstreet, James
Page, W.F.
Pillans, P. J.
Pace, B.
Ramsey, John
Roberts, John
Riley, William
Robbins, William
Roberts, Joseph H.
Rattan, Thomas
Richardson, D. M.
Shelton, Horatio
Slack, Amos P.
Stephens, George
Schalelford, Mrs. Mahala F.
Smirh, George
Spead, Mr.
Smith, Mrs Ann
Smith, Alex
Shields, Robert
Spred, Mattias
Stover, Sr., John
Stark, Amos
Stone, John
Still, Joseph
Schakle, Bluford
Jones, James
Starrett, James
Shannon, Samuel
Tyres, Elisha
Thomas, Jesse E.
Thomson, James A.
Thompson, William
Taylor, R. H
Turner, John
Thomas, John C.

Thomas, David G.
Thompson, Nancy
Turney, Moses
Taylor, Claxson, J.
Turner, Henry
Thresher, Franklin
Turner, William
Throckmorton, Robert M.
Trimble, Mrs. Martha
Underwood, Ann
Underwood, Elijah C.
Van Pool, Obed.
Vivian, James
Vielliers, Henri H.
Wall, Preston H.
Wells, Oliver
Wright, John W.
Williams, Philip
Wells, Person
Wells, Rezin
Wells, Rev. R.
Williams, George
Woods, Elisha
Wilson, William
Wison, Miss Mary J.

Wabb, D.
Wright, Fisher
Williams, J. M.
White, William T.
Wheeler, Thomas
Wood, David L.
Wilt, Eli W.
Whitley, Alex
Wilson, David C.
Walker, Thomas E.
Williams, Jesse
Ward, J. C.
Whittenberg, Iraneus
Waldrip, Andrew B.
Waldrip, William
Walker, Albert G.
Williamson, John
Wood, James A.
Williams, James C.
Williams, John D.
Williams, William L.
Yarborough, Jno. O.
Zimmerman, James M.

****

From The Northern Standard for February 20, 1847

obituaries
Randolf C. Harris died at his residence in Bowie County, on February 4, 1847. He was 44 years old and had come to Texas in 1837 from South Alabama

commercial announcement
drugs, medicines, paints etc. for sale by E. S. Look in Clarksville

land for sale
town lots for sale by L. Goodard in Town of Buffalo in Henderson County, on the north side of the Trinity River, 47 miles below Dallas

town lots for sale by Smith & Mitchell and L. Goodard in Town of Bazzett, on a bluff on the west side of the Trinity, 50 miles below Dallas

town lots in Town of Albion, on Red River, offered by George S. Park, Edward West, Henry Little, W. M. Harrison, Bennet H. Martin, E.M. Jones, J. J. Montgomery and W. T. Montgomery

lost headright certificate
Lost headright certificate by Curtis C. Jordan in Lamar County
****

From The Northern Standard for February 27, 1847

agricultural news
The editor is indebted to Dr. W. H. Boyce for a specimen barrel of Bowie County flour, from wheat raised upon his plantation of Red River and which is manufactured at the Dr.'s own mill

professional card
Dr. G. W. Wooten has his office on the east side of the Clarksville Public Square

administration of estates
John D. Thomas has been appointed executor of the Estate of Richard Thomas of Lamar County

W. M. Williams has been appointed administrator of Estate of John Fiser of Lamar County

Kiziah Martin has been appointed executrix of the Estate of Thomas T. Martin of Lamar County

Matilda Drew has been appointed administrator of the Estate of Joseph J. Dew in Red River County; George Lawton is her agent

John Barkman in Bowie has been appointed administrator of Estate of Mary Morris

Frances Crabtree and James Gillet have been appointed administrators of the Estate of Solomon Crabtree in Lamar County

sports news
challenge by Robert Smith to Major Smith, Col. Gordon and Ragland Davis for a horse race.

lawsuit filed
notice of filing of legal action entitled *John Ballard against William Baker and David G. Ball* in Red River County District Court regarding purchase of unsound horse before Justice of the Peace, A. M. Crooks of Red River County; notice given by Wade H. Vining, Clerk of Court, and Edward West, Sheriff

strays
Washington Gray and William Tigert have appraised at $20 at a hearing before Joseph A. Clark, Justice of the Peace of Titus County the horse found by Smith B. Cherry; notice by Jefferson Cook, Court Clerk

William M. Peacock and John Peacock have appraised the horse found by Ewing Ellison at $20 before E. G. Rogers; Justice of the Peace of Titus County; notice by Jefferson Cook, Court Clerk

J. B. Daniel and Jno. C. Glass have appraised at $37 before James Daniel, Justice of the Peace of Titus County, the horse found by R. C. Harris; notice by Jefferson Cook, Court Clerk

J. D. Thomas and Abraham Payne have appraised at $10 at hearing before Robert M. Worthham, Justice of the Peace of Lamar County, the horse found by William Yates; notice by John R. Craddock, Court Clerk

W. R. Brown and James Richey have appraised at $30 at hearing before F. Morrison, Justice of the Peace of Lamar County, the horse found by Gibson May; notice by John R. Craddock, Court Clerk

lawsuit filed
legal notice in Lamar County District Court in action entitled *Alexander Mabane, William Tinnin and Alexander W. Hodge, executors of Estate of L. W. Tinnin against William N. Porter, John B. Craig, John T. Harmon, William C. Young, James Bourland, Mansell W. Matthews, Albert G. Kimbell, George Wright and Travis G. Wright* to apportion the Estate's debt; notice given by Jacob Long, Clerk of Court, by Sheriff Reddin

Russel

notice by Jacob Long, Clerk of Lamar County Court, of complaint of *William Davis, administrator of the Estate of Thomas Davis against Abram Mittower, John Emberson, Joshua Bowerman and Isaac Williamson* on promissory notes

notice of complaint styled *Joshua F. Johnson against George B. Clifton* for action for debt; notice given by Wade V. Vining, Clerk in Red River, and Edward West, Sheriff

lands for sale
J. B. Darnall advertises 11,000 acres of land for sale in north Texas
****

From The Northern Standard for March 6, 1847

newspaper business
Editor acknowledges his thanks to Judge [John] Mills and R. M. Hopkins, Esq.

public notice
notice from Young & Morgan, attorneys, that they are the agents for the dissolving firm of Look and Peters

commercial announcements
for sale by Henry Gooding at the Star Hotel in Clarksville or George C. Gooding, post master, Fort Towson for cash or for good terms on produce for a close carriage of large size in good condition; price is $500, its original cost in Peterburg, Va

Holmes and Russel announce auction on general assortment of hardware, tin ware, shoes etc

STAR HOTEL -- formerly the property of the late Col. James H. Johnson. We call attention to the card of the host of the Star Hotel, Henry Gooding; He reopens the house with a fine assortment of good things and the determination to do the best he can for his customers. We take the occasion to say that travelers, who may favor him with their presences, will find him to be a most agreeable landlord and will be well fed and attended to.

Lost headright certificate
Hiram Baker and Caroline Baker, administrators of the Estate of David Sample, give notice of lost headright certificate for 640 acres in Red River County

****

From The Northern Standard for March 13, 1847

school news
notice by Mrs. Weathered of Examinations at Clarksville Academy. She will be assisted by Mrs. Graham

administration of estates
William H. Boyce appointed administrator of Estate of Isham J. Boyce in Bowie County;

military news
notice from St. Clair Denny, Paymaster, U.S. Army that he will be in Clarksville for the purpose of paying off unpaid obligations of Col. Young's Regiment and Captain McGarrah's Detachment

notice that General James H. Rogers of Texas Militia will be forming enlistments in Red River County

****

From The Northern Standard for March 20, 1847

commercial announcements
advertisement for sale of lumber by Montgomery, Barnett & Co.

advertisement by William Perry for his hotel, the Soda Lake Hotel in the town of Jefferson: "Every means will be offer comfort to the tired, traveler; his table and larder will be furnished with the best the country will warrant; stables connected with the hotel are large, airy and commodious and horses will be taken care of by an experienced person; charges are on a moderate scale suited to the hard times; the ladies department will be under the superintendence of Mrs. Perry who will devote her whole attention to her guests

advertisement of George W. Wright of Paris, Lamar County of Lamar Hotel, a 'house of public entertainment; his building are

new, large and commodious; his stables supplied with plenty of
corn hay and fodder and careful, attentive ostlers."

E.S. Look advertises Sand's Extract of Sarsaparilla
****

From The Northern Standard for March 27, 1847

public notice
E. S. Look calls upon those who owe him to pay him

married
on February 24, 1847, by the Rev. F. W. Hobbs, J. W. Mone to
Miss M. Duvall

on March 2, 1847, by Judge Latimer, J.D. Wren to Miss
Isabella Simpson

on the 4th day of March, 1847 by the Rev J. W. Hobbs, Mr H. J.
Allen to Mrs Angelina Ann Adams

land for sale
notice by Charles Fenton Mercer of the Texas Association
offering land in North Texas to be settled by immigrants

commercial announcement
advertisement by Joseph Bartlett of his ferry at Fenton on the
Trinity

stray
notice by George Lawton, Clerk of Court, that strays found by
Jeremiah Monk were assessed by Marcus G. Settle, Justice of
the Peace of Red River County, on appraisal of Levit Cady and
Daniel Waters at $15 for the mare, $20 for the colt

notice by George Lawton, Clerk of Court, stray found by James
Backsten was assessed at hearing before Solomon Bryant,
Justice of the Peace of Red River County on appraisal of D. S.
R. Matthews and E. Bateman Waters at $ 16.25

church news
notice that the Red River Cumberland Presbyterian Church will
meet in Clarksville on Friday of the third Sabbath of April; Rev.
James Sampson's opening sermon beginning at 11:'clock

notice by J. W. Fields to the preachers of the Eastern Texas Conference to come to the Courthouse in Clarksville where they will be assigned where they are boarding

professional card
Dr. W.F. T. Hart is returning to practice in Red River County, where he has been 6 years previously in his 14 years of experience

stop payment
James Tomberlin says his check to Wm. W. Vining or Thomas Vining for a horse , saddles etc was without consideration

commercial announcement
notice by S. Carey that he has purchased entire stock of drugs and medicine of Chrisman and Alexander in Jefferson and will be sold as cheap as they can at Shreveport at the sign of "the Golden Mortar"

****

From The Northern Standard for April 1, 1847

newspaper business
S. K. McGowan is *The Standard's* representative in Bonham

election news
results of election for Militia Officer in Clarksville
for Colonel:
Hugh F. Young   59; Lovell Coffman   43

for Lieutenant Col:
John W. West 69; W. P. Cornelius 25

for Major:
George W. Hart 57; F.M. Sims 40

Municipal elections
Mayor: H. Gooding

Assessors: R.H. Graham; S.S. Turner; E .S. Look; Charles Durfee; E.M. Smith; B. C. Bagby; John A. Bagby

Town Constable: Adam Ribble

B. H. Epperson was elected County Commissioner for the
vacancy on the resignation of John R. Bedford
****

From The Northern Standard for April 8, 1847

hostilities with Mexico
Red River volunteers -- In compliance with the call from the
Secretary of State, our citizens have again turned out for war
and with a zeal that never flags; when honor calls, they are
prepared to do service for their country. Old Red River is up
and ready. On Monday last there being 80 names on the rolls,
the company proceeded to organize. Col. Sam'l W. Sims was
almost unanimously elected captain."Our Red River Boys are a
stout company. We will guarantee that they will do their duty in
any emergency". This District always does its duty. It always
tenders unhesitating obedience to the laws, it always pays its
apportionment of the taxation, even when others do not, and it
always finds men for the service of the Country, when they are
called for. The fact is that the Old Red River district is
sound to the core and cannot be excelled by the same amount of
population anywhere

Red River Volunteers
Colonel   Samuel Sims
1st Lieut.   John W. West
2nd Lieut.   J. J. Snider
3nd Lieut.   F.M. Sims
1st Sarg.   J. M. Bevins
2nd Sarg   J. H. Harris
3rd Sarg   T.P. Hightower
4th Sarg   A.P. Corley
1st Corporal   W. W. White
2nd Corporal   David C. Russel
3rd Corporal   Wright Stanley
4th Corporal   James T Patrick

married
on March 3, 1847 by the Rev. James Graham, Dr. W. T. F.
Coles to Martha A. Bourland, all of Lamar County

commercial announcement
notice by J. K. Oliver and R. Chatfield of lately arrived goods
for sale

public notice
notice by J. M. Morphis that accounts of Ragsdale and Wright have been put into his hands for collection

The following are described as owning patents for lands in Fannin and notice by William H. Hunt are to meet with S. K. McGowen:

Bennet T. Logan	Sussanah Walker
James H. Haslett	Elijah Young
Josiah Hart	Jordan Ward
Jesse M. Boyd	William B. Williams
George W. Bagby	Justin Ferry
Henry Bivens	Bukley L. Berland
Rufus A. Clark	Louis Richardson
W. Carroll Click	John L. Lovejoy
James Dennis	Alex E. Ross
John Dennis	Joseph Williamson
Charles W. Sadler	Felix R. Foster
William M. Williamson	Robert C. Fleming
John Kuykendall	James Hellfinger

****

From *The Northern Standard* for April 15, 1847

letters at Post Office
letters left at Clarksville Post Office

Agar, Mr.	Sulivas, Adam
Albright, Alfred	Britten, Joseph
Anthony, James B.	Bell, Samuel
Allen, Hugh	Bryan, Dr. J. H.
Anderson, James	Bedford, John R.
Akin, John B.	Baccus, Enoch
Arrington, Joel	Barnes, Talton T.
Adams, James	Bryarly, Thomas F.
Allen, Alfred	Bowerman, Joshua
Allen, attorney	Boots, William
Bartlett, William	Burnett, Isham
Berry, William H.	Cox, Hiram W.
Black, Miss Elizabeth	Craig & Norris
Burnes, Mrs Jane R.	Collins, C.P.
Bowers, Tomisher	Collins, Commodore A.
Blevins, William	Carroll, Ferdinand

Clark, James
Clark, Mr. Nancy
Clark, John T.
Carter, John C.
Clampett, L. D.
Coincon, F. X.
Campbell, Esq
Campbell, John
Corbit, Nathaniel
Donnell, E. F.
Eads, John
Epperperson, R. J.
Fuqua, Joshua
Farmer, John
Farmer, David C.G.
Gare, Thomas W.
Gilliam, James
Gray, William
Graham, Rev. James
Graham, Mrs. Eliz.
Graham, Thomas
Graham, Lilly
Harland, N. R
Hunt, Mrs. Ann
Hedge, Robert
Hannah, Richard H.
Harris, Henry B.
Hardy, William T.
Harmon, Samuel
Hamilton, James
Holt, T. C.
Hunt, Green T.
Henderson, James
Hickey, M. B.
Haning, Aron
Hudson, Mrs. Sally
Horton, William
Jones, Alfred H.
Johnson, Mrs. Clarissima
Jones, Jacob B.
Jacobs, William
Keen, William
Karber, Peter
Long, Tobias

Long, James
Long, William R.
Lindley, Jacob
McBride, Rev. C.
Martin, Thomas
Marler, H.
McCasland, J.D. F.
Mills, J. T.
Moore, L.P.
Mauker, Allen
Marshall, Stephen
Maxwell, Nicholas
Maban, J. A.
Montgomery, Elizabeth R.
Mimm, Gideon
Martin, Matthew W.
McCarty, Joseph
Morgan, William
Mathis, Daniel
Norris, James
Nitt, Isaac
Nall, Robert
Norman, John
Newcombe, William
Otwell, John R.
Osburn, William
Price, Thomas
Powel, Nathan
Patterson, Isaac H.
Peters, John
Reynolds, Lemuel M.
Robinson, Fontaine
Robertson, Elridge
Richey, James
Rhome, H.
Reed, John
Reed, Joseph
Richard, Wilson
Rice, A. J.
Ragin, Caleb
Roland, Samuel
Ryder, Miss Mary
Scott, William
Williams, A. M.

196

Stewart, John
Snell, I. F.
Sublen, Capt. G.A.
Stallings, Abraham
Sedicum, F.
Shearer, Spencer
Shearer, Sarah A.
Spencer, Arthur
Spears, Dickson
Stacy, B.F.
Stephenson, George H.
Stockelager, P.A.
Sutherland, N.T.
Simpson, John
Stephenson, Alexander
Staley, Joseph
Smith, William
Tune, David J.
Talbot, A.G.
Thompson, Franklin
Turley, William
Thomas, Elijah
Thomas, Washington
Thomas, William,
Long, James

Tankerley, Richard
Tuggle, Jackson
Todd, Col. W. S.
Tinnin, I. W.
Tinnin, W. H.
Ursery, J. E.
Victor, Palangue Monsieur
Vice, Nathaniel
Vanlandingham, Alfred
Wall, John
Whiteside, W. H.
Whitesides, Wm. N.
Whitesides, Mrs. Florinde
Wyman, Mrs. Martha
Williamson, Clark
Wilkins, George
Willaims, Joseph
West, John
Whitaker, Robert
Ward, A.M.
Ward, Sarah
Ward, James
Westerman, Benjamin

A.M. Crooks
****

From The Northern Standard, April 22, 1847

church news
appointments of Presbyterian Conference of East Texas: For the Clarksville District were Daniel Payne and F. W. Stowall, Andrew Davis in Dekalb, James Graham in Paris, J. H. Biggs, M.F. Cole and Jefferson Shook in Bonham and Dallas, Daniel Shook in Kingsborough; George West is Bible Agent

San Augustine District – J. W. Fields
Jasper Liberty District – N. W. Berks
Trinity District –   K. Wilson
Nagidoches District –   P. W. Hobbs
Angelina District –   to be named
Wesleyan College Dist.   J. T. P. Davis

Marshall District -- H.E. K. Lacy
Rusk Circuit -- S.A. Williams
Henderson Circuit -- William Craig
Shelbyville Circuit– E. P. Chisholm
Also mentioned in the article were F. Wilson and Rev. J. M. Baker

obituary
Major John M. Allen, U. S. Marshall for Texas

land for sale
Sheriff's sale advertised by Edward West for sale of lands, adjoining Solomon Wargenner in Blossom Prairie, near A.W. Latimers, known as the property that Ira Poor purchased from Sherrod Roland, on which judgments by B. H. Martin and John Fowler have executed.

hostilities with Mexico
letter received from Charles P. Scott, of the Red River Volunteers, dated San Antonio on March 18, 1847, reporting that company has started for Monterey

letters left at post office
letters from Fort Towson Post Office

Allen, Col. Wm. F.
Archer, Creed
Cobb, R. T.
Colbert, Miss Malinda
Eastman, Dr. A. Perry
Early, Elbert
Evens, Abraham
Frazier, David
Feeny, Robert
Gay, William B.
Gage, C. W.
Greenwood, Jerreson
Glass, John C.
Halsey, A.A.
Kinney, Stephen
Meredith, William
Meadow, Richard
Mulligan, James
Murphy, Thomas G.
Mabane, Alexander

Nall, Miss Livia
Osman, John
Ouchetchya, Charles
Porter, Alex L.
Parker, John H.
Pickings, James
Perry, Rev. Moses
Pitchlyn, Thomas J.
Powers, Michael
Powel, Erwin
Simmons, E. L.
Scott, John T.
Shannin, James
Stewart, Wiley
Tiner, Jesse
Thompson, William
Tushkahimitah or Asanochi
Turnbull, Robert
Turnbull, Turner B.
Thompson, Giles

Robinson, Capt John
Richards, Martin
Reynolds, L. M.
Wills, Hamp
Worthington, Chessly
Wilson, David
Williams, William
Walker, Geo. W.

Whitney, A.H.
Ward, Dr. J.
Williamson, Clark
Wilson, Thomas
Wallace, Joseph M.
Wilson, Hurly

Geo. Gooding, P.M.

land for sale
sale of town lots in Boston, Bowie County by L. M. Rice, Commissioner
****

From The Northern Standard, April 29, 1847

land for sale
William M. Harrrison offering land for sale

stray
John Ware advertises that he found a stray mule
****

From The Northern Standard, May 5, 1847
public notice
notice by William H. Boyce that he has appointed James N. Smith, Esq. his agent while away

lost headright certificate
Hiram Baker and Caroline Baker give notice of lost headright certificate of David Sample
****

From The Northern Standard, May 13, 1847

obituary
Joseph Mather, born in Ireland, died of typus fever at home in Pine Bluff, Red River County on April 29, 1847

commercial announcement
advertisement by Oliver & Chatfield for "ready made clothing"and blacksmith tools in Clarksville store

stop payment
notice by F.B. Gunn to stop payment on note he gave S.S. Booth for the purchase of land

stray
notice by Richard R. Crook, Clerk of the Court of Red River County, that a horse was taken up by John T. Harris, living about five miles west of Tarrant, was appraised before R.R. Crook and William Fatherred in hearing before Lewis J. Crook, Justice of the Peace
****

From *The Northern Standard*, May 19, 1847

election news
Jesse Robinson of Sabine County announces candidacy for Governor

newspaper business
Joseph A. Clark is now in charge of advertising *The Western Argus* in Bonham, together with John Shaffer

professional card
T. J Rogers ((Jefferson) and J. H. Rogers (Daingerfield) are in partnership practicing law

commercial announcement
A.L. Davis is making the best quality of wheat fans and is selling them at his farm, five miles west of Clarksville

hostilities with Mexico
E. Jones seeking payment for goods furnished to Col. Young's Regiment for which he has not been paid and tells the soldiers to settle their accounts at the following places:

G. A. Everts of Bonham for Captain Dagley's Company
H. D. Woodsworth Esq. in Paris for Capt. Gillette'
Capt. Smith Clarksville for his own company
Capt. Rice of Boston for his own Company

sporting news
horse race in Parish between J. J. Musgrove's mare *Purity* and Col. R. M. Jones mare, *Choctaw Filly*

administration of estates
Stephen D. Raney is appointed administrator for Estates of William Wellborn and Charles C. Wellborn in Red River Probate

crime news
news item: about four weeks previously, three men named Adkins, McDonald and MacGuire (last two from Houston County, Alabama) murdered two men named Bronton and Moore in Leon County on the west side of the Trinity River, allegedly because they would not join in some "villainy". Mr. Randolf, Sheriff of Houston County and a large number of citizens pursued them to Alabama, then to Leona where they delivered themselves up for trial to Mr. Garner, the magistrate of that place, whom they thought would give them a sham trial and acquit them. He would not, which led to more violence, including Black Hardin, Garner's son in law, killing both MacDonald and McGuire

On Saturday, May 1, the jail in Soda Lake was broken and James Beck, Gideon Flynt, A.V. Keener and the Negro Bacchus, all having been committed as felons to await trials, escaped
****

From The Northern Standard, May 26, 1847

Indian news
eight horses stolen by Indians within two miles of county seat of Grayson County on the night of May 7th. Pursuit was made by Mr. Bingaman and Mr. Clark, both of whom had just emigrated to the county and had been settled there but a few days, and they killed two of the three Indians and crippled a third

crime news
on Thursday, April 22nd last, at a wedding held at the home of Mr. John Wilkinson on the Sabine River, Shelby County, the 72 guests were seized with violent sickness, twelve of whom died. Arsenic, mixed in the cake by accident, reckless carelessness or diabolical, is suspected
****

From The Northern Standard, June 2, 1847

Indian news
report from - Col D. Mitchell, who is surveying the Upper Trinity region, writes us that he has just returned from a surveying trip on Noland's River and that he saw plenty of Indians that were very friendly and that Col. Tho. I. Smith's rangers are all remaining at their old posts

strays
notice by J. R. Craddock that stray found by Gibson May has been appraised at $30 by William R. Brown and James Richey at hearing before F. Morrison Justice of the Peace in Lamar County

notice by J. R. Craddock that stray found by John L. Dillingham has been appraised at $15 by William L. Hamilton and Willard Stowell at hearing before F. Morrison, Justice of the Peace Lamar County

administration of estates
John A. Talbot has been appointed administrator of Estate of William McFarlin of Bowie County

lands for sale
notice by W. Nicks Anderson on behalf of Charles Fenton Mercer & Associates for sale of lots at Pine Bluff on the eastern bank of the Trinity

public notice
George Gordon gives notice that no one is to collect wood from his property
****

From The Northern Standard, June 9, 1847

election news
Notice by Col. Hugh F. Young regarding location of polling places and person in charge in election of officers to be held at

Beat No.1 at Millville –	Marcus G. Settle
Beat No.2 at John Robbins --	R .J. Sims
Beat No.3 at Wm. Humphreys --	B. Crownover
Beat No.4 at Davis N. Barry's--	W. W. Foreman

Beat No.5 at Clarksville --   A. M.Crooks
Beat No.6 at Clarksville --   James W. Sims
Beat No.7 at Thomas O. Benge's -- J. C. English
Beat No.8 at John Stiles --   John Stiles

strays
notice by J. R. Craddock that stray found by Richard G. Miller has been appraised at $15 by John Jacobs and Robert Glass at hearing before John T. Harmon, Justice of the Peace in Lamar County

notice by J. R. Craddock that stray found by Elizabeth Crow has been appraised at $25 by Cyrus Holman and Joel W. Magee at hearing before Brad C. Fowler, Justice of the Peace in Lamar County

notice by J. R. Craddock that stray found by David Williams has been appraised at $30 by J. A. Askey (his mark) and James W. Morgan at hearing before Ervin Thompson, Justice of the Peace in Lamar County
****

From The Northern Standard, June 16, 1847

Masonic news
notice by John E. Long, secretary of the Masonic Lodge, that the Festival of St John the Baptist will be celebrated in Paris

professional cards
notice by Drs. Look and Dr. Cornelius of a partnership to practice medicine

Dr. A.B. Hoy, dental surgeon, is in Clarksville for a few days

commercial announcement
C. Asberry has opened a photographic studio at Dr. Look's house and will take Daguerreotypes

notice by N. R. Harland & Co of his tan yard and saddler's shop at Bluff Spring, Lamar County

administration of estates
E. R. Miller is appointed administrator of the Estate of Atlas Dodd in Lamar County

203

strays
notice by J. R. Craddock that stray found by George Kenedy has been appraised at $20 by Lee Foster and E. F. Anderson at hearing before John L. Dillingham, Justice of the Peace in Lamar County

notice by J. R. Craddock that stray found by Hiram M. Halsey has been appraised at $5 by John Davis and William Clark at hearing before John L. Dillingham, Justice of the Peace in Lamar County

notice by J. R. Craddock that stray found by Benjamin Schoenover has been appraised at $15 by Wm. L. Hamilton and John M. Roberts at hearing before F. Morrison, Justice of the Peace in Lamar County

notice by J. R. Craddock that stray found by John L. Dillingham has been appraised at $15 by William Cage and Thomas E. Wesern at hearing before F. Morrison, Justice of the Peace in Lamar County
****

From The Northern Standard, June 22, 1847

election news
The Standard endorses George T. Wood of Liberty as Governor

local news
De Morse reports en route to court in Jefferson that he visited Mr. Booth's at Dalby's Spring, about 35 mile south of Clarksville, where he drank the noted spring water

agricultural news
De Morse acknowledges the receipt of heads of rye which are from 8 ½ inches to 9 1/4 inches long and very heavy. They were from the farm of John Butler near Clarksville.

July 4 celebration
celebration of the Anniversary of American Independence by the citizens of Red River County at Thomas O. Bunge's: The committee of Joseph N. Burns, James Gilliam, James B. Wooten, appointed for the day, has selected
Thomas J. Scurry, Esq. to read the Declaration of Independence and Burrel P. Smith, Esq, as the orator of the day

court news
report on meeting, chaired by David S. Kaufman, of the Bar of Eastern Texas generally, some thirty counties represented, where a Committee, chaired by W. S. Todd of Bowie County, was appointed to prepare a request to the U.S. Congress and the Legislature of the State of Texas to hold a session of court each year in Henderson, Rusk County, the only Federal District Court being in Galveston and the Supreme Court of Texas sitting in Austin. The members of the Committee were:

Bennett H. Martin of Red River
Charles De Morse of Red River
B. W. Gray of Titus
Samuel F. Mosley of Cass
Andrew Allen of Harrison

Benjamin G. Burke of Sabine
Richard S. Walker of San Augustine
L. D. Evans of Fannin
A. S. Thurston of Harrison

additional attorneys at meeting were:
W. P. Hill
Amos Morrill
J. C. McGonigal
G.M. Adams
Granville Lewis
Richard D. Walker
M.D. Rogers
James A. Simpson
David Stinson
R.N. Good
John B. Mabane

Jas. M. Clough
D. Fields
John W. Ellet
Edward Clark
Alexander Frazier
W. H. Bristow
T. T. Gamage
George Lane
James H. Rogers
J. C. Everett
Thomas J. Rogers

Those not at meeting but who support petition
John T. Mills
B.P. Donlevy
W.B. Scurry
R. Scurry
B. P. Smith
J. W. Latimer

B. H. Epperson
Wm. C. Young
S. H. Morgan
A. J. Russell

married
in Clarksville on June 12, 1847 by the Rev. J. W. P. McKenzie,

Stephen D. Raney to Miss Elizabeth Russell

at Pine Bluffs, Red River County, May 17, 1847 by Marcus G. Settle, Esq., Joseph J. Smith to Mrs. Mary K. Ryder

obituary
at Monterey, Mexico, on the 26th of April, Wm. W. Vining, aged 28 years, son of Wade H. and Martha Vining of this vicinity

Major William Armstrong, the well known Indian Agent, died in Doaksville, Choctaw Nation on May 19, 1847 of billious chills

professional cards
T. J. Rusk and A. J Thruston; Rusk's office will be in Nachdoches and Thruston in Marshall; will attend the courts of Harrison and all of the Sixth Judicial District

Byrd W. Gray will practice in all the courts of the 8th Judicial District and Upshur and Cass Counties; his office is in Mount Pleasant, Titus County

public notice
Notice from assessor and collector of taxes in Red River County, A. Jackson Titus, for citizens to settle up their taxes with him, or in his absence, with George F. Lawton

school news
Notice from M. W. Weatherred and E.A. Graham denying that the Clarksville Female Academy was leaving town, even though Mr. Weatherred was going to cultivate a farm outside of town
****

From The Northern Standard for June 30, 1847

election news
B. Gooch announces his candidacy to be representative of Red River County in next legislature

Chas. De Morse announces his candidacy to be representative of Red River County in next legislature

Fourth of July celebrations
Fourth of July... The procession upon the 5th of July will be formed at the Star Hotel at half past 10 o'clock a.m. The ladies are respectfully requested to meet there and take part in the procession. Mr Gooding has proffered the necessary room for their convenience

school news
Female Institute. We learn from Col. William S. Todd that the institution now known as the Ringwood Female Seminary will move from Boston to Clarksville and occupy "the elegant residence and grounds presently occupied by Mr. M. Harrison Esq. and a two story and a half building for the school, sleeping rooms and dining hall will be erected immediately. The Editor is pleased to see the movement. The character of the Ringwood Institute is so high and with the very excellent institution of Mrs Weathered & Graham, both in our Town, the place will present such opportunity for education as seldom found west of the Mississippi."

agricultural news
Turnip . . . a turnip from Dr. Burris of Blossom Prairie, measuring 39 inches in circumference

land for sale
Thomas Shannon has a thousand acres of Becknell Prairie to sell, part of the headright of William Becknell, about six miles west of Clarksville

runaways
From Jno. S. Herring, two slaves, John almost 25 years old and very stout and Ruben, about 22 years of age and very light complexion

administration of estates
William H. Kimbell has been appointed administrator of the Estate of William R. Smith of Henderson County

strays
notice by J. C. McGonigal that stray found by G. H. Glover has been appraised at $50 by Wilson Wright and Lewis H. Walker at hearing before A.M. Poer, Justice of the Peace in Red River County

notice by George T. Lawton that stray found by Francis M. Hillburn has been appraised at $40 by A. Jackson Titus and James Burkham at hearing before John A. Bagby Justice of the Peace of Red River County

notice by Jefferson Cook that stray found by G. W. Halgrass has been appraised at $20 by B. W. Gray and M.C. Martin, at a hearing before Graven Batwell, Justice of the Peace of Titus County

notice by George F. Lawton that stray found by Richard F. Gidden has been appraised at $20 by Isaac Morgan and N.B. Hutchinson at hearing before N.G. Butler, Justice of the Peace in Red River County
****

From The Northern Standard for July 3, 1847

letters at post office
notice by A.M. Crooks, P.M. of letters left in Clarksville Post office

Arnett, John
Adams, Isaac
Allen, Hugh
Mulligan, Thomas M.
Addison, Malcolm H.
Anthony, James B.
Autry, Lewis
Austin, Richard
Aimes, Charles
Barnett, James
Baker, Solomon
Bedford, John R.
Benton, William H.
Blair, Capt. James
Beene, William
Butle, Olvy J.
Bryant, Robert R.
Baler, James
Webb, S.
Bourling, Maj. James

Boules, J. L.
Barroy, Mrs. Polly
Barton, John G.
Blauton, David
Bailey, William
Barker, Emmanuel
Blackburn, James
Bishop, O. H.
Barnett, Martin
Brown, Miss Sarah Jane
Byrd, Abel
Baker, Thomas C.
Barker, Wilson
Brown, M. J.
Barnett, Alex. M.
Boyd, George C.
Barker, Elizabeth
Batrs, Mrs. E. L.
Bishop, Joseph
Corley, Samuel
Clark, James

Cain, Miss Lucy
Crewdon, William M.
Care, John
Dickson, Reynolds
Clemens, Andrew E.
Caudle, Mrs. M.
Corbett, Nathaniel
Cooper, Henry
Cass, Mrs.
Cullum, John
Culberson, J. F.
Cole, D. W.
Crutchfield, David M.
Cleveland, Gen. Benjamin
Cline, Isaac
Clinton, James
Cullen, Asa
Davidson, Ellis
Dixon, Enoch
Dawthet, Ambrose
Day, Edward
Denny, Maj. St. Clare
Davis, Dr. John
Donnell, Rev. T.F.
Dite, George
Dewit, Clinton, Chap. #6
Duncan, William B.
Enox, David F.
Edmonson, Mr.
Fulbright, Daniel
Fulbright, D.& C.
Fulbright, Sawyer Elias
Flemon, William
Graham, John
Gaiter, Col. F.
Gregg, Mrs. Mary
Gilbert, Mr. (Pine Creek)
Green, James W.
Guest, A.N.
Goock, Hartford
Gilbert, James
Grangen, John
Garrison, John C.
Green, M. T. C.

Griffin, Benjamin
Goodall, James F.
Gilliam, H. O.
Guest, Martin
Guest, Isaac
Harris, William S.
Haughton, William M. S.
Hannah, Richard
Heath, James
Halbert, Joel
Hail, Joshua
Hansford, John M.
Hitl, Thomas
Hail, John W.
Henderson, John
Hill, Abner
Hodges, William
Hodges, Robert
Heath, James
Hawker, Henry
Hill, Ephraim
Howard, Christopher
Hill, Barnard
Hargen, John
Hanyell, Daniel B.
Hollard, Andrew J.
Hubard, Mr.
Hubard, Fulbright
Hemingway, R. C.
Hardway, Miss Mary A.
Johnson, John W.
Johns, C.R.
Johnston, Miss Mary Annie
Jones, Miss Mary
Johnson, Jonathan
Keasey, Dr. Stephen
Kellam, James W.
Kelvey, Rev. H. B.
Keith, William S.
Marshall, Stephen
Kilbreth, Rev. James
Lyon, William
Lyon, Miss Maria T.S.
Lee, James

Lasson, Abay
Lynn, B.F.
Langley, Samuel
Lewis, Samuel
Lowden, Thomas
Liha, William
McAnear, Alex
Mather, Joseph
Maffett, John
Morrison, James P.
Morgan, Dr. W. N.
Morgan, John F.
Moore, John G.
McCrourie, James
Montgomery, L. M.
Miller, Martin G.
Moss, Miss Hester
Moore, Rev. E.D.
McAnear, Samuel
Mathews, Mrs. Ann
McGuire, G.
McCarty, E.C.
McGill, James
McGill, Anderson
Myers, Miss Charlotte
Monkhouse, John
Mees, James
Matthews, M. W.
McBride, Charles
Mathers, James
Nall, Dr. James M.
Newborn, Thomas J.
Newcomb, William
Othwell, John R.
Osburn, William
Oural, John
Potter, Mrs. Matilda
Pickins, B.F.
Parks, Mrs. Elizabeth
President of East Texas Conference
Powell, Nathaniel
Pinter, Thomas H.
Purkis, John Todd

Penick, Chalres J.
Paine, Bishop Robert
Revier, W. K.
Rodgers, Gen. J. H.
Rowland, Burgess G.
Rowlett, Dr. Daniel
Recorde, James P.
Rotter, George
Reed, Miles
Reed, Mrs. Mary
Roley, Charles
Richards, W.G.
Richey, Mrs. Jane
Rankin, Thomas
Ransom, Richard
Saige, Edward N.
Sutton, J. Edgar
Scott, William
Williams, J. R.
Williams, A.N.
Smith, Robert E.D.
Stovall, Warren
Spencer, Oliver
Stroud, Allen
Shelton, John
Smith, E.M.
Shearer, Spencer
Smith, Jackson
Sampson, Rev. James
Stors, Capt. Joshua
Stintham, Thomas B.
Stephens, Thomas
Stuart, John
Shannon, T. J.
Scott, William
Stacey, John S.
Scantling, Fielding
Spears, Dickson
Stonham, James
Smithers, Isaac
Sheriff of Red River County
Tone, George N.
Teague, William
Terry, John

Thomas, Marrion
Tabin, Anson
Thomas, Henry
Thomas, John
Thomas, John D.
Thompson, Miss Jane
Turley, William
Usry, James
Vernoy, G.
Vice, Nathaniel
Vaught, J. B.
White, Samuel D.
White, W. W.
Whittaker, Robert
Ward, Augustus
Woollin, Rev. J. C.

Whitington, William T.
Wasson, Hiram
Wasson, Aroander
Wilkinson, John L.
Willison, Thomas
Waggoner, Daniel
Warhop, Mrs. Elizabeth
Webb, A.W.
Warren, James F.
Warren, Col.
Williamson, Clark
Williams, Philip G.
Williams, Mrs. Elizabeth
Williams, Rev. E. B.
Williams, A.N.

administration of estates
H. Matthiessen and M.D. Woodsworth have been appointed administrators of Estate of Joseph Mather

hostilities with Mexico
letter from S. W. Sims from Mexican War: "The Regiment is now almost complete, nine full companies having been mustered in some time since and with another to be mustered in today or tomorrow. We had our election for field officers on the 11th instant and it resulted in the election of John C. Hays, Colonel Commandant and H. Harper of this place [San Antonio] Lieutenant Col. Wm. H. Bourland was elected Major. We are under orders of Capt. Howe. The company was mustered into service on May Day. We have 94 men the strongest company in the regiment. The volunteers are generally in good health, no sickness except measles, except one case and that has proven fatal. Capt. Dagly of Fannin was buried at the Catholic Graveyard yesterday at 5:00 p.m. with the honors of war. He was taken with a congestive chill the day before his death and died with the second chill.
P.S. The Rev. Sam'l Corley has been appointed by Col. Hays as a chaplain of our regiment. The Parson s very popular in our regiment and in San Antonio
****

From The Northern Standard for July 10, 1847

election news
Jesse J. Robinson of Sabine County is a candidate for Governor

Gen. E. H. Tarrant is candidate for Lt. Governor

Col L. D. Henderson is a candidate for senator for the Counties of Red River, Bowie Titus and Cass

B.Gooch is a candidate for Representative of Red River County in the next legislature of the state

Fourth of July celebrations
celebration of our National Anniversary took place in Savannah in this county on the 2nd. The ceremonies were opened by the reading of the Declaration of Independence by Thomas Scurry, Esq., which was done in a audible voice and in an impressive manner. Then followed an oration by B. B. Smith, Esq. The meats were cooked in excellent style under the supervision of our old friend, Jas. Atkinson, Esq. A Ball closed the enjoyments of the day.
In Clarksville, the celebrations were had on the 5th. The Declaration of Independence was read by A. J. Russell, Esq and the oration given by B. H. Epperson, Esq.

legal news
The house of Mr. Brooks, the surveyor and one of the first three inhabitants, who alone were the residents of the present county of Upshur two years ago, was the first one we [De Morse and the other lawyers riding the circuit] came to after leaving the Cypress. A half mile beyond is the town of Gilmer. We arrived at Gilmer on Monday morning and found Judge Roberts and District Attorney Walker punctual in their attendance. On getting into Town, we found that the Hon. Kaufman and several gentlemen from Harrison County. In the course of the morning arrived Mr. Van Zandt, the candidate for Governor whom we mentioned as having been at Jefferson. We found here Judge Hart of Nacogdoches, an old acquaintance we had not seen for some years. We also met here Col. Haden Edwards of Nacogdoches, who is a candidate for the senator in the State Legislature and was making the tour of his district.

commercial announcements
Brackney and Collins have a furniture shop in Paris

Oliver & Chatfield advertise medicines, glassware in Clarksville
****

From the Northern Standard of July 17, 1847

election news
The *Standard* endorse George T. Wood for Governor

Berry H. Durham, of Jefferson is a candidate for Senator for the Counties of Red River, Bowie, Titus and Cass

John A. Bagby is candidate to be representative of Red River County in the next legislature of the state

Charles De Morse candidate to be representative of Red River County in the next legislature of the state

De Morse praises E. H .Tarrant as candidate for Lieutenant Governor

Letter from James Rogers to De Morse regarding Wood's candidacy

commercial announcement
Clarksville Gin Manufactory. . . a new branch of mechanical employment in our neighborhood. It has performed to the expectations of Mr. Patterson and he has enlarged his capacity for business with a co-partnership with Mr. J. J. Snider of our Town, a notice of which will be found in this day's paper. Mr. Patterson is telling us that he constantly is receiving orders from a distance, including orders from the Choctaw Nation and he has a much business before him as he could desire

letters at post office
letters at Fort Towson Post Office
Brown, W.   Colbert, Holmes
Colbert, Silas   Drecher, Frederick
Cotter, Miss Susan   Doss, Thomas C.
Carter, George W.   Fisher, Col.Charles
Cat, Luther F.   Fisher, S.D.

213

Folsom, Lyman
Green, B.H.
Gilbert, R.S.
Huey, E.G.
Hollis, Joseph
Hays, Thomas
Harris, Miss Sarah
Jones, A .J.
Jones, Miss Kasiah
Latta, R.H.
Lancaster, Joseph
McKinney, Miss Marsha
McKinney, Hon. A.
Mitchell, Joseph G.
McHenry, Henry
Malone, John P.
Marer, John P.
Meyers, D. L.or N.T.
Nail, Liuccinder

Norris, John H.
Norris, Joshua
Osman, John B.
Oakchist, Chareston
Pitchlyn, Susan
Perkins, Mrs. Elli
Riker, N.M.
Reynolds, Mrs. Julia A.
Reynoldst, Mrs P.
Revere, William
Rogers, Lovely
Rutter, William
Thompson, William
Thom, James
Vermillion, H.F.
Woodward, H.G.
Ward, Samuel

George C. Gooding, P.M.

hostilities with Mexico
Notice by Hugh F. Young, Colonel and Commandant, and his adjutant R. J. Sims for the election of Lieutenant Colonel and other officers on August 7 at:

Beat no.1 at Millville   Wm. Scurlock
Beat no.2 at Jno. Robbins   William Guest
Beat no.3. at William Humphries John Humphries
Beat no.4 at David N. Barry's   A.R. Dickson
Beat no.5 at Clarksville   B.C Bagby

administration of estates
Probate Order entered by J. B. Wooten, Presiding Judge, Red River County Probate and entered by George Lawton, Clerk regarding estate of Edward M. Dean, by administratix, Sarah Mullins, formerly Sarah Dean

notice that Wm. M. Kimbell has been appointed administrator of the Estate of Wilson Smith.

lawsuit filed
notice from B. H. Doss, the Clerk of Lamar County District

Court, given under order of William H. Wynne, Justice of the Peace to William Witt to appear in action commenced him by Reuben W. Williams for money owed.

Notice from B.H. Doss, the Clerk of Lamar County District Court, given under order of William H. Wynne, Justice of the Peace of Henderson County to James Bourland, Garnishee, to appear in action commenced by E. B. Wade
****

From The Northern Standard of July 24, 1847

newspaper business
Editor thanks Gilbert Ragin for the paper from New Orleans

hostilities with Mexico
report from the Red River Volunteers by Lafayette Weatherred

church news
notice by the Rev. James Sampson of camp meetings to be held at Hopewell, Shiloh, at Bullard's Creek

runaway
notice by John G. Chambers of runaway slave
****

From The Northern Standard of July 31, 1847

weather
Matagorda Herald reports of violent storm "accompanied with more severe lightning and thunder than we have ever experienced." A small dwelling house at the upper end of town, opposite the church, owned by Mr. F. Waldeman and occupied at that time by himself and family, was struck and almost completely demolished. Mrs. Walderman was mutilated by the timbers and splinters and later died. She was sitting at the time in a rocking chair with four young children --one an infant --on the floor around her. At the dwelling house of W. W. Stewart, Esq. Mr. Stewart's son, a young man, was seriously injured. The church in the same neighborhood was struck. The Rev. Mr. Ives was in the vestry room, "and could not have been more than 5 feet from the course of the [lightning]"

agricultural news
Received mastodon cotton bolls from plantation of S. B. McKenzie

Editor has some grapes raised by Mr. Echlinger of Indian Point

election news
list of candidates
for Representatives for Fannin, Hunt, Grayson and Collins
T. J. Shannon
Daniel Montague
P. J. Pillans
S. K. McGowen
–, Backus

for Senator for Lamar and Hopkins
William M. Williams

for Representatives for Lamar and Hopkins
Wm. H. Bourland
S. R. Campbell
J. E. Hopkins

for Representatives for Bowie and Cass
Col. John Wilson
S. F. Mosley

for Representatives for Harrison and Panaola
Col J. A. Simpson
Charles Livingston
Col. T. T. Gammage
Capt E. M. Wilder
Col. M.V. Mann
Capt E.J. Thompson
James F. Taylor
B. B. Taylor

for Senate for Harrison and Panaola
Edward Clark
James McCown

for Senate for Red River and Titus
Berry H. Durham

for Representatives for Red River and Titus
John A. Bagby
Charles De Morse

letter from O. Hendrick in Marshall to Charles De Morse,
George Gordon, S. H. Morgan, J. J. Ward and Edward West
regarding election for Governor

professional card
Dr. A. J. Redding, late of Marine Hospital in St Marks Florida,
has opened his office at Pine Bluff

administration of estates
R.G. Miller appointed administrator of Estate of S. Peck

strays
notice of stray from Pickett & Stephens

notice by J.R. Craddock that stray found by John C. Bates has
been appraised at $25 by P.S. McKinley and A.J. Perriman at
hearing before J.A. Dillingham, Justice of the Peace in Lamar
County

filing of lawsuit
notice by W. H. Vining to sheriff Edward West of Red River
County to summon Samuel Riker in connection with a note
given to A. Baker & Co.

notice by W.H. Vining to sheriff Edward West of Red River
County to summon Samuel Riker in connection with a note
given to William Garquot, Lames A. Garquot, Henry Parish,
Samuel Parish and Peter Courtney, New Orleans merchants

notice by W.H. Vining to sheriff Edward West of Red River
County to summon Samuel Riker and Daniel Riker in
connection with notes given to William Henderson and William
Gaines

commercial announcements
notice from Isaiah Wells for books, cloths, shoes, saddles etc.
for sale and will advance on beeswax, gin receipts and Cotton

Patterson and Snider advertise Clarksville Cotton gin

E.S. Look has black varnish for saddles

****

From The Northern Standard of August 14, 1847

local news
Ebenezer Allen, formerly of Clarksville and Secretary of State of Republic of Texas is in town

obituary
John R. Bedford Esq., in Laredo, about June 1; he was from Clarksville and, before that, Boone County, Mo.

newspaper business
prospectus for new paper in Town, *The Western Star*, a Whig paper founded by W. J. F. Morgan

agricultural news
an ear of corn from the plantation of John Robbins, 11 and ½ inches long has 976 grains and weighs one pound nine ounces; cotton bolls from Wm. S. Johnston; largest measures 6 inches and 3/8th of a inch around; sweet potatoes from the farm of E. P. Wallis; muskmelon from Mr. A. J. Rice, weighing twenty five pounds and measuring 35 and ½ inches.

lost property
notice of lost land certificate by William Becknell in Red River County

strays
notice by George W Lawton that two strays found by A. J. Titus have been appraised at $35 and $30 by Thomas O. Benge at hearing before John A. Bagby, Justice of the Peace in Red River County
****

From The Northern Standard of August 21, 1847

sporting news
notice of horse race in Clarksville between the horses of A. J. Titus and J.K. Oliver by J .C. Hart, secretary of the Clarksville Racing Association

obituary
Mrs. Mary Malvina Doss at her residence in Paris on August 9, 1847. She was 21 years of age, the wife Benjamin H. Doss and the daughter of Reuben W. and L. R. Reynolds.
****

From The Northern Standard of August 28, 1847

land for sale
S. W. Simms has property for sale

commercial announcement
Alfred & Co of New Orleans lists C. C. Alexander, T .J. and W. P. Cornelius of Clarksville, A.M. and L.C. Alexander of Paris and Joseph Harrison of Bonham and Isles of Pine Bluff as references

school news
advertisement W. W. Weatherred and E. A. Graham for Clarksville Female Academy
****

From The Northern Standard of September 4, 1847

election news
letter by L. D. Barry of Clarksville to De Morse re election

administration of estates
Thomas Dennis is appointed administrator of the Estate of James Dennis

lost headright certificate
Allen Urguhart gives notice of lost head right certificate
****

From The Northern Standard of September 18, 1847

election news
Letter to the Editor from D. M. Short, W.F. Echols, L.H. Ashcroft of Shelbyville enclosing communication from Maj. James Reiley of Henderson regarding upcoming elections

obituary
Col. Zach Miller at his home in Lamar, aged 29 on August 12

219

From The Northern Standard of September 25, 1847

election news
Gubernatorial Candidate George Wood will address the citizens at James E. Hopkins in Hopkins County, at Jesse Shelton's and at Erwins in Honey Grove

river news
report by the Grand Jury of Bowie County calling for cooperation with other counties to clear Red River of a raft. Bowie proposes sending D. M. Chisolm and N.D. Ellis as their representatives. The report was signed by Carro Epperson, Chairman. The Committee consists of:

John C. Dalby	Jacob H. Collom
Bluet Stewart	Hiram H. Dalton
Betrnd E. Elliot	Benjamin White
Hardin R. Reynolds	James Wise
Evan T. Watson	Alfred M. Jordan
Francis B. Gunn	John Tisdale
James Aikin	
Samuel Bobo	

****

From The Northern Standard of October 2, 1847

land for sale
advertisement by D. K. Jamison for the sale of his premises of 300 acres

desirable residence for sale by S. W. Sims, 3/8 of a mile from the courthouse in Clarksville, 10 acres --part in cultivation; house in good condition; good cistern and out houses attached; situation is a pleasant one and convenient to anyone wishing to do business in town

stray
notice by B.F. Hawkins that he lost a horse

notice by Jefferson Cook that two strays found by G. W. Neal have been appraised at $20 each by John M. Crane and John Hightower at hearing before W. W. Hickey, Justice of the Peace of Bowie County

lost property
lost land certificate by George Brinlee of Bowie County for land in Red River County

sporting news
J. C. Hart calling for subscriptions for next racing season and the announcement of a upcoming race

commercial announcement
notice by Montgomery Barnett and Co. selling lumber. Its agent in Paris is H. D. Woodsworth

administration of estates
Curtis Jordan is appointed administrator of Estate of Thomas Jordan in Lamar County

L. W. House is appointed administrator of Estate of R. C. Harris of Bowie County
****

From The Northern Standard of October 9, 1847

agricultural news
Texas flour --. Editor has a sample of flour manufactured at Ellison's Mill in Titus County,

letters left at post office
letters left at Clarksville Post Office

Allen, Ebenezer
Asbury, Charles J.
Arrington, Martha or
Alabama Ridge
Adair, Robert
Allison, William
Armstrong, Matthew
Atwood, Simon
Bottles, James C.
Barnes, J.W.
Briarly, Thomas F. or
Bryarly, Minerva A.
Brown, Matthew
Brown, John

Berry, John S.
Brandon, Elizabeth
Batemen, Micajah M.
Bloodworth, John
Boiles, America
Barkman, John
Byers, Adam Meek
Barker, Wilson F.
Bridgman, J.C.
Burge, Zipiah
Barnard, Calvin
Batt, Mr. or Mrs.
Bailey, James C.
Bradley, Edward

Balls, William
Bibins, James or Peter Ringo
Clevenger, Elias
Clampitt, Elisha
Clampet, L.D.
Clark, Thomas C.
Coffman, Lovel
Clark, James
Carr, H.B.
Collins, William
Crutchfield, Davis M.
Caldwell, S.W.
Crealy, William
Carter, Armstead
Chaffin, T.B.
Crittendon, William
Daren, John
Daren, Mrs. N.L.
Davis, William W.
Dean, Levi
Dean, Elias
Dowdy, Martin
Ellisom, Ewing
Easkridge, Harvey
Fleming, P.H.
Fleming, Perry
Farier, William B.
Ferguson, Pleasant M.
French, L.
Files, John
Gage, E. H.
Gordon, John
Green, Roland
Gaffney, William
Gilbert, Wiley
Gibson, J.P.
Gugn, William
Gray, Pleasant
Gless, Rachel, E.
Hicklin, Martha
Hales, Jesse P.
Holmes, Hardy B.
Hadden, H. B.

Harris, William
Hughart, Edward
Hunt & Black
Hemingway, R. C.
Hemingway, Mrs. L. J.
Hogue, James
Hoy, A.B.
Horn, William
Hawkins, William
Hutchinson, N. B
Hamilton, R. Wm.
Irion, William S.
Johnson, Mrs. Sarah
Jackson, Calvin
Jackson, G. B.
Jones, H. W.
Jones, Henry
Jones, James C.
Jones, James L.
Jones, Mary C.
Jones, Thomas
Johns, Clem R.
Jacobes, Harry
Kelly, Mrs. Martha
Keith, Abijah
Knight, William
Kinney, Stephen
King, James
Lynch, James
Laney, George
Lynn, Joseph
Lanier, A.S.
Lewis, John S.
Lee, James
McLoughlin, Joseph
May, Mary A.
McClure, W.S.
Martin, W.C.
Moffett, John
Murphy, Dubart
Mather& Stats
Mason, George
McCashland, J.D.
McCrury, James

Martin, J.W.
Moore, Parker
McAnier, John
McMillan, Dr. L.B.
Montgomery, Mary A.
Morgan, Charles
Norman, John
Nunn, Julian L.
Neal, Mathias G.
Newton, William M.
Petty, John M.
Powell, Nathan
Porter, B.E.
Pryor, L.
Price, R.E.
Price, John
Parlier, Littleton
Priestly, Catherine
Rusk, James
Reilly, John P.
Richards, L.
Rainey, Mary
Rainey, S.D.
Shannon, Samuel
Smith, E.M.
Smith, M.
Sinclear, Clayton C.
Sampson, William M.
Scurlock, William
Shelton, Irv
Shelton, Jesse
Suttle, M.G.
Stewart, John
Scarborough, Winny
Stors, Joshua
Smiley, Samuel
Smith, Joseph
Stanfill, Ervin or

William Bowlin
Shannon, Davies
Sims, George K.
Shook, Mrs. Mary A.
Stonham, Mrs. Ellen
Steel, John
Smith, William D.
Tus, Tumagga, sub chief at Red River
Tune, William
Thom, Josiah
Trigg, Edward S.
Tucker, Jefferson
Vernoy, C.
Van Zandt, Hon. Isaac
Wallis, Miss Mary J.
Wallis, William M.
Ward, James
Ward, Dr. William
Whitaker, Robert
Wheeler, Richard C.
Ward, H.
Winslow, John
Woods, John
Wood, Gen. George T.
White, Lewis L.
White, William W.
Walker, Samuel N.
Williams, Thomas
Williamson, Clark
Whiteman, David W.
Wenner, Martin
Webb, John
Warren, J. H.
Waggoner, Daniel
Yarborough, Stephen

A.M. Crooks P.M.

commercial announcement
advertisement for the Paris Hotel, William Owens. Room was a $1.75 per day, horse $.25

strays
notice by J. C. McGonigal and his deputy S. H. McFarland of stray found by James P. Alord has been appraised at $25 by William Wright and Alford M. Jordan at hearing before M.A. Poer, Justice of the Peace in Bowie County

notice by E. Hopkins that stray found by William Wilkins has been appraised at $20 by John Hart and George Wilkins and claimed by Merideth Hart at a a hearing before William Wilkins, Justice of the Peace in Hopkins County

lost property
notice by Charles Syms of lost land certificate, in Natchodoces County, of Abraham Gibson and acquired from the estate of John Van Vaughn

notice by Alfred L. Hulm of lost land certificate in Bowie County

administration of estates
William Pirtle is appointed administrator of Estate of Benjamin Pirtle in Titus County

Moses W. Johnson is appointed administrator of Estate of Samuel Johnson in Titus county

Booker F. Mullins is appointed administrator of Estate of Bennet Caudle in Titus County

Benjamin Gooch appointed administrator of Estate of H. F. Eskridge in Titus County

Nancy Cherry is appointed administrator of Estate of Jno. V Cherry in Titus County

lawsuit filed
notice by W. H. Vining, Clerk of the Court of Red River County, to Edward West, Sheriff, to summon Elizabeth Greenman, formerly known as Elizabeth Pettijohn, to appear in action by Sylvester Greenman for divorce

notice by W. H. Vining, Clerk of the Court of Red River County, to Edward West, Sheriff to summon Vincent B. Tims to

appear in court in action by James Conkling, Noah T. Conkling, William K. Belcher, and Henry Calhoun, all of New York, in an action against him and Johiah H. Donk for debt
****

From The Northern Standard of October 16, 1847

election news
Bowen Waller of Austin and John A. Hainey are running for Lieutenant Governor

notice by John A. Bagby, Chief Justice of Red River County as to election precincts for upcoming civil elections
Precinct no.1   Solomon Bryant
Precinct no.2   John Stiles
Precinct no.3   A.M. Crooks
Precinct no.4   Malcolm G. Settle
Precinct no.5   Reddick J. Syms
Precinct no.6   Benj. Crownover

newspaper business
Agents for *The Standard* are:
Gen. E. H. Tarrant in Navarro County
Dr. H. Graham and C. Allen in Buffalo, Henderson County
William P. Knight, Greenville, Hunt County
S. McGowan, Bonham, Fannin County
John R. Craddock and Jacob Lake in Paris, Lamar County
Eldridge Hopkins, PM in Tarrant, Hopkins County
B. W. Gray in Mount Pleasant, Titus County
J. J. Williams in Boston, Bowie County
Thomas Watson, Cass County
R. P. Grump in Jefferson

sporting news
results of horse race at Clarksville track: S.G. Novel's horse beat E. Finnin's in first race; Jno. Lorings' horse won in the second race

commercial announcement
O. Lewis and E.C. Hart doing business as O. Lewis & Co. of Shreveport, La. gives T.G. Wright as reference

professional card
William H. Johnson, Attorney at Law in Mount Pleasant, Titus

County

military news
by Order of Gen. Hugh F. Young, elections for officers are set at following locations with the following locations with precinct captains
Beat no.1 at Millville   Charles C. Settle
Beat no.2 at Jno. Robbins   Lovell Coffman
Beat no.3 at William Humphries Benj. Crownover
Beat no.4 at David N. Barry's   Lewis D. Barry
Beat no.5 at Clarksville   B. C. Bagby
****

From The Northern Standard of October 23, 1847

election news
candidates for Sheriff of Red River County are:
Lewis D. Barry
Hugh F. Young
John H. Duke
Col. Robert S. Hamilton

candidates for Probate Judge, Red River County, are:
Jackson M. Montgomery
John A. Bagby

notice by Jas. B. Wooten that sickness will prevent him from visiting Red River, Cass and Titus Counties prior to the election

legal news
Editor reports of court proceeding in Hunt County including meeting candidates for office, Col. McGarrah of Collins and Col. Jack. He stayed in Greenville at an "excellent tavern" kept by Mr. Knight

commercial announcement
"75 cords of fire wood wanted--Apply at this office immediately": Charles De Morse
****

From The Northern Standard of October 30, 1847

election news
General Lamar is a candidate for the Legislature of Nueces

County

newspaper business
Editor is indebted to B.P. Smith, Esq. of Clarksville, and V. B. Timms and Mr. H. Von Bibber of Shreveport for New Orleans newspapers

agricultural news
notice by William Ward of Public sale of "corn, cattle, hogs and farming utensils"

farm for rent
Richard M. Hopkins advertises his 500 acre farm for rent near Clarksville

public notice
warning by Geo. Gordon for people not to take wood from his property

military news
notice by S. H. Morgan that he will be in Fannin to obtain powers of attorneys from members of Col. Young's company
****

From The Northern Standard of November 6, 1847

election news
election results in Red River County and Titus
Governor: Wood, Darnell, Van Zandt, Miller, Robinson
Lieutenant Governor: Tarrant, Greer, Waller, Haynie
Floating Senator: Bourland
Senator: Wooten and Durham
Representative: Stout. Gilliam, De Morse, Epperson, Gooch
Chief Justice: Stiles, King
Probate Judge: Montgomery, Bagby

in Lamar County
Representative: Wm. M. Bourland, S.R. Campbell; Johnson Wren, A. Skidmore, Harvey Shelton, D.O. Norton

in Fannin, County
Representative: Shannon, Gogart, Montague, McGarrah and Pillans
****

From The Northern Standard of November 13, 1847

public notice
Dissolution of Partnership between John A. Talbott and A. L. Mulm
****

From The Northern Standard of November 20, 1847

river news
advertisement for the Old Steamer *Victress*, R.J. Hickerstaff, Master; J.J. Smith is the agent in Pine Bluff

land for sale
William Ward advertises land for sale his place about 2 1/4 miles south of Clarksville

commercial announcement
advertisement for Porter's Bluff Inn, run by R.H. Porter

administration of estates
Edward West is appointed administrator Estate of William W. Vining of Red River County
****

From The Northern Standard of November 27, 1847

farm for rent
Jno. T. Mills advertises his farm for rent

stray
notice by T. P Hightower that four of his horses either strayed or were stolen

elections
letter, marked "advertisement", from L. D. Barry regarding politics and critical of Robert Weatherred
****

From The Northern Standard of December 4, 1847

elections news
a response, also marked "advertisement", from Robert Weatherred regarding politics and critical of L. D. Barry

228

land for sale
notice by Margaret A. Cornelius of Mill Creek, Bowie County that she will offer her farm for public bid.

commercial announcement
advertisement by James Gilmer that he will buy hides and peltries. He will be aboard the *Belle of Illinois*
****

From The Northern Standard of December 11, 1847

newspaper business
Editor is indebted to Mr. Bell of Deaksville for a copy of the Washington Union

river news
report on the Raft Convention. Among the attendees and those appointed to a Committee of 30 were:

from Arkansas
Hon. Edward Cross; Capt C. K. Cheatam; Judge H. K. Brown; M. V. Cheatam; Capt. William Wynn; Judge Jas. Trigg; Allen W. Blevins; William W. Andrews

from Bowie County
N.D. Ellis; D. M. Chisholm; Col. Charles Lewis; Caro Epperson; Dr. William Boyce; Dr. J. W. Fort

from Red River County
William Trimble; Charles De Morse; Capt T.G. Wright; A. J. Titus; A H. Latimer; William M. Harrison; R. C. Bagby; W.R. Scurry; Jas. W. Sims; John T. Mills; George F. Lawton

from Hopkins County
Capt J. E. Hopkins; Eldridge Hopkins

lost property
notice by Alfred L. Hulm of Bowie County of lost land certificate

notice that Charles Sims is going to apply for a new land certificate on behalf of Absalom Gibson as administrator of Estate of John Van Vaught in Nacadoches

notice of lost land certificate by Bartholomew W. Millhollon in Lamar County

administration of estates
Benjamin Gooch is appointed administrator of the Estate of H. F. Eskridge of Titus County

notice from Joseph M. Mabane and Robert W. Mabane regarding Estate of Alexander Mabane

Booker T. Mullins is appointed administrator of Estate of Bennet Caudle of Titus County

notice by William McCuiston regarding Estate of John C. McCuiston in Lamar County

Nancy P. Cherry is appointed administrator of the Estate of Jno.V. Cherry of Titus County

commercial announcement
Isaiah Wells is looking for cotton to buy
****

From The Northern Standard of December 18, 1847

river news
additional representatives from Lamar to the Raft Convention are: George W. Wright; James Morphis and Dr. John Davis

obituary
funeral oration for Mary Jane Martin, consort of Col. B. H. Martin, will be preached at the Presbyterian Church in Clarksville by the Rev. J. W. P. McKenzie

public notice
notice to those in Fannin and Lamar Counties who are indebted to J. J. Williams to settle up with N. B. V. Manion, Esq.

land for sale
notice of lot for sale in new town of Taos, Texas by R.H. Porter
****

From The Northern Standard of December 25, 1847

agricultural news
Red Irish potatoes--- Editor was presented by the sons of A.W. King, Esq. of Red River County with several potatoes of this type

Christmas gift -- We acknowledge the receipt of a superb quarter of mutton from Thos. L. Cowan, Esq.

school news
Clarksville Female Institute. . . The reputation of Mrs. Todd as an instructress of the higher branches of Female Education, including the graces of deportment, as well as of mind, is too well established to need commendation.

obituary
died at her residence in Red River County, Malinda K. Henderson, consort of L. D. Henderson. She was 39 and had six children. She was the daughter of Col. David Hardin, originally of Kentucky and late of Mississippi

1848

From The Northern Standard for January 8, 1848

postal news
new Post Office-- A new post office has been established at the house of M. W. Matthews, Esq., in Hopkins County. M. W. Matthews, the Post Master, is our Agent

letters left at Clarksville post office

Aikin, William B	Brown, H. K.
Abel, Green B.	Brown, Stephen or Matthew
Austin, A.S.	Brown, Alexander
Armstrong, Matthew	Barnett, Alfred
Allen, David	Bernard, Calvin
Balley, James	Bourland, W. H.
Becknell, John	Bourland, James
Bryarly, R. J.	Byrd, Abel
Bryarly, Thomas F.	Byers, Wesley
Bradford, H.H.	Bruton, Benj. or Elijah

Boyd, Robert
Bell, Howard T.
Blakley, John
Barker, William
Baker, Thomas C.
Bridge, James
Blanton, Wesley
Ballard, B.
Barnes, James W.
Barnes, William M.. M.D.
Benton, William
Couchman, John D.
Cherry, Miss Margaret
Cooper, Calvin
Clampett, Elijiah
Culley, Dr. S.C.
Cook, Elijiah
Cock, B.F.
Clevenger, Elias
Cozart, Miss Danell
Casden, E. J.
Clark, Frank H.
Cornelius, Henry
Cunningham, Jas. R
Davidson, Josiah
Dean, Levi
Donnell, Rev. S. F.
Dobbins, Samuel C.
Dumas, Lawrence W.
Dewran, Jesse
Evans, D.L.
Evans, William
Fulbright, Daniel N.
Fulbright, Martha
Forte, James
Fryer, George W.
Fisher, Joseph
Freeman, Polly
Fuller, James S.
Hudson, Sarah J.
Hudson, William R.
Hudson, John Hill
Hains, William S.
Harris, William

Hearling, Mrs. Mary
Hobbs, J. C.
Harrison, James W.
Harland, N. R.
Halkins, William W.
Harrison, John
Hill, Ephraim
Hill, Marinda
Hillis, John M.
Grant, William
Gordon, Joseph
Gordon, G. Pope
Green, Roland
Gray, Eli
Gosset, John
Graham, B.F.
Jackson, Sarah M.
Jackson, Calvin
Johnson, William H.
Johnson, J. F.
James, Col L. M
Jarman, Robert F.
King, William W.
King, James N.
King, Amelia
King, Anderson
King, Permella
Lock, James
Loving, J.D.
Laboou, Peter
Laws, George S.
Latimer, J.
Morrow, Bethel C.
Mollett, Hohn L.
Mitchell, Alexander or
Mr. Grinning
McCarty, Joseph
Matthews, John
Nethery, Robert
Neugent, Jacob L.
Odle, Joseph
Park, William A.
Poindexter, Esquire
Poindexter, Bartley

232

Paris, Thomas H.
Parks, William
Pope, James
Provine, James
Pirkey, Solomon H.
Pickens, B.F.
Powell, Nathaniel
Pruet, Christopher
Peters, Lemeul
Perry, C.B.
Ritchie, James
Rogers, Andrew
Rogers, John K.
Rogers, John W.
Russell, James W.
Rutledge, J. S.
Rosson, William H.
Redding, Dr. A..J.
Reins, Dr. John W.
Smith, Harriet E. M.
Smith, Samuel
Smith, Solomon
Sims, Bradford
Seight, John
Stout, W.B.
Speaks, John D.
Shook, Rev Daniel
Sheppard, Marion

Smiley, Samuel
Starnes, Aaron or
Thomas Simmons
Snell, James F.
Snell, Stephen
Thom, John
Tucker, Jefferson
Vowel, William
Van Dyke, L. D.
Verlon, G. W.
Waggoner, Daniel
Winlock, William H.
Windel, Johnson P.
Warrewn, James F.
Wells, Isiah W.
White, Mrs. V.P.
West, Edward, Sheriff
Whittington, William T.
Westerman, Wilson or
Philip J. Smith
Wilkins, Mrs. Mary
Wooten, William
Welch, Daniel
Walker, James T.

A. M. Crooks PM

lost property
notice by Wilson McSrorey of a lost land certificate

notice by John Gregg of lost land certificate for land awarded James Berkham in Hopkins County

strays
notice by Jefferson Cook of stray found by Thomas Pope, which has been appraised at $20 by Grayner S. Lacy and John W. Burns at hearing before William Burk in Titus County

election news
notice by John Stiles, Chief Justice of Red River County appointing the following as Election Officers for election of County Commissioners

Precinct no.1 Solomon Bryant
Precinct no.2 Isaac Morgan
Precinct no.3 John A. Bagby
Precinct no.4 Marcus W. Caudle
Precinct no.5 Lovell Coffman
Beat no.6.   Benj Crownover

school news
notice by Mrs. Elizabeth A. Todd and Mrs Anne Ellet of opening of new term of Clarksville Female Institute

professional card
Dr. K. Ellet, M.D. will have his office and practice the healing arts at the late residence of H. Graham in Clarksville

farm for rent
advertisement by J. W. West, to rent his farm five miles east of Clarksville
****

From The Northern Standard, for January 15, 1848

court news
Hon. John T. Mills will be returning to his native South Carolina for a short visit

professional cards
notice by B. H. Martin, S. H. Epperson and O. Lewis have joined into the firm of Martin, Epperson and Lewis and will practice in 8th Judicial District and Cook County

Drs. Martin and Gilliam have opened an office for the practice of medicine in Paris, Lamar County

military news
A line of forts established from the Red River to the Rio Grande:
The first company is stationed on the Elm Fork of the Trinity River and ranges to Red River. It is commanded by Capt Fitzhugh
The second is stationed at the Waco Village, 40 miles above the falls of the Brazos, and is commanded by Capt M. T. Johnson
The third is at the mouth of the Llano, sixty miles above Austin

on the Colorado, and is commanded by Capt H.R. McCullough
There are also stations on the Medina 24 miles north west of
San Antonio, commanded by Capt. William G. Crump; at
Fredericksburg is Capt S. Highsmith; on the Saco, 60 miles
north of San Antonio, is the unit commanded by Jas. P. Gillet
and on the Rio Grande at Laredo by M. B. Lamar and Capt. S. P.
Ross.

lawsuit filed
notice by Edward West, Sheriff and W. H. Vining, Clerk of the
District Court of Red River, of a summons issued to Isaac N.
Brewer on the petition of Jepha Vining who cites Brewer and
John Bull for trespass
****

From The Northern Standard, for January 29, 1848

newspaper business
Charles De Morse appoints Edward West and J. C. Hart as his
agents while he is out of town
****

From The Northern Standard, for February 5, 1848

political news
letter from W.B. Stout to De Morse regarding matters at Austin

strays
notice by Jefferson Cook of stray found by J. N. Ewinder has
been appraised at $17.50 by S. W. Musgrove and W. Gray at
hearing before W. J. Hamilton, Justice of the Peace in Titus
County

notice by Jefferson Cook of stray found Henry Duryby has been
appraised at $ 25 by Joseph M. Cartwright and Joel M. Sansand
at hearing before William Burk, Justice of the Peace in Titus
County

notice by J. C. McGonigal that stray has been appraised by J.
McFarland and C.M. Akin at hearing before J. C. Moore, Justice
of the Peace in Bowie County.
****

From The Northern Standard, February 12, 1848

Indian news
report of Indian fight . . . A party of Comanches stole horses from Capt. Gillett on the Saco. Lieutenant Cozzens with twelve men went in pursuit of them, overtook them, and engaged in hand to hand combat, killing seven. Two of the rangers were killed and Lieutenant Cozzens was dangerously wounded with an arrow in the side. One of the most exciting Indian fight since Col. John Hays

political news
proceedings of Democratic party meeting in Clarksville : meeting was called to order by Thomas J. Cornelius and Thomas A. Bagby was appointed Chair and John K. Oliver as secretary
on motion made by Gen. William C. Young to elect delegates to represent them in the State Democratic Convention to be held in Austin: James Gilliam, William B. Stout; Charles De Morse, James Wooten, and Simpson H. Morgan were selected. Thomas J. Cornelius, Ira Poor, Gen. William C. Young, R. Scurry, John K. Oliver, George Gordon and William S. Todd were appointed to Committee to draft resolutions for meeting

three men were appointed as a committee for each precinct
Precinct No. 1 A. J. Titus, Thomas L. Cowan and A.W. King
Precinct No.2 John Styles, James McGowan, John Cameron
Precinct No.3 W. P. Crittendon, Nelson Deak and A. J. Russell
Precinct No.4 William Scurlock, William A. Park and Gideon Mimms
Precinct No.5 Martin Guest, T. C. Forbes, Lovel Coffman
Precinct No.6 B. Crownover, D. Fullbright and Wm. Humphreys

Central Committee:
on motion made by Gen. William C. Young , William S. Todd, Charles De Morse, John K. Oliver, George Gordon, John Bagby William R. Scurry were selected for Central Committee

sporting news
challenge by J. C. Hart for horse race
****

From The Northern Standard, February 19, 1848

stray
notice by J. C. McGonigal, by his deputy W. S. McFarland, of stray caught by Joseph Loony and appraised at $ 35 by David Garret and Cookman Watson at hearing before William B. Williams, Justice of the Peace in Bowie County
****

From The Northern Standard, February 26, 1848

military news
Col. Hays and some of his men had a brush with Padre Jaranta, at a place called San Juan. Although the guerillas far exceeded the Texans,they did not wait for more than the first charge but fled in great confusion.

administration of estates
Reuben W. Reynolds and Henry Trimble appointed administrators of Estate of Andrew B. Smith in Lamar County

stray
notice by George F. Lawton of stray found by W. M. Pickett living four miles east of Clarksville has been appraised at $40 by J. W. Finn and James Ballard at hearing before S. Bryant, Justice of the Peace of Red River County
****

From The Northern Standard, March 4, 1848

stray
notice by George W. Lawton of stray found by William M. Dillard has been appraised at $ 20by William Lawrence and James Ballard at hearing before S. Bryant ,Justice of the Peace of Red River County

commercial announcement
notice by G. W. Wright that his horse *Tom Benton* for stud
****

From The Northern Standard, March 11, 1848

professional cards
W. H. Johnson and B. W. Gray practicing as Johnson & Gray, Attorneys at Law at Mount Pleasant, Titus County

Dr. R. R. Rogers has moved permanently to Clarksville and has his office for medicine on the east side of the Square

stop payment
stop payment on note given by Martin Guest to one Musey, first name not provided

runaway
notice by A. M. M. Upshaw of the Chickaw agency that he has taken up a runaway slave by the name of Aaron who says he belongs to Mr. John Landrum of Rusk County; a white man was also taken who said his name was George Washington Carr, but later learned his name was Clarke

administration of estates
R. G. Miller and Sarah E Miller have been appointed administrators of the Estate of Z. B. Miller of Lamar County

lawsuit filed
notice by W.B. Guest, Constable of Red River County to William A. Vowell, that Milas Bagwell has commenced an action against him for a sum less than $100 in an action pending before R. J. Sims, Justice of the Peace

commercial announcement
notice by Brackney and Collins that they have opened a cabinet and furniture making shop in Paris, Lamar County

strays
notice by George F. Lawton, Clerk, that a mule taken up by Charles Morgan has been appraised at $40 by Ellis Littlepage and William Welch at a hearing before A.M. Crooks, Justice of the Peace in Red River County

notice by George F. Lawton, Clerk, that a horse taken up by Peter Ringo has been appraised at $20 by John Mcrory and William Leahy at hearing before B. Crownover in Red River County

notice by George F. Lawton, Clerk, that a horse taken up by C.

C. Wellborn has been appraised at $25 by William C. Young and T.O. Renge at hearing before John A. Bagby, Justice of the Peace in Red River County

notice by George F. Lawton, Clerk, that three horses taken up by S.D. Rainey have been appraised at a combined $60 by A. E. Clemmons and R.W. Mathis at hearing before John Stiles, Justice of the Peace in Red River County

****

From The Northern Standard, March 18, 1848

newspaper business
Edward West and J. C. Hart are De Morse's agents when he is out of town

election news
George W. Smythe of Jasper County has been has been elected Commissioner General of the Land Office

public notice
notice of ordinances of Town of Clarksville by John A. Bagby, Mayor

****

From The Northern Standard, March 25, 1848

lawsuit filed
notice to Christopher Brooks by Sheriff Reddin Russel of Lamar County, by his deputy F. Miles, that a suit has been filed against him by Henry G. McDonald regarding land in Lamar County in the office of John T. Harmon, County Surveyor, on land surveyed by James Bourland, Deputy surveyor. Judge is J. Long

lost property
Wilson McCorey reports his land certificate is lost or stolen and he will apply for a new one

****

From The Northern Standard, April 1, 1848

school news
advertisement by Mrs. Weathered and Mrs. Graham on behalf of Clarksville Academy

administration of estates
J.P. Hale has been named administrator of the Estate of Joshua Hudson, Red River County

stray
notice by George F. Lawton, Clerk, that a horse taken up by W. M. Pickett, 4 miles east of Clarksville, has been appraised at $40 by K. W. Finn and James Ballard at hearing before S. Bryant, Justice of the Peace in Red River County

lawsuit filed
notice from W. H. Vining, Clerk of the Red River Court by his deputy John W. Chenoweth, certified by Sheriff Edward West, of summons to W. K. Revere to answer complaint of Willis Dean of Lamar
****

From The Northern Standard, April 8, 1848

letters at Clarksville post office

Aikin, James
Arnold, Mrs. Ann P.
Allen, David
Anthony, Henry
Asberry, Robert Esq.
Bep, John
Baird, John
Britain, Rev. John
Blanton, C.W.
Blanton, David
Ballard, Bartley
Beaty, Mrs. N.
Bledsoe, A.
Bedford, William H.
Bankston, Asa
Binkerstaff, J. S.
Bryant, William
Barnett, E.D.
Byers, Wesley
Baptist, any man
Butts, Mrs. Elizabeth
Barker, Wilson H.
Banus, Dr. M.

Barnard, Calvin
Chepler, James
Crick, Elijah
Corley, Rev. Sam
Clampett, Elisha
Chism, J. C.
Cargill
Clark, Robert A.
Campbell, B. M.
Campbell, John
Camnam, Bundry M.
Clack, Miss Martha
Clemmons
Cooper, Mrs. Lucy A.
Catlin, Jacob J.
Compton, Thomas
Caldwell, S. W.
Cusons, F.C.
Cooper, Samuel
Doods, John C.
Davis, William
Duncan, William B.
Donnell, Samuel F.

Duran, Jesse
Durca, William
Ellis, M.D.
Funderburg, W.B.
Felps, William
France, Alfred
Fleming, Perry H.
Fowler, A. J.
Gray, Susan
Gregg, William
Glass, Eliza R.
Glass, A .J.
Gray, Eli 2
Gwin, William
Garrison, Thomas F. 3
Gill, W. H.
Gelpin, James P.
Graham, John
Green, Turner L.
Harris, Newton
Harrison, William M.
Harden, Samuel
Hooker, Samuel C.
Hobbs, William
Hudson, Jno. H.
Henderson, James
Henderson, Alexander
Henderson, Mary J.
Hornback, George
Hoy, Dr. A.H.
Hightower, Charnell
Harrison, John
Hill, Barnard
Johnson, Mrs. Amanda
Johnson, Peter
Johnson, P. H.
Johnson, Joshua
Jennings, James
Johnson, Enos B.
King, Elijah W.
King, Elijah
King, Armstead
King, Young
Laws, John

Lawson, J.D.
Lahey, William
Langhorn, H.M.
Lewis, William C.
Loring, Mary E.
Loop, Dr.
Lawrence, William
Lock, Richard
Lawrence, Alexander
Link, J. J.
McPherson, Capt. J. H.
Mathis, J. S.
Mathis, R.W.
Mitchell, H.
Mathis, S. B.
Mimms, Gideon
McLain, James A.
Miller, T. H.
McReynolds, James
Mobly, Meyers
McCoy, Ephraim D.
McCarley, G. W.
Morton, William
McMillen, B.L.
May, John
Mc Connell, Jas. G.
McHam, Jerrit
Marshall, William
Morrow, C.B.
Murrin, John
Maulding, James R.
Methias, Mawry
Norral, L.
Newland, John S.
Nevill, Samuel C.
Newson, Letey
Newburn, Thomas J.
Netherly, Robert
Odle, Joel
Osbrooks, Lewis
Price, Henrietta Mary
Price, Elias
Price, Richard E.
Patterson, Isaac H.

Powell, Nathan
Powell, O.C.
Peryman, Austin
Pope, James
Ponder, Mr.
Perry, Col. James
Pariner, Jno. F.
Prince, Curtis
Shannon, T. J.
Smith, Reeves
Smith, Burill
Sims, George K.
Sims, Samuel W.
Shaw, Eli
Smith, Drury J.
Smathers, Isaac
Scurry, Thomas J.
Seague, William
Street, M.B.
Stephen, A.F.
Stephenson, Alexander
Speers, Isaac
Simpson, John

Stout, W.B.
Spencer, Shers
Thomas, T.M.
Thomas, Miss
Thomas, Warfield
Talbott, Miss A. E.
Vowel, William A.
Williams, David
Williams, J. J.
West, Terrel
Wagley, Joseph
Waites, James
Wright, Maj. J.P.
Ward, Matthias
Ward, Dr. William
Whiteman, J
Wheat, brickmason
Wiggons, Mrs. Mary
Winston, William C.
Westerman, William F.

John A. Bagby P.M.

administration of estates
notice by George F. Lawton, Clerk of Court, by order of J. M. Montgomery, Probate Judge, that Charles Jones, administrator of the Estate of Isaac Jones, to heirs Lodida Jones, H. W. Jones, Jun., James Winter and Minerva Winter, Charles Jones, Jun, Isaac Jones, Jun., William Jones and Wesley Jones
****

From The Northern Standard, April 15, 1848

stray
notice by J. Cook, Clerk, of stray found Ruben D. Collins which has been appraised at $25 by Rufus Morton and Thomas Wilson at hearing before William Sure, Justice of the Peace in Titus County

professional card
law partnership of Geo. W. Paschal of Grapevine and S.A.

Paschal of San Antonio

****

From The Northern Standard, April 22, 1848

newspaper business
editor thanks Isaiah H. Wells of Line Hills and J. K Oliver

obituary
in Clarksville, of pneumonia, Elza Durfee, aged 22, consort of Charles Durfee

runaway
reward for runaway slave named Burton, offered by John G. Chambers, in Titus county near Daingerfield

administration of estates
Thomas R. Starns appointed administrator of Estate of Aaron Starns of Titus County

James J. Ward appointed administrator of the Estate of James W. Green of Red River County

****

From The Northern Standard, April 29, 1848

strays
notice by J. C. McGonigal, Clerk of the County Court of Bowie County, by Deputy Clerk S. H. McFarland, that stray found by H.A. Runnels has been appraised at $ 25 by A. L. Hulme and S. H. Byrne at hearing before John Loop, Justice of the Peace in Bowie County

notice by John R. Craddock, Clerk, that stray found by Penanrum Brown has been appraised at $15 by H.R. Latimer and Mat. W. Martin at hearing before Brad C. Fowler, Justice of the Peace in Lamar County

notice by John R. Craddock, Clerk, that stray found by Henry H. Heatherley has been appraised at $ 30 by R.H. Doss and Wm. Woolridge at hearing before W. H. Wynne, Justice of the Peace in Lamar County

election news
candidates for Office of Sheriff of Red River County:
Lewis D. Barry, Col. Hugh F. Young, John H. Duke and Col. Robert S. Hamilton.

John M. Bivins is candidate for Assessor of Red River County
****
The issues of *The Northern Standard* for May 6, 13, 20 and 27, 1848 are not legible
****

From The Northern Standard, June 3, 1848

political news
report of Rep. David Kaufman speech on the slave question in United States House of Representatives

crime news
Convicted --The retrial of the slave Nelson for the murder of Lucky took place at the courthouse on Thursday, a special term being held for the purpose. He was found guilty as before and on Friday morning was sentenced to be hanged on Friday next

Indian fight
extract from a letter written by Samuel C. Whiting, a member of Capt. Veache's Company of Rangers stationed at the Rio Grande

stolen slave
notice by R. H. Porter that his slave Mary was stolen as they camped near the place of G. W. Morgan on the Brazos river

sports news
notice by J. C. Hart, secretary to the Clarksville Subscription Club, for races at the Clarksville course

stray
notice by E. Hopkins, Clerk that a stray has been taken up by John Hopkins which has been appraised at $16 by John Terrel and A. Herrin at hearing before Peter Visor, Jstice of the Peace of Hopkins County Court

commercial announcements
C. C. Alexander advertises dress goods and fancy article at new store in Clarksville

advertisement by Henry Gooding for the his Star Hotel in Clarksville

advertisement by G. W. Wright for his hotel, the Lamar Hotel, in Paris

notice that the Constitution of the State of Texas and the Court rules could be purchased at 25 cents per copy at: C. C. Alexander and Oliver & Chatfield in Clarksville; at the store of A.M. Alexander of Paris; at the store of L. A. Alexander in Bonham; at the store of R. P. Crimp in Jefferson, at the store of M.M. Knight of Greenville, at the store of Dr. B. Grahm in Buffalo and from Elridge Hopkins in Tarrant, B. W. Gray in Mount Pleasant and R. Morton and White Oak

Alfred & Co. , wholesale grocers of Shreveport, list their references as C. C. Alexander and T. J and W. P. Cornelius of Clarksville; A.M. and L.C. Alexander and Ragsdale & Wright in Paris; Joseph Harrison and Pace & Bro. in Bonham; Berthelet; Heald & Co in Doaksville, Choctaw Nation and Chas. P. Stewart of Mayhew, Choctaw Nation.

C. Lewis & Co, wholesale grocers of Shreveport, lists as references Messrs Graham, Bagby & Co of Clarksville, Capt T.G. Wright of Red River and P. Colbert of the Choctaw Nation
****

From The Northern Standard, June 10, 1848

election news
County Clerk -- A. .J. Titus
Sheriff   Lewis D. Berry, Col. Robert Hamilton

crime news
the Negro Nelson, convicted of the murder of Luckey, was hung yesterday at about 1 o'clock PM.

strays
notice by John R. Craddock, Clerk, that stray found by E. F. Anderson has been appraised at $15 by R. Q. Hudson and J. O. Logan at hearing before John A. Dillingham, Justice of the Peace in Lamar County

notice by John R. Craddock, Clerk, that stray found by Stewart Brewer has been appraised at $30 by John L. Dillingham and M.S. Boyd at hearing before John A. Dillingham Justice of the Peace in Lamar County

notice by James Boggs that stray found by P. M .Harrison has been appraised at $40 by N.G. Ballard and G.B. Mason at hearing before A. J. Hunter, Justice of the Peace in Henderson County

notice by James Boggs that stray found by Ephraim Gutherieng has been appraised at $65 by J.P. Moore and J. L. Gossett at hearing before James Stephenson Justice of the Peace in Henderson County

military news
notice by Brig. Gen. James H. Rogers, First Division, Texas Militia as directed by H. E Young regarding drilling dates

obituaries
Dr.Walter Fostgate, native of New York, at Victoria. He had been a surgeon in the Texas Revolution and had attended De Morse on occasion

Littleton W. House in Bowie, born in 1810 in Middle Tennessee

William Knight, died of hydrophobia . He resided on Frances Square in Francesville
****

From The Northern Standard, June 17, 1848

religious news
Notice by A. E. Clemmons that he will preach at the Presbyterian Church on the 3rd Sabbath in June.

married
by the Rev. A. Davis, Burrel P. Smith, Esq. to Sarah Henderson, daughter of L. D. Henderson of this vicinity

obituary
William K. McKenzie son of the Rev J. W. P. McKenzie from a horse falling on him
****

From The Northern Standard, June 24, 1848

Masonic news
notice by V. H. Vining, Secretary of the Brethren of Masonic Fraternity will have celebration in memory of St. John the Baptist

lawsuit filed
notice by James M. Riggs, Clerk of the District Court, by his deputy T. A. Henderson, that James A. Johnson, Sheriff of Navarro County, has been instructed to notify the unknown heirs of Edward Davis to answer a lawsuit in Corsicana brought against them by W.F. Henderson, Robert M. Tyers, John R. Henry and John Karner

strays
Charles De Morse gives notice that some of his cattle have strayed

notice by J. C. McGonigal, Clerk of Bowie County, by his deputy S. H. McFarland, that a stray taken up by James R. Boyce was appraised at $60 by J. M. Kimble and E. S. Tansor at a hearing before D. M. Chisholm, Justice of the Peace of Bowie County

notice by James Boggs, Clerk of Bowie County, that a stray taken up by Walter Farrel was appraised at $25 by F. W. Bridges and Peter High at a hearing before J. L. Austin, Justice of the Peace of Henderson County

obituaries
Thomas Johnson, editor of *The National Vindicator,* on June 16th at his residence in Brenham, Washington County

Capt. George W. Jewell in Paris, Lamar County on June 20th
****

From The Northern Standard for July 1, 1848

Indian news
The portion of the Comanche tribe, under the chief Santa Anna, came into Austin last Wednesday. The old chief professed much friendship. He alleged for the main reason for coming

into the settlements was that the buffalo had left their ranges farther north and had come down in this direction and that it was necessary for them to follow the herd in order for their subsistence.

agricultural news
ten bales of wool were received in this City [Houston], on Thursday last, from Limestone County near Springfield. It was sheared from 1600 head of sheep, owned by Mr. Harris. These sheep were driven by him from Missouri. It is put up neatly in bales weighing 750 lbs each and consigned to C. Ennis in this city, with instructions to ship it to New York.

Prussian Rye -Texas Growth – Judge Ochiltree has furnished us with several green heads of Prussian rye from the plantation of William A. Lawrence at Mound Prairie in Anderson County. It is said that the seeds were introduced into Alabama by the Hon. Dixon H. Lewis, three years ago.

Texas resources
iron ore -- Last week, Mr. W. M. Freeman of Cass County presented us with a specimen of Texas Iron, separated from the ore by Mr. Nash near the southwest corner of Cass County

military news
The following is a list of ranging Companies, their stations and their Captains on the frontier of Texas

Capt. Fitzhugh's Company on the East Fork of the Trinity, with a detachment 30 miles above near Red River;
Capt. Johnson's Company on the west fork of the Trinity, with a detachment on the Leon, 30 miles distant;
Capt. Conner's Company on the Navasoto, between the Brazos and the Trinity;
Capt. Ross's Company at Waco Village, detachment on the Leon 30 miles distant;
Capt. McCulloch's Company, Hamilton valley, 60 miles north of Austin;
Capt. Highsmith's Company on a fork of the Sandy, 18 miles from Fredericksburgh and near the Enchanted Rock;
Capt.Crump's Company on the Medina, 20 miles south of San Antonio;
Capt. Gillet's Company on Arroyo Saco, 60 miles southwest of San Antonio

Capt. Veach's Company on the Rio Grande, above the Presidio Crossing;
Capt. Lamar's Company at Laredo, on the Rio Grande;
Capt. Sutton's Company, near San Patricio, on the Nuces, detachments at Corpus Christi

administration of estates
Benjamin Booth appointed administrator of Estate of Nelson J. Staats of Red River County

election news
John Stiles, Chief Judge of the County of Red River, gives notice that, pursuant to the authority given him by the order of George T Wood, Governor, of the following election officers and precincts

Precinct no.1	John Stiles at Levi G Childers
Precinct no.2	A. J. Titus at Solomon Bryant
Precinct no.3	Clarksville at A.M. Crooks
Precinct no.4	Pine Creek at M. W. Caudle
Precinct no.5	John Robbins at L. Coffman
Precinct no.6	William Humphries at Thomas Patterson

commercial announcements
advertisement by A. J. Russell for the Clarksville Male Academy

advertisement by Frank Clark for music sheets

advertisement by Oliver Ingles who has sides of bacon for sale

advertisement by L. W. Yeager that he makes signs and carriage painting

advertisement by Thomas Stevenson for his watch store and repairs in Clarksville

advertisement for furniture store by James B. Shanahan

advertisement by John P. Dale, a tailor

advertisement by Bagby and Garrison for their tin ware manufactory advertisement by Thomas R.Wilson of his saddlery shop

professional card
Murray & Latimer, Eighth Judicial District
J. Murray and J. W. Latimer

stop payment
notice by Sarah Hamilton stopping payment to note to Charles Warfield

public notice
Burrell P. Smith, Major Fulbright, George Young and Isaiah H. Wells have notary power conferred by John Stiles, Chief Judge of Red River County

strays
notice by J. Cook, Clerk, that a stray taken up by Lindsey Burk was appraised at $55 by J. M. Cartwright and John Humphreys at a hearing before William Burk, Justice of the Peace of Titus County

notice by J. Cook, Clerk, that a stray taken up by Samuel McCrory was appraised at $30 by Rufus Goodwin and Daniel McCall at a hearing before J. W. Dabbs, Justice of the Peace of Titus County

lawsuit filed
notice by Cyrus K. Holman, Sheriff of Lamar County to James M. Morphis that he is to file an answer in the action pending before Brad C. Fowler, Justice of the Peace, in action commenced against him by John R. Craddock

From The Northern Standard for July 8, 1848

legal news
article responding to criticism of Judge John Mills

professional card
J. P. Morgan, M.D. has opened his office in Clarksville

administration of estates
Jonathan Bateman has been appointed administrator of Estate of Isaac Bateman in Red River County

stray
notice by J. Cook, Clerk of stray taken up by Samuel McCrorey and appraised at $30 by Rufus Godwin and Daniel McCall at hearing before J. W. Dabbs, Justice of the Peace of Red River County

****

From The Northern Standard for July 15, 1848

letters left at Clarksville Post Office

Aldridge, Moses
Bell, Willson
Byrd, John A.
Blanton, C. W.
Bicker, Hiram
Burgess, Franklin
Burghen, Youn
Butryan, Richard
Breaken, William
Bates, Elizabeth M.
Bain, John
Blackurn, James
Blackwell, Wiley
Burden, Nathaniel
Breedin, C. C.
Bateman, Evan
Barnard, Culver
Calhoun, Miss Mary
Churchill, John
Chatfield, Richard
Chatfield, Andrew
Clanton, Martha
Cooke, Benjamin
Cadwell, Samuel
Chism, William V.
Clemmons, Rev F.A.
Collins, William
Cornelius, Matthew
Clapp, William
Campbell, Mrs. Ann G.
Campbell, Francis A.
Corley, Rev. Samuel

Danton, John
Duty, Henry
Donley, S.P.
Dean, Jesse
Dean, Levi
Daniel, Alice
Darnell, Foster S.
Dale, Thomas
Duranagho, Robert B.
Ennis, N.F.
Ellis, N.D.
Epperson, B. H.
English, Campbell
Edmonson, Samuel
Funderburg, William B.
Fleming, B. M. C.
Gregg, Thomas
Green, Rolin
Glass, J. A.
Grant, Mr.
Gilbreath, James G.
Holbrook & Roman
Hogan, Woodson
Husbands & Buchanan
Houston, Robert
Harland, N. R.
Johnson, Mrs. Amanda
Johnson, Peter B.
Jenkins, Charles
Jones, Dennis
Ingram, Messrs M. and W.
Kelley, Mrs. Suzzanne
King, Miss Eliza Ann

Lawson, I.D.
Lacey, Jacob J
Levins, Nicholas
Lahey, William
Lee, William
McCarley, Robert
McFarland, James
Miller, W.G.
McNeil, Jesse
Maren, John or Posey Tensey
MaCleash, J.
Martin, William
Mathis, W.R.
McLaurin, James
McCartney, B. H.
McCarty, M.S.
McKuller, William
Main, John
Norville, S.G.
Morris, James
Philips, James
Philis, William
Pope, James
Patrick, Loughley Jane
Parks, Elizabeth
Putnam, B. R.
Parkinson, Benjamin
Pearson, James
Price, Elizabeth
Post Master
Rohn, Jane
Remmington, Mr.
Robson, John
Reeves, J. H.
Redding, A. J.
Redding, W. P.
Russell, N.M.
Russe, John
Ripley, Ambrose
Rice, Elias

Rice, A. J.
Rice, William L.
Rogers, John K.
Sherry, Barnard
Sampson, Rev. James
Stewart, Joseph S.
Sawns, Israel
Sparks, A.
Sims, Samuel
Smith, M.
Smith, Thomas
Smith, James
Singleton, A. J.
Skerry, Richard
Stephens, Mrs. A. F.
Smith, Russell P.
Sutton, Thomas
Stearns, Aaron
Seals, William
Smith, John S.
Travelstead, Lt. E.C.
Travelstead, Anthony
Turggle, John H.
Talton, John F.
Tate, James M.
Tucker, Jefferson
Thomas, F.M.
Terry, John
Wilkinson, Mrs. Mary
Withington, William T.
Whitson, Mrs. Esther
Ward, James
Ward, William
West, Edward
Walker, J. W.
Wims, W.
Wellborn, Charles C.

John A Babgy P.M.

****

From The Northern Standard for July 22, 1848

newspaper business
William F. Henderson Esq. *The Standard's* Agent in Corsican, Navarro County

agricultural news
potatoes... We are indebted to John Moore for some specimens of Irish potatoes, the largest that we have ever seen in this district

election news
notice from W.B. Stout's withdrawal as a candidate

notice of Democratic Mass meeting (still calling themselves the Democratic Republicans) to ratify nominations to the Baltimore Convention for President and announcing a free barbeque as well. Notice given by:

William C. Young	James Gilliam
George C. Bagby	Isaiah King
Geo. Gordon	Shelby Crawford
A. J. Titus	E.M. Smith
James Latimer	Edward West
W.R. Scurry	A. J. Latimer
J. W. P. McKenzie	John Ware
Granville Lewis	John A. Bagby
A.R. Dickson	B.P. Smith
R. Scurry	P. Duty
R. M. Hopkins	William Crittenden
J. C. Hart	Jesse Adams
Chas. De Morse	Nelson Doak
A. J. Russell	

commercial announcement
advertisement by Frank C. Clark the sale of books and newspapers in Clarksville

strays
notice by J. C. McGonigal, Clerk, of stray taken up by Presely Maulding and appraised at $30 by James P. Alford and William Nunn, at hearing before John Loop Justice of the Peace of Bowie County
****

From The Northern Standard for July 29, 1848

newspaper business
thank you to Gilbert Ragin for providing copy of New Orleans *Commercial Times*

election news
notice by the Democratic Electors for the State of Texas, James B. Miller and T.G. Broocks for the Eastern District and William C. Young and M. A. Dooley for the Western District, shall vote for Lewis Cass of Michigan and William O. Butler for President and Vice President of the United States

list of officers elected by Democratic Mass Meeting in Clarksville
President: R. Scurry
Vice Presidents: William Bourland of Lamar County, Martin Glover, Esq. of Bowie County, James F. Hopkins Esq. of Hopkins County, Hon. James Gilliam of Red River County, James J. Ward of Red River County, Maj. James W. Sims of Red River County
Secretaries: B.P. Smith, Esq., John M. Bivins, Esq.

Charles De Morse gave a speech in support of General Cass.

commercial announcement
advertisement by Thomas Stevenson of jewelry store

advertisement by S. H. Clark for house, sign and carriage painting

advertisement by John P. Dale, tailor, located on the southwestern corner of the Public Square

school news
Notice by Eliza A. Todd of reopening of term of Clarksville Female Institute

Notice of reopening of Clarksville Male Academy by A. J. Russell
****

From The Northern Standard for August 5, 1848

obituary
former resident of Clarksville, Miss Sarah E. Darnell, aged 28 years, died in Holly Spring Mississippi on July 4

election news
notices of candidacy for August elections–

County Clerk: Ballard C. Bagby
Chief Justice: Hugh F. Young
Assessor: John M. Bivins
Sheriff: Lewis D. Barry and Col. Robert S. Hamilton

Raise the tall poles. . . Our fellow citizen, J. C. Hart, raised on yesterday morning, by his grocery at the corner of the Public Square, a tall spire of the forest, at which about 70 feet from the ground, dances a white banner upon which the words are displayed "Liberty & Democracy --Cass & Butler"

Mass Meeting to be held in Paris of Lamar Democrats. Ladies especially invited; barbecue and speech by Elector William C. Young by Committee of:

	R.W. Reynolds
Thomas C. Yates	Richard G. Miller
Matthias Click	James C. Record
John A. Rutherford	E. W. Upshaw
William M. Williams	John Onstot
Isaac J. Powell	W. H. Millwee
Joseph Baker	Isaiah Davis
John Strenzil	Robert B. Francis
Jason Wilson	John F. Griffin
W. H. Bourland	George Wilson
Randolf Scott	Parker S. Doss
Jacob Lyday	William Skidmore
Abram Skidmore	James Bourland
H. R. Latimer	J. W. Latimer
Henry B. Heatherly	
John T. Harmon	

married
by the Rev. Samuel Corley, J. B. Dinwiddie to Miss Sarah Jane Gilliam, daughter of James Gilliam, Esq
****

From The Northern Standard for August 12, 1848

newspaper business
Wm. F. Henderson, Esq. is *The Standard's* agent in Corsicana, Navarro County

election news
it has been a very close election for the County. The following are known to be elected:

Chief Justice: Hugh F. Young
County Clerk: George F. Lawton
Sheriff: Robert S. Hamilton
Assessor: John M. Bivins

Joseph Srygley and August King were probably elected County Commissioners

gathering of Democrats in Huntsville – addresses were given by Gen. Davis of Liberty; the Hon. H. J. Jewett of Leon; F. S. Stockdale of Grimes County and Messrs W.A. Leigh and A.P. Wiley of Huntsville

agricultural news
large peaches. John Wooten presented us three large peaches raised upon his plantation, weighing nearly a pound each

commercial announcement
Thomas Stevenson advertises watches and jewelry at his store on Public Square

Frank H. Clark advertises he has 50 copies of "Pictorial John Donkey " from 4th of July
****

From The Northern Standard for August 19, 1848

results of Red River election
Chief Justice: Young –(333 votes)

Sheriff: Hamilton (283), Barsa (259)

County Clerk: Lawton (289), Bagby - (251)

256

Assessor: John M. Bivins (300), West (292)

County Commissioners : Stiles (290), Srygley (264), Humphries (256), I. King (210), A. King (197), J. Walker (177), Crittenton (174) and Fulbright (119)

END NOTES

1. A bit about De Morse might aid the visualization of the scenes De Morse depicts. A 1941 volume entitled *Charles De Morse, Pioneer Editor and Statesman*, by Ernest Wallace, is a complete biography of this journalist. It is based, in part, on information from De Morse's granddaughter, Isabella De Morse Latimer, as well as from an article De Morse himself wrote in the *Standard* in 1872 about the early days. Helpful also is Lorna Sheppard's *An Editor's View of Early Texas*, published by Eakin Press

Born in Leicester, Massachusetts, on January 31, 1816, he was christened Charles Denny Morse, the middle name being his mother's maiden name. His forebears on both sides had been English settlers who, in the 1600s, had sought religious freedom in New England.

De Morse's early years were in Leicester, a community in transition from an agriculture economy to cotton manufacturing. Charles' father was an innkeeper there. Morse's mother was to die at the age of 29. Widower Morse, his sister, also widowed, and young Charles moved to New Haven, Connecticut, where again the elder Morse operated an inn. Some years later, they moved a third time, to New York City. Here, Morse ran the well-known colonial era Tontine Coffee House at the foot of Wall Street, then, as now, the heart of the nation's financial market.

It was in New York that Charles began to "clerk" for the New York law firm of Inglis and Van Wyck. Van Wyck, Morse's mentor at the firm, had a brother-in-law, also a lawyer, named Samuel Maverick who had just gone to Texas and fight in the Revolution against Mexico. Young Morse had a desire for something different. Inspired by Maverick's letters home, Morse joined a brigade of volunteers ready to sail for Texas and glory.

En route, their vessel, the Brig *Watawomkeag* was taken by a British warship who thought the Americans were pirates. After a month in jail, they were tried in Nassau and acquitted. During Morse's detention there, however, a British officer made a clerical error that "re-christened" him Charles De Morse rather than Charles D. Morse. Viewing the error as a mystical *merger* of his long-dead mother's maiden name, "Denny", with the paternal "Morse", he immediately began using this new name exclusively and later had it changed legally to "De Morse".

Reaching New Orleans and after some more adventures, De Morse and the other new recruits traveled by land from New Orleans to the war front. En route, they met the captain of the schooner *Independence*, one of several vessels which comprised the new Republic's Navy, who signed De Morse up as a first lieutenant of marines. De Morse almost got to fight in the famous battle of San Jacinto. Hurrying to the front, he was close enough to hear the booming of the cannons before the battle ended in victory for the Texans. Later, De Morse was to exchange his commission in the Navy to become a major in the Texas Army, a title he would called for the next two decades.

De Morse was six feet tall and lanky, which made him look even taller. He had a large forehead, extended by beginning baldness, which gave the impression that he had a brain larger than others. A short brown square-cut moustache was his only facial hair, and he was meticulous in his dress and habits: linen suits, with black string ties, in summer; dark and conservative suits in the winter. He was well-mannered, did not smoke and apparently drank rarely. He was not a churchgoer, but was certainly a believer in the Deity.

2. Its earliest settlers, of course, were Indians, as long as 2,500 years ago. The Caddos lived there when the Spanish and French probed the area, but departed at the end of 1700s because of an epidemic and the belligerence of the neighboring Osages tribe. By the 1820s, Indian newcomers from the East -- Shawness, Delaware and Kickapoo, pushed by an expanding white population -- settled along creeks that still bear their name. They remained there barely a decade before the wave of settlers pushed them west and north into the Indian Territory across the Red River.

3. American hunters and Indian traders had come to Red River county as early as 1815, claiming that it was part of the Louisiana Purchase of 1803. In 1818, the Jonesborough and Burham's Settlements were made. It took Claigborne Wright, six months on a keel boat he made himself, the *Pioneer*, to come all the way from Tennessee, with his family and his two married slaves, Jin and Hardy Wright. They put down stakes along the Red River, near Pecan Point, in 1816, joining George and Alex Wetmore and William Mabbit who had settled there earlier that year. By mid 1820s, the settlers had begun to move from the river locations to the prairies. In 1833, James Clark and his wife Isabella Hanks Clark founded Clarksville.

4. *The Standard* was full of news, advertisements, notices, announcements etc. from many more towns than just Clarksville. De Morse kept up the practice of law during the time he published *The Standard.* Then, judges and lawyers, usually twice a year, would ride the "circuit", going from county to county, spending a week or more in each county seat, trying cases. De Morse welcomed the chance to visit the Red River Valley, the Upper Trinity and the Upper Cross Timber regions of North Texas, as far south as Dallas and Fort Worth, the edge of the frontier in Texas in those days. He sold subscription there and gathered stories and advertisements, which reveal to us the identities of thousands of other citizens of Northeastern Texas from 1842 through 1848.

5. Within three years, by 1851, it had all doubled. The population of the county had increased to 5,374 and the State to 200,000.

6. The United States of the 1850's was what one would describe as a Christian country. The 1850 Census showed there to be 36,011 churches in America and 210 more in the District of Columbia and the Territories. Church property exceeded $86 million dollars in value and there was one church for every 557 free inhabitants, one for every 646 with the slave population included. In 1854 in Texas, , there were some 9,000 Baptists of all types, 6,000 Presbyterians, 2,000 Episcopalians, 20,000 Methodists and an unknown number of Lutherans. Except among the Mexican population, Roman Catholics were rare in Texas. However, their numbers elsewhere in the Nation were growing with immigration.

7. In 1815, the Rev. William Stevenson, a frontier minister who rode the religious circuit for the Missouri Conference of the Methodist Church, made a pastoral visit to the home of Claiborne Wright of Pecan Point, a member of the newly arrived Anglo Americans who that had drifted below the Red River into Texas. Records indicate that Stevenson's preachings to Wright and friends in 1815 constituted the first Protestant sermons given in Texas. The sermons were to earn him a marker in the Clarksville Public Square.

8. And brother of General James Rogers Clark, the American leader who captured the Ohio region from the British.

9. The Rev. John Witherspoon Pettigrew McKenzie, a graduate of the University of Georgia, came as a Methodist missionary to the Choctaws at Fort Towson in the Indian Territory, just north of the Red River. During his first year among the Indians, Dr. McKenzie crossed the Red River to establish Methodist Societies in Jonesboro, Clarksville and DeKalb. Tradition has it that McKenzie and a Rev. John Lemeul Lovejoy organized the first Methodist Episcopal Church, South, in Clarksville in 1838. It was located just south of the Square on what today is known as east Church Street.

10. Called the Shiloh Cumberland Presbyterian Church, it had at first been located at the Shiloh Community, about six miles east of Clarksville. Later, it moved to Clarksville and merged with other congregations to become the First Presbyterian Church of Clarksville.

11 Many in North Texas considered alcohol an evil, needing to be suppressed. Actually, it was a national movement. The United States Supreme Court upheld government's right to ban liquor in order to prevent "idleness and debauchery". Chapters of The Sons of Temperance formed in every county, including Red River, and their members preached, prayed and lobbied for a ban on alcohol. The efforts were not wasted. In 1854, the Texas Senate terminated all licenses to sell alcohol, and permitting each county, upon the vote of its citizenry, the choice whether to allow the sale of alcohol or not, and if so, the terms. Most voted for a version of what came to be known as the "Quart law", prohibiting the sale of ardent liquors in bottles less than a quart size, except for medicinal, mechanical or sacramental purposes".

12. Indeed, timbering could be a livelihood of its own. Surplus trees could be cut down, saw milled and sold to the settlers to the west on the treeless prairie.

13. Fortunately, Clarksville and Red River County were blessed with all the ingredients for an endless supply of brick including the all important clay.

14. Clarksville still has its public square i.e., where four blocks--Broadway, Pecan, Main and Locust--face inward to form a square, inside which there once was a Court House. Malls --public squares outside of town -- and giant discount

stores with huge parking lots have drained the traditional downtown public squares of their business and bustle, Clarksville being no exception.

15. The first school in town was Clarksville Academy, founded in 1842 by the Rev. James Sampson. It was co-educational, although the sexes were educated in separate rooms. Other schools followed, among them, the Clarksville Male Academy, or, as it was later renamed, the Clarksville Classical Mathematical and Mercantile Academy.

16. Two schools concentrated on young women, instructing them "in the higher branches of Female Education including the graces of deportment, as well as of mind". One was the Clarksville Female Academy. It had been begun as the Pine Creek Academy by Robert and Martha W. (Maum) Weatherred in 1840 at Pine Creek, 15 miles north of Clarksville. The other had moved to town from Lamar County, changing its name from the Ringwood Female Seminary to the Clarksville Female Institute. The school had been begun in 1844 by Eliza A. Todd for the daughters of wealthy planters and had an elementary, high school and the beginning of a college curriculum, with a special emphasis on French.

17. Being a religious school, discipline was rigid. Four students were assigned to a room, and they had to take turns at night to study before the single oil lamp in the room. The courses were rigorous, including the languages needed to read the New and Old Testaments in their own tongues, Hebrew, Latin and Greek. There was mandatory chapel before dawn and after dusk. The students took oaths not to gamble, use tobacco or alcoholic beverages, or miss class or chapel. There was little chance that any McKensie College student would appear at the post examination balls, given by the girls schools in Town. Among their promises were not to leave school without permission and not to dance.

18. The Mississippi River, gateway to points eastward, was five days away by stage via "Mr. Hanger's line of Mail Stages, from Clarksville to Little Rock, connecting Northern Texas with the world east of the Mississippi." The coaches were said to be "comfortable and regular in their passage" and were especially recommended to "immigrants with families, desiring to come to northern Texas, [who] will find this the

most comfortable and expeditious route, coming up the Arkansas and White rivers and thence by stage here." Another stage route was from Clarksville to Jefferson (the most important port of the time in Texas) where one could connect to passage to Shreveport. The stage stopped at Mt. Pleasant and Daingerfield en route.

19. Northern Texas was huge and its population few. Only the mail -- and newspapers which were delivered by mail - could connect them all together. Postal service was a top priority, as evidenced by the following announcement in *The Standard* of January 28, 1843, several years before Texas joined the U.S.:

"We are happy to inform our readers that the mail routes have all been taken and that there is now every expectation of having an uninterrupted communication with the different sections of the Republic. The rates of postage have been raised about one-fourth higher, and with the $12,000 appropriated by the last Congress, together with the revenue derived from the postage, it will be sufficient to keep this important branch of the Government in an efficient state."

The schedule was not complicated, once one learned the destinations along the route:

"Mail from Fulton, Ark, via Boston and Dekalb, arrives Friday evening, leaves Tuesday morning; mail from Fort Towson, Choctaw Nation [Oklahoma] arrives Monday morning, leaves Sunday morning; mail from Houston, via Nacogdoches and San Augustine, arrives Friday evening, leaves Tuesday morning; mail from Warren, Prairie country, via Fort English, Paris and Ward's Post Office, arrives Sunday evening, leaves Monday morning; mail from Warren, river posts, via Lexington, Raleigh, Franklin, Jonesboro and Pine creek, arrives Monday evening, leaves Tuesday evening."

There was no mail delivery at the time. The postal patron came to the letters, not *vice versa*. The *Standard* regularly printed a "List of Letters" to let the addressee know they had mail.

20. It marked the end of one world order and began a

new one, one still encircling the world, spreading the message of Liberty. Sadly, the enthusiastic celebration of the holiday is in decline some places these days. This would have disappointed John Adams, second President of the United States. He had been involved in the Continental Congress in 1776 advancing the resolution of the Colonies to be independent from Great Britain. From the beginning, Adams had exhorted Americans to celebrate it as their "Day of Deliverance, by solemn Acts of Devotion to God Almighty. It ought to be solemnized with Pomp and Parade, with Shows, Games, Sports, Guns, Bells, Bonfires and Illuminations from one End of the Continent to the other from this Time forward forever more."

21. The following order of march was observed:
1. Clarksville Band; 2. National Colors; 3. Speaker of the Day and Reader of the Declaration of Independence; 4. Ladies in sections of two; 5. Sabbath schools in sections of two; 6. Public schools in sections of two; 7. Soldiers of the War of 1812; 8. Soldiers of the Texas Revolution; 9. Soldiers of the War with Mexico; 10. Mayor and Common Council; 11. Citizens on foot

22. Mens' clubs --fraternal organizations, often with female "sisterhoods" as their auxiliaries, sponsored a number of community events. They included the anti alcohol Sons of Temperance; the Knights Templars, another fraternal order of Freemasons, claiming descent from the Knights Templar founded in the 1100's to protect the Holy Land; the Independent Order of Odd Fellows, an international movement, started in and still active in America; and the Masons, another order that could trace its beginnings to the other side of the Atlantic. All could turn out in considerable force.

23 It was not, however, officially celebrated on the last Thursday in November until 1863. Before then, customarily, the Governor would declare a day to be one of general Thanksgiving for the blessings the people had received and urge the citizens and clergy to observe it as such.

24. How many in Dallas--once called the City of the Three Forks of the Trinity--know the location of those river beds today? Dams, lakes, flood control, irrigation and development, all have done their part to the withering of Texas rivers: the Brazos, Colorado, Sabine, Trinity, Guadalupe, San Antonio, Nueces, Rio Grande and, of particular importance to the people

of Clarksville and the Red River Valley, the Red River, with its Sulphur Creek.

25. You will not find Roland on the map today, or even in the memory of the oldest citizen. But, it was there, at Roland, where the Red River planters and Clarksville merchants received the seed, equipment, manufactured goods and other necessities and luxuries they had been ordered the autumn before.

26. Although the best way to market, river transportation was still a very difficult, often unreliable, route. The river was not deep and it was obstructed in places, with accumulated fallen trees and growths of vegetation, called *rafts*. Usually, the river began to rise in January or February, peak in mid-spring and then decline until, by early summer, boats became rare. Sometimes, late fall would bring some more rains and the river would again be briefly "boatable." For example, in the spring of 1846, the river was reported as "running red" which, we are told, "indicated a good stage for boats". Presumably, the river was gaining the color, for which it was named, from the red clay in the banks, not usually washed into the water, unless it was swollen.

27. Without sufficient cotton, the mills in England and New England would close, their citizens would be idle and hungry, and they would have no goods to sell to the people of the American and English countryside, which, after all, was the basis of their economies

28. What really made wheat attractive, however, was a bit of farm equipment that would revolutionize agriculture, the reaper invented by Cyrus McCormick. With it, a single man, with three horses, could cut 15 acres a day. Before that, a farmer could not get enough help to harvest wheat, either because the needed men were working at their own farms or because using slaves would interfere with the cultivation of the more important staple, cotton. A second invention that made wheat farming attractive was the thresher. Raising and cutting more acres of wheat resulted in more bushels that had to be threshed before milling. Technology allowed the small farmer to utilize a "wagon like vehicle of unusual appearance", called Emery's Wheat Thresher, which, according to an advertisement in the *Standard*, was "highly commended for portableness and

of their comparative performance, being worked by two horses and threshing 250 bushels a day."

29. Some of the vegetables raised were positively world record-breaking, confirming once again that everything in Texas is bigger and better: a muskmelon, weighing 25 pounds and measuring 35 ½ inches around one way and 37 the other; a sweet potato, measuring 18 inches in length, and 21 inches in circumference and weighing 13 pounds; turnip sprouts, one 26 inches around, weighing five pounds; the other 24 inches around, weighing 8 ½ pounds; a mammoth gourd, measuring in circumference five foot nine inches and holding more than five buckets of water; radishes, 18 inches around, and weighing 4 3/4pounds; another one weighs 2 1/2 pounds; an ear of corn 11 ½ inches long, with 976 grains and weighing one pound nine ounces; cotton bolls 6 inches and 3/8th around; a beet, measuring 22 inches around and weighting 11 pounds; 5 pound peaches; and an eggplant which measured around the middle 22 ½ inches.

30. *The Standard* of October 29, 1842 reported that "as for the corn crop, there is more than the population can consume and, if our neighbors are in want, we can supply them with all they require, and cheap at that."

31. Sugar could be made from the dried stalks. Maturing in fewer than a 100 days, from time of sowing of seed, it could be used either for sugar or feeding livestock. It was said to yield 4,500 gallons of "vinegar" or "syrup" to the acre, a rich molasses which, De Morse pronounced, as having the taste of the sugar houses molasses.

32. Not only were the hogs used for food -- pork (salted, boiled or as bacon) was a three times a day staple in those days -- but they were also boiled down to make oil. While inferior to the best sperm whale oil, ironically enough, it was, according to De Morse, far superior to any other oil in Texas. An oil factory slaughtered between 60 and 100 hogs a day and the lard manufactured into oil and candies.

33. Northern Texas got off easily, compared to the normally warmer South At Galveston, for example, the ground froze and pools of water were covered with ice half an inch thick. One man perished of cold on the prairie below the town

and another nearly lost his life. The shoreline of Galveston Bay was literally strewn with frozen fish, forced upon the beach in the surf by the violence of the wind.

34. De Morse tells of one storm in *The Standard* of December 9, 1848:

> "*Oaks of at least a half a century standing about our house, which had no appearance of having suffered before from any cause, were dropping their heavy branches with a sullen crash, laying fences low before them. A stately pecan which was the front yard ornament of a neighbor and perhaps the largest tree about Town, is a perfect "sight", the least imaginable resemblance to its proportions on Tuesday at mid-day. As for the ornamental growth in the yards which had not yet attained much size- the Arbor Vitae, the magnolia, the Weeping Willow, their heads are bowed to the ground and rest upon it the weight which the stems are insufficient to hold erect. Bushes and vines are trailing low in their frozen suits.*"

35. THE DROUGHT.--*It is now 8 or 9 weeks since this region of the country has been visited by anything like a good, seasonable rain. Springs and creeks are dried up and the few cisterns almost exhausted. Man and beast are in a state of suffering. Most of the citizens of Clarksville are dependent upon hauling water two or three miles, from holes in the creek, which will, we are told, soon be exhausted. Crops are seriously injured; planters say they will not make more than half their crop of cotton.*" *The Standard*, September. 4, 1844

36 "*We have never before in our lives witnessed such continuous rains, as has poured down on this region for the past 6 or 8 months, and it still comes almost daily and the mud and the water stand in our streets, as though it were mid winter. It is, indeed, most disagreeable, and, for months, it has been a matter of wonder that the country around us has not been sickly. The crops, of course, are suffering. Cotton, unless we have some dry weather in the next few days, will be hardly a fourth crop and, even if the rain ceases, will not be more than a half crop. Wheat in this county, Lamar and Fannin is a failure.*" *The Standard*, June 30, 1849

37. One cannot help but see, over the 18 year time span, a pattern of periods, 2 to 3 years each in duration, that alternate between good and bad weather for North Texas. Abnormal weather in 1843 and 1844 was followed by three years of "normal" weather (1845-48), which, in turn, was followed by wet and cool aberrant weather for 2 ½ years (1849-1851). Normal weather returned in latter half of 1851, continued in 1852 and 1853, to be replaced by another 2 ½ year span of unusually hot and dry weather (1854-56), and concluded with a third period of normalcy, 1857 and 1858. Do we experience such alternating patterns today? Do we blame this on a fickle Mother Nature or perhaps an unrecognized El Nino or La Nina?

Another suggestion that emerges from a review of these 18 years of weather reports is that Northern Texas is much warmer today than it was in the 1840's and 1850's. The winters seemed colder and ice skating was a popular sport some winters around Clarksville, something that would surprise many today. Temperatures in the summer hot spells of the period were in the 90 degree to 100 degree range for brief periods. Compare this to our summers now that routinely have a dozen days with temperatures in the 100's. Is this proof of global warming?

38. There were town and county elections. During the days of the Republic of Texas (1842-1845), there were also elections to the executive and legislative bodies in Austin. When Texas became a state, there were then state and national elections. De Morse was an avid Democrat and he always reported on the political scene.

39. A frequent notice in *The Standard* was for lost or mislaid land certificates, prior to application made for a new certificate. The history of land grants in Texas goes back to Spanish and Mexican times. Its purpose was to encourage colonization of the vast vacant region. At different times, different governments issued different certificates for Texas citizens of a certain era who settled in Texas for three years. The Republic of Texas reconfirmed the Spanish and Mexican grands and extended the practice. For example, heads of families living in Texas on March 4, 1836 were granted first class head rights of one league and one labor (4,605.5 acres), and single men, seventeen years or older, received one-third of a league (1,476.1 acres). Second class head rights of 1,280 acres went to heads of families and 640 acres to single men who immigrated to Texas after the Texas Declaration of

Independence but before October 1, 1837. Third class head rights of 640 acres for heads of families and 320 acres for single men went to recipients who immigrated to Texas after October 1, 1837 but before January 1, 1840. In 1841, fourth class head right certificates of 640 acres for family heads and 320 acres for single men were granted to immigrants to Texas between January 1, 1840, and January 1, 1842. In all, more than thirty six million acres were granted by the Republic in the form of these certificates.

The Republic also granted lands for military service. For example, certificates of 640 acres each were given to all persons who had engaged in specific battles in the War for Independence.

40. Lost and strayed horse notices also can be a valuable resource for someone seeking to find his Texas ancestors. Each notice tells who found the horse, the two citizen appraisers who fixed a value to the stray and then the Justice of the Peace and his Clerk who confirmed the appraisal.

41. When someone died, an administrator (or an executor if there were a will) was appointed by the Court. Notice was given by the fiduciary in a newspaper like *The Standard,* that all those indebted to the estate should make their identities known and pay off their obligations. and that similarly, all creditors of the estate should come forward and file their claims against the estate within the period proscribed by law, 12 months, or risk having their claims barred. De Morse, who was a lawyer himself, warned fiduciaries, that if they neglected to give this statutory notice then they themselves would be responsible to pay late claims. This, of course, accounted for a great deal of business for *The Standard*, which was really the only newspaper in the region. We are also the beneficiaries of that requirement as it preserves the names of the those who died, where they lived and often the names of their spouses and children.

42. The Texas courts handled all types of civil litigation, from divorce to foreclosures. As in modern jurisprudence, the Court obtained "jurisdiction" over a defendant no longer residing within the Judicial District by serving him or her by "publication" -- that is, by a notice of the commencement of the lawsuit published in a newspaper a proscribed number of times.

43. This notice is similar to the stop payment order on a check today. Texas did not have banks or checks so individuals gave each other notes that would be cashed by people or institutions who knew the maker of the note.

44. Letters were not delivered to the home as sometimes is done now. In Texas, in the 1840s, residents checked with the post office for their mail. Mail not picked up was noticed in the paper with the warning that, unless picked up in 90 days, they would be sent to the General Post Office as "dead letter". Happily, these notices provide us with the names of many residents, who were not noteworthy enough to get into the regular columns.

INDEX OF PERSONAL NAMES

A

A. Baker & Co - 8/7/47
AARON, slave -3/11/48
ABEL, Green B.-10/10/46; 1/8/48
ABBOT, William O. - 10/7/43
ADAIR, Robert - 10/9/47
ADAM, slave boy - 10/2/44
ADAMS, Mrs. Angelina Ann -3/27/47
ADAMS, Benjamin -10/10/46
ADAMS, Fitch - 2/13/47
ADAMS, G.M.- 6/22/47
ADAMS, Isaac -7/3/47
ADAMS, James - 4/15/47
ADAMS, Jeremiah - 5/15/44
ADAMS, Jesse - 1/13/ 44; 7/22/48
ADAMS, John, -endnote 20
ADAMS (no first name given) 7/15/46
ADDISON, Malcolm H.- 7/3/47
ADKINS, (no first name given)-5/19/47
ADRIANCE, Cornelius - 2/13/47
AGAR, Mr. - 4/15/47
AGULIER, Ulysses - 8/20/42; 8/27/42; 7/20/43; 1/13/ 44; 7/31/44; 3/6/45; 5/30/45;6/28/45; 7/26/45; 8/2/45; 11/23/45; 1/21/46; 7/1/46
AIKIN, James - 9/25/47;- 4/8/48
AIKIN, WILLIAM B. -1/8/48
AIKINS, ALFRED -9/10/42
AIMES CHARLES [SEE AMES]-8/20/42; 9/3/42; 7/6/43; 7/3/47
AIMS, COLIN- 8/20/42
AKE, FELIX G.-7/15/46
AKIN, John B - 4/15/47
AKIN, C.M.- 2/5/48
AKTINSON, James- 5/11/43
ALABAMA Ridge - 10/9/47
ALBRIGHT, Alfred - 4/15/47
ALBRIGHT, William - 10/10/46
ALBRISALA, Alfred- 11/19/45
ALDRIDGE, Moses - 7/15/48
ALEEN, Ebenezer [see Allen]- 5/29/44
ALEXANDER, A.- 1/14/46
ALEXANDER, A.M. - 8/28/47; 6/3/48
ALEXANDER, Angeline- 3/16/44
ALEXANDER, B.D - 3/23/43
ALEXANDER, C.C. -6/3/46; 7/15/46; 8/28/47; 6/3/48
ALEXANDER, CHRISMAN & -

273

3/27/47
ALEXANDER, Daniel T. - 9/3/42
ALEXANDER, Electra - 1/14/43
ALEXANDER, Mrs. E.- 7/15/46
ALEXANDER, Isaac W.- 7/26/45
ALEXANDER, James M.- 4/3/44
ALEXANDER, L.C. - 8/28/47; 6/3/48
ALEXANDER'S - 4
ALFORD, James - 2/3/44; 7/22/48
ALFRED & CO - 8/28/47; 6/3/48
ALLEN, SOLOMON,& WARGENNER, - 4/22/47
ALLEN, A. D. - 10/17/46
ALLEN, Alfred - 5/13/45; 4/15/47
ALLEN, Andrew - 6/22/47
ALLEN, C.- 10/16/47
ALLEN, David -1/8/48 ;4/8/48
ALLEN, Dixon- 2/13/47
ALLEN, Ebenezer - 8/20/42; 12/10/42; 1/14/43; 7/6/43; 10/14/43; 7/3/44; 11/27/44; 12/26/44; 2/6/45; 8/14/47; 10/9/47
ALLEN, H. J.-3/27/47
ALLEN, H.M. - 5/4/43
ALLEN, Hiel S. -1/21/46
ALLEN, Hugh - 7/26/45; 10/10/46; 4/15/47; 7/3/47
ALLEN, Jane -12/17/42

ALLEN, Jesse - 7/3/44
ALLEN, Maj. John M. - 4/22/47
ALLEN, Jno. T - 5/13/46
ALLEN, Jonathan -1/21/46
Allen, R. C.-10/10/46
ALLEN, Thomas - 10/17/46
ALLEN, Col. Wm. F. - 4/22/47
ALLEN, William K.-1/21/46
ALLEN, William - 12/17/42; 7/6/43; 10/17/46
ALLEN, Attorney - 4/15/47
ALLENON, Perry -2/13/47
ALLEY, D. N. - 4/6/43; 4/20/43; 8/21/44; 10/16/44; 12/12/44; 2/6/45, 5/13/46
ALLIN, William [see Allen] 7/26/45
ALLIS, William - 5/13/45
ALLISON, William - 10/9/47
ALORD, James P.[see Alford] - 10/9/47
AMES, Charles [see Aimes] 12/3/45
ANDERSON, Andy - 10/9/44; 1/23/45
ANDERSON, E.F.- 6/16/47; 6/10/48
ANDERSON, James - 2/13/47; 4/15/47
ANDERSON, N.- 4/17/44
ANDERSON, R. G.- 10/7/43
ANDERSON, T. A.-12/26/44
ANDERSON, Dr. W. -2/6/47
ANDERSON, W. Nicks - 6/2/47
ANDERSON, William - 5/27/46; 7/1/46

ANDERSON Col. -8/7/44
ANDREW, Bella - 8/8/46
ANDREWS, C .K - 10/29/42
ANDREWS, William B.- 7/15/46
ANDREWS, William S.- 1/14/46
ANDREWS, William W.- 12/11/47
ANTHONY, HENRY - 4/8/48
ANTHONY, JAMES B.- 4/15/47; 7/3/47
APPERSON, PETTY - 2/13/47
ARCHER, CREED -4/22/47
ARMISTEAD, L.A. U.S.A,- 10/17/46
ARMITIN, Thomas - 2/13/47
ARMSTRONG, Matthew - 10/9/47; 1/8/48
ARMSTRONG, Septemus - 2/13/47
ARMSTRONG, Maj. William 6/22/47
ARNETT, John -7/3/47
ARNOLD, M.. - 1/23/47
ARNOLD, Mrs Ann P.-4/8/48
ARNOLD, Bird -10/10/46
ARNSPIGER, M.D.- 2/13/47
ARRINGTON, Joel - 4/15/47
ARRINGTON, Martha - 10/9/47
ASANOCHI - 4/22/47
ASBERRY C. - 6/16/47
ASBERRY, Robert Esq.- 4/8/48
ASBURY, Charles J - 10/9/47
ASBY, M. J. - 5/29/44
ASHBROOKS, Henry - 1/28/43

ASHCROFT, L.H.- 9/18/47
ASHLEY, A.-11/19/45
ASHLEY, Alvin -7/15/46
ASHLOCK, Meridith - 2/13/47
ASKEY, J.A. - 6/9/47
ASKINS, Capt. Wesley - 11/19/45
ATKINS, (no first name given) - 4/20/43
ATKINSON, JAMES -8/20/42; 7/10/47
ATKINSON, JOSEPH - 4/9/44
ATKINSON, MARY - 10/2/44
ATWOOD, Simon -10/9/47
AUDREY, John -11/11/43
AUSTIN, A.S.-1/8/48
AUSTIN, J. L.-6/24/48
AUSTIN, Richard -7/3/47
AUTRY, L -7/15/46
AUTRY, Lewis -9/11/44; 7/3/47
AVERY, James -9/24/42
AYRES, E. H.- 10/2/44

B

BABB, David - 5/29/44
BACCHUS, a slave-5/19/47
BACCUS, Enoch - 4/15/47
BACKSTEN, James -3/27/47
BACKUS, Mr.- 8/7/47
BACON, James A. –10/28/43
BADGER, Laura - 9/5/46
BADGMAN, James W.- 1/23/45
BAGBY, Amanda - 12/24/45
BAGBY, B. C.-11/28/46; 4/1/47; 6/30/47; 7/17/47;

8/7/47; 10/16/47
BAGBY, Ballard C.- 3/2/43; 5/11/43; 5/18/43; 5/30/45; 6/7/45; 11/12/45; 12/24/45; 8/5/48
BAGBY, George -12/10/42; 3/2/43; 6/8/43; 5/13/45; 4/8/47; 7/22/48
BAGBY, J.A.. - 1/23/47
BAGBY, Maj. John A.- 12/24/45; 1/14/46; 6/10/46; 8/8/46; 10/17/46; 10/24/46; 4/1/47; 7/17/47; 8/14/47; 10/16/47; 10/23/47; 1/8/48; 2/12/48; 3/11/48; 3/18/48; 4/8/48; 7/15/48; 7/22/48
BAGBY, R.[B?] C.-12/11/47
BAGBY, Thomas A.- 2/12/48
BAGBY, (no first name given)- 8/9/45; 11/6/47
BAGBY & GARRISON -7/1/48
BAGBY, GRAHAM & CO - 6/3/48
BAGER, Miss Mary Anne - 2/13/47
BAGLEY, Thomas A. - 9/21/43; 10/28/43; 1/5/47
BAGWELL, G. W.- 1/14/46
BAGWELL, Milas. -3/11/48
BAILES, Alfred -5/15/44; 12/12/44; 12/26/44; 1/23/45
BAILEY, Francis B. - 10/10/46
BAILEY, Isaac - 5/29/44; 7/15/46
BAILEY, John - 5/13/45
BAILEY, William -7/3/47
BAILEY, (no first name given) - 2/4/46

BAILY, Claibourne C.[Baley] - 10/7/43
BAILY, Isaac J [see also Bailey] -4/3/44
BAILY, J. -[see also Bailey] 7/31/44
BAILY, J. C.-7/15/46
BAILY, James - 2/13/47; 10/9/47
BAIN, John - 7/15/48
BAIRD, Andrew S.- 1/23/45
BAIRD, John -4/8/48
BAIRD, William - 10/15/42
BAKER A. - 8/7/47
BAKER, Caroline - 7/20/43; 3/6/47; 5/5/47
BAKER, Hiram - 7/20/43; 3/6/47; 5/5/47
BAKER, Rev. J. M. - 4/22/47
BAKER, Col. J. Y.- 1/23/45
BAKER, Joseph - 8/5/48
BAKER, Samuel -9/21/43
BAKER, Solomon -7/3/47
BAKER A. & CO - 8/7/47
BAKER, Thomas C,- 12/10/42; 5/13/46; 7/3/47; 1/8/48
BAKER, William - 2/27/47
BALER, James -7/3/47
BALEY, Claborn - 7/3/44
BALL, D. G. - 7/8/46
BALL, David G. - 2/27/47
BALL, Elisha - 5/29/44
BALL, James - 11/6/44
BALL, John - 11/5/42, 4/9/44
BALL, Dr. S. H.- 8/8/46
BARNARD, Calvin - 10/9/47; 4/8/48

BARNARD, Culver - 7/15/48
BARNES, J. W.- 10/9/47
BARNES, James W.-1/8/48
BARNES Joseph - 10/17/46
BARNES, Talton T.- 4/15/47
BARNES, Thomas L - 5/13/45
BARNES, William- 7/15/46; 10/10/46; 7/1/46; 8/8/46; 1/8/48
BARNET, E.D.- 1/14/43; 4/8/48
BARNET, Salina - 5/18/43
BARNETT, Alex M -7/3/47
BARNETT, Alfred -1/8/48
BARNETT, James -7/3/47
BARNETT, (first name not given)-3/6/45
BARNETT, Martin -10/10/46; 7/3/47
BARNETT, MONTGOMERY AND CO; -3/20/47
BARNEY, Henry - 5/29/44
BARNEY, Lucien - 5/29/44; 10/2/44
BARREN, W. -9/3/42
BARRET, George -9/21/43
BARRON, S.D. - 2/13/47
BARROY, Mrs. Polly -7/3/47
BARRY, D. N.- 12/24/45
BARRY, David N.- 7/17/47; 10/16/47
BARRY, Davis [d?] N.- 6/9/47
BARRY, James B.-11/19/45
BARRY, L. D.-11/23/45; 12/24/45; 1/21/46; 7/1/46;9/4/47; 11/27/47; 12/4/47

BARRY, Lewis D.- 10/16/47; 10/23/47; 4/29/48; 8/5/48
BARRY, Margaret M.- 1/13/44
BARRY, Dr. -5
BARSA - 8/19/48
BARTLETT, Joseph -3/27/47
BARTLETT, William - 4/15/47
BARTON, John B.- 4/3/44
BARTON, John G.-7/3/47
BARZELL, Allen -10/10/46
BASHAM, Wm. C.- 4/3/44
BASIN, George - 8/20/42
BASIN, Henrietta - 8/20/42
BASKINS, John - 7/3/44
BATEMAN, Evan - 7/15/48
BATEMAN, Isaac -7/8/48
BATEMAN, J.-11/23/45
BATEMAN, James W. - 10/7/43; 7/3/44;
BATEMAN, Jonathan - 1/21/46 ;7/8/48
BATEMAN, Micajah M. - 10/9/47
BATES, Elizabeth M. - 7/15/48
BATES, James- 5/13/45; 7/26/45
BATES, John C. - 8/7/47
BATRS, Mrs. E. L.-7/3/47
BATSOE, Felix -11/19/45
BATT, Mr.- 10/9/47
BATT, Mrs. - 10/9/47
BATTLE, C. W. - 5/13/45
BATTLE, Jethro O.-11/19/45
BATWELL, Graven -6/30/47
BAYARLY, Thos. F. - 8/20/42; 8/27/42;

BAYLESS, H.- 7/24/44;
1/21/46; 7/1/46; 8/8/46;
1/15/47
BAYLOR, John R.-8/28/44
BAYLOR, Judge (no first name given) -9/21/43
BEAL, R.R.- 5/29/44
BEAN, John - 5/13/46; 10/17/46
BEAN, Thomas C - 1/9/45; 7/12/45; 7/26/45;1/21/46
BEARD, Andrew - 4/3/44
BEARD, W. H. - 1/28/43
BEARD & Cochran - 11/6/44
BEAT, William - 10/7/43
BEATY, Mrs. N.- 4/8/48
BEATY, William S.- 7/26/45
BECK, James -5/19/47
BECKNELL, John -1/8/48
BECKNELL, Wm. Capt.- 9/11/44; 2/13/45; 8/2/45; 11/23/45; 1/14/46; 1/21/46; 4/1/47; 6/30/47
BEDFORD, John R.- 12/10/42; 1/14/46; 1/21/46; 7/1/46;8/14/47; 4/15/47; 7/3/47; 8/14/47
BEDFORD, Dr. R. - 1/23/47
BEDFORD, William H.- 4/8/48
BEEKAM, Mary - 10/2/44
BEEMAN, Mrs Sarah Ann - 2/13/47
BEEN, John - 2/13/47
BEENE, William -7/3/47
BELCHER, William K.- 10/9/47
BELL A.H. Miss - 10/2/44

BELL, Amelia - 3/20/44; 5/1/44
BELL, Daniel - 1/13/ 44; 5/1/44
BELL, David G.- 5/29/44
BELL, Davis - 7/6/43
BELL, H.L.-10/10/46
BELL, Howard T.-1/8/48
BELL, John T. - 1/23/47
BELL, P.- 5/29/44
BELL, Samuel - 4/15/47
BELL W.H.- 10/7/43
BELL, Willson -7/15/48
BELL, Mr. -12/11/47
BENGE, Thomas O. - 8/14/47;6/9/47
BENGE, William B. - 10/7/43
BENNER, Alex'r -9/3/42
BENTON, John Jr. -9/3/42
BENNET, J. - 5/13/45
BENNET, Joshua -1/21/46
BENNET, E.H.-10/10/46
BENTON, James- 2/23/43
BENTON Jesse - 10/17/46
BENTON, Jesse Jr, - 6/8/43
BENTON, John - 7/15/46
BENTON, Nathaniel G.- 7/15/46
BENTON, W. H. - 5/8/44
BENTON, William H.- 10/10/46; 7/3/47; -1/8/48
BENY, Eleanor - 1/13/ 44
BEP, John -4/8/48
BERKHAM, James -1/8/48
BERKS, N. W. 4/22/47
BERLAND, Buckley L.- 4/8/47
BERNARD, [see Barnard]

Calvin-1/8/48
BERRIS, W. M.. -9/3/42
BERRY, Capt. E.- 8/8/46
BERRY, James - 8/20/42
BERRY, John S.- 10/9/47
BERRY, Lewis .- 8/2/45; 6/10/48
BERRY, William H - 4/15/47
BERTHELET, HEALD &- 6/3/48 CO
BESKY (no first name given) 10/1/42
BEVINS, J. M.- 4/8/47
BIBINS, James - 10/9/47
BICKER, Hiram - 7/15/48
BIGGS, J. H - 4/22/47
BILL, Slave - 3/23/43
BILLEY, Wesley-- 1/23/45
BILLINGSBY, Mrs. Ann W.- 11/12/45
BILLINGSBY, Capt. James - 11/12/45
BILLINGSBY, Jesse - 7/3/44
BINGAMAN , (first name not given)- 5/26/47
BINION, John [see also Binnian and Binnion] - 7/3/44
BINKERSTAFF, J. S.-4/8/48
BINNIAN, John - 5/13/45
BINNION, John -10/9/44
BIRD, Isaac - 7/6/43
BIRD, James - 11/5/42
BIRD, Maj. Jonathan - 8/8/46; 2/13/47
BIRDWELL, Zachariah - 9/3/42, 1/25/43
BIRPHEN, Rev. - 7/6/43
BISHOP, H. V.- 2/13/47

BISHOP, Joseph -7/3/47
BISHOP, O. H.-7/3/47
BISHOP, William N.- 12/3/45
BIVENS, Henry - 4/8/47
BIVINS, John M.- 4/29/48; 7/29/48; 8/5/48; 8/12/48; 8/19/48
BLACK, Abram -1/21/46
BLACK, Miss Elizabeth - 4/15/47
BLACK, Jacob- 9/24/42; 1/9/45; 1/21/46
BLACK, John D.- 4/3/44; 1/21/46; 5/13/46; 2/13/47
BLACK, Joseph -12/5/46
BLACK, Mary -1/21/46
BLACK, William - 2/13/47
BLACK, Hunt & - 10/9/47
BLACKBURN, James - 7/3/47; 7/15/48
BLACKWELL, James A.- 7/15/46; 10/10/46
BLACKWELL, Wiley 7/15/48
BLAGG, James P.- 5/15/44
BLAGG, Samuel- 5/15/44
BLAIR, Andrew J. J.- 7/3/44
BLAIR, James
BLAKLEY, John-1/8/48
BLANKENSHIP, Nancy - 5/29/44
BLANLON, William -7/15/46
BLANTON, Benjamin- 2/23/43
BLANTON, C..W. - 4/8/48; 7/15/48
BLANTON, David- 4/8/48
BLANTON, Francis L.- 7/27/43

BLANTON, Jacob -10/14/43
BLANTON, Lemeul -9/24/42
BLANTON, Wesley -1/8/48
BLAUTON, David -7/3/47
BLEDSOE, A.-4/8/48
BLEDSOE, Adalina - 8/27/42
BLEDSOE, George B. - 10/15/42
BLEDSOE, William - 8/27/42
BLEVINS, Allen W.-12/11/47
BLEVINS, William - 4/15/47
BLOODWORTH, John - 10/9/47
BLYTH [E.}, William 10/28/43; 1/14/46 BLYTHE, Samuel- K. - 2/3/44
BLYTHE, William T.- 1/14/46
BOB, slave - 10/7/43; 3/20/44; 10/30/44; 5/13/45
BOBBER, G. W.- 10/17/46
BOBO, Samuel- 9/25/47
BOGGS, James- 6/10/48; 6/24/48
BOILES, America - 10/9/47
BOLIN, Gerney L.-11/19/45
BONNER, C.B. -9/3/42
BONNER, George S.- 10/2/44; 1/14/46; 10/10/46
BOOKER, Jas -1/5/47;
BOOTH, Benjamin - 1/21/46; 7/1/48
BOOTH, James -4/3/44
BOOTH, R.- 8/9/45
BOOTH, S. S.- 5/12/47
BOOTH, Thomas - 2/13/47
BOOTH, Capt.(no first name given) -4/17/44
BOOTH, (first name not given)- 6/22/47
BOOTS, William -10/9/44; 6/3/46; 6/17/46; 4/15/47
BORBAC, James - 2/13/47
BORGER, Young - 10/2/44
BORLAND, Robert - 11/5/42
BOSWORTH, W. J. - 6/28/45; 7/12/45
BOTTLES, James C.- 10/9/47
BOUFNAN, Samuel- E. - 10/29/42
BOULER, John - 11/6/44
BOULES, J. L. -7/3/47
BOURLAND, Benjamin F 1/28/43; 6/15/43
BOURLAND, James - 9/14/43; 10/7/43; 12/12/44; 11/12/45; 12/24/45; 2/27/47; 7/17/47; 11/6/47; 1/8/48; 3/25/48; 8/5/48
BOURLAND, John - 10/29/42
BOURLAND, Jno M. - 5/18/43
BOURLAND, Martha A.- 4/8/47
BOURLAND, W. H. - 1/8/48;8/5/48
BOURLAND, William - 7/3/47; 8/7/47; 11/6/47; 7/29/48
BOURLING, Maj.-7/3/47 James
BOUTON, David - 10/15/42
BOWDEN, William M.- 10/10/46
BOWERMAN, Capt. Joshua - 7/13/43; 3/9/44;7/3/44; 2/6/45; 11/19/45; 2/13/47; 2/27/47; 4/15/47

BOWERMAN & MITTOWER - 2/6/45
BOWERS, Elijah D. - 5/13/46
BOWERS, Harriet, Sophronia Jane - 9/26/46
BOWERS, Thomas L. - 4/6/43
BOWERS, Tomisher- 5/13/46; 10/10/46; 4/15/47
BOWERS, W. P.- 7/6/43
BOWERS, William - 10/15/42; 9/26/46; 10/17/46
BOWIE, Daniel - 10/7/43
BOWLES, G. W.-12/26/44
BOWLIN, William - 10/9/47
BOX, James F. -10/15/42; 7/20/43; 7/31/44; 5/30/45; 6/28/45; 8/2/45; 11/23/45; 1/21/46
BOX, R.W. - 3/20/44
BOX, Thos. F.- 1/13/44
BOYCE, Isham J.-3/13/47
BOYCE, James R.-6/24/48
BOYCE, Dr. W. H. -2/4/43; 11/27/44; 2/27/47
BOYCE, Dr. William - 3/13/47; 5/5/47; 12/11/47
BOYD, George C.-7/3/47
BOYD, Jesse M.- 4/8/47
BOYD, M.S. -6/10/48
BOYD, Robert -1/8/48
BRACKEN, Lemuel - 3/20/44
BRACKNEY, John 10/28/43
BRACKNEY & COLLINS . - 7/10/47; 3/11/48
BRACKSON, Rev W.- 10/2/44
BRACKTEEN, Rev. William 4/6/43

BRADBURY, John - 5/27/46
BRADDLEY, Thomas L.[see Bradly]--10/10/46
BRADFORD, H.H.-1/8/48
BRADLEY, Edward - 10/9/47
BRADLY, Thomas C.- 2/13/47
BRADSHAW, James - 3/20/44
BRADY, Zephanish - 2/13/47
BRANDON, Elizabeth - 10/9/47
BRANSOM, Charles - 4/6/43
BRASHAM, Jas, - 3/2/43
BRATEN, John D.- 1/14/46
BRAVELL, Robert - 2/13/47
BRAZELTON, John -7/15/46
BREAKEN, William - 7/15/48
BREDON, W.W.- 2/13/47
BREDWELL, Elijah M.- 7/15/46
BREEDIN, C. C. - 7/15/48
BRETTAIN, Bartlet - 10/10/46
BREWER, Isaac N. - 10/23/44; 1/15/48
BREWER, Jno..- 8/20/42
BREWER, N. -11/18/43
BREWER , Stewart -6/10/48
BRIARLY, J. H.- 10/17/46
BRIDGES, F.W. -6/24/480
BRIDGES, James -1/8/48
BRIDGMAN, J.C.- 10/9/47
BRINLEE, George -10/2/47
BRISTOW, W.H. - 6/22/47
BRITAIN, Rev. John -4/8/48
BRITAIN, M.J.-10/10/46

281

BRITTEN, Joseph - 4/15/47
BRITTON, Joseph - 5/13/46
BROGDEN, (no first name given)- 10/7/43
BROMLEY, Samuel-10/10/46
BRONTON (first name not given)-5/19/47
BROOCKLIN, Katherine - 10/17/46
BROOKFIELD, E. H.- 10/17/46
BROOKS, Bevin -4/17/44
BROOKS, Christopher - 3/25/48
BROOKS, Miss P.- 8/8/46
BROOKS, Pamela - 4/17/44
BROOKS, T.G.- 7/29/48
BROOKS, Thomas - 5/13/45; 7/26/45; -11/19/45; 1/14/46
BROOKS, Travis G.- 10/29/42
BROOKS, Z.-10/10/46
BROOKS, Mr. -7/10/47
BROTHERTON, John - 1/23/45; 11/19/45
BROTHERTON, William W.- 3/23/43
BROWN, Alexander -1/8/48
BROWN, Cicero -11/19/45
BROWN, George A.- 12/5/44; 5/13/45
BROWN, Mrs. H. - 5/13/45
BROWN, H. K -12/11/47; 1/8/48
BROWN, Jeffrey - 5/1/44
BROWN, John - 7/6/43; 2/13/47; 10/9/47
BROWN, M. J.-7/3/47
BROWN, Matthew - 4/6/43; 1/14/46; 10/9/47; 1/8/48
BROWN, Penanrum -4/29/48
BROWN, Polly - 8/27/42
BROWN, Miss Sarah Jane - 7/3/47
BROWN, Sarah M.-10/10/46
BROWN, Squire - 2/13/47
BROWN, Stephen - 1/13/ 44; 1/8/48
BROWN, W. - 7/17/47
BROWN, W. R. - 2/27/47
BROWN, Wm. B. - 8/8/46
BROWN, William -10/29/42; 7/27/43; 5/8/44; 6/2/47
BROWNING, J. E.- 1/28/43
BROWNING, James 10/15/42; 1/16/45; 1/13/44; 7/24/44
BROWNING, Sam'l - 1/13/44; 5/29/44; 6/26/44; 7/26/45
BROWNING, W.D.- 7/27/43
BRUMET, (first name not given)- 11/19/45
BRUMLY, Elizabeth - 10/2/44
BRUMLY, Thomas - 1/14/43
BRUMMITT H.- 6/3/46
BRUMMITT, John W.- 2/13/47
BRUNE, E. - 11/25/43
BRUTON, Benj. -1/8/48
BRUTON, David -5/25/43; 5/30/45
BRUTON, Elijah -1/8/48
BRUTON, Isaac - 8/9/45
BRUTON, Joseph R.- 7/3/44
BRYAN, Dr. J. H - 4/15/47
BRYAN, John N. -1/21/46

BRYAN, Col.- 1/16/45
BRYANT, H. E. - 10/15/42
BRYANT, John -2/13/47
BRYANT, L. D. -3/2/44
BRYANT, Robert R.-7/3/47
BRYANT, S. - 2/19/48;-
3/4/48 ; 4/1/48
BRYANT, Solomon - 4/3/44;
8/2/45; 11/23/45; 1/21/46;
8/8/46; 10/24/46; 3/27/47;
10/16/47; 1/8/48;7/1/48
BRYANT, William -
10/17/46; 4/8/48;
BRYARLY, Minerva A. -
10/9/47
BRYARLY, R. J. [T?]-1/8/48
BRYARLY, R. T.- 2/23/43;
5/27/46
BRYARLY, Thomas F.-
10/9/44; 1/14/46; 4/15/47;
10/9/47; 1/8/48
BRYZZUL, Allen - 7/6/43
BUCHANAN, HU0SBANDS &
7/15/48
BUEL, Daniel G. -10/10/46
BULL, John -1/15/48
BUNDREN, Isaac -10/10/46
BUNDRESS, Isaac- 10/15/42
BUNGE, Thomas O.-6/22/47
BURDEN, Nathaniel -7/15/48
BURESS, Jas. E. - 7/6/43
BURGE, Zipiah - 10/9/47
BURGESS, Franklin -7/15/48
BURGHEN, Youn - 7/15/48
BURK, Lindsey -7/1/48
BURK, William-1/8/48;
2/5/48; 7/1/48
BURKE, Benjamin G.-
6/22/47

BURKE, Samuel -6/29/43
BURKE(no first name given)
11/20/44
BURKHAM, Charles -
3/16/43; 6/3/46
BURKHAM, James - 3/16/43;
12/24/42; 8/2/45; 11/23/45;
6/3/46; 6/30/47
BURLESON, General -6/5/44
BURNES, Mrs. Jno. R. -
4/15/47
BURNES, Thomas L. -
4/6/43; 7/6/43; 3/11/46
BURNETT, A.G. - 7/6/43
BURNETT, E. D. - 1/23/47
BURNETT, Isham- 7/6/43;
4/15/47
BURNEY, David F.-
10/17/46
BURNHAM, James - 3/9/44
BURNS, John W. -1/8/48
BURNS, Joseph N.- 6/22/47
BURNS, Thomas L.-7/31/44;
5/30/45; 6/28/45; 8/2/45;
11/23/45; 1/21/46
BURNS, Uriah - 10/17/46
BURNS, Wiley - 11/19/45
BURRIS, Wm. M. Dr. -
12/8/43; 6/15/43; 5/15/44;
7/1/46; 6/30/47
BURTON, I.-11/19/45
BURTON, (no first name
given) -4/22/48
BUSH, (no first name
given)-5/25/43
BUSH, Evan - 7/6/43
BUTLE, Olvy J.-7/3/47
BUTLER, J.-7/15/46
BUTLER, James - 2/13/47

BUTLER, John - 8/21/44; 10/16/44; 5/13/45; 6/22/47
BUTLER, N.G.-6/30/47
BUTLER, Nathan G, - 12/24/46; 1/5/47;
BUTLER, Reese - 5/13/46
BUTLER, William O.- 7/29/48; 8/5/48
BUTRYAN, Richard - 7/15/48
BUTTS, August J. - 2/4/43, 5/8/44
BUTTS,, Mrs. Elizabeth - 4/8/48
BYERS, M. - 3/20/44

C

C. LEWIS & CO - 6/3/48
CA[L?}DWELL, Samuel- 7/15/48
CADY, Levit -3/27/47
CAGE, William - 6/16/47
CAIN, Lucy A. R.-10/10/46; 7/3/47
CALDWELL, Isaac - 2/4/43
CALDWELL, J. A - 10/29/42; 12/24/42
CALDWELL, S. W. - 11/19/45; 10/9/47; 4/8/48
CALDWELL, Sam - 1/14/46;
CALHOUN, Henry -10/9/47
CALHOUN, Miss Mary - 7/15/48
CALMES, George - 5/29/44
CALVIN (slave)- 12/10/45
CAMERON, John - 12/8/43; 10/7/43; 5/29/44; 2/12/48
CAMNAM, .Bundry M. - 4/8/48
CAMPBELL, Mrs. Ann G. - 7/15/48
CAMPBELL, B. M -4/8/48
CAMPBELL, Francis A. - 7/15/48
CAMPBELL, John - 5/25/43; 7/27/43; 4/3/44; 5/13/45; 4/15/47
CAMPBELL, Robert - 7/15/46; 10/10/46;
CAMPBELL, S. R.- 8/7/47; 11/6/47
CAMPBELL, Samuel R.- 1/14/46
CAMPBELL, Esq. - 7/15/46; 2/13/47; 4/15/47
CAMPBELL, Major (first name not given)- 5/25/43
CAMPBELL AND GILLET - 1/14/46
CANADA, Jesse -7/15/46
CANADAY, Henry M. - 2/13/45
CANDLE, (Caudle) John - 12/19/46
CANDLE, Linda M.-10/9/44
CANDLE,(Caudle) Marcus W. -12/19/46
CANE, Miss L.-11/19/45
CARBOW, Henry - 5/13/45
CARDEL, Polly A.- 10/2/44
CARE, John-7/3/47
CAREY, S.-3/27/47
CARGILL, -4/8/48
CARNELL, W.G.- 10/17/46
CARNES, Jas. H. Col. - 2/23/43
CARNEY, E. W.-7/15/46

CARPENTER, S. E.- 2/13/47
CARR, George Washington - 3/11/48
CARR, H.B. - 10/9/47
CARR, John - 2/13/47
CARROLL, Daniel J. - 7/26/45
CARROLL, Ferdinand - 4/15/47
CARROLL, Jacob - 2/13/47
CARSON, Charles - 5/29/44
CARSON, John - 5/29/44, 6/3/46
CARTER, Armstead - 10/9/47
CARTER, Colbert. - 1/23/47
CARTER, George W. - 7/17/47
CARTER, J.C.- 1/14/46
CARTER, Gen. James- 3/2/43
CARTER, John -11/19/45
CARTER, John B. - 8/20/42
CARTER, John C. - 4/15/47
CARTER, John R. - 10/15/42
CARTER, (slave) - 7/27/43
CARTWRIGHT, J. M.-7/1/48
CARTWRIGHT, Joseph - 2/3/44; 8/2/45
CARTWRIGHT, Joseph M. - 2/5/48
CARVER, Benjamin -7/15/46
CASBEER, John [Casber]- 1/14/46, 10/10/46
CASDEN, E.J. -1/8/48
CASS, Lewis - 7/29/48; 8/5/48
CASS, Mrs.-7/3/47
CASTLEDINE, John -8/21/44
CASTLEDINE, Henry- 7/27/43

CAT, Luther F.- 7/17/47
CATLIN, Jacob J. -4/8/48
CATON, Cynthia -12/5/46
CAUDLE, Bennet -10/9/47; 12/11/47
CAUDLE , John A. 3/11/46, 12/19/46
CAUDLE, Mrs. M.-7/3/47
CAUDLE, M. W.-7/1/48
CAUDLE, Marcus W. - 3/11/46, 6/3/46;6/17/46; 12/19/46; 1/8/48
CAVE, W. J.- 7/3/44
CHACK, Rev. Levi - 3/2/44; 3/9/44
CHAFFIN, T.B. - 10/9/47
CHAFFLIN, Charles - 2/13/47
CHALMERS, Dr. John G. - 1/23/47; -7/24/47
CHAMBERS, John -4/22/48 .
CHAMBERS, John G.- 7/26/45
CHAMBERS, Dr.(first name not given)- 6/7/45; 1/21/46
CHANDLER, Alfred -6/5/44
CHANEY, Garrison - 10/10/46
CHAPMAN, John - 12/5/44
CHARBOUTNE, James - 10/10/46
CHARLES FENTON MERCER & ASSOCIATES - 6/2/47
CHARLES, Col.(first name not given)-- 1/16/45
CHATFIELD, Andrew - 7/15/48
CHATFIELD, R.- 4/8/47
CHATFIELD, Richard -

7/15/48
CHATFIELD, OLIVER & -
5/12/47; 7/10/47; 6/3/48
CHATFIELD, R. & Co. -
8/29/46
CHAWANS, J. C.-7/31/44
CHEATAM, Capt C. K. -
12/11/47
CHEATAM, M. V.-12/11/47
CHEATHAM, Cyrus -
10/10/46
CHENOWETH, John W. -
4/1/48 .
CHEPLER, James -4/8/48
CHERRY, J. V. - 10/15/42
CHERRY, James -10/9/44
CHERRY, Rev. John -
11/19/45
CHERRY, Jno.V. -10/9/47;
12/11/47
CHERRY, Miss Margaret -
1/8/48
CHERRY, Nancy- 10/9/47;
12/11/47
CHERRY; Smith B - 2/27/47
CHILDERS, Levi - 1/23/45;
7/1/48
CHISHOLM, Mrs Cynthia -
11/19/45
CHISHOLM, D.M.- 9/25/47;
12/11/47; 6/24/48
CHISHOLM, E.P. - 4/22/47
CHISM, J. C.-4/8/48
CHISM, V. William -7/15/48
CHRISMAN & ALEXANDER -
3/27/47
CHURCHILL, John -7/15/48
CLACK, Miss Martha -4/8/48
CLAMPET, L.D. -4/15/47;

10/9/47
CLAMPETT, Elijah -1/8/48
CLAMPETT, Elisha -10/9/47;
4/8/48
CLANTON, Martha -7/15/48
CLAPP, William -7/15/48
CLARK,, Benjamin - 1
CLARK, Edward - 6/22/47;
7/31/47
CLARK, Frank H.- 1/5/47;-
1/8/48; 7/1/48; 7/22/48;
8/12/48
CLARK, Gilbert - 3
CLARK, Isabella Hanks -
1;endnote 3
CLARK, James - 1; 3;
4/15/47; 7/3/47; 10/9/47;
endnote 3
CLARK, James Rogers -
endnote 8
CLARK, John T.- 4/15/47;
4/8/48
CLARK, Joseph A.-5/19/47
CLARK, Nancy - 4/15/47
CLARK, Robert A - 4/8/48
CLARK, Rufus A.- 4/8/47
CLARK, S. H.- 1/5/47;
7/29/48
CLARK, Thomas C. -
2/27/47; 10/9/47
CLARK, William - 2/13/47;
6/16/47-
CLARK, (first name not
given)- 5/26/47
CLARKE, (first name not
given) -3/11/48
CLEMENS, Andrew E. -
7/3/47
CLEMMONS , A.E.. -3/11/48;

6/17/48
CLEMMONS, Rev F.A.-
7/15/48
CLEMMONS, (first name not given) -4/8/48
CLEVELAND, Gen. Benjamin C. -7/3/47 .
CLEVENGER, Elias - 10/9/47; 1/8/48
CLICK, Matthias - 8/5/48
CLICK, W. Carroll - 4/8/47
CLIFTON, George B - 2/27/47
CLINE, Isaac -7/3/47
CLINTON, George B.- 1/5/47;
CLINTON, James - 6/22/47; 7/3/47
COBB, R. T. 4/22/47
COBB, Richard T. - 1/23/47
COCK, B.F. -1/8/48
COFFMAN, John 2/13/47
COFFMAN, L.-7/1/48
COFFMAN, Levi - 1/5/47;
COFFMAN, Lovell - 4/1/47; 10/9/47; 10/16/47; 1/8/48 ; 2/12/48
COINCON, F. X.- 4/15/47
COLBERT, Holmes - 7/17/47
COLBERT, P. - 6/3/48
COLBERT, Miss Malinda - 4/22/47
COLBERT, Silas - 7/17/47
COLE, D.W.-7/3/47
COLE, M.F. -4/22/47
COLES Dr. W.T. F.- 4/8/47
COLLINS, Commodore A - 4/15/47
COLLINS, C.P.- 4/15/47

COLLINS , Ruben D -4/15/48
COLLINS, William - 10/9/47; 7/15/48
COLLINS, BRACKNEY & .- 7/10/47; 3/11/48
COLLOM, Jacob H. - 9/25/47
COLTON, Michael G. - 2/13/47
COMPTON, Thomas -4/8/48
CONANT, S.D. - 2/13/47
CONKLING, James -10/9/47
CONKLING, Noah T. - 10/9/47
CONNER, Capt.-7/1/48
COOK, D.C.- 2/13/47
COOK, Elijah -1/8/48
COOK, J,-4/15/48; 7/1/48
COOK, Jefferson - 2/27/47; 6/30/47; 10/2/47; 1/8/48; 2/5/48
COOKE, Benjamin -7/15/48
COOPER, Calvin -1/8/48
COOPER, Henry - 7/3/47
COOPER, Mrs. Lucy A. - 4/8/48
COOPER, Samuel- -4/8/48
CORB[I] ETT, Nathaniel - 4/15/47;7/3/47
CORLEY, A.P.- 4/8/47
CORLEY, Rev. Samuel - 7/3/47; 7/15/48; 4/8/48; 8/5/48
CORNELIUS, Henry -1/8/48
CORNELIUS, Margaret A. - 12/4/47
CORNELIUS, Matthew - 7/15/48
CORNELIUS, T. J. - 8/28/47;

4/8/48;
CORNELIUS, W. P. - 4/1/47;
8/28/47; 6/3/48
CORNELIUS, Dr.- 6/16/47;
6/3/48
CORNELIUS, Thomas J. -
2/12/48
COTTER, Miss Susan -
7/17/47
COUCH, George - 2/13/47
COUCHMAN, John D.-1/8/48
COURTNEY, Peter - 8/7/47
COWAN, J.D. -5/13/45
COWAN, Thomas - 4/3/44;
5/1/44; 7/15/46; 12/18/47;
2/22/48
COX, George W.- 1/5/47
COX, Hiram W - 4/15/47
COX, Hugh. -2/6/47
COZART, Miss Danell -
1/8/48
COZZENS, Lt. - 2/12/48
CRABTREE, Frances -2/27/47
CRABTREE Solomon -
2/27/47
CRADDOCK, J. R.- 2/27/47;
6/2/47; 6/9/47; 6/16/47;
8/7/47; 10/16/47; 4/29/4;
6/10/48;
CRAIG & NORRIS - 4/15/47
CRAIG, John B. - 2/27/47
CRAIG, William -4/22/47
CRANE, John M..–10/2/47
CRAVENS, Miss Zerelda -
2/13/47
CRAWFORD, Shelby -
7/22/48
CREALY, William - 10/9/47
CREWDON, William M. -

7/3/47
CRICK, Elijah -4/8/48
CRIMP, R.P . - 6/3/48
CRITTENDON, W.P. -2/12/48
CRITTENDON, William -
10/9/47; 7/22/48
CRITTENTON - 8/19/48
CROOKS , A..M - 2/27/47;
4/15/47; 6/9/47;
10/9/47;10/16/47; 1/8/48; -
3/11/48; 7/1/48
CROOK, Lewis J. - 5/12/47
CROOK, R.R. - 5/12/47
CROOK, Richard R.- 5/12/47
CROSS, Hon. Edward -
12/11/47
CROW, Elizabeth - 6/9/47
CROWNOVER, B. - 6/9/47;
2/12/48; 3/11/48
CROWNOVER, Benjamin,-
1/5/47;10/16/47; 1/8/48
CRUMP, Capt. William G. -
1/15/48; 7/1/48
CRUTCHER, William -
1/15/47
CRUTCHFIELD, David M. -
7/3/47; 10/9/47
CULBERSON, J. F.-7/3/47
CULLEN, Asa -7/3/47
CULLEY, Dr. S. C -1/5/48
CULLUM, John -7/3/47
CUNNINGHAM, Jas. R -
1/8/48
CUNNINGHAM, John -
2/13/47
CUNNINGHAM, William. -
1/23/47
CUSONS, F.C.-4/8/48

D

DABBS, J. W - 11/5/42, 6/7/45; 7/1/48
DAGICY, Miss H. - 5/29/44
DAGLEY, Thos -4/3/44
DAGLEY, Wm. -4/3/44
DAGL[E]Y, Capt-5/19/47; 7/3/47
DAIL, William - 5/29/44
DAKEN, Jacob - 5/13/45
DALBY, Col. J. C.-1/21/46
DALBY, John C. -9/25/47
DALBY (no first name given)-9/4/44
DALE, C. C.- 4; 5/13/45,
DALE, Charles C.-6/8/43; 10/28/43
DALE , J.P.- 4
DALE, John P. -7/1/48; 7/29/48
DALE, Martilda - 6/3/46
DALE, Rebecca-12/24/46
DALE, Thomas - 6/3/46; 5/48
Dalton, Hiram H. -9/25/47
DANIEL, Alice - 7/15/48
DANIEL J. B. - 2/27/47
DANIEL, James - 2/27/47
DANIEL, L. W.- 5/13/45
DANIEL, Lewis W. -10/9/44
DANIELS, Jesse - 6/14/45; 1/21/46; 8/8/46
DANIELS, William C. - 1/14/43
DANTON, John - 7/15/48
DAREN, John - 10/9/47
DAREN, Mrs. N. - 10/9/47
DARING, A.P. -1/14/43

DARNELL, Foster S.- 7/15/48
DARNALL, J. B.- 2/27/47
DARNALL, J. H. -12/10/42
DARNELL, Miss Sarah E. - 8/5/48
DARNELL, -11/6/47
DARNALL & DICKSON - 5/13/45; 6/28/45; 12/24/45; 6/3/46
DAVENPORT, James - 3/13/45
DAVIDSON, Ellis -7/3/47
DAVIDSON, James L. - 10/10/46
DAVIDSON, Josiah -1/8/48
DAVIS, Rev. A.-6/17/48
DAVIS, A. L.-5/19/47
DAVIS, Andrew - 4/22/47
DAVIS, Edward- 6/15/44; 6/24/48
DAVIS, Greenville - 10/2/44
DAVIS, H.E.- 1/23/45
DAVIS, Isaiah - 8/5/48
DAVIS, J. T. P.- 4/22/47
DAVIS, John - 10/29/42; 1/14/43, 10/2/44; 6/16/47; 7/3/47; 12/18/47
DAVIS, Dr. John H. - 3/2/43; 11/2/43;
DAVIS, John W. II - 5/27/46
DAVIS, Joseph - 7/1/46
DAVIS, Josiah - 6/3/46
DAVIS, Malinda - 12/24/45
DAVIS, Ragland - 2/27/47
DAVIS, Thomas - 2/27/47
DAVIS, William - 11/2/43; 1/14/43; 4/20/43;10/9/44; 5/13/45; 5/31/45; 12/24/45;

1/14/46; 5/27/46; 1/21/46;
2/27/47; 10/9/47; 4/8/48
DAVIS, Gen. - 8/12/48
DAVIS, Rev. - 5/13/46
DAVIS (grocery)-7/15/46
DAVISON, Israel- 10/7/43
DAVISON, Josiah - 1/23/45
DAVISON, Wm. - 10/7/43
DAVIT, Salina - 8/27/42
DAVIT, Samuel K. - 8/27/42
DAWSON, Israel - 1/13/ 44;
1/14/46
DAWSON, James L.- 8/28/44
DAWTHET, Ambrose -7/3/47
DAY, Edward -7/3/47
DAY, Samuel -11/28/46
DAY, Sarah A.-11/28/46
DE MORSE, Charles – v; 1;
3; 6;- 9; 11; 12; 13; 8/20/42;
1/1/43;1/14/43; 5/11/43;
6/8/43; 4/17/44; 8/21/44;
12/26/44; 1/9/45; 2/20/45;
3/6/45; 3/13/45; 5/30/45;
6/7/45; 7/5/45; 8/9/45;
11/12/45; 12/24/45; 1/14/46;
2/4/46; 10/24/46; 12/19/46;
6/22/47; 6/30/47; 7/17/47;
10/23/47; 11/6/47; 12/11/47;
1/29/48; 2/5/48; 2/12/48;
6/24/48; 7/22/48; 7/29/48;
endnotes 1; 4; 31; 32; 34;
38; 41
DEAK, Nelson - 2/12/48
DEAN, Asa - 11/4/43
DEAN, Edward M - 5/18/43;
7/17/47
DEAN, Elias - 10/9/47
DEAN, George - 6/3/46
DEAN, Irene - 1/14/46

DEAN, James - 6/3/46
DEAN, Jesse; - 7/15/48
DEAN, Joab A. - 6/3/46
DEAN, Levi D. - 7/6/43;
7/3/44; 6/3/46; 10/9/47;
1/8/48; 7/15/48
DEAN, Mary - 10/30/44
DEAN, Mrs. Sarah -5/18/43;
11/19/45; 6/3/46;7/17/47
DEAN, Speer – 6/3/46
DEAN, Susanah -11/4/43
DEAN, Thomas -10/9/44;
6/3/46
DEAN, Willis -4/1/48
DEARING, A.D.- 4/3/44
DEARING, Albion [Allen?]-
10/10/46
DEARING, Allen J.- 1/13/ 44
DEARMEN, G. - 2/13/47
DEARMEN, John - 2/13/47
DEARMEN, Taylor - 2/13/47
DEGREFFENRAID, William
B. - 2/13/47
DENNIS, Colby - 12/24/45
DENNIS, James - 7/10/44;
4/8/47; 9/4/47
DENNIS, John - 12/24/45;
4/8/47
DENNIS, Thomas - 7/10/44,
12/24/45; 9/4/47
DENNY, Maj. St. Clair
3/13/47; 7/3/47
DENSON (no first name
given) - 2/4/43
DENTON, John B. - 3/16/43;
5/29/44
DENTON, Mary - 8/20/42
DENTON W.C. - 6/3/46;
7/1/46

DENTON, William C. -2/6/45
DENTON, Parson - 2/13/47
DERDON, John - 7/6/43
DERN, Lynette - 1/28/43
DERRICK, Simon - 3/11/46; 12/19/46
DERRYBERY, H.M. - 5/13/45
DEVENPORT, James B.- 10/10/46
DEVILLE, Patrick - 10/17/46
DEWIT, Clinton, -7/3/47
DEWRAN, Jesse -1/8/48
DICK, Joseph -9/10/42
DICKENS, John S. -2/13/47
DICKENS, Townsend - 1/14/46
DICKSON, A.R.- 7/17/47; 7/22/48
DICKSON, J. A. - 10/7/43
DICKSON, James - 1/14/43; 8/14/44
DICKSON, Miranda A. - 11/4/43
DICKSON, P.- 7/3/44
DICKSON, Reynolds -7/3/47
DICKSON, Sarah Eliza - 1/21/43
DILLARD, Matthew - 9/28/43; 3/2/44; 5/29/44
DILLARD, William M. - 3/4/48
DILLINGHAM, J. A.- 2/4/43; 10/2/44; 8/7/47
DILLINGHAM, J. E. [A or L?] -2/13/47
DILLINGHAM, J. P.[A or L?] 12/31/42
DILLINGHAM, John - 11/26/42; 2/3/44

DILLINGHAM John L.- 6/2/47; 6/16/47; 6/10/48;
DILLINGHAM, Nancy W. - 7/6/43; 2/3/44; 5/27/46; 6/3/46; 7/1/46
DILLON, H. K.- 7/26/45
DINWIDDIE, J. B.- 8/5/48
DINWIDDLE, Mary Anne - 6/3/46
DIRCKS, I. H.- 5/30/45; 6/28/45; 8/2/45; 11/23/45; 1/21/46
DIRCKS, J. H. - 11/12/45
DIRCKS,, J. W.- 7/3/44
DIRCKS, John Henry - 3/11/46; 3/18/46; 3/25/46
DIRCKS, (first name not given) - 2/4/46
DIRKSON, James A.- 1/23/45
DITE, George -7/3/47
DIXON, Enoch -7/3/47
DOAK & TITUS - 5/29/44
DOAK, D.- 4/17/44
DOAK, N.- 1/30/45
DOAK, Nelson -2/13/45; 7/22/48
DOAK, (no first name given) 2/4/46
DOAK & TIME [Titus?]- 2/24/44
DOBBINS, Samuel C -1/8/48
DODD, A. -9/21/43, 4/3/44
DODD, Atlas - 6/16/47
DONALD, Dan - 10/7/43
DONEL; James -2/13/47
DONK, Johiah H.-10/9/47
DONLEVY, B.P.- 6/22/47
DONLEY, S.P.- 7/15/48

DONNELL, E.F.- 4/15/47
DONNELL, REV. Samuel F. - 7/3/47; 1/8/48; 4/8/48
DONOHO, Mary W.- 12/3/45, 1/7/46
DONOHO, Wm - 8/20/42; 3/9/43; 4/6/43; 9/21/43; 1/13/ 44; 4/24/44; 7/24/44; 8/21/44; 8/28/44; 10/16/44; 11/20/44; 11/12/45; 12/3/45; 1/7/46
DONOHO, Mrs.- 4;5
DONOHO, (no first name given)-9/24/42
DOODS, John C -4/8/48
DOOLEY, George W. - 5/13/46
DOOLEY, M.A. - 7/29/48
DOOLEY, Wm. - 1/23/47
DOOLITTLE, Harrison - 10/17/46
DORON, Thom.7/6/43
DORSEY, Greenberry W.- 11/25/43

DREW, Joseph J. - 2/27/47
DREW, Matilda - 2/27/47
DRIVER, John -10/10/46
DRY, Amos - 2/23-43
DRYER, John 12/10/42
DUKE, John H. - 11/19/45; 10/23/47; 4/29/48
DUKE, Rev. - 1/28/43
DUKE, Mr. -6
DULANEY, William - 5/29/44
DUMAS, Lawrence W. - 1/8/48
DUNCAN, A. D - 4/6/43;

DOSS B. H.-11/7/46; 7/17/47; 4/29/48
DOSS, Benjamin H. - 8/21/47
DOSS, J. W -10/10/46
DOSS, James W.- 7/26/45
DOSS, Mark . - 2/23/43; 7/6/43; 10/14/43
DOSS, Mrs. Mary Malvina - 8/21/47
DOSS, Parker S.- 8/5/48
DOSS, Thomas J. - 7/6/43; 7/17/47
DOUGLASS, W.-7/3/44
DOWDY, Martin - 10/9/47
DOWDY, Thomas - 12/31/42
DRAGON, John - 10/7/43; 1/23/45
DRAPER, Parson -11/19/45
DRAPER, Daniel - 10/2/44
DRECHER, Frederick - 7/17/47
DRENNON, E.-- 7/3/44
DRENON, David - 7/6/43

4/20/43; 12/12/44
DUNCAN, Charles R.- 10/9/44
DUNCAN, Garnet - 12/24/45
DUNCAN, George - 10/7/43
DUNCAN, H.S.-10/9/44
DUNCAN, James - 5/29/44
DUNCAN, John J. - 5/31/45
DUNCAN, Rob't - 10/7/43
DUNCAN, William B.- 7/3/47; 4/8/48
DUNCAN, William R.M. - 11/6/44
DUNNON, Hickman -

2/13/47
DURAN, Jesse -4/8/48
DURANAGHO, Robert B - 7/15/48
DURCA, William -4/8/48
DURFEE, Charles - 4/1/47; 4/22/48
DURFEE, Elza -4/22/48
DURHAM, Col. B.H. - 1/7/46
DURHAM, 11/6/47
DURHAM, Berry H. - 7/17/47; 8/7/47
DUTY, Henry -11/23/45; 1/21/46; 7/15/48
DUTY, M.T. - 10/17/46
DUTY, P.- 7/22/48
DUTY, Philip - 4/9/44; 5/11/43; 1/7/46
DUVALL, Miss M.-3/27/47
DWIGHT, Jonathan E. - 1/23/47
DYE, Jacob - 1/23/47; 2/13/47
DYE, Kelsey. - 1/23/47
DYER, Abia -6/29/43
DYER, D.H.- 6/15/43; 6/22/43; 6/26/44; 2/17/44; 2/6/45
DYER, Geo. W. - 7/12/45
DYER, John M. -1/13/ 44
DYER, Gen. John H - 2/4/43; 7/6/43;
DYER, William -6/29/43; 3/9/44; 4/24/44
DYKE, L. D. - 1/13/ 44

E

EADS, John - 4/15/47
EAKRIDGE, H.F. -10/10/46
EARLE, Samuel - 8/8/46
EARLEY, Col. Gilbert - 5/13/46 t
EARLY, E. -4/17/44;
EARLY, Elbert - 2/23/43; 6/29/43; 4/22/47
EASKRIDGE, Harvey - 10/9/47
EASTER, Jas.- 7/6/43
EASTMAN, Dr. A. Perry - 4/22/47
EASTWOOD, John - 4/27/43
ECHOLS, W.F.- 9/18/47
EDMONSON, Caroline - 3/9/44
EDMONSON, Isabella - 10/17/46
EDMONSON, Col. R.-12/5/46
EDMONSON, Samuel - 7/15/48
EDMONSON, T.B.- 4/17/44
EDMONSON, Turner B.- 1/14/46
EDMONSON, William - 1/14/43; 3/9/44
EDMONSON, Mr.-7/3/47; 8/7/47
EDWARDS, Col. Haden. - 7/10/47
EDWARDS, Thomas C.- 10/10/46
ELI, slave - 6/8/43
ELIOT, J. -3/27/44
ELLET, Mrs Anne - 6/3/46; 1/8/48
ELLET, J. W. -1/21/46
ELLET,, John W.- 4/6/43;

6/22/47
ELLET, Dr. K. MD. -1/8/48
ELLIOT, B. E.-10/10/46
ELLIOT, Bertrand E. -
7/31/44; 9/25/47
ELLIOT, E.G. USA -
10/17/46
ELLIOT, R. M. - 11/19/45
ELLIOT, W.A.- 10/9/44
ELLIOT, William -10/10/46;
12/11/47;4/8/48;7/15/48
ELLIS, John - 10/17/46
ELLIS, N.D.- 11/12/45;
9/25/47;
ELLIS, Peter - 7/6/43
ELLIS, Richard Judge -
7/24/44; 1/16/45; 1/5/47
ELLIS, S. H.- 2/6/45; 2/20/45
ELLIS, William B.- 5/13/45
ELLIS & VAN DYKE -
2/20/45
ELLISOM, Ewing - 2/27/47;
10/9/47
ELLISON'S MILL - 10/9/47
ELMORE, Christopher -
10/16/44
ELY, Maj. F. B. - 2/10/44;
3/9/44; 3/27/44; 6/15/44
EMBERSON, J.- 3/20/44
EMBERSON, John - 9/10/42;
3/9/44; 2/27/47
EMERSON, Margaret. -
1/23/47
EMERY'S Wheat Thresher -
endnote 28
ENGLISH, Col. J. C. -
10/15/42; 5/11/43; 7/10/44;
7/1/46; 6/9/47
ENGLISH, Bailey - 10/29/42

ENGLISH, Campbell -
11/23/45; 7/15/48
ENGLISH, Elizabeth -
11/23/45
ENNIS, C. -7/1/48
ENNIS, N.F.- 7/15/48
ENOX, David F.-7/3/47
EPPERSON, B.H.- 4/1/47;
6/22/47; 7/10/47; 7/15/48
EPPERSON, Caro - 5/13/45;
9/25/47; 12/11/47
EPPERSON, Mark - 8/8/46
EPPERPERSON, R.J.- 4/15/47
EPPERSON, S. H - 1/15/48
EPPERSON, Col. -11/28/46
EPPERSON, (first name not
given) 11/6/47
ERWIN, Samuel - 1/14/43;
2/3/44; 5/13/45
ERWIN, (first name not
given) - 9/25/47
ESKRIDGE, H. F.- 5/29/44;
10/9/47; 12/11/47
ESKRIDGE, Susan - 5/29/44
ESPIE, Robert - 7/26/45
ESTES, James - 7/26/45,
1/14/46
ESTILL, Rev. Milton - 3.
ESTIMAUVILLE, Sohia -
5/29/44
ETHRIDGE, Godfry - 7/1/46
EVANS, D. L [L. D.?] -
1/8/48
EVANS, John - 2/17/44
EVANS, L.D.- 8/9/45;
6/22/47
EVANS, W.- 2/13/45
EVANS, WM. C -
10/9/44;2/13/47; 1/8/48;-

EVANS, Col.(first name not given)-- 6/7/45
EVANS, Capt.(first name not given)- 6/3/46
EVENS, Abraham-4/22/47
EVENS, Jesse - 4/3/44
EVERETT, J. C. - 6/22/47
EVERTS, G. A. - 5/19/47
EVERTS, Judge G - 6/7/45
EWELLS, T.-12/26/44
EWINDER, J. N.- 2/5/48
EWING, Clayton -10/9/44
EWING, Jon. B. S. - 9/3/42
EWING, William -7/12/45; 10/10/46

F

FAGAN, James - 5/1/44
FAILING, Elizabeth - 2/13/47
FANNING, William - 10/10/46
FARIER, William B. - 10/9/47
FARIS, John - 1/23/45
FARIS, (no first name given)- 11/19/45
FARISS, George - 12/17/45
FARMER, David C.G.- 4/15/47
FARMER, John - 4/15/47
FARMER, Thomas - 1/14/43
FARQUHART, John L - 4/3/44
FARREL, Walter -6/24/48
FARRET, John -5
FARRINGTON, Maj. R.- 1/23/47

FARRIS, Joseph -12/17/42
FATHERRED, William - 5/12/47
FEENY, Robert - 4/22/47
FELPS, William -4/8/48
FENLY, Jas. D.- 5/29/44
FERGUSON, P.M.- 7/3/44
FERGUSON, Pleasant M. - 10/9/47
FERGUSON, Richard - 10/15/42
FERN, Lawrence W. - 2/3/44
FERR, James - 12/31/42
FERRIN, W. H. 2/13/47
FERRY, Justin - 5/13/45; 4/8/47
FIELD, William - 5/29/44
FIELDEN, Calvin - 3/13/45
FIELDS, D. - 6/22/47
FIELDS, J. W.-10/10/46; 3/27/47; 4/22/47
FIELDS, Rev. Washington - 5/27/46
FIGUERS, Bartholomew - 11/5/42
FILES, John - 10/9/47
FILLER, George - 5/13/45
FINDLEY, D.C.- 7/26/45
FINLEY, C.- 7/15/46
FINLEY, William L.- 3/23/43; 10/9/44
FINN, J. W. - 2/19/48
FINN, K. W.- 4/1/48
FINN, Richard - 5/15/44
FINNIN; E.- 10/16/47
FISER, John - 2/27/47
FISH, Nathan S.- 1/14/46
FISHBACK, Isaac H.- 6/19/44; 6/19/44; 7/3/44;

1/23/45; 2/13/45; 6/7/45
FISHER, Col. Charles - 7/17/47
FISHER, Miss E. - 10/17/46
FISHER, Jesse - 1/14/46
FISHER, Joseph -1/8/48
FISHER, S.D. - 7/17/47
FITCH, C. H - 2/13/47
FITCH, Richard A. - 2/13/47
FITZGERALD, Elizabeth - 1/13/ 44
FITZGERALD, Jabaz - 1/13/ 44
FITZGERALD, Wm - 4/3/44
FITZPATRICK, F.G - 1/28/43
FITZHUGH, Gabriel - 5/13/46
FITZHUGH, (no first name given)- 7/3/44
FITZHUGH, Capt.- 1/15/48; 7/1/48
FLACK, M.C.. - 1/23/47
FLATT, William - 7/26/45
FLATTERY, M.Y.- 2/13/47
FLEMING, B. M. C. -7/15/48
FLEMING, J. J.-10/10/46
FLEMING, P.H. - 10/9/47
FLEMING, Perry - 10/9/47; 4/8/48
FLEMING, R. C. -10/10/46
FLEMING, Robert C. - 11/6/44; 4/8/47
FLEMING, Thom. B - 10/10/46
FLEMING, W.-10/10/46
FLEMING. W. H.- 5/13/45
FLEMING. William -1/14/43
FLEMON, William -7/3/47
FLOYD, James B. -11/19/45
FLOYD, Robert F.- 5/29/44

FLYNT, Gideon -5/19/47
FLYNT (no first name given) 10/16/44
FOGG, Lafayette - 1/28/43
FOLLONER, Alsey - 5/13/45
FOLSOM, Lyman - 7/17/47
FORBES, T. C.- 2/12/48
FORBES, Thomas -12/24/42; 1/14/43; 11/11/43;
FORD, J. - 8/9/45
FOREMAN, Solinda - 2/13/47
FOREMAN, (first name not known)- 2/4/46
FOREMAN, W. W.- 7/3/44; 7/31/44; 5/30/45; 6/28/45; 12/24/45; 6/9/47
FOREMAN, William - 4/24/44
FORT, Dr. J. W.-7/24/44; 5/13/45; 12/11/47
FORT, Joseph M.- 1/23/45
FORTE, James -1/8/48
FOSTER, Felix R.- 4/8/47
FOSTER, G. W.- 10/17/46
FOSTER. John H.-11/19/45
FOSTER, Lee - 6/16/47
FOSTGATE, Dr. Walter - 6/10/48
FOWLER, A. J. - 11/ 26/42; 3/23/43; 4/8/48
FOWLER, B.C.- 2/4/43
FOWLER, Brad C. -9/17/42; 4/20/43; 6/8/43; 3/18/46; 6/9/47; 4/29/48; 7/1/48
FOWLER, Elizabeth - 10/15/42
FOWLER, J. A. - 12/10/42
FOWLER, Col J. H. -1/28/43;

4/3/44; 1/14/46
FOWLER, J. S.-10/9/44
FOWLER, John - 4/22/47
FOWLER, Mrs. Kezziah - 2/2343; 3/2/43
FOWLER, R. O.-10/10/46
FOWLER, Rebecca - 7/3/44
FOWLER, Robert B - 4/20/43
FOWLER, Wm. - 2/23-43
FOWLKEN, E. K.- 10/17/46
FOYE, James - 5/29/44
FRAGER, Enoch -10/10/46; - 10/10/46
FRALEY, Andrew -11/19/45
FRALEY, C..L -10/10/46
FRALEY, David W.- 4/3/44
FRANCE, Alfred -4/8/48
FRANCES, Negro woman - 11/20/44
FRANCIS, Robert B.- 8/5/48
FRANKLIN, Lucretia - 11/19/45
FRANKS, Littleberry B.- 7/27/43
FRASELS, Robert - 10/15/42
FRAZIER, Alexander - 6/22/47
FRAZIER, Charles A.-7/15/46
FRAZIER, David - 4/22/47
FRAZIER, E.- 7/27/43
FRAZIER, E. N.- 4/20/43
FRAZIER, Ebenezer - 3/23/43
FRAZIER, Sweeney - 10/17/46
FREEMAN, Polly -1/8/48
FREEMAN, W. M. -7/1/48
FRENCH, L. - 10/9/47
FRY, Benjamin J.- 10/16/44
FRY, Lucinda - 10/16/44

FRYER, George W. -1/8/48
FUGATE, Rubin M.-10/9/44
FULBRIGHT, C.-7/3/47
FULBRIGHT, D. -7/3/47; 2/12/48
FULBRIGHT, Daniel N - 7/3/47; 1/8/48
FULBRIGHT, Martha -1/8/48
FULBRIGHT, Maj.-7/1/48
FULBRIGHT - (first name not given) 8/19/48
FULLER, Berkley J. - 4/13/43
FULLER, James S. -1/8/48
FULLER, Joel C. -10/10/46
FULLERTON, J. M.-10/9/44
FULLERTON JOHN M. - 2/6/47
FULLERTON, W. N.[M?]- 6/26/44; 1/14/46
FULLERTON WILLIAM W. - 10/9/44; 2/6/47
FULTON, C.T.[H?]- 10/17/46
FULTON, G. H- 10/17/46
FULTON, Samuel - 9/10/42; 10/29/42; 7/6/43; 3/9/44; 2/20/45;12/24/45; 6/3/46
FULTON, W. M. - 2/4/43
FUNDERBURG, W.B.-4/8/48
FUNDERBURG, William B. - 7/15/48
FUQUA, Joshua - 4/15/47
FUQUA, Nathan -11/19/45
FURNACE, Benjamin J. - 10/17/46

G

GAFFNEY, William - 10/9/47
GAGAHAN, James. - 2/6/47
GAGE, C. W.- 4/22/47
GAGE, E. H. - 10/9/47
GAINES, William - 8/7/47
GAITER, Col. F.-7/3/47
GALLA, J. C.-12/26/44
GALLA[O?]WAY, D. - 10/15/42
GALLOWAY, Charles - 11/28/46
GALLOWAY, Daniel - 4/6/43
GAMIGAW, J.C. - 1/14/43
GAM[M]AGE, T. T.- 6/22/47; 8/7/47
GARE, Thomas W.- 4/15/47
GARETT, William - 12/24/45
GARNER, Bashaell - 7/3/44
GARNER, James M. - 7/3/44
GARNER, Napoleon - 12/10/42
GARNER, Thomas -11/19/45
GARNER, Magistrate (first name not given)-5/19/47
GARQUOT, William - 8/7/47
GARQUOT, James A. - 8/7/47
GARRET, David -2/19/48
GARRET, Elizabeth - 12/24/45
GARRET, George - 12/24/45
GARRET, Kitarah - 12/24/45
GARRISON, John C.-7/3/47
GARRISON, Lloyd M. - 5/8/44
GARRISON, Thomas F. -3; 4/8/48

GARRISON, BAGBY & - 7/1/48
GARROUTH, John R. -4/3/44
GARVIN, James H.-10/10/46
GARVIN, W.G.- 2/4/43
GAY, William B.- 1/23/47; 4/22/47
GELPIN, James P.-4/8/48
GEORGE, Fleming - 3/23/43; 4/6/43; 12/16/43
GEORGE, Jesse H - 7/1/46
GEORGE, Presley S. - 7/1/46
GEORGE, (no first name given)-2/6/45; 1/21/46
GERDIS, Catherine - 12/24/45
GERDIS,, E. - 12/24/45
GIBBONS, Pamela Jane - 11/2/43
GIBSON, Abraham - 10/9/47
GIBSON, Absalom -12/11/47
GIBSON, J.P. - 10/9/47
GIBSON, Joseph P.- 5/13/45
GIBSON, Robert A. 2/13/47
GIBSON, Roland - 7/26/45
GIDDEN, Richard F - 1/14/43; 6/30/47
GIDEON, Isaac - 1/30/45; 2/6/45
GILBERT AND SWIGLEY - 11/28/46
GILBERT, James -7/3/47
GILBERT, M.S. - 7/1/46
GILBERT, Michael. - 1/23/47
GILBERT, R. R. - 5/13/46
GILBERT, R.S. - 7/1/46; 7/17/47
GILBERT, Richard S. -

6/3/46; 6/17/46; 7/1/46; 11/28/46
GILBERT, Wiley - 10/9/47
GILBERT, Mr. -7/3/47
GILBERT & CO - 12/3/45
GILBREATH, James G. - 7/15/48
GILL, Mrs. Jane Chandler - 9/26/46
GILL, W. H.- 4/8/48
GILL, William H.- 9/26/46
GILLAM, SIMON -1/14/43
GILLET, JAS, P[S?].- 1/15/48
GILLET, Jas. S. - 2/23/43; 2/13/45; 6/7/45; 1/14/46
GILLET, James - 2/27/47
GILLETT, Capt.- 2/12/48; 7/1/48
GILLETTE, Capt.(first name not given)-5/19/47
GILLIAM, H.O.-7/3/47
GILLIAM, Col. James - 5/30/45; 6/7/45; 8/2/45; 12/3/45; 4/15/47; 6/22/47; 2/12/48; 7/22/48; 8/5/48; 7/29/48
GILLIAM, Miss Sarah Jane - 8/5/48
GILLIAM, Dr. (first name not given) - 1/15/48
GILLIAM, (first name not given)- 11/6/47
GILLILAND, Allen -10/10/46
GILLUM, Dudley -12/10/42
GILL[I]AM, James - 3/2/43
GILMER, James-12/4/47
GLASS, A .J.- 4/8/48
GLASS, Eliza R.- 4/8/48
GLASS, J. A. - 7/15/48
GLASS, J. C.-1/21/46
GLASS, John C.- 5/29/44; 2/27/47; 4/22/47
GLASS, Robert - 1/23/45; 6/9/47
GLEN, George - 5/29/44
GLENDENEN, Matthew - 2/13/47
GLENN, James B.- 2/13/47
GLENN, John -10/10/46
GLESS, Rachel, E. - 10/9/47
GLOVER, G. H. -6/30/47
GLOVER, Gatewood - 1/23/45
GLOVER, John - 6/14/45
GLOVER, M. -2/20/45
GLOVER, Mrs. Mary Ann - 5/13/45; 11/19/45
GLOVER, Martin - 3/16/43; 3/23/43; 7/13/43; 8/21/44; 7/29/48
GLOVER, William -1/14/43; 5/29/44; 11/13/44; 5/13/45; 5/31/45
Goddard, L. -11/7/46
GODLEY, M. D. G. - 10/14/43
GODLY, Frances - 10/17/46
GODSY, B.J. - 2/13/47
COFFE, D.J.-11/19/45
GOGART, - 11/6/47
GOINS, Live - 4/6/43
GOLDING, James - 5/29/44
GOOCH, B. - 4/17/44;6/30/47; 7/10/47
GOOCH, Benjamin - 1/28/43; 6/15/43; 5/15/44; 8/21/44; 8/28/44; 5/30/45; 6/28/45; 11/12/45; 2/13/47;

10/9/47;12/11/47
GOOCH, Elizabeth - 5/13/45
GOOCH, (first name not given) - 11/6/47
GOOCK, Hartford -7/3/47
GOOD, R.N.- 6/22/47
GOODALL, James - 1/14/46; 7/3/47
GOODARD, L.- 2/20/47
GOODE[A]LL, James P.- 10/10/46
GOODIN, A.H. - 6/21/45
GOODING, George C.- 6/7/45; 10/17/46; 3/6/47; 4/22/47; 7/17/47
GOODING, H. - 4/1/47
GOODING, Henry - 3/6/47; 6/3/48
GOODING, Mr. (first name not given)-6/30/47
GOODMAN, Archibald - 6/29/43
GOODMAN, George- 10/10/46
GOODWIN, Rufus -7/1/48
GORDON, E. - 2/11/ 46
GORDON, Catherine - 2/11/46
GORDON, G. Pope -1/8/48
GORDON, George - 8/20/42; 9/3/42; 12/10/42; 3/9/43; 4/6/43; 4/20/43; 5/11/43; 3/20/44; 5/8/44; 7/24/44; 1/16/45; 2/6/45; 1/14/46; 2/4/46; 6/17/46; 1/5/47; 6/2/47; 8/7/47; 10/30/47; 2/12/48
GORDON, Jas. H. - 5; 7/6/43

GORDON, John - 5; 10/9/47
GORDON, Joseph H - 4/13/43, 7/1/46; 1/8/48
GORDON, Julian - 2/13/47
GORDON, Col. (first name not given)- 2/27/47
GOSSERT, Presly - 5/29/44
GOSSET, John -1/8/48
GOSSETT, J. L. - 6/10/48
GOUGH, James H.-10/10/46
GRAFT - 6
GRAGG, John - 7/3/44
GRAHAM, A.N.- 10/2/44
GRAHAM Dr. B.- 6/3/48
GRAHAM, B.F. -1/8/48
GRAHAM, Charles - 12/24/45
GRAHAM, E. A.- 6/22/47; 8/28/47
GRAHAM, Mrs. Eliz.- 4/15/47
GRAHAM Ellen. - 1/23/47
GRAHAM, Dr. H. - 10/16/47; 1/8/48
GRAHAM, Rev. James - 4/15/47;4/22/47; 4/8/47
GRAHAM, Jane -11/ 26/42
GRAHAM, John - 8/8/46; 7/3/47; 4/8/48
GRAHAM, L - 5/29/44
GRAHAM, Lilly - 4/15/47
GRAHAM, R. B.[H] - 7/6/43; 5/13/45; 11/28/46; 4/1/47
GRAHAM, Robert M. - 1/7/46
GRAHAM, Thomas - 4/15/47
GRAHAM, Mrs.-3/13/47; 6/30/47; 4/1/48

GRAHAM, (no first name given)- 3/23/43
GRAHAM, BAGBY & Co. - 6/3/48
GRAND, Stephen - 1/23/45
GRANGEN, John -7/3/47
GRANT, S. - 12/24/45
GRANT, William -1/8/48
GRANT, Mr. (first name not given) -7/15/48
GRAVES, Robert C. - 10/15/42
GRAY, B.W.- 4/17/44; 7/3/44;12/12/46; 6/30/47; 10/16/47; 3/11/48; 6/3/48
GRAY, Byrd W.- 6/22/47
GRAY, Eli -1/8/48; 4/8/48
GRAY, Elizabeth -12/3/42
GRAY, Pleasant - 10/9/47
GRAY, Susan - 4/8/48
GRAY, Thomas -12/3/42
GRAY, W. J.- 1/23/45; 5/13/45
GRAY, W. M. - 7/6/43
GRAY, Washington - 2/27/47
GRAY, William - 4/15/47
GRAY, JOHNSON & . - 3/11/48
GREAVES, Jon S.- 1/23/45
GREEN, Benedict F.[H]- 11/19/45; - 7/17/47
GREEN, Benjamin - 10/2/44
GREEN, J. W.- 4/20/43, 10/24/46
GREEN, James W.- 8/20/42; 3/2/43; 7/6/43; 1/23/45; 10/10/46; 10/24/46;7/3/47; 4/22/48

GREEN, M.T. C.-7/3/47
GREEN, Roland -10/9/47; 1/8/48; 7/15/48
GREEN, Turner L.- 4/8/48
GREENMAN, Elizabeth - 10/9/47
GREENMAN, S.P.-10/10/46
GREENMAN, Sylvester - 10/9/47
GREENWELL, W. H - 7/6/43
GREENWOOD, Garrison - 5/13/45
GREENWOOD, Jerreson - 4/22/47
GREER, B. H. - 1/23/47
GREER, (first name not given) - 11/6/47
GREGG, Jacob -11/19/45
GREGG, John-1/8/48
GREGG, Mrs. Mary -7/3/47
GREGG, Thomas - 5/13/46; 10/10/46; 7/15/48
GREGG, W.- 1/13/ 44
GREGG, William - 8/20/42;1/14/43; 7/31/44; 2/20/45; 5/30/45; 6/28/45;8/2/45; 4/8/48
GREY, Timothy - 7/26/45
GRIFFIN, Benjamin -7/3/47
GRIFFIN, H. H- 6/22/43, 6/15/43
GRIFFIN, J.- 3/20/44
GRIFFIN, James -11/19/45
GRIFFIN, John F.- 3/23/43; 8/5/48
GRIFFIN, Thomas -11/19/45
GRIFFITH, Evan -11/19/45
GRIFFITH, Dr. L. E.- 3/2/43

GRIFFITHS, Dr. E. L.- 3/23/43
GRIGGS, Andrew - 1/23/45
GRIGGS, D. P - 5/29/44
GRIMES, James Hon. - 10/29/42
GRIMM, J. W - 7/3/44
GRINDER, William G.- 11/19/45; 7/15/46; 7/15/46; 11/28/46
GRINDER, Mr. (first name not given)-12/19/46
GRINNING, -1/8/48
GROMBER, A.G. - 2/23/43
GRUMP, R.P - 10/16/47
GUDRIAN, Chas. F.M.- 5/13/45
GUEST, A.N.-7/3/47
GUEST, Isaac -5/29/44; 7/6/43; 8/14/44; 8/8/46; 7/3/47
GUEST, Joseph - 1/14/43; 1/28/43; 8/8/46
GUEST, Martin - 1/14/43; 1/28/43; 7/3/47; 2/12/48; 3/11/48
GUEST, W.B. -3/11/48
GUEST, William- 7/17/47
GUGN, William - 10/9/47
GUM, Martha - 6/26/44
GUNN, F.B.- 5/12/47
GUNN, Francis B.- 9/25/47
GUTHERIE, R.H. 2/13/47
GUTHERIENG, Empraim - 6/10/48
GUTHRIE, James - 12/24/45
GWIN, William -4/8/48
GWINN, Pleasant M.- 10/9/44

H

H. LITTLE & CO - 6/21/45; 1/28/46; 2/4/46; 5/13/46; 6/3/46
HADDEN, H. B. - 10/9/47
HAGER, J.R. - 2/23/43
HAGOOD, Cephas - 2/13/47
HAIL, John W. - 7/3/47
HAIL, Joshua - 7/3/47
HAIL, Stephen S.- 1/14/46
HAINEY, John A.- 10/16/47
HAINS, William S. -1/8/48
HALBERT, Joel - 2/6/45; 5/13/45; 5/31/45; 7/12/45; 7/3/47
HALBERT, John - 2/6/45; 5/13/45; 5/31/45;
HALBROOK, (first name not known) - 4/3/44; 7/3/44
HALE, Abedage - 1/23/45
HALE, J. C - 5/11/43
HALE, J.P.-4/1/48
HALES, Jesse F. -12/24/46; 1/5/47; 10/9/47
HALGRASS, G. W.-6/30/47
HALKINS, William W. - 1/8/48
HALL, A.-10/9/44
HALL, A.M.- 12/5/44
HALL, J. H[T/]. -12/12/44
HALL, J. T.- 7/26/45
HALL, P. F. - 5/29/44
HALL, Preston H..-2/20/45
HALL, William - 7/3/44
HALLBROOK, J. R.- 7/1/46
HALM, Rob't S. - 4/6/43
HALSEY, A.A. - 4/22/47

HALSEY, Hiram M. - 6/16/47
HAMILTON Ebenezer R - 10/7/43
HAMILTON, James - 2/23/43; 4/15/47
HAMILTON, Joseph - 5/15/44
HAMILTON, M.- 1/14/46
HAMILTON, Martha P.- 5/15/44
HAMILTON, R.W. - 7/6/43; 11/20/44; 3/11/46; 3/25/46; 10/10/46; 12/5/46; 10/9/47
HAMILTON, Col. Robert S.- 3/20/44; 7/10/44; 1/23/45; 7/26/45; 1/14/46; 1/21/46; 1/28/46; 12/5/46;10/23/47; 4/29/48; 6/10/48; 8/5/48; 8/12/48; 8/19/48
HAMILTON, Sarah -7/1/48
HAMILTON, W. E. -1/14/43
HAMILTON, W.F. -5/11/43; 1/28/46; 3/11/46; 12/5/46;
HAMILTON, W. J.- 8/20/42; 1/14/43; 1/13/44; 4/17/44; 2/5/48
HAMILTON, W.L. - 5/8/44; 6/2/47; 6/16/47 HAMILTON, William C.- 5/15/44 .
HAMILTON, (first name not given) - 2/4/46
HAMILTON, M'KINDER & CO.- 1/7/46
HAMILTON AND RAINEY - 11/19/45, 2/4/46
HAMLIN, (first name not given)- 1/15/47
HAMMERICK, Joseph- 11/2/43
HAMMOCK, A. J. - 7/6/43

HAMMOCK, Andrew J.- 1/14/46
HAMMOCK, J. - 10/15/42
HAMMOCK, Jackson - 7/3/44
HAMPTON, John - 10/15/42
HAMPTON, (first name not given- 1/28/43
HANCOCK, Joseph - 4/3/44; 5/29/44; 7/3/44
HAND, B.- 10/17/46
HANDY, Nelson H.- 5/13/45
HANGER, Mr. - endnote 18
HANING, Aron - 4/15/47
HANNAH, Richard H.- 4/15/47; 7/3/47
HANSFORD, John M. - 7/3/47
HANYELL, DanielB.- 7/3/47
HARBOL, David - 2/13/47
HARDAWAY, H.- 1/14/46
HARDEN, Samuel - 4/8/48
HARDIN , Allen G.- 5/13/46
HARDIN, Black - 5/19/47
HARDIN, Col. David - 12/25/47
HARDIN, Sarah W. M - 10/10/46
HARDKINS, G. W. - 10/7/43
HARDWAY, Ainsworth - 10/17/46
HARDWAY, Miss Mary A. - 7/3/47
HARDY, Martin - 2/13/47
HARDY, William T - 4/15/47
HARGEN, JOHN - 7/3/47
HARGRAVE, J. B. - 10/17/46

HARLAND, N.R - 3/18/46; 6/17/46; 4/15/47; 6/16/47; 1/8/48; 7/15/48
HARLIN, N. R. - 2/4/43
HARMAN, HENRY J. - 1/14/43
HARMAN, MATILDA- 1/14/43
HARMON, Catherine E.- 11/2/43
HARMON, J. T (see also, Harmon, John T). - 2/23/43; 10/2/44; 2/13/45; 12/24/45
HARMON, John T -1/13/ 44; 3/9/44; 7/3/44; 2/27/47; 6/9/47; 3/25/48; 8/5/48
HARMON, Joseph - 10/7/43
HARMON, M. - 7/26/45
HARMON, Samuel - 4/15/47
HARMON, William - 10/10/46
HARNEY, William R. - 10/17/46
HARPER, Elijah - 2/13/47
HARPER, H.-7/3/47
HARPER, Peter -1/28/43; 6/15/43
HARRELL, Richard - 2/13/47
HARRELSON, James - 7/15/46
HARRIET, runaway slave - 9/24/42
HARRIS, Alfred -9/4/44,
HARRIS, Daniel - 6/14/45
HARRIS, E. P.-12/26/44
HARRIS, Henry B.- 4/15/47
HARRIS, J. H.- 4/8/47
HARRIS, John - 6/14/45; 5/12/47
HARRIS, Joseph B -11/19/45

HARRIS, Nath.- 7/3/44
HARRIS, Newton -10/10/46; 4/8/48
HARRIS, R.-11/7/46
HARRIS, R. C.-9/4/44; 5/18/43; 6/19/44; 10/17/46; 2/27/47; 10/2/47
HARRIS, Randolf C. - 2/20/47
HARRIS, Miss Sarah - 7/17/47
HARRIS, Virgil K.- 1/23/45; 10/10/46
HARRIS, William J. - 2/13/47; 7/3/47; 10/9/47; 1/8/48
HARRIS (first name not given) -7/31/44; 7/1/48
HARRISON, J. W. (see also, Harrison, John W.) - 5/29/44
HARRISON, James W.(see also, Harrison, J. W.) - 10/17/46; 1/8/48
HARRISON, John -1/8/48; 4/8/48
HARRISON, John W. (see also, Harrison, J. W.) - 10/29/42; 10/17/46
HARRISON, Joseph - 8/20/42; 8/28/47; 6/3/48
HARRISON, Mrs. Louisa K - 3/2/43; 10/17/46
HARRISON, M. -6/30/47
HARRISON, P.M. -6/10/48
HARRISON, Philip - 8/8/46
HARRISON, W. C. - (see also, Harrison, William C.) 1/13/ 44; 3/9/44

HARRISON, W. M.- 8/20/42; 10/15/42; 5/11/43; 1/13/ 44; 2/17/44; 5/15/44; 2/13/45; 6/21/45; 1/7/46; 5/6/46; 10/24/46; 11/28/46; 4/29/47; 12/11/47; 4/8/48
HARRISON, William C. (see also, Harrison, W.C.) - 9/10/42; 10/17/46; 10/24/46
HARRISON, W. M. (see also, Harrison, William M.) - 2/4/46; 10/24/46; 2/20/47
HARRISON, William M. (see also,
HARRISON & GRAHAM)- 1/7/46
HART, E[J?].C.- 10/16/47
HART, G. W.(see also, Hart, Geo. W.)- 3/6/45; 11/23/45
HART, Geo, W. (see also, Hart, G. W.)-2/13/45; 4/1/47
HART, J. C -9/10/42; 10/1/42; 10/15/42; 11/5/42; 3/16/43;4/6/43; 4/27/43; 6/8/43; 9/28/43; 11/2/43; 11/18/43; 3/9/44; 5/1/44; 5/29/44; 6/5/44; 6/19/44; 7/3/44;9/11/44; 11/6/44; 11/13/44; 2/13/45; 3/6/45; 6/21/45; 6/28/45; 7/12/45; 11/23/45; 12/3/45;12/17/45; 1/14/46; 1/28/46; 2/11/46; 3/11/46; 8/21/47; 10/2/47; 1/29/48; 2/12/48; 3/18/48; 6/3/48; 7/22/48; 8/5/48
HART, John- 10/9/47
HART Josiah, - 2/13/47; 4/8/47

HART, Merideth - 10/9/47
HART, Wm. F. T (see also, HART, William,, W. F. T. and Dr. Hart.). - 1/14/43; 3/9/44; 5/8/44; 2/13/45; 3/27/47
HART, William (see also, Hart, Wm. M. W. F. T and Dr. Hart.)- 9/21/43; 10/21/43; 10/17/46
HART (first name not given) - 5/25/43
HART, DR.(see also, Hart, William, Wm. M, and W.F.T Hart.)-1/14/43; 10/28/43; 5/15/44
HART, Judge -7/10/47
HART & CO. - 10/23/44
HARTELL, William - 8/8/46
HARTFIELD, Asa - 10/7/43
HARTKNAPP, Chas. - 7/6/43
HARTY, Dennis - 5/13/45
HARTY, Dorothy - 5/13/45
HARVEY, E. L. -9/10/42
HARVEY, J. H.- 1/9/45
HARVEY, Louisa J. T - 2/13/47
HARVICK, Sarah - 4/6/43
HASLETT, James H.- 4/8/47
HAUGHTON, William M. S. 7/3/47
HAUSE, Vardeman - 2/13/47
HAWKER, Henry - 7/3/47
HAWKINS, B.F.-10/2/47
HAWKINS, William - 1/14/43; 1/23/45; 7/26/45;1/21/46;10/9/47
HAYDEN, John W. - 2/4/46
HAYDEN, Moses - 7/3/44

HAYES, William J (see also Wm. J. Hays)- 7/6/43
HAYGOOD, O.S.- 8/8/46
HAYGOOD, S.G. - 2/13/47
HAYMAN, John -1/21/46
HAYNES, L. C.-12/26/44
HAYNIE - 11/6/47
HAYS, Col. John C-7/3/47; 2/12/48; 2/19/48
HAYS, Thomas - 7/17/47
HAYS, Wm, J. - 7/5/45; 1/15/47
HAZELWOOD, Richard - 10/14/43
HEADER, Col. L. D. -9/28/43
HEALD , BERTHELET & CO. - 6/3/48
HEARLING, Mrs. Mary - 1/8/48
HEATH, James - 6/26/44; 7/26/45; 7/3/47
HEATH, Richard B.- 5/13/45; 7/26/45
HEATHERLY, Henry . - 4/29/48; 8/5/48
HEATHERLY, Thomas Col. - 7/24/44; 1/16/45; 1/23/45; 8/8/46
HEDGE, John H.- 1/5/47
HEDGE, Robert - 4/15/47
HEFFLEFINGER, James - 3/23/43; 12/16/43; 11/19/45
HEFFLEFINGER, (no first name given) - 4/6/43
HEFNER, Alfred - 4/3/44
HELLFINGER, James - 4/8/47
HELLMAN, C.K. - 8/8/46
HEMINGWAY, Mrs. L. J. - 10/9/47

HEMINGWAY, M.C.- 10/17/46
HEMINGWAY, R. C. - 10/10/46; 10/17/46; 1/5/47; 7/3/47; 10/9/47
HEMPHILL, S. - 7/3/44
HEMPHIL, Chief Justice - 4/20/43
HENDERMAN, M.C.- 1/23/45
HENDERSON, Alexander - 4/8/48
HENDERSON, Archibald - 1/23/45
HENDERSON, Frank - 9/21/43
HENDERSON, Gen J.P. - 12/10/42 , 11/20/44
HENDERSON, James - 12/5/44; 4/15/47; -4/8/48
HENDERSON, John - 7/3/47
HENDERSON, L.D.- 4/6/43; 12/10/45; 7/10/47; 12/25/47; 6/17/48
HENDERSON, Malinda K. - 4/3/44; 12/25/47
HENDERSON, Mary J.- 4/8/48
HENDERSON, Sarah -6/17/48
HENDERSON, T.A. -6/24/48
HENDERSON, W.F. -6/24/48
HENDERSON, William - 10/10/46; 8/7/47; 7/22/48
HENDRIX, John - 10/17/46
HENDRICK, O.- 8/7/47
HENDRICK, Sol. B - 5/13/45
HENELY, Daniel - 2/13/47
HENELY, Henry - 2/13/47
HENRY C.J.- 8/8/46

HENRY, James - 2/13/47
HENRY, John R.- 6/24/48
HENSLEY, Charles -6/3/46; 10/10/46
HENSON, Jeremiah -9/11/44
HERBERT, Capt. C. C.- 1/23/47
HERRICK, Dr. I. - 8/20/42; 3/9/43; 12/16/43; 8/28/44
HERRIN, A. - 6/3/48
HERRING, Jno. S.-6/30/47
HERRINGTON, John - 5/29/44
HERRON, John M - 2/13/47
HERVEY, Samuel B - 3/9/44
HICKERSTAFF, R.J. - 11/20/47
HICKEY, M. B.- 4/15/47
HICKEY, W.W.-10/10/46; 10/2/47
HICKLIN, Barnet - 6/29/43
HICKLIN, Martha - 10/9/47
HIGH, Peter -6/24/48
HIGHSMITH, Capt. S. 1/15/48; -7/1/48
HIGHTOWER, Charnell - 4/8/48
HIGHTOWER, John -10/2/47
HIGHTOWER, T. P. - 4/8/47; 11/27/47
HILBURN, C.E. - 11/6/44
HILL, Aaron - 10/17/46
HILL, Abner - 7/3/47
HILL, Barnard - 4/6/43; 7/15/46; 7/3/47; 4/8/48
HILL, Elizabeth Mrs.- 1/23/45
HILL, Ephraim - 7/3/47; 1/8/48

HILL, H. B.-11/19/45
Hill, J. B. (see also Hill, Joshua B) -9/3/42
HILL John -8/28/44
HILL, Joshua B. (see also HILL, J. B)--11/19/45
HILL, Marinda -1/8/48
HILL, Mrs. Sarah E. -- 7/6/43
HILL, W. P. - 6/22/47
HILL (first name not given) 11/20/44
HILLBURN, Francis M.- 6/30/47
HILLIS , S. W. (see also Hillis, Samuel and Sam W) 6/19/44
HILLIS, John M. -1/8/48
HILLIS, Sam W. (see also Hillis, Samuel and S.W.) - 11/6/44
HILLIS, Samuel (see also Hillis, Sam W. and S.W.) - 8/2/45;11/23/45; 1/21/46; 10/10/46
HINES, R.E.- 6/7/45; 6/14/45; 8/9/45
HINSTON, A. L - 1/14/43
HITL, Thomas - 7/3/47
HITZBUGH, William - 2/13/47
HOBBS, J. C. -1/8/48
HOBBS, Rev. J.W.-3/27/47
HOBBS, Jonathan T. - 1/14/43
HOBBS, Mary - 5/29/44; 10/2/44
HOBBS, P. W. -4/22/47
HOBBS, Preston W.-

11/19/45
HOBBS, Thomas - 2/13/47
HOBBS, William -4/8/48
HOCKER, Henry C.- 5/30/45; 6/28/45; 11/23/45; 1/21/46
HODGE, A.M. (see also Hodge, Alexander) 1/13/44; 5/29/44; 7/12/45
HODGE, Alexander - 3/2/43;12/24/45; 10/17/46; 2/27/47
HODGES, J. S.- 10/17/46
HODGES, Robert - 7/3/47
HODGES, Mrs. Sally Ann - 2/13/47
HODGES, William - 7/3/47
HOGAN, G.M.- 1/23/45
HOGAN, Woodson - 7/15/48
HOGUE, James - 10/9/47
HOKE, A. N - 5/29/44
HOLBROOK, R. J.- 7/12/45; 8/2/45; 1/28/46; 2/11/46
HOLBROOK & ROMAN - 7/15/48
HOLCOMB, Frank S.- 1/28/43
HOLCOMB, Louis - 7/27/43
HOLCOMBS, A.F.- 8/8/46
HOLDERY, G. W. - 2/13/47
HOLEMAN, Cyrus - 4/3/44
HOLLARD, Andrew J. - 7/3/47
HOLLIS, Joseph - 7/17/47
HOLLOWAY, Barnes - 10/29/42
HOLLOWAY, James -2/6/45
HOLLOWAY, Jane - 10/29/42
HOLLOWAY, Mrs. June [John, Jane?]-1/21/46;

8/8/46
HOLLOWAY, William - 8/8/46
HOLMAN, Cyrus - 6/9/47; 7/1/48
HOLMES & RUSSEL - 3/6/47
HOLMES, Hardy B. - 10/9/47
HOLT, T.C.- 4/15/47
HOMER, Robert - 5/29/44
HOMER, Dr.- 5/13/46
HOMES ,James - 1/5/47
HOOKER, Samuel - 10/15/42; 4/8/48
HOOKER, William - 10/17/46
HOPKINS, A.N.- 4/6/43; 11/2/43; 4/17/44; 5/29/44; 10/2/44
HOPKINS, David -10/10/46
HOPKINS, E.- 10/9/47; 6/3/48
HOPKINS, Eldridge - 4/17/44; 10/17/46; 10/16/47; 12/11/47; 6/3/48
HOPKINS Henry -4/17/44
HOPKINS Iss. E. - 7/6/43
HOPKINS, Capt J. E. - 9/21/43; 8/7/47; 12/11/47
HOPKINS, James - 9/25/47; 7/29/48
HOPKINS, John - 6/3/48
HOPKINS, L - 10/1/42
HOPKINS, R. - 10/15/42; 11/5/42; 9/21/43; 2/6/45; 7/26/45; 12/10/45; 1/7/46; 2/11/46;
HOPKINS, R. M.- 3/6/47; 7/22/48

HOPKINS, Richard -
10/10/46; 10/30/47
HOPKINS,S.M. - 1/5/47;
HOPPES, M. Charles -
2/13/47
HORG, E. H.- 1/23/45
HORN, Benny - 5/29/44
HORN, William - 10/9/47
HORNBACK, George -4/8/48
HORTON, William - 4/15/47
HOUNSKELL, Joseph- 4/6/43
HOUSE, L.W. -10/2/47
HOUSE, Littleton W. -
6/10/48
HOUSTON, Maarmakuke T. -
7/6/43
HOUSTON, Robert - 7/15/48
HOUSTON, Sam - 12/26/44
HOUSTON, W.B.- 10/17/46
HOWARD, Christopher -
7/3/47
HOWARD, David - 5/29/44
HOWARD, Wm. C - 5/29/44
HOWE, A. J. - 2/13/47
HOWE, Capt.-7/3/47; 7/3/47
HOWLING, Joel W.- 6/3/46
HOY, DR. A.B.- 6/16/47;
10/9/47; 4/8/48
HOYMAN, John - 1/9/45
HUBARD, Fulbright - 7/3/47
HUBARD, Mr.- 7/3/47
HUBBARD, Thomas -
2/13/47
HUBBARD, Walter G.-
1/14/46
HUDLY, Thomas Capt.-
7/27/43
HUDRIC, H.G. - 2/13/47
HUDSON, A.B. - 7/6/43

HUDSON, John Hill -1/8/48
HUDSON, Jno. H.-4/8/48
HUDSON, Joshua -4/1/48
HUDSON, R.Q. -6/10/48
HUDSON, Mrs. Sally -
4/15/47
HUDSON, Sarah J. -1/8/48
HUDSON, Wiley - 10/17/46
HUDSON, William -10/9/44;
1/8/48
HUEY, E.G. - 7/17/47
HUFFER, Samuel - 8/20/42;
7/24/44; 8/7/44; 8/21/44;
8/28/44; 10/9/44; 11/19/45
HUGHART, E.D. (see also
Hughart, Edward)- 4/9/44
HUGHART, Edward -
4/24/44; 10/23/44;
12/19/44; 10/9/47
HUGHES, Isaac - 4/17/44;
5/13/45
HUGHES ,James - 2/6/47
HUGHES, Joel - 8/9/45
HUGHES, Moses M. -2/6/47
HUGHES, Robert - 7/6/43;
7/26/45
HUGHES, Simon P.- 2/3/44
HUGHES, Vade -5/25/43
HUGHES, William -
10/15/42; 1/14/43; 7/31/44
HULL, Dr.- 8/29/46
HULME, A. L. - 4/29/48
HULM[E?], Alfred L-
10/9/47; 12/11/47
HUMPHREYS, John -8/8/46;
7/17/47; 7/1/48
HUMPHRIES, William -
8/20/42; 5/11/43; 7/20/43;
1/13/ 44; 7/31/44; 5/30/45;

8/2/45; 11/23/45; 1/21/46;
6/9/47; 7/17/47; 10/16/47;
2/12/48; 7/1/48
HUMPHRIES, (first name not given) - 8/19/48
HUNDENWICK, W.- 5/29/44
HUNT, Mrs. Ann - 4/15/47
HUNT, Green T.- 4/15/47
HUNT, John -7/15/46
HUNT, William - 9/5/46; 10/17/46; 4/8/47
HUNT, first name not given 1/30/47
HUNT & BLACK - 10/9/47
HUNTER, A. J. - 6/10/48
HUPPER, Langhouse - 7/15/46
HUSBANDS & BUCHANAN - 7/15/48
HUTCHINSON, N.B.-6/30/47

I

INGLES, Oliver -7/1/48
INGLISH, Bailey - 10/7/43
INGLISH, Campbell - 7/3/44
INGLIS AND VAN WYCK. - endnote 1
INGRAHAM, Wm. C. (see also Ingram, W. C.)- 5/29/44
INGRAM, M - 7/15/48
INGRAM, W. - 7/15/48
INGRAM, W. C. (see also Ingraham, Wm. C.)--9/17/42
IRBY, Edward- 3/2/43
IRION, William S. - 10/9/47
IRVINE, M. A. - 8/8/46
ISAAC, runaway slave -

9/24/42; 2/20/45
IVES ,Rev. -7/31/47

J

JACK, P.C.- 6/5/44
JACK, Wm. H.- 9/11/44; 9/11/44
JACK, Col.- 10/23/47
JACKSON, Americe - 11/26/42
JACKSON, Calvin - 10/9/47; 1/8/48
JACKSON, Charles - 7/6/43; 5/29/44; 10/2/44; 5/13/45; 5/13/46
JACKSON, D.C. - 5/29/44
JACKSON, Daniel R - 8/27/42
JACKSON, E.T.- 10/17/46
JACKSON, Edmund - 10/15/42
JACKSON, G. B - 10/9/47
JACKSON, Isaac N. - 3/25/46
JACKSON, James - 7/26/45
JACKSON, John -9/3/42
JACKSON, Rachael - 9/3/42
JACKSON, Samuel -10/10/46
JACKSON, Sarah M. -1/8/48
JACKSON, Slocomb - 7/6/43
JACKSON, T. H.- 7/26/45
JACKSON, Thomas - 9/3/42
JACOBES, Harry - 10/9/47
JACOBS, John - 0/17/46; 6/9/47
JACOBS, Samuel - 10/10/46
JACOBS, William - 4/15/47
JAMES, Henry - 10/15/42

JAMES, Jarret - 6/15/43
JAMES, Col L. M -1/8/48
JAMES, W.- 1/23/45
JAMES, Wm.- 5/29/44
JAMISON, D .K - 2/4/43;10/2/47
JANES, Charles - 8/20/42
JANES, H.S.(see also, Janes, Henry S.) - 7/5/45
JANES, Henry S. (see also, Janes, H. S.) - 9/25/44; 12/12/44
JANES, Jesse - 8/20/42
JANES, M. H (see also, Janes, Massack H.) 9/25/44
JANES, Massack H. (see also, Janes, M. H.) -6/15/43; 12/12/44
JARANTA, Padre - 2/19/48
JARMAN, Robert F -1/8/48
JASON, Whitney - 2/23-43
JEFF, a Negro man -11/20/44
JEFFERIES, Benjamin J - 7/15/46
JEFFERS, J. J.- 4/17/44
JEFFERS, James - 10/17/46
JEFFERSON. P.- 2/6/45
JEFFRIES, James R.- 10/17/46
JEFFUS, Samuel - 6/28/45
JENINGS James - 6/3/46, 7/1/46
JENKINS, Charles - 7/15/48
JENNINGS, James H. 2/13/47; 4/8/48
JENNINGS, John - 2/13/47
JENNINGS -(first name not given)--11/20/44
JERNEGAN, Curtis –1/28/43

JESSE,(slave) -12/19/46
JEWELL, Capt George W.- 6/24/48
JEWETT, H. J. - 8/12/48
JEWETT, J. G. (see also Jewett, John G.)- 10/29/42
JEWETT, John G. (see also Jewett, J.G)-9/24/42
JITT, William - 2/13/47
JOE, Slave- 7/27/43
JOHN, Slave - 6/30/47
JOHNS, C R -12/10/42; 12/3/42; 4/6/43; 5/25/43; 2/6/45; 5/13/45; 8/8/46; 7/3/47
JOHNS, Clem R. - 10/9/47
JOHNS, J.G.- 5/13/45
JOHNS, S.B. - 7/24/44; 7/5/45
JOHNSON, A. J.. - 1/23/47
JOHNSON, Miss A.S. (see also Johnson, Alexander S.) - 7/20/43;11/11/43; 12/3/45; 10/17/46
JOHNSON, Alexander S. (see also Johnson, A. S). - 6/14/45
JOHNSON, Mrs. Amanda – 4/8/48;7/15/48
JOHNSON, B.-5/13/45
JOHNSON, B. W.- 8/8/46
JOHNSON, Benjamin - 5/6/46
JOHNSON, Clarissima - 4/15/47
JOHNSON , Cyrus - 10/2/44
JOHNSON, E.- 7/3/44
JOHNSON, E.M. - 10/29/42; 7/3/44

JOHNSON, Enoch S.-
10/10/46
JOHNSON, Enos B - 4/8/48
JOHNSON, G. C.- 8/14/44
JOHNSON, Harris - 6/28/45
JOHNSON, Isaac H.- 5/29/44
JOHNSON, J. F. - 6/21/45;
5/27/46; 6/10/46; 1/23/47;
1/8/48
JOHNSON, J. S.- 1/28/43
JOHNSON, James - 6/15/43;
1/28/43
JOHNSON, James A. [H?]-
6/24/48
JOHNSON, James. H. (see
also Johnson, James) -
9/10/42; 9/24/42; 2/4/43;
5/11/43; 6/8/43; 5/15/44;
6/19/44; 6/26/44; 10/30/44;
1/23/45; 2/6/45; 1/5/47;
1/23/47; 3/6/47
JOHNSTON, James S.-
11/28/46
JOHNSON, John - 7/26/45;
11/19/45; 1/14/46
JOHNSON, John S. - 2/13/47
JOHNSON, John W. - 7/3/47
JOHNSON, Jonathan -
7/3/47
JOHNSON, Joshua F -
2/27/47; 4/8/48
JOHNSON, Brig. Gen.
Lindlay - 12/2/43; 6/28/45
JOHNSON, Lucius - 7/27/43
JOHNSON, Capt. M.T. -
1/15/48
JOHNSON, Martin - 3/2/43
JOHNSON, Miss Mary Annie
7/3/47

JOHNSON, Moses W.-
10/9/47
JOHNSON, Nancy - 5/29/44
JOHNSON, Nathan - 2/13/47
JOHNSON P. B - 1/28/43
JOHNSON, P. H. [B.?]-
4/8/48
JOHNSON, Peter - 5/13/45;
6/3/46; 6/17/46; 4/8/48
JOHNSON, Peter B. 7/15/48
JOHNSON, Riley - 1/23/45
JOHNSON, Samuel - 10/9/47
JOHNSON, Mrs. Sarah -
10/9/47
JOHNSON, Thomas -6/24/48
JOHNSON, W. - 7/10/44
JOHNSON, W. H. - 3/11/48
JOHNSON, W. R.- 10/17/46
JOHNSON, Wm. - 6/15/43;
9/28/43; 10/14/43; 5/1/44;
8/7/44
JOHNSON, William P.-
2/13/47
JOHNSON, William H.-
10/16/47
JOHNSTON, Wm. S.- 8/14/47
JOHNSON (first name not
given) - 5/13/45
JOHNSON, Capt.-7/1/48
JOHNSON & AIK - 5/6/46
JOHNSON & GRAY -
3/11/48
JOHNSON'S Southern
Minstrels - 7
JOLLEY, James - 11/19/45
JONAKIN, Malinda - 7/26/45
JONES, A. E.- 7/3/44
JONES, A. J. - 7/17/47
JONES, Alfred H .- 4/15/47

JONES, Isaac N. - 7/1/46
JONES, Jacob B - 4/15/47
JONES, James - 2/13/47
JONES, James C - 10/9/47
JONES, James L. - 10/9/47
JONES, Jesse - 11/4/43
JONES, John - 2/23/43; 2/13/47
JONES, John H. B. [W.?]. 2/13/47
JONES, Miss Kasiah - 7/17/47
JONES, Lodida - 4/8/48
JONES, M. W.- 7/1/46
JONES, Miss Mary -7/3/47; 10/9/47
JONES, Col. R. M.- 5/25/43; 12/12/46; 5/19/47
JONES, Gen. T. W.- 1/14/46
JONES, Theodore - 2/13/47
JONES, Thomas - 10/9/47
JONES, Wesley - 4/8/48
JONES, William - 4/8/48
JONES, William E.- 6/15/44; 1/21/46
JONES, William M - 2/13/47
JORDAN Alfred M. - 9/25/47; 10/9/47
JORDAN, Curtis -12/24/46; 10/2/47
JORDAN, Ellennor - 5/8/44
JORDAN, John - 7/3/44
JORDAN, Levi [see also Jourdan] - 5/25/43, 5/8/44
JORDAN, Thomas - 10/9/44;10/2/47
JORDAN, William L. - 7/15/46; 10/10/46
JOSEPH HARRISON & CO. - 8/20/42; 2/4/43
JOUETT, J. G. (see also Jouett, John G.)- 1/28/43
JOUETT, John G. (see also Jouett, J.G.)- 2/23/43; 3/2/43; 12/3/45
JOUETT, Thomas - 2/23-43
JOURDAN,[Jordan?] Levi - 12/5/44
JOURNEY, Nathaniel T.- 12/10/42
JOY, George - 5/13/46
JULIEN, James - 7/26/45

K

KARBER, Peter - 4/15/47
KARBER, (first name not given) - 3/6/45
KARNER, John - 6/24/48
KAUFMAN, David S.- 7/12/45; 1/14/46; 3/25/46; 10/17/46; 6/22/47; 7/10/47; 6/3/48
KEAN, John - 2/13/47
KEAR, James - 5/29/44
KEASEY, Dr. Stephen - 7/3/47
KEATHERLY, James - 7/6/43
KEEN, J. W.- 2/13/47
KEEN, William - 4/15/47
KEEN, Miss - 2/13/47
KEENER, A.V.-5/19/47
KEETH, Gabriel - 7/6/43
KEITH, A.- 1/5/47
KEITH, Abijah - 10/9/47
KEITH, M.- 7/1/46
KEITH, Stephen - 11/23/45

KEITH, Wm. S. - 10/7/43; 7/3/47
KELLAM, JAMES W.- 7/3/47
KELLER, MITCHELL - 6/26/44; 10/30/44
KELLEY, MRS. SUZANNE - 7/15/48
KELLY, HENRY. - 1/23/47
KELLY, Jesse - 11/2/43
KELLY, Mrs Martha - 10/9/47
KELSEY, H.B - 12/10/42
KELVEY, Rev. H.B.- 7/3/47
KENDALL, Ann Morlab - 12/17/45
KENDALL, James - 12/17/45
KENDELL, Benjamin - 10/15/42
KENDELL, Joseph - 10/15/42
KENDRIX, Martha - 5/29/44
KENNEDY George - 6/16/47
KENNER, Nancy - 8/20/42
KERLEY, Wm. G. - 10/30/44
KETCHIN, Gabriel - 7/5/45
KEY, David P - 5/4/43
KEYS, WILLIAM - 10/17/46,
KILBRETH, REV. JAMES - 7/3/47
KIMBELL, A.G.(see also Kimbell, Albert G)- 8/27/42; 9/3/42; 1/28/43; 6/15/43; 6/19/44
KIMBELL, Albert G.(see also Kimbell, A. G) - 12/24/45; 2/27/47
KIMBELL, John -10/9/44; 6/14/45

KIMBELL, William H.- 6/30/47
KIMBELL, Wm. M.- 7/17/47
KIMBLE, J. M. - 6/24/48
KIMBLE, John [see Kimbell] 4/3/44; 11/19/45
KINCAIDE, George N.- 1/14/43
KINCHELO William - 2/20/45
KINEY, James - 1/28/43
KING, A.W. - 5/11/43; 1/9/45; 3/18/46; 12/25/47; 2/12/48
KING, Amelia -1/8/48
KING, Anderson - 1/8/48
KING, Armstead - 4/8/48
KING, August - 8/12/48; 8/19/48
KING, Elijah - 4/8/48
KING, Miss Eliza Ann - 7/15/48
KING, Elizabeth - 1/14/43
KING, I.. - 8/19/48
KING, Isaiah - 7/22/48
KING, Jas. - 7/6/43; 2/13/47; 10/9/47
KING, James H. - 11/11/43; 11/20/44; 7/15/46; 1/8/48
KING, JOHN - 5/29/44; 7/15/46
KING, L.S.- 7/3/44
KING, Lewis T. - 9/10/42
KING, Miss Margaret - 2/13/47
KING, Nathaniel - 5/29/44
KING, O.H.- 5/11/43; 4/17/44
KING, Permella -1/8/48

KING, W. - 4/8/48
KING, Wm.- 2/13/45; 2/13/47
KING, William W. -1/8/48
KING, YOUNG - 4/8/48
KING (first name not given)- 2/4/43; 11/6/47
KINGS, Daniel - 7/12/45
KINGSBURY, Rev. Cyrus - 1/13/ 44
Kinnar, Nancy - 7/6/43
KINNEY, James - 5/13/45
KINNEY, Stephen - 2/6/45; 4/22/47; 10/9/47
KINZEY [IE], Dr. Stephen - 8/20/42; 10/29/42; 4/13/43; 7/6/43;4/3/44; 7/3/44; 7/26/45
KITCHENS, Pharough - 2/13/45
KITEREL, John - 4/20/43
KLINE [Klein], Charles F.D.- 1/23/45, 1/14/46; 7/15/46; 10/10/46
KNIGHT, M.M. - 6/3/48
KNIGHT, WILLIAM - 10/9/47; 10/16/47; 6/10/48
KNIGHT, Mr.- 10/23/47
KNOZ, William -2/13/47
KOHN & RHINE - 8/29/46
KORN, D .R.- 6/19/44
KUSTER, Washington - 4/3/44
KUYKENDALL, John - 4/8/47
KUYKENDALL, Sarah - 12/5/44

L

L. W. PERRY & CO - 2/13/45; 7/1/48
LABOOU, Peter -1/8/48
LACEY, Jacob J - 7/15/48
LACEY, Wm. Y - 8/20/42
LACY, Grayner S.-1/8/48
LACY, H.E. K. - 4/22/47
LADY, Milton W. - 2/13/47
LAHEY, William - 4/8/48; 7/15/48
LAKE, Jacob - 10/16/47
LAKIN, Samuel L. -11/11/43
LAMAR, Edmund - 1/23/45
LAMAR, M. B. - 1/15/48
LAMAR, Rebecca Ann - 9/14/43
LAMAR, Samuel - 5/13/45
LAMAR, Capt.-7/1/48
LAMAR, General - 10/30/47
LAMB, John C. - 12/24/45
LANCASTER, Joseph - 7/17/47
LANDRUM, J. - 2/13/47
LANDRUM, John. - 3/11/48
LANE, David - 2/13/47
LANE, George - 6/22/47
LANE, J. W.- 1/5/47
LANEY, George - 10/9/47
LANGFORD, E. N. (see also Langsford, Eli or Elinor) - 10/9/44
LANGFORD, Eli (see also Langsford, E..N.) - 7/6/43; 10/10/46
LANGFORD, Elinor (see also Langsford, Eli or E. N.) - 8/27/42

LANGFORD, M. H. - 2/13/47
LANGFORD, Rosetta - 4/3/44; 6/26/44
LANGHORN, H.M. - 4/8/48
LANGLEY, SAMUEL- 10/10/46; 7/3/47
LANIER, A.S. - 10/9/47
LANIER, Archer B.- 7/6/43
LARRENCE, James - 2/13/47
LARY, Henry J. - 10/28/43
LASSON, Abay - 7/3/47
LATIMER, H. R.- 8/20/42; 4/6/43; 5/11/43; 6/7/45; 8/9/45; 4/29/48; 8/5/48
LATIMER, A.H.- 1/14/43; 4/27/43; 6/29/43; 7/6/43; 8/9/45; 4/22/47; 12/11/47
LATIMER, A. J. - 7/22/48
LATIMER, Ann - 8/16/45
LATIMER, Isabella De Morse -endnote 1
LATIMER, J. -1/8/48
LATIMER, J. W. -11/23/45; 1/14/46; 6/22/47; 7/1/48; 8/5/48
LATIMER, James - 12/10/42; 2/17/44; 5/30/45; 6/7/45; 8/16/45; 7/22/48
LATIMER, Mary - 8/16/45
LATIMER, Judge - 3/27/47
LATIMER, Master (first name not given)--6/15/43; 6/22/43
LATIMER, (first name not given)- 10/15/42
LATIMER, BAGBY & CO - 5/8/44; 2/6/45
LATIMER & JOHNSON - 12/24/42

LATIMER, MURRAY & - 7/1/48
LATTA, R.H. - 7/17/47
LAURENCE, Mrs. - W.2/13/47
LAWDEN, Malinda - 10/2/44
LAWES, Roseanne - 8/20/42
LAWLER, James E. - 10/10/46
LAWRANCE, McD.- 7/3/44
LAWRENCE, Alexander - 4/8/48
LAWRENCE, D.H.- 1/23/45
LAWRENCE, O. W.- 1/23/45
LAWRENCE, William - 1/14/43; 3/4/48;4/8/48;
LAWS, George S. - 1/8/48
LAWS, John - 4/8/48
LAWSON, J.D.- 4/8/48; 7/15/48
LAWTON, GEORGE. - 10/15/42;2/ 24/44; 10/2/44; 3/20/44; 5/29/44; 8/16/45; 2/4/46; 3/11/46; 6/3/46; 6/17/46; 8/8/46; 12/5/46; 12/19/46; 12/24/46 ;1/5/47; 2/6/47; 2/27/47; 3/27/47; 6/22/47; 6/30/47; 7/17/47; 8/14/47; 12/11/47; 2/19/48; 3/4/48; 3/11/48; 4/1/48; 4/8/48; 8/12/48; 8/19/48
LAWTON, I. D.- 11/4/43
LAWTON, Isaiah - 10/1/42; 10/15/42
LAWTON (no first name given) - 12/16/43
LEACH, Marcus - 5/29/44
LEAHY, William. - 3/11/48
LEAL, Charles - 10/10/46

LEDBETTER, Jas. - 10/2/44
LEE, Abner - 7/3/44
LEE, Andrew - 9/10/42
LEE, Charles - 2/13/47
LEE, Daniel W .- 6/3/46
LEE, E. W.- 1/28/43
LEE, J. T (see-also Lee, James. Thos) - 7/5/45; 1/14/46
LEE Jacob - 10/17/46
LEE, James - 7/3/47; 10/9/47
LEE, James. Thos (see-also Lee, J. T.) -6/15/43; 6/22/43; 10/7/43; 12/9/43; 2/17/44; 10/9/44; 2/27/45; 3/13/45
LEE, John - 2/13/47
LEE, Peter - 2/13/47
Lee, R.W. (see-also Lee, Roswell, W.T.) - 8/27/42; 10/15/42; 5/13/45; 3/18/46; 6/3/46
Lee, Robert - 2/13/47
LEE, Roswell W. (see-also Lee, R.. W.) . - 3/2/43
LEE, Sussanah - 5/13/46
LEE, Terrence - 6/8/43
LEE, Thos. D. - 1/16/45; 2/6/45; 2/27/45; 3/6/45; 3/13/45; 7/5/45; 1/14/46; 10/17/46
LEE, William - 7/15/48
LEE, Mrs.-5
LEECH, Evander - 12/24/46; 1/5/47
LEGWOOD, Thomas Y. - 10/15.42
LEIGH, W.A. - 8/12/48

LEMMON C.- 10/17/46
LENON, Wm - 4/3/44
LENOX, Wm.- 5/29/44
LEONARD, Elizabeth - 2/13/47
LERNAY, D.- 7/3/44
LEVEN (no first name given)- 3/6/45
LEVINS, Nicholas - 7/15/48
LEWELLING, Thomas- 10/10/46
LEWIS, C. - 6/3/48
LEWIS, Charles Col. - 10/15/42; 1/13/ 44; 7/24/44; 1/16/45; 5/13/45; 1/21/46;12/11/47
LEWIS, Dixon H -7/1/48
LEWIS, Frances - 11/19/45
LEWIS, Granville - 6/22/47; 7/22/48
LEWIS, John S. - 10/9/47
LEWIS, Capt. Mark B.- 9/21/43
LEWIS O. - 10/16/47; 1/15/48
LEWIS, Reuben - 2/13/47
LEWIS, Samuel - 7/3/47
LEWIS, W. W. - 10/22/42
LEWIS, William C. - 2/13/47; 4/8/48
LEWIS, Slave - 5/25/43; 10/7/43
LIHA, William - 7/3/47
LILLEY, Hugh B - 1/14/43
LILLY, Noah - 8/21/44
LINCICUM, Grant - 7/24/44
LINDLEY, Jacob - 4/15/47
LINDSAY, Mrs. E.M.- 1/21/46

LINK, J. J.- 4/8/48
LINN, B. F. - 5/11/43; 4/3/44
LINN, Judge - 7/26/45
LITTLE, Henry - 2/4/46; 10/24/46; 2/20/47;
LITTLE, John - 5/4/43
LITTLEPAGE, Ellis. - 3/11/48
LIVELY, Anderson - 2/13/47
LIVINGSTON, Charles - 8/7/47
LLOYD, Richard - 2/13/47
LOCK, James -1/8/48
LOCK, John - 2/13/47
LOCK, Richard -3/2/43; 4/8/48
LOCKE, John - 5/13/46
LOCKETT, Richard R.- 1/14/46
LOCKHART, P. -4/3/44
LOCKS, Miss Sussanah. - 2/6/47
LODGE, Constantine - 5/13/46
LOGAN, Bennet T - 4/8/47
LOGAN, Charles - 9/3/42, 5/4/43
LOGAN, J. O. - 6/10/48
LOGAN, James - 8/28/44
LOGAN, Matthew T. - 5/1/44
LOGWOOD, Thomas Y.- 2/20/45; 6/14/45
LONG, Ben - 9/21/43
LONG, J.(see also Long, Jacob or James)- 5/15/44; 2/6/45; .2/13/45; 12/24/45; 8/8/46; 11/28/46; 3/25/48
LONG, Jacob (see also Long, J.) - 10/7/43; 2/6/45; 6/14/45; 2/27/47
LONG, James - 4/15/47
LONG, Tobias - 4/15/47
LONG, John E. - 6/16/47
LONG, William R.- 4/15/47
LONGWISH, Rubie - 10/10/46
LOOK, Dr. E. S.- 3/9/43; 1/13/ 44; 12/5/44; 2/6/45; 3/13/45; 6/21/45; 7/5/45; 6/17/46; 11/28/46; 1/5/47; 2/20/47; 3/20/47; -3/27/47; 4/1/47; 6/16/47; 8/7/47;
LOOK, Marinda, - 6/21/45
LOOK & GRIFFITH - 1/7/46
LOOK & HALL -1/13/ 44; 8/28/44
LOOK & PETERS - 3/6/47
LOONEY, M. - 1/9/45; 3/6/45
LOONEY, William -1/21/46
LOONY, Joseph - 2/19/48
LOOP, John - 5/13/45;1/23/47;4/29/48; 7/22/48
LOOP[K?], Dr.- 4/8/48
LORING, John - 9/21/43; 4/9/44; 5/29/44; 1/9/45; 1/30/45; 5/31/45; 7/12/45
LORING, Mary E.- 4/8/48
LORINGS, Jno - 10/16/47
LOSSON, Abey - 5/13/46
LOTT, John -12/10/42
LOUGHBOROUGH, P.S. - 12/24/45
LOVE, James Col. - 10/29/42

LOVE, Thomas - 8/8/46
LOVEJOY, J .S. - 2/23/43
LOVEJOY, Rev. John L - 11/5/42; 6/15/43; 10/17/46; 12/12/46; 4/8/47; endnote 9
LOVEJOY, L .J.- 4/17/44
LOVING, J.D. - 1/8/48
LOVING, James - 5/29/44
LOVING, John B - 6/21/45
LOVING, Oliver - 5/29/44
LOWDEN, Thomas - 11/19/45; 7/3/47
LOWE, Manson - 2/13/47
LOWELL. Joseph - 10/15/42
LOWHON, Hugh, M.- 10/10/46
LUCAS, George F. - 2/13/47
LUCKEY -6/10/48
LUCKY - 6/3/48
LUCK[E]Y, Hugh - 5/29/44; 1/14/46; 5/6/46
LUCY, R. J.- 1/14/46
LUDLOW, J. R.- 1/28/43
LUDWIG, J. F.- 10/17/46
LUNN, William - 5/13/45
LUPTON, Jonathan W. - 12/24/42
LUPTON, Joseph - 10/9/44; 11/19/45
LYDAY, A.- 10/9/44
LYDAY, Andrew - 2/13/47
LYDAY, Jacob - 8/5/48
LYDAY, Joseph - 3/9/44; 1/23/45
LYNCH, Rebecca - 6/19/44
LYNCH, James - 2/13/47; 10/9/47
LYNCH, Joab - 6/19/44, 1/14/46

LYNCH, P. - 6/3/46; 7/1/46
LYNN, Benj. F.- 7/6/43; 7/3/44; 1/23/45; 11/23/45
LYNN, B.F.- 7/3/47
LYNN, Joseph - 10/9/47
LYON, Miss Maria T.S. - 7/3/47
LYON, William - 7/3/47

M

M'FARLAND, Jackson - 11/23/45
M'GOWEN, S.K. - 2/13/47
M'MAHON, TROTTER & PEARSALL - 1/13/ 44
MABAN [E?], J. A.- 4/15/47
MABANE, Alexander -9; 12/10/42; 1/13/ 44; 7/12/45; 11/12/45; 12/24/45; 2/27/47; 4/22/47; 12/11/47
MABANE, Geo - 4/17/44; 10/30/44
MABANE, J .H. - 9/3/42
MABANE, John B.- 6/22/47
MABANE, Joseph M. - 12/11/47
MABANE, Robert W. - 12/11/47
MABANE (first name not given) - 2/4/43MABBIT, William –endnote 3
MACGUIRE, (first name not given)-5/19/47
MACLEASH, J - 7/15/48
MADDEN, Robert -1/14/43
MADDIN, R.W. - 3/20/44
MADDOX, N. -11/ 26/42

MAFFETT, John - 7/3/47
MAGEE, Joel W. - 6/9/47
MAGRY, R.P.- 5/29/44
MAHLIN, J.G. -9/10/42
MAIN, John - 4/3/44;7/15/48
MAINOR, J.- 5/29/44
MAJORS, Eveline S.- 4/6/43
MAJORS, John P.- 10/17/46
MALONE, John P. - 7/17/47
MANION, A.B. - 3/2/43; 5/29/44; 5/31/45
MANION, N. B.V.- 12/18/47
MANLEY, Moore G. - 7/3/44
MANLEY, Mrs. S.F.- 7/3/44
MANN, Col. M.V.- 8/7/47
MANSON, Andrew - 9/21/43
MANZE, W.H. - 7/1/46
MARAN, Wm. H.- 5/29/44
MAREN, John - 7/15/48
MARER, John P. - 7/17/47
MARKS, Morgan - 11/28/46; 12/19/46
MARLER, H.- 5/29/44; 4/15/47
MARLER, W.S.- 1/23/45
MARMUTH, Matilda - 10/2/44
MARROW, W. H. - 8/21/44
MARRS, , Jeremiah - 2/13/47
MARS, J. R. - 2/13/47
MARS, James H. - 2/13/47
MARS, , Samuel W. - 2/13/47
MARSHALL, J. G.- 10/10/46
MARSHALL, Stephen - 4/15/47; 7/3/47

MARSHALL, William - 6/10/46; 4/8/48
MARTIN, B[ennet]. H. - 8/20/42; 11/26/42; 12/10/42; 3/23/43; 7/6/43; 7/20/43; 9/28/43; 1/13/ 44; 2/17/44; 4/17/44; 5/29/44; 1/16/45; 5/13/45; 11/23/45; 2/4/46; 10/24/46; 2/20/47; 4/22/47; 6/22/47; 12/18/47; 1/15/48
MARTIN, Clark -11/20/44
MARTIN, Gabriel N.- 2/4/43; 12/12/44
MARTIN, Hardy - 7/3/44
MARTIN, Kiziah - 1/14/43; 2/27/47
MARTIN, J. R. - 6/10/46
MARTIN, J.W. - 10/9/47
MARTIN, John B. - 2/13/47
MARTIN, Joseph -7/15/46
MARTIN, M.C.- 6/30/47
MARTIN, Mary Jane - 12/18/47
MARTIN, Dr. Matthew M. - 11/19/45
MARTIN, Matthew W.- 4/15/47; 4/29/48
MARTIN, Thomas - 1/14/43; 10/10/46; 2/27/47; 4/15/47
MARTIN, W.C - 10/9/47
MARTIN, William C.- 10/7/43; 10/28/43; 5/13/45; 1/14/46; 5/29/44; 7/15/48
MARTIN, Dr.- 1/15/48
MARTIN, EPPERSON AND LEWIS - 1/15/48
MARY - 6/3/48
MASH, Seaving - 10/7/43

MASON, G.B. - 6/10/48
MASON, George, - 10/9/47
MASON H.- 1/5/47;
MASON, H. D.- 12/3/42;
2/3/44; 12/12/46
MASON, Henry D. -
10/10/46
MASON, PATSY - 12/10/42
MATHER, JOSEPH - 1/14/46;
5/12/47; 7/1/46; 7/3/47
MATHER & STATS -
1/23/45; 10/9/47
MATHERS, James -1/23/45;
7/3/47
MATHEWS, Mrs. Ann 7/3/47
MATHEWS, Elbert - 3/9/44
MATHEWS, Isaac - 8/20/42
MATHEWS, James - 3/6/45
MATHEWS, Joseph -10/7/43;
11/19/45
MATHEWS, Dr. Mansel W.
10/15/42, 7/6/43, 10/7/43;
4/17/44 9/11/44; 11/12/45;
12/24/45;7/3/47
MATHEWS, R. L. -11/23/45,
1/21/46
MATHEWS, Robert E--
7/20/43
MATHEWS, Wm.--10/9/44
MATHIS, Daniel - 4/15/47
MATHIS, J. S.-4/8/48
MATHIS, R.W. - 3/11/48;
4/8/48
MATHIS, S. B.- 4/8/48
MATHIS, W.R. - 7/15/48
MATLOCK, Gideon C -
10/17/46
MATTHEWS, D.S.R.-3/27/47
MATTHEWS, David R.-
10/10/46
MATTHEWS, John -1/8/48
MATTHEWS M. W -
10/10/46
MATTHEWS [see also
Mathews], Mansell W. -
2/27/47
MATTHEWS, Richard H.-
10/10/46
MATTHEWSON, Robert -
2/13/47
MATTHIESON & COLES -
1/23/45
MATTHIESON, U.- 1/23/45
MATTHIESSEN, H. -7/3/47
MAUDLING, Maj. John -
6/7/45
MAUDLING, P. -1/21/46
MAUKER, Allen - 4/15/47
MAULDING, James R.-
4/8/48
MAULDING, Presely -
7/22/48
MAVERICK, Samuel-
endnote 1
MAXWELL, Nicholas -
2/4/46; 12/24/46; 1/5/47;
4/15/47
MAY, A. J. - 2/13/47
MAY, Gibson - 2/27/47;
6/2/47
MAY, John - 4/8/48
MAY, Joshua - 2/13/47
MAY, Mrs M.A. R -7/15/46
MAY, Mary A. - 10/9/47
MAYFAN, Larkin -11/19/45
MAYFIELD, J. S. - 3/2/43;
3/9/43
MAYLIE, M. Saunders -

8/8/46
MAYO, Wm. - 8/20/42
MAYS, John - 4/3/44
MAYS, Wm.-1/14/43; 7/31/44
MC FARLAND, S. H.- 10/9/47
MC CONNELL, Jas. G.- 4/8/48
MCADAMS, William - 8/20/42
MCANEAR, Alex - 7/3/47
MCANEAR, John H.- 6/5/44
MCANEAR, Samuel - 7/3/47
MCANIER, Mrs Elizabeth - 7/27/43
MCANIER, John -10/9/47
MCANIER, Mary- 7/27/43
MCBRIDE, Rev. C.- 4/15/47
MCBRIDE, Charles - 7/3/47
MCCALL, David - 7/6/43; 7/1/48
MCCARDLE, A.-1/21/46
MCCARLEY, G. W. - 4/8/48
MCCARLEY, Robert - 7/15/48
MCCARRINACK, Hardy - 7/6/43
MCCARTNEY, B.H.- 7/15/48
MCCARTY, E.C. - 7/3/47
MCCARTY, J. H. (see also McCarty John H.) - 5/29/44
MCCARTY, John H. - (see also McCarty J. H) 2/23/43
MCCARTY, Joseph - 4/15/47; 1/8/48
MCCARTY, M.S. - 7/15/48
MCCARTY, William -

7/12/45
MCCASLAND, J.D. F - 4/15/47; 10/9/47
MCCLENDON, Jackson - 1/14/46
MCCLISH, James -1/14/43
MCCLOSKEY, J.J.-1/21/46
MCCLOSKEY, John - 8/8/46
MCCLURE, A.B - 3/2/43
MCCLURE, W.M[S.?]. - 8/7/44
MCCLURE, W.S. - 10/15/42; 6/15/43; 6/29/43; 10/14/43; 1/13/ 44; 7/3/44; 7/10/44;1/23/45; 1/30/45; 2/6/45; 5/13/45; 10/9/47
MCCONAL, William - 11/26/42
MCCOREY, Wilson - 3/25/48
MCCORMACK, Hardy - 12/9/43
MCCORMICK ,Cyrus - endnote 28
MCCOWAN, James - 10/10/46
MCCOWN, Roger - 1/14/43
MCCOWN, William - 8/20/42
MCCOY, Ephraim D -4/8/48
MCCOY, James - 3/16/43
MCCRACKIN, Ovid - 7/6/43
MCCRORRY, James - 1/5/47
MCCRORRY, John - 1/5/47
MCCRORY, Samuel -7/1/48
MCCROURIE, James - 7/3/47
MCCRURY, James - 10/9/47
MCCUISTON, John C -

12/11/47
MCCUISTON, William - 12/11/47
MCCULLEN, Theodotia M.- 5/29/44
MCCULLOUGH, Capt. H.R. - 1/15/48; 7/1/48
MCCULLOUGH, Sam - 7/3/44
MCCURLEY, George W.- 4/24/44; 7/3/44
MCCURLY, Jn.- 7/20/43; 1/13/ 44; 2/20/45
MCDONALD, A.W. (see also McDonald, Alex) 5/13/45; 11/19/45
MCDONALD, Alex (see also McDonald, A. W.) 1/23/45
MCDONALD, Charles - 2/13/47
MCDONALD, DR. H. - 3/9/44
MCDONALD Henry G. - 3/25/48
MCDONALD, Thomas - 2/13/47
MCDONALD, V.- 10/10/46
MCDONALD - (first name not given)-5/19/47
MCDONALL, Dan'l. - 10/7/43
MCDUFFIE, John - 2/13/47
MCFARLAND, J.- 2/5/48
MCFARLAND, James M. Dr.- 5/13/45; 7/15/48
MCFARLAND, Robert - 10/9/44
MCFARLAND, S. H. - 4/29/48; 6/24/48

MCFARLAND, W. S.- 2/19/48
MCFARLANE, A.W.- 5/29/44
MCFARLANE, B.C.- 5/29/44
MCFARLANE, Jacob - 12/9/43
MCFARLAN[D?], S.M [H.?]- 8/8/46
MCFARLIN, William - 4/6/43; 6/2/47
MCGARRAH - 11/6/47
MCGARRAH, Col.- 10/23/47
MCGARRAH, Capt. - 3/13/47
MCGEE, Newman - 3/2/43
MCGILL, Anderson - 7/3/47
MCGILL, James - 7/3/47
MCGONIGAL, J. C.- 6/22/47; 6/30/47 10/9/47; 2/19/48; 2/5/48; 4/29/48; 6/24/48; 7/22/48
MCGOWAN, James - 2/12/48 MCGOWAN, S.K. - 4/1/47; 4/8/47; 8/7/47; 10/16/47
MCGUIRE, G.- 7/3/47
MCHAM, Jerrit - 4/8/48
MCHENRY, Henry - 7/17/47
MCINTOSH, James - 10/17/46
MCINTYRE (no first name given)- 3/13/45
MCK BALL, William - 3/23/43
MCKAY, Daniel, B.- 8/8/46
MCKAY, M - 10/17/46

MCKEAN, (first name not given) --9/21/43
MCKEE, Alexander - 7/26/45
MCKELLER ,Archibald. - 2/6/47; 2/13/47
MCKENNI, Mrs. M.- 1/13/44
MCKENZIE, Abner (see also McKinzie, A.H).- 8/20/42
MCKENSZIE, Charles - 7/15/46
MCKENZIE, Rev. J. W. P. - 3;6; 11/ 26/42; 12/10/42; 1/21/43; 11/2/43; 5/29/44; 1/9/45; 12/5/46; 12/5/46; 6/22/47; 12/18/47; 6/17/48; 7/22/48; endnote 9
MCKENZIE, Sam'l B. - 7/6/43; 1/14/46; 8/7/47
MCKENZIE, William K.- 6/17/48
MCKINLEY, P.S.- 8/7/47
MCKINNEY, Hon. A - 7/17/47
MCKINNEY, Collin - 5/13/45
MCKINNEY, Daniel - 2/13/45
MCKINNEY, Edwin - 10/17/46
MCKINNEY, J.A. (see also McKinney, John A.)- 6/7/45; 6/14/45; 7/5/45
MCKINNEY, John A.(see also McKinney, J. A)- 4/6/43; 10/28/43; 5/31/45
MCKINNEY, Miss Marsha - 7/17/47

MCKINNEY, William - 8/8/46
MCKINZIE, A.H. (see also McKinzie, Abner)- 8/20/42
MCKNIGHT, William - 10/15/42
MCKOWN, Robert P - 10/17/46
MCKULLER, William- 7/15/48
MCLAIN, James A.-4/8/48
MCLAUGHLIN, Henry - 7/15/46
MCLAUGHLIN, Joseph - 7/15/46
MCLAURIN, James - 7/15/48
MCLOUGHLIN, Joseph - 10/9/47
MCMAHON, TROTTER AND PEARSELL -10/15/42
MCMILLAN, H. - 7/15/46
MCMILLAN, Hiram - 12/19/46
MCMILLAN, Dr. L. B. - 10/9/47
MCMILLEN, B.L.- 4/8/48
MCMINN, John - 4/6/43
MCMULLEN, James - 10/17/46
MCNEALY, Friar - 2/13/47
MCNEIL, Jesse - 7/15/48
MCPETERS, Jonathan - 10/9/44
MCPHERSON, Charles T. - 3/23/43
MCPHERSON, Capt. J. H.- 4/8/48
MCRAE, Colon D.- 12/5/46

324

MCRAE, Robert, -12/5/46
MCRAE, William L.- 12/5/46
MCREE, Nancy L. - 10/10/46
MCREYNOLDS, James - 4/8/48
MCRORY, John . - 3/11/48
MCSPADIN, W.B. - 7/6/43
MCSROREY, Wilson-1/8/48
MCWRIGHT, (no first name given)-7/15/46
MEADOW, Richard - 4/22/47
MEADOWS, J. J.- 7/6/43
MECHEM, Joel - 2/13/47
MEEK, John - 10/1/42, 10/15/42
MEES, James - 7/3/47
MELTON, A.G.- 5/11/43; 3/6/45
MERCER, Charles Fenton - 8/21/44; 3/27/47
MERCHANT, Berry - 1/5/47
MEREDITH, William - 4/22/47
MERREAL, C.- 5/29/44
MERRICK, James C. - 2/13/47
MERRILL, Benj. -7/31/44
MERRILL, D - 10/17/46
MERRILL, David - 1/14/46
MERRILL, Everly C.-11/2/43
MERRILL, Wm. - 8/20/42
MERVEN, John -11/19/45
METHERLY H. - 2/6/47
METHERLY Thomas. - 2/6/47
METHIAS, Mawry - 4/8/48
MEYERS, D. - 2/23/43; 2/13/45
MEYERS, D. L. - 7/17/47
MEYERS, N.T. - 7/17/47
MILES, A.- 5/29/44
MILES, F . -3/25/48
MILHOLLAND, R.W.- 10/30/44
MILLER, Andrew, - 1/14/46
MILLER, E. R.- 2/13/45; 6/16/47
MILLER, James B.- 7/29/48
MILLER, Martin G. - 7/3/47
MILLER, Nicholas - 2/13/47
MILLER, R. G. (see also Miller, Richard G.)- 9/17/42; 3/9/44; 8/7/47; 3/11/48
MILLER, Richard G. (see also Miller, R. G.)- 12/17/42; 12/10/42; 10/21/43; 11/19/45; 6/9/47; 8/5/48
MILLER, Sarah E. -3/11/48
MILLER, T. H.- 4/8/48
MILLER, W.G. - 7/15/48
MILLER, Wm. G.- 5/29/44
MILLER, Z. B. - 4/17/44; 3/11/48
MILLER, Col. Zach - 9/18/47
MILLER, -11/6/47
MILLHIN, George - 5/18/43
MILLHOLLON, Bartholomew -12/11/47
MILLICAN, Elijah -2/6/45
MILLIGAN (first name not given)- 10/15/42
MILLIGAN, William - 1/5/47
MILLIKIN, Sarah - 4/3/44

MILLS, EDWARD - 2/13/47
MILLS, HON. JOHN T.-
8/27/42; 9/3/42; 2/23/43;
3/23/43; 4/6/43; 4/20/43;
9/28/43; 4/24/44; 8/7/44;
12/26/44; 5/13/45; 5/30/45,
6/7/45; 6/28/45; 1/21/46;
6/10/46, 6/17/46, 7/8/46;
3/6/47; 4/15/47; 6/22/47;
11/27/47; 12/11/47;
1/15/48; 7/8/48
MILLS, Robert -10/9/44
MILLSTEAD, John - 5/8/44
MILLWEE, W.H.- 8/5/48
MILNER, Thomas W.-
8/8/46
MIM (first name not given) -
2/4/43
MIM[M?]}S, Gideon -
4/15/47; 2/12/48; 4/8/48;
8/20/42; 1/28/43; 1/13/44;
1/14/46
MITCHELL, Alexander -
1/8/48
MITCHELL, Col. D.- 6/2/47
MITCHELL, E. H. - 5/29/44;
7/3/44
MITCHELL, H.- 4/8/48
MITCHELL, Joseph G -
7/17/47
MITCHELL, M.M.- 8/8/46
MITCHELL, Mrs. Mary -
8/8/46
MITCHELL, R .P.- 5/13/45
MITCHELL, Smith -
10/24/46
MITCHELL, Wm. S. -
7/20/43; 1/13/44; 7/31/44
MITCHELL (first name not
given) -7/31/44
MITCHELL SMITH & -
2/20/47
MITOWER, A[bram]. -
5/29/44; 10/30/44; 2/6/45;
12/24/45; 2/27/47
MOBLY; Meyers - 4/8/48
MOFFETT, John - 10/9/47
MOLLETT, Hohn L. -1/8/48
MONCEY, Jeremiah -
5/13/45
MONE, J. W. -3/27/47
MONK, J. - 5/29/44
MONK, Jeremiah -3/27/47
MONKHOUSE, J. - 7/3/44,
7/26/45
MONKHOUSE, John - 7/1/46;
10/10/46; 7/3/47
MONROE, Joseph -11/19/45
MONTAGUE, Daniel -
10/15/42; 8/7/47
MONTAGUE, (no first name
given) - 11/6/47
MONTGOMERY, Elizabeth
R. - 4/15/47
MONTGOMERY, J. J (see
also Montgomery, Jackson)
- 2/4/46; 10/24/46; 2/20/47
MONTGOMERY, J. R. -
4/8/48
MONTGOMERY, Jackson
(see also Montgomery, J.) -
5/13/45; 10/23/47;
MONTGOMERY, John J. -
8/8/46
MONTGOMERY, L. M.-
7/3/47
MONTGOMERY, Mary A. -
10/9/47

MONTGOMERY, T.S.- 10/10/46
MONTGOMERY, W. T. (see also MONTGOMERY, William T.) - 2/4/46, 6/26/44, 10/24/46; 2/20/47
MONTGOMERY, William T (see also Montgomery, W. T.)-9/17/42
MONTGOMERY, BARNETT & CO -3/20/47; 0/2/47
MONTGOMERY,(no first name given) 11/6/47
MONTIEW, S. - 5/29/44
MOONEY, Edward - 2/13/47
MOONS, Uriah - 8/20/42
MOORE, Abel -1/14/43
MOORE, Alfred - 1/14/46
MOORE, Allison - 7/1/46
MOORE, Amanda -11/20/44
MOORE, B. -11/ 26/42; 5/13/45
MOORE, Curtis - 2/6/45
MOORE, Mrs. E. B.- 10/17/46
MOORE, Elizabeth - 7/1/46
MOORE, Rev. Ephraim D. - 3/16/43; 7/3/44; 10/10/46; 2/6/47; 7/3/47
MOORE, G.B.- 10/10/46
MOORE, Isaac - 11/2/43; 3/9/44; 8/21/44; 5/13/45
MOORE, J. C.- 2/5/48
MOORE, J.P. -6/10/48
MOORE, James -1/14/43
MOORE, John G. -5/29/44; 8/21/44; 1/23/45; 7/3/47; 7/22/48
MOORE, Joseph P.- 1/13/ 44
MOORE, Joshua - 11/2/43; 3/9/44
MOORE, L. P [V.?]- 4/15/47
MOORE, L.V.- 11/2/43; 3/9/44; 5/29/44; 10/2/44
MOORE, Levin - 5/13/45
MOORE, Mary [Jane]- 3/9/44; 2/6/47
MOORE, Miles - 10/17/46
MOORE, Parker - 10/9/47
MOORE, R. P -3/9/44
MOORE, Samuel -11/19/45
MOORE, Thomas - 2/13/47
MOORE, West -3/9/44
MOORE, Whitfield - 3/9/44
MOORE, Wm. H, - 4/6/43
MOORE (first name not given)-5/19/47
MOORE, Dr. -5
MOORES, Charles Col.- 7/24/44
MOORES, Elizabeth - 2/6/47
MOORES, William- 2/6/47
MORAN, William H - 11/11/43;11/19/45
MORE, B.D.-11/19/45
MORE, Edward - 2/13/47
MORGAN, Charles - 10/9/47; 3/11/48;
MORGAN, G. W - 6/3/48
MORGAN, Isaac- 6/30/47; 1/8/48
MORGAN, Dr. J. P.- 7/8/48
MORGAN, J. F.- 7/6/43
MORGAN, James - W 6/9/47
MORGAN, John - 12/31/42; 10/10/46; 7/3/47

MORGAN, Joseph - 10/15/42
MORGAN, Joshua - 12/31/42
MORGAN, Mary F. -9/24/42
MORGAN, Peter -9/24/42
MORGAN, S.B.(see also Morgan, Sam and S.C.) - 5/13/45
MORGAN, S. H. (see also Morgan, Sam and S.B.) - 8/14/44; 6/10/46; 7/1/46; 7/15/46; 10/24/46; 6/22/47; 8/7/47; 10/30/47
MORGAN, Samuel (see also Morgan, S.B. or S. H) - 5/29/44
MORGAN, Simpson H. - 2/12/48
MORGAN, Dr. W. N. -7/3/47
MORGAN, W. J. F. - 8/14/47
MORGAN, William - 4/15/47
MORGAN & CLARK - 5/13/45, 7/15/46MORGAN,YOUNG & - 3/6/47
MORPHIS, J. M.- 4/8/47
MORPHIS, James - 1/5/47; 12/18/47; 7/1/48
MORREY, Daniel - 2/13/47
MORRILL, Amos - 10/15/42; 12/8/43; 4/13/43; 11/4/43; 1/13/ 44; 9/11/44; 10/9/44; 1/9/45; 2/6/45; 2/20/45; 7/26/45; 11/19/45; 6/10/46; 6/22/47
MORRIS, D. - 4/9/44
MORRIS, Daniel - 11/5/42
MORRIS, James - 7/15/48

MORRIS, John - 10/17/46
MORRIS, Jonathan - 7/3/44
MORRIS, Joseph - 4/3/44; 1/14/46
MORRIS, Mary - 2/27/47
MORRIS, Thomas J.- 10/10/46; 12/19/46
MORRISON, D. W.- 11/19/45; 2/13/47
MORRISON, F. 2/27/47; 6/2/47; 6/16/47
MORRISON, James P.- 7/3/47
MORROW, Bethel C. - 7/26/45; 1/8/48
MORROW, C.B.- 4/8/48
MORROW, Cicero - 2/13/47
MORSE, Charles Denny - endnote 1
MORSE, William - 1/14/43
MORTON, Cynthia - 11/4/43
MORTON, John - 10/15/42; 10/29/42; 12/10/42;12/17/42; 1/14/43; 11/4/43;
MORTON, R. - 6/3/48
MORTON, Rufus - 11/4/43; 7/3/44; 5/30/45; 6/28/45; 8/2/45; 11/23/45; 1/21/46; 4/15/48
MORTON, William - 4/8/48
MOSES, Henry Philip - 2/13/47
MOSESHOUSE, James - 1/7/46
MOSLEY, Daniel - 2/13/47
MOSLEY, S. F.- 8/8/46; 8/7/47
MOSLEY, Samuel F.-

11/19/45; 6/22/47
MOSLEY, Lieutenant - 6/17/46
MOSS, Miss Hester - 7/3/47
MULLENS (no first name given)- 10/16/44
MULLIGAN, James - 4/22/47
MULLIGAN, Thomas M.- 7/3/47
MULLINS, B. W.- 10/10/46
MULLINS, Booker.- 10/9/47; 12/11/47
MULLINS, Sarah- 7/17/47
MULLINS, T.B.- 1/23/43
MULM, A. L. - 11/13/47
MURPHY, Dubart -10/10/46; 10/9/47
MURPHY, James -12/17/42
MURPHY, Mary -12/17/42, 7/6/43, 5/13/45
MURPHY, Thomas G - 2/11/46;4/22/47-
MURRAY, J.-7/1/48
MURRAY, MAY - 10/2/44
MURRAY, RICHARD S.- 7/26/45
MURRAY & LATIMER - 7/1/48
MURRELL, John A. - 8/7/44
MURRIN, John -4/8/48
MUSEY, (first name not given). -3/11/48
Musgrove, J. J.-6/5/44; 10/9/44; 5/19/47
MUSGROVE S. W - 2/5/48
MUSGROVE Mr. (first name not given)-12/5/46
MUSGROVE & VERNOY - 5/1/44

MYERS, Aaron -11/19/45
MYERS, Miss Charlotte - 7/3/47
MYERS, D.- 4/17/44
MYERS, Gibson Dr. 10/28/43
MYLOR, Chas.- 5/29/44

N

N. R. HARLAND & CO - 6/16/47
NAIL, Mrs Anne - 2/13/47
NAIL, Liuccinder - 7/17/47
NAKCISSA, Jouett, - 12/3/45
NALL, James - 5/1/44; 7/3/47
NALL John - 10/2/44, 12/3/45
NALL Joseph - 6/19/44, 10/2/44
NALL, Miss Livia - 4/22/47
NALL Martin G.- 5/13/45; 7/26/45; 12/3/45; 4/15/47
NALL Wm.- 7/3/44
NALL, Robert - 7/26/45, 4/15/47
NANCY, slave -12/19/44; 12/26/44
NANTZ, Drury - 10/7/43
NASH, -7/1/48
NATHAN, slave - 1/5/47;
NEAL, G.W.–10/2/47
NEAL, Mathias G. - 10/9/47
NEAL (first name not given] 11/20/44
NEEDHAM, Lewis - 4/6/43,

8/9/45
NEELY, Samuel - 10/7/43, 7/26/45
NELSON, John E [M?]- 7/26/45
NELSON, John M -11/27/44
NELSON - 6/3/48; 6/10/48
NETHERY, Robert -1/8/48; 4/8/48
NEUGENT, Jacob L. -1/8/48
NEVILL, Alexander - 7/20/43; 10/7/43; 1/13/ 44; 7/31/44; 5/13/45; 5/30/45; 6/28/45; 8/2/45; 11/23/45; 1/21/46;12/12/46
NEVILL, Samuel C.- 4/8/48
NEWBERN, Sarah —5/8/44; 11/27/44; 5/31/45
NEWBE[O or U?]RN, Thomas J. -10/7/43; 5/8/44; 10/2/44; 11/27/44; 2/6/45; 5/31/45
NEWBORN, Thomas J. - 7/3/47
NEWBURN, Thomas J.- 4/8/48
NEWCOMBE, William - 4/15/47; 7/3/47
NEWELL, Isaac J.,- 8/8/46
NEWLAND, John S.- 4/8/48
NEWLAND, Wm. H. - 3/20/44
NEWSON, Letey - 4/8/48
NEWTON, Hervy -2/13/47
NEWTON, William M. - 10/9/47
NICHOLSON, Elizabeth - 8/27/42
NICHOLSON, John J. -

8/27/42
NICKERSON, John J.- 5/29/44
NICKLE, Roland - 7/1/46
NIDEVER, John - 3/23/43
NITT, Isaac - 4/15/47
NOLAN, John -9/21/43
NOLIN, Lewis -3/23/43
NORMAN, John - 4/15/47; 10/9/47
NORRAL, L. - 4/8/48
NORRIS, James - 4/15/47
NORRIS, John H. - 7/17/47
NORRIS, Joshua - 7/17/47
NORTHINGTON, Marshall W. -10/14/43
NORTON, D.O.- 11/6/47
NORTON, David O. - 6/15/43; 5/29/44; 7/24/44; 10/2/44
NORVILLE, S.G - .7/15/48
NORWOOD, George -7/15/46
NOTT, J.- 5/29/44
NOVEL, S.G.- 10/16/47
NOWELL, I. J.- 10/2/44
NUGENT, John - 7/3/44
NUNN, Julian L - 10/9/47
NUNN, William - 7/22/48
NUTT, George W. - 2/20/45

O

O. LEWIS & CO - 10/16/47
O'NEAL, James - 10/15/42; 12/10/42
OAKCHIST, Chareston - 7/17/47
OCHILTREE, Judge -

11/20/44; 12/26/44; 7/1/48
ODELL, Steven -7/15/46
ODLE, Joel - 4/8/48
ODLE, Joseph -1/8/48
OFSPRING, John- 10/10/46
OGDEN, Abraham - 9/28/43
OGDEN William D -11/7/46
OGLE, David - 2/13/47
OLDHAM, H. F.- 2/13/47
OLERHLSON, William M.- 7/26/45
OLGESBY, (no first name given)- 4/3/44
OLIVER, J - 7/6/43; 4/8/47; 8/21/47; 4/22/48
OLIVER, John -8/8/46; 10/17/46; 2/12/48
OLIVER, Minerva Ann - 8/27/42
OLIVER Sarah Ann R. - 8/8/46
OLIVER & CHATFIELD - 4; 5/12/47; 7/10/47; 6/3/48
ONEAL, W.P.- 7/6/43
ONSTOT; Griffin - 1/28/43
ONSTOT John,- 8/5/48
ORR, Rev. Green - 1/28/43; 1/14/46
ORTON, B.B.- 7/6/43
OSBROOKS, Lewis - 4/8/48
OSBURN, William - 4/15/47; 7/3/47
OSBURN[E}, Bushred W. - 9/3/42; 10/15/42; 10/14/43
OSMAN, John - 4/22/47; 7/17/47
OT [H.?]WELL, John R.- 4/15/47
OTHWELL, John R.- 7/3/47

OUCHETCHYA, Charles - 4/22/47
OURAL, John - 7/3/47
OVERSTREET, James - 2/13/47
OVERTON, Richard - 7/26/45; 11/19/45
OWENS, William- 10/9/47

P

PACE, B. - 2/13/47
PACE, D. K. - 9/3/42, 4/17/44
PACE, Rhoda - 10/2/44
PACE, Urias -9/24/42
PACE & BRO. - 6/3/48
PAGE, W.F.- 2/13/47
PAINE, Bishop Robert - 7/3/47
PAIRAM, James - 5/29/44
PALEW, E. L.- 10/2/44
PALMER, H.S.- 8/8/46
PARAM, Richard - 7/26/45
PARINER, Jno. F.- 4/8/48
PARIS, Thomas H. -1/8/48
PARISH, Henry - 8/7/47
PARISH, Leam - 1/23/45
PARISH, Samuel - 8/7/47
PARK, George S. -12/3/45; 2/4/46; 10/24/46; 2/20/47
PARK, Thomas - 8/8/46
PARK, William A. -10/7/43; 7/3/44; 1/8/48; 2/12/48
PARKER, John H.- 4/22/47
PARKER, Rebecca H.- 10/10/46
PARKER, Westly - 7/6/43

PARKER, (no first name given)- 2/16/43
PARKINSON, Benj.- 1/28/43
PARKS, Charles W. - 1/14/43
PARKS, Mrs. Elizabeth - 1/14/43; 7/3/47; 7/15/48
PARKS, James- 10/10/46
PARKS, William -1/8/48
PARKS, Dr. - 8/20/42
PARLIEN, Maj. Wm..- 1/23/45
PARLIER, Littleton - 10/9/47
PARRIS, Thaddeus - 1/14/46
PARRISH, J. C.- 7/3/44
PARRISH, Wm. D. - 5/13/45
PARVIS, John T.- 7/3/44
PASCHAL, Geo. W - 4/15/48
PASCHAL, S.A Paschal - 4/15/48
PASSON, J. -1/21/46
PATITTIE, N. H - 6/14/45
PATRICK, James - 7/6/43; 1/13/ 44; 4/8/47
PATRICK, Jane - 7/15/48
PATRICK, Susannah- 10/10/46
PATTERSON, Isaac H.- 11/28/46; 4/15/47; 4/8/48
PATTERSON, J. H.-10/9/44
PATTERSON, John -1/14/43; 1/28/43
PATTERSON, Thomas - 7/1/48
PATTERSON, Tilmon - 1/5/47
PATTERSON, Mr. - 7/17/47
PATTERSON & SNIDER - 8/7/47
PATTON, C. R. -8/21/44
PATTON, John - 10/10/46
PATTON, N. B - 6/14/45
PATTON, Napoleon - 11/26/42
PATTON, Samuel B.- 1/13/44
PAUL, Z. M.-11/ 26/42
PAXTON, John -10/14/43
PAXTON, Johnson - 11/5/42
PAXTON, W .J. -1/21/46
PAYNE, Abraham - 2/27/47
PAYNE, Daniel - 4/22/47
PAYNE, Rhoda - 5/29/44
PAYNE (no first name given)- 2/23/43
PEACOCK, John Peacock, - 2/27/47
PEACOCK, William - 1/21/46; 2/27/47
PEAKE (no first name given)- 2/4/43
PEARSON, James - 7/15/48
PEARSON, John T.- 4/6/43
PECK, S.- 8/7/47
PECK, Samuel - 7/6/43, 10/21/43
PEEBLES, Ephraim - 10/28/43
PEG, slave -7/24/44
PENICK, Charles J. -7/3/47
PERKINS, Mrs. Elli - 7/17/47
PERKINSON, B. H.- 4/3/44
PERRIA, William - 7/26/45
PERRIMAN, A.J. - 8/7/47
PERRY, C.B.- 10/10/46;

1/8/48
PERRY, Col. James - 4/8/48
PERRY, Josiah D. - 10/7/43, 4/3/44
PERRY, L. W.- 4/20/43; 4/17/44
PERRY, Rev. Moses - 4/22/47
PERRY, William -12/12/46; 3/20/47
PERRY, William Mrs. - 12/12/46
PERRY, Mrs -3/20/47
PERRY, L. W. & Co. - 2/13/45
PERYMAN, Austin -4/8/48
PETERS, E. M.– 1/16/45
PETERS, Dr. John S. - 3/2/43; 6/8/43; 1/13/ 44; 5/13/45; 7/26/45; 6/17/46; 4/15/47
PETERS, L.- 1/13/ 44
PETERS, Lemeul -1/8/48
PETERS, Richard - 10/10/46
PETERS, Maj. S.M. - 1/14/43; 3/9/43; 9/21/43, 1/16/45, 3/13/45
PETERS, Stephen -7/31/44
PETERS, William - 7/26/45; 12/24/45; 7/26/45
PETERS LOOK &- 3/6/47
PETTEGREEW, James C.- 5/13/45, 11/19/45
PETTIJOHN, Elizabeth- 10/9/47
PETTIJOHN, John D - 3/23/43
PETTUS, Col. Wm. -8/21/44
PETTY, John M. - 10/9/47

PETTY, Nathan - 11/25/43
PETTYJOHN, Jas. G.- 7/6/43
PEYTON, Alexander - 9/21/43
PHILLIPS, A.- 10/17/46
PHILIPS, James - 7/15/48
PHILIPS, William - 7/15/48
PICKENS, B.F. -1/8/48
PICKENS J - 10/17/46
PICKETT, W. M. - 2/19/48; 4/1/48
PICKETT & STEPHENS - 8/7/47
PICKINGS, JAMES - 4/22/47
PICKINS, B.F.-7/3/47
PILLANS, P. J.- 3/13/45; 6/10/46; 10/24/46; 2/13/47; 8/7/47; 11/6/47
PINCHAM, Peter -1/14/43
PINKHAM, Melvin Miles - 10/17/46
PINKSTON, John - 6/14/45
PINTER, Thomas -1/21/46; 7/3/47
PIRKEY, Solomon H. - 1/8/48
PIRTLE, Benjamin - 10/9/47
PIRTLE, Henry - 12/24/45
PIRTLE, William - 10/9/47
PITCHLYN, Susan - 7/17/47
PITCHLYN, Thomas J. - 4/22/47
PLUMMER, Mrs. H. - 2/16/43
POE, Adam T - 3/23/43
POER, A.M. - 6/30/47
POER, M.A. - 10/9/47
POER Solomon - 7/8/46
POINDEXTER, Bartley -

1/8/48
POINDEXTER, Esquire - 1/8/48
POLITE, William - 10/17/46
POLK. William - 6/15/44
POLLARD, George - 10/10/46
POLLOCK , L. J - 10/15/42
PONDER, Mr.-4/8/48
POOR, Eliza - 1/14/46
POOR, Ira S.- 6/15/43, 6/22/43; 4/3/44; 1/14/46; 4/22/47; 2/12/48
POPE, James -1/8/48; 4/8/48; 7/15/48;
POPE, Sarah - 9/17/42
POPE, Thomas -1/8/48
PORTER, Alex L.- 4/22/47
PORTER, B.E. - 10/9/47
PORTER, James M - 10/17/46
PORTER, R.H.-11/20/47; 12/18/47; 6/3/48
PORTER, Robert - 2/4/43
PORTER, William N. - 12/24/45; 6/17/46; 2/27/47
POSEY, Leaden - 1/14/46
POTTEETSR, T. R.H., - 2/13/45
POTTER, Harriet - 8/20/42
POTTER, Mrs. Matilda - 7/3/47
POTTER, Robert - 8/20/42; 9/3/42; 5/18/43; 12/3/45
POTTER, William - 10/10/46
POTTS, Joseph B - 10/17/46
POTTS, Rev. Ramsey - 4/6/43
POTTS, Thomas - 10/17/46

POWEL, Erwin - 4/22/47
POWELL, Isaac J - 8/5/48
POWELL, John M.- 10/10/46
POWELL, Matthew N. - 5/13/45
POWELL, Nathan - 4/15/47; 7/3/47;10/9/47; 1/8/48; 4/8/48
POWELL, O.C.- 4/8/48
POWERS, Michael - 4/22/47
POWERS, Samuel E. -2/6/45; 12/24/45
PO[O?]ER Martin A.- 10/22/42; 11/19/45; 7/8/46; 8/8/46
PREALY, George -11/19/45
PRICE, Henrietta Mary - 4/8/48
PRICE, Elias -4/8/48
PRICE, Elizabeth - 7/15/48
PRICE, John - 1/13/ 44; 10/9/47
PRICE, R.E. - 1/14/46; 10/9/47
PRICE, Richard E.- 4/8/48
PRICE, Robert - 2/4/43; 3/16/43
PRICE, Thomas - 4/15/47
PRICE, William- 10/10/46
PRIESTLY, Catherine W- 10/10/46; 10/9/47
PRINCE, Ann - 10/2/44
PRINCE, Curtis - 4/8/48
PRINCE, Orestes- 10/10/46
PRIOR, John - 1/14/46
PROCTOR, Lucinda - 11/26/42
PROVINE, James -1/8/48
PRUET, Christopher -1/8/48

PRY, Peter - 10/15/42
PRYOR, L. - 10/9/47
PURKIS, John Todd -7/3/47
PUTNAM, B. R.- 7/15/48

R

RAGIN, Caleb - 4/15/47
RAGIN, Gilbert -5; 7/24/47; 7/29/48;
RAGSDALE & WRIGHT - 4/8/47; 6/3/48
RAINES -(first name not given) 5
RAINEY, Mary - 10/9/47
RAINEY, S.D. - 10/9/47; 3/11/48
RAMSEY, John 2/13/47
RANDOLF, Sheriff (first name not given)-5/19/47
RANEY, Stephen D. - 5/19/47; 6/22/47
RANKIN, Thomas -7/3/47
RANSOM, Richard -7/3/47
RATTAN, Thomas - 2/13/47
READ, (first name not given) -1/30/47
RECORD, James C.- 8/5/48
RECORDE, James P.-7/3/47
REDDING, Dr. A. J. -8/7/47; 1/8/48; 7/15/48
REDDING, W. P.- 7/15/48
REED, John - 4/15/47
REED, Joseph - 4/15/47
REED, Mrs. Mary -7/3/47
REED, Miles -7/3/47
REEVES, J. H. - 7/15/48
REILEY, Maj. James - 9/18/47
REILLY, John P. - 10/9/47
REINS, Dr. John W. -1/8/48
REMMINGTON, Mr. - 7/15/48
RENGE, T.O.- 3/11/48
REVERE, W. K.-7/3/47; 4/1/48
REVERE, William - 7/17/47
REYNOLDS, Mrs. Julia A. - 7/17/47
REYNOLDS, Hardin R. - 9/25/47
REYNOLDS, L. M. - 4/22/47
REYNOLDS, L. R. - 8/21/47
REYNOLDS, Lemuel M.- 4/15/47
REYNOLDS, Mrs. P. - 7/17/47
REYNOLDS, R.W.- 8/5/48
REYNOLDS, Reuben W. 8/21/47; 2/19/48
RHOME, H.- 4/15/47
RIBBLE, Adam - 4/1/47
RICE, A. J.- 4/15/47; 8/14/47; 7/15/48
RICE, Elias.- 7/15/48
RICE, L. M.- 4/22/47
RICE, William L.- 7/15/48
RICE, Capt.(first name not given)-5/19/47
RICHARDS, L - 10/9/47
RICHARDS, Martin 4/22/47
RICHARDS, W.G.-7/3/47
RICHARDSON, D. M.- 2/13/47
RICHARDSON, Louis - 4/8/47
RICHEY, James - 2/27/47;

4/15/47; 6/2/47
RICHEY, Mrs. Jane -7/3/47
RIGGS, James M. -6/24/48
RIKER, Daniel - 8/7/47
RIKER, N.M. - 7/17/47
RIKER, Samuel - 8/7/47
RILEY, William - 2/13/47
RINGO ,Peter - 1/5/47;
10/9/47; 3/11/48
RIPLEY, Ambrose.- 7/15/48
RITCHIE, James -1/8/48
ROBBINS, John - 6/9/47;
7/17/47;
8/14/47;10/16/47;7/1/48
ROBBINS, William - 2/13/47
ROBERTS, John - 2/13/47;
6/16/47
ROBERTS, Joseph - 2/13/47
ROBERTS, Joseph H. -
2/13/47
ROBERTS, Judge. -7/10/47
ROBERTSON, Elridge -
4/15/47
ROBINSON, Fontaine -
4/15/47
ROBINSON, Jesse -5/19/47;
7/10/47
ROBINSON, Capt. John -
4/22/47
ROBINSON (first name not given)- 11/6/47
ROBSON, John- 7/15/48
ROGERS, Andrew -1/8/48 .
ROGERS, E. G. - 2/27/47
ROGERS, J. H. - 5/19/47
ROGERS, James - 7/17/47
ROGERS, Gen. James H. -
3/13/47; 6/22/47; 7/3/47;
6/10/48

ROGERS, John K. -1/8/48;
7/15/48
ROGERS, John W. -1/8/48
ROGERS, Lovely - 7/17/47
ROGERS, M.D.- 6/22/47
ROGERS, Dr. R.R. -3/11/48
ROGERS, T. J -5/19/47
ROGERS, Thomas J -
6/22/47
ROHN, Jane - 7/15/48
ROLAND, Samuel - 4/15/47;
ROLAND, Sherrod - 4/22/47
ROLEY, Charles -7/3/47
ROMAN, HOLBROOK & -
7/15/48
ROSS, Alex E.- 4/8/47
ROSS, Capt. S.P. -1/15/48
ROSS, Capt.-7/1/48
ROSSON, William H. -
1/8/48
ROTTER, George -7/3/47
ROWLAND, Burgess G.-
7/3/47
ROWLAND, Thomas M. -
1/5/47;
ROWLETT, Dr. - 9/14/43
ROWLETT, Dr. Daniel -
7/3/47
RUBEN, slave - 6/30/47
RUNNELS, H.A. - 4/29/48
RUSK, James - 10/9/47
RUSK, T..J.- 6/22/47
RUSSE, John.- 7/15/48
RUSSEL, David C. - 4/8/47
RUSSEL, Reddin - 2/27/47;
3/25/48
RUSSEL HOLMES & - 3/6/47
RUSSELL, A. J.- 6/22/47;
7/10/47;2/12/48; 7/1/48;

7/22/48; 7/29/48
RUSSELL, Miss Elizabeth - 6/22/47
RUSSELL, James W -1/8/48
RUSSELL, N.M. - 7/15/48
RUTHERFORD, John A.- 8/5/48
RUTLEDGE, J. S. -1/8/48
RUTTER, William - 7/17/47
RYDER, Miss Mary - 4/15/47; 6/22/47

S

SADLER, C. W.- 2/4/43, 3/13/45
SADLER, Charles W.- 4/8/47
SADLER, James - 3/16/43
SADLER, William S.- 3/13/45
SAIGE, Edward N.-7/3/47
SAMPLE, David - 7/20/43; 3/6/47; 5/5/47
SAMPSON, James Rev. - 11/26/42; 12/10/42; 4/6/43, 6/15/43; 6/22/43; 11/4/43; 3/27/47; -7/3/47; 7/24/47; 7/15/48; end note 15
SAMPSON, William M. - 10/9/47
SANDLER, William -10/9/44
SANDLIN, A. K.- 10/28/43
SANFORD, D.- 5/29/44
SANSAND, Joel M..- 2/5/48
SANTA ANNA, Chief -7/1/48
SARAH - 5/31/45
SARGEANT, Levin S. - 1/14/46
SATTATHITE, Thomas - 6/15/43
SAUNDERS, Clarke - 7/12/45
SAUNDERS, S.- 5/29/44
SAVEGH, J. H.-12/26/44
SAWNS, Israel - 7/15/48
SAWYER, Elias -7/3/47
SAWYER, Horace - 5/29/44
SCANTLING, Fielding - 7/3/47
SCARBOROUGH, D.B.- 7/26/45; 1/14/46
SCARBOROUGH, Winny - 10/9/47
SCHAKLE, Bluford - 2/13/47
SCHALELFORD, Mrs. Mahala F. - 2/13/47
SCHILLEE, I. - 10/17/46
SCHOENOVER, Benjamin - 6/16/47
SCOTT, Charles P. - 4/22/47
SCOTT, John T. - 5/13/45; 4/22/47
SCOTT, Joseph - 10/7/43
SCOTT, N. - 5/29/44
SCOTT, Nehimiah - 10/29/42
SCOTT, Randolf - 8/5/48
SCOTT, Sarah A.- 5/29/44; 10/17/46
SCOTT, Solomon J. - 1/14/43; 7/6/43
SCOTT, William - 7/26/45; 4/15/47; 7/3/47
SCURLOCK, Wm.- 1/28/43; 2/4/43; 5/11/43; 3/2/44; 6/26/44; 11/20/44; 10/10/46; 7/17/47; 10/9/47; 2/12/48

SCURRY, R.- 6/22/47; 2/12/48; 7/22/48; 7/29/48
SCURRY, Thomas. - 6/22/47; 7/10/47; 4/8/48
SCURRY, W.B.- 6/22/47
SCURRY, W.R. - 7/13/43; 12/11/47; 7/22/48
SCURRY, William R.- 1/21/43; 2/4/43; 3/9/43; 3/23/43; 7/27/43; 1/13/ 44; 4/17/44; 12/26/44; 1/9/45; 5/13/45; 7/26/45; 8/9/45; 8/16/45; 1/14/46
SEABBREY, Mrs. W. - 10/17/46
SEAGUE, William -4/8/48
SEALS William- 7/15/48
SEAREY, L.C.- 5/13/45
SEAREY, Merit - 5/13/45
SEAWRIGHT, John - 5/29/44; 1/23/45
SEAWRIGHT, Wm. M.- 5/29/44
SEBRING, R. D.-8/21/44
SEDICUM, F.- 4/15/47
SEED, Campbell - 1/23/45
SEIGHT, John -1/8/48
SELFE, William - 10/15/42; 5/13/45
SELVETER, John - 12/5/44
SETTLE, Anne -3/9/44
SETTLE, Charles C. - 10/16/47
SETTLE, Malcolm [Marcus?] G.- 10/16/47
SETTLE, Marcus G.-3/9/44; 3/27/47; 6/9/47; 6/22/47
SEWARD, R. B.- 10/17/46
SEWELL, Joseph -12/10/42

SEWELL, Richard-11/19/45
SHAFFER, John -5/19/47
SHAFFER, Phillip - 6/19/44
SHANAHAN, James B.–5; 6/5/44; 7/1/48
SHANAHAN'S AND BRIM'S CABINET SHOP -5;
SHANNI [O?]N, James - 4/22/47
SHANNON, Davies - 10/9/47
SHANNON, James - 3/13/45
SHANNON, Jefferson - 7/6/43
SHANNON, T. J.- 7/1/46; 7/3/47; 8/7/47; 10/9/47
SHANNON, Thomas - 7/31/44; 6/30/47
SHANNON, Samuel - 2/13/47
SHANNON, - 11/6/47
SHARKEY, J. S.- 2/20/45
SHARP, Ann. -2/6/47
SHARP, Anthony -1/14/43
SHARP Jesse M. - 1/13/ 44; 10/30/44
SHARP, John . - 2/6/47
SHARP, M.T.- 11/25/43
SHARP, William L.- 11/23/45; 1/14/46
SHAW, Eli - 4/8/48
SHAW, James Esq. - 10/29/42
SHEARER, Sarah A.- 4/15/47
SHEARER, Spencer -4/3/44; 7/3/44; 4/15/47; 7/3/47
SHECK, A.- 7/3/44
SHEEKS, Adam - 2/23/43
SHELL, James M – 8/14/44

SHELTON, E. J.- 1/14/46
SHELTON, H. W. - 3/6/45
SHELTON, Harvey- 11/6/47
SHELTON, Horatio - 2/13/47
SHELTON, Irv - 10/9/47
SHELTON, J. - 2/ 24/44
SHELTON, Jesse -10/29/42;
11/26/42; 12/10/42; 1/14/43;
6/8/43; 12/16/43; 1/13/44;
4/3/44; 9/25/47; 10/9/47
SHELTON, John -7/3/47
SHELTON, J. & Co. -2/24/44;
3/20/44; 5/29/44; 11/20/44;
2/6/45; 6/28/45
SHEPPARD, Lorna - endnote 1
SHEPPARD, Marion -1/8/48
SHERMAN, Maj. Gen.-
Sidney- 6/28/45
SHERRY, Barnard - 7/15/48
SHIDMORE, Mary - 10/2/44
SHIELDS, Robert - 2/13/47
SHOOK, Daniel - 4/22/47;
1/8/48
SHOOK, Rev. J. H.- 10/2/44
SHOOK, Jefferson -4/22/47
SHOOK, Mrs. Mary A.-
10/9/47
SHOOK, Rev. Nathan.-
12/5/44;11/19/45
SHORT, D. M.- 9/18/47
SHREWSBURY, Charles -
10/7/43
SHULTS, John W.- 8/8/46
SILKWOOD, Mrs. P. -
10/15/42
SIMMONS, E. L. - 4/22/47
SIMMONS, James - 10/7/43
SIMMONS, Thomas-1/8/48
SIMMS, C.H. - 10/7/43

SIMMS, S. W. - 8/28/47
SIMONS, Benjamin S. -
5/15/44; 11/19/45
SIMONS, Catherine -
5/15/44
SIMONS, Elisha -7/6/43;
1/13/ 44; 3/2/44; 10/9/44
SIMONS, John P.- 5/15/44
SIMONS, Jones - 7/6/43
SIMONS (no first name
given) -10/28/43
SIMPSON, Miss Isabella -
3/27/47
SIMPSON, Col J. A.- 8/7/47
SIMPSON, James A.-
6/22/47
SIMPSON, John -6/26/44;
4/15/47; 4/8/48
SIMS, Bradford -1/8/48
SIMS,[see also Syms]
Charles -12/11/47
SIMS, Mrs. E.A - 1/23/45
SIMS, F.M. - 5; 4/1/47;
4/8/47
SIMS, George K.-10/9/47;
4/8/48
SIMS, Maj. James W.
8/20/42; 5/11/43; 8/7/44;
6/9/47; 12/11/47; 7/29/48
SIMS, Mary -1/21/46
SIMS, Mat F. - 10/7/43;
1/13/ 44; 5/29/44; 5/31/45
SIMS, R. J.- 6/9/47;
7/17/47; 3/11/48
SIMS [see also Syms],
Reddick J.-1/21/46
SIMS, S. W.-7/3/47 ;10/2/47
SIMS, Samuel W.-3/20/44;
8/7/44; 8/9/45; 12/24/45;

1/14/46; 2/4/46; 6/17/46;
4/8/47; 4/8/48; 7/15/48
SIMS, Col. W. - 8/20/42;
7/24/44;
SIMS, Wm.- 7/6/43
SINCLAIR, Charles -11/19/45
SINCLAIR, Daniel --6/19/44
SINCLAIR, Samuel M.- 7/6/43
SINCLEAR, Clayton C .-
10/9/47
SINGLETON, A. J.. - 7/15/48
SINLANGH, John- 10/10/46
SKERRY, Richard.- 7/15/48
SKIDMORE, A. - 11/6/47
SKIDMORE, Abram - 8/5/48
SKIDMORE, William - 8/5/48
SKINNER, James - 1/14/46
SKINNER, Livingston -
10/15/42
SKINNER, Thomas - 5/4/43
SLACK, Alfred- 3/2/43
SLACK, Amos P. - 2/13/47
SLATON, W.L - 10/17/46
SLAYTON, H.S. - 3/6/45;
3/13/45
SLAYTON, Lucy- 7/6/43
SLAYTON, Sanford G -
12/31/42
SLEAN, Thom. E.- 1/23/45
SLINGSAND, William -4/9/44
SLOAN, A.M.- 1/14/46
SLOAN, B.S. - 3/2/43
SLOORS, Joshua - 1/14/46
SMATHERS, Isaac -1; 3/13/45;
7/3/47; 4/8/48
SMIDER, Joseph -11/19/45
SMILEY, Edward - 5/13/45
SMILEY, Samuel - 10/9/47;
1/8/48

SMITH, Alex - 2/13/47
SMITH, Andrew B. - 2/19/48
SMITH, Mrs Ann - 2/27/45;
2/27/45; 2/13/47
SMITH B. B [P.?] -7/10/47
SMITH, B.P.- 6/21/45;
6/10/46; 6/22/47;10/30/47;
7/22/48; 7/29/48
SMITH, Burrel P - 1/15/47;
6/17/48;6/22/47; 4/8/48;
7/1/48
SMITH, C.M. -7/3/44
SMITH, Caleb -10/9/44;
10/10/46
SMITH, Cannon -2/13/45
SMITH, Charlotte - 1/5/47
SMITH, Drury J.- 4/8/48
SMITH, E.M. -10/15/42;
11/26/42; 5/11/43; 7/6/43;
10/7/43; 12/9/43; 1/13/ 44;
4/9/44; 12/26/44; 1/9/45;
11/19/45; 12/3/45;
12/24/45; 4/1/47; 7/3/47;
10/9/47; 7/22/48
SMITH, Mrs. Elizabeth -
1/21/46
SMITH, F.- 5/29/44
SMITH, F. P.- 7/26/45
SMITH, Francis -- 10/15/42
SMITH, George - 7/31/44; -
10/24/46; 2/13/47
SMITH, Harriet E. M. -
1/8/48 SMITH, Henry -
12/12/46; 1/5/47
SMITH, Isaac - 5/13/45
SMITH, J. J. -11/20/47
SMITH, J. W. - 8/8/46
SMITH, Jackson,-7/3/47
SMITH, James - 6/8/43,

7/24/44; 8/21/44; 10/9/44; 1/16/45; 2/13/45; 5/13/45; 1/14/46; 5/5/47; 7/15/48
SMITH, James Reves - 7/26/45
SMITH, Jesse A.-6/5/44
SMITH, John - 10/9/44; 12/24/45; 1/5/47; 7/15/48
SMITH, Joseph J. - 10/2/44; 6/22/47; 10/9/47
Smith, M - 10/9/47; 7/15/48
SMITH, Martha Ann - 11/26/42; 5/4/43
SMITH, Mrs. Mary.-1/14/43; 2/6/45; 7/26/45, 11/19/45
SMITH, Mitchell - 7/3/44
SMITH, Philip J.-2/27/45; 1/8/48
SMITH, Mrs. Polina - 5/13/45
SMITH, R.E. D.- 10/10/46
SMITH, Reeves - 4/8/48
SMITH, Robert - 10/15/42; 2/27/47; 7/3/47
SMITH, Russell P.- 7/15/48
SMITH, S.F.- 3/13/45
SMITH, Sampson - 12/17/45; 12/19/46
SMITH, Samuel -7/6/43; 1/23/45; 2/13/45; 5/13/45; 6/24/46; 1/5/47; 1/8/48
SMITH, Scott - 3/23/43
SMITH, Solomon -1/8/48
SMITH, Sterling - 2/4/46
SMITH, T.F.- 2/4/43, 5/29/44
SMITH, Col. Thom.-1/28/43; 4/6/43, 4/24/44;6/2/47; 7/15/48
SMITH, William - 4/15/47; - 6/30/47; 10/9/47
SMITH, Wilson - 7/17/47
SMITH, Capt(first name not given)- 5/19/47
SMITH, Major - 2/27/47
SMITH, Mrs. (first name not given)- 7/24/44
SMITH & DARNELL - 7/3/44
SMITH & MITCHELL - 7/8/46, 10/24/46; 2/20/47
SMYTHE, George W. - 3/18/48
SNELL, James F.-1/8/48
SNELL, I. [J.?]F.- 4/15/47
SNELL, Stephen -1/8/48
SNIDER, J. J.- 4/8/47; 7/17/47
SNIDER, PATTERSON & - 8/7/47
SOULS, Hannibal Seth - 5/13/45
SOUTH, Benjamin - 11/27/44
SOUTH, C.- 1/23/45
SOUTH, Charles - 10/15/42; 10/7/43
SOUTH, E.- 10/17/46
SOUTH, S. - 5/29/44
SOUTH, Wm.- 10/7/43; 5/29/44; 1/23/45
SOUTHLAND, Mary - 8/8/46
SOWELL, Joseph - 2/4/43
SOWELL, Louisa - 2/4/43
SOWELL, Richard - 2/4/43, 6/14/45
SPAIN, L. D.- 4/3/44
SPARKS, A.. - 7/15/48
SPARKS, Wm.- 10/15/42
SPEAD, Mr. - 2/13/47

SPEAK, John W.- 5/13/45
SPEAKS, John D - 1/8/48
SPEAKS, Thomas- 5/29/44
SPEARS, Mrs A. -11/19/45
SPEARS, Dickson - 4/15/47; 7/3/47
SPEERS, Isaac - 4/8/48
SPENCE, James P.- 10/17/46
SPENCER, Ambrose Jr.- 10/29/42; 3/23/43
SPENCER, Arthur - 4/15/47
SPENCER, Asbury, - 3/13/45
SPENCER, Oliver H. - 1/14/43; 10/7/43; 1/13/44; 7/3/44; 1/14/46; 7/3/47
SPENCER, Shers -4/8/48
SPILLMAN, Daniel - 7/26/45
SPRED, Mattias - 2/13/47
SRYGLEY, Joseph - 8/12/48; 8/19/48
ST. CLAIR, Charles - 1/14/46
STAATS, Nelson J - 7/1/48
STACEY, John S.-7/3/47
STACY, B.F.- 4/15/47
STAITS, Nelson -2/3/44
STALCUP, Joseph - 10/7/43
STALCUP, Rhesa - 10/7/43
STALCUP, William - 1/14/46
STALEY, Joseph - 4/15/47
STALLINGS, Abraham - 7/6/43; 7/3/44; 4/15/47
STANDERFER, Jesse M – 4/3/44, 5/29/44
STANDS, MATHER & - 1/23/45
STANFIELD, J. W. O - 10/29/42
STANFILL, Ervin - 10/9/47
STANLEY, F.-1/18/43

STANLEY, Fermay - 10/15/42
STANLEY, John D - 6/28/45
STANLEY, Wright - 4/8/47
STARK, Amos - 2/13/47
STARKES, Aaron - 5/8/44
STARKES, Susan - 5/8/44
STARKEY, J.S.– 3/6/45
STARKEY, John Maj. - 1/16/45; 3/6/45
STARKS, C.- 11/19/45
STARNS, Aaron - 1/8/48; 4/22/48
STARNS, Thomas R.- 4/22/48
STARRETT, James - 2/13/47
STATS, MATHER& -10/9/47
STEARNS, Aaron. - 7/15/48
STEEL, John - 10/9/47
STEINSON, John - 5/29/44
STELE, John - 10/17/46
STEPHEN A.F.- 10/10/46; 4/8/48
STEPHENS, Mrs. A. F.- 7/15/48
STEPHENS, George- 10/10/46; 2/13/47
STEPHENS, Isham - 4/6/43
STEPHENS, Jr. John,- 7/6/43
STEPHENS, Jno. - 5/8/44
STEPHENS, Nancy - 5/8/44
STEPHENS, Thomas -7/3/47
STEPHENS, Priscilla - 9/24/42
STEPHENS, PICKETT & - 8/7/47
STEPHENSON, Alexander - 4/15/47; 4/8/48
STEPHENSON, George H -

4/15/47
STEPHENSON, James - 9/28/43; 6/10/48
STERING, Robert D.- 7/26/45
STERLING, James A. - 7/6/43
STERNE, A. - 10/29/42
STEVENS, John -9/24/42
STEVENSON, Elizabeth - 4/3/44
STEVENSON, Thomas - 7/1/48; 7/29/48
STEVENSON, Rev. William endnote 7
STEWART, Bluet -9/25/47
STEWART, Chas. P. -4/13/43; 6/3/48
STEWART, James- 10/10/46
STEWART, John - 4/15/47; 10/9/47
STEWART, Joseph S. - 7/15/48
STEWART, M.- 7/1/46
STEWART, W.W. - 7/31/47
STEWART, Wiley - 4/22/47
STEWART, William P - 10/17/46
STEWART, Willis - 12/24/45
STILES - (no first name given)- 11/6/47; 8/19/48
STILES, H.- 4/17/44
STILES, John - 8/20/42; 5/11/43; 7/20/43; 11/11/43; 1/13/ 44; 7/3/44; 7/31/44; 3/13/45; 5/30/45; 6/28/45; 7/1/46; 8/8/46; 10/24/46; 12/24/46; 1/5/47; 6/9/47; 10/16/47; 1/8/48; 3/11/48; 7/1/48
STILL, G. W.- 3/20/44

STILL, Joseph - 2/13/47
STINSON, David - 6/22/47
STINTHAM, Thomas B.- 7/3/47
STOCKDALE, F.S. - 8/12/48
STOCKELAGER, P.A.- 4/15/47
STONE, John - 2/13/47
STONEHAM, Henry - 4/6/43
STONEHAM, James - 4/6/43; 3/9/44
STONEHAM, Polly - 3/9/44
STONEHAM, William - 4/6/43
STONHAM, Mrs. Ellen - 10/9/47 -
STONHAM, James -7/3/47
STORES, J.- 5/29/44
STORS, Augustus - 7/6/43
STORS, Capt. Joshua - 7/3/47; 10/9/47
STOUT, Mary Halen - 11/19.45
STOUT, Henry -10/28/43
STOUT, Sarah Isabella, - 11/23/45
STOUT, Matilda - 11/19/45;11/23/45
STOUT, William B. – 8/20/42, 9/10/42, 10/1/42; 10/15/42; 11/5/42; 2/4/43; 2/23/43; 3/16/43; 4/6/43; 4/27/43; 5/11/43; 6/8/43; 7/20/43; 7/27/43; 10/21/43; 10/28/43; 11/4/43; 1/13/ 44; 3/9/44; 5/8/44; 6/26/44; 7/31/44;10/16/44;10/30/44; 12/26/44; 2/13/45; 3/6/45; 5/30/45; 14/45;6/28/45;

8/2/45; 8/9/45; 11/19/45;
11/23/45; 12/3/45; 1/21/46;
6/10/46; 7/1/46; 12/19/46;
2/6/47; 1/8/48; 2/5/48;
2/12/48; 4/8/48; 7/22/48
STOUT,(first name not given)
- 11/6/47
STOVALL, Warren -7/3/47
STOVER, John Sr. - 2/13/47
STOWALL, F. W. - 4/22/47
STOWELL, Willard - 6/2/47
STREET, M.B.-4/8/48
STREME, John - 5/13/45
STRENZIL, John - 8/5/48
STROUD, A - 4/3/44
STROUD, Allen -10/10/46; 7/3/47
STUART, C.-11/19/45
STUART, Charles -1/14/43
STUART, Edward - 8/27/42
STUART, John -5/4/43; 7/3/47
STUART, Polly - 8/27/42
STUART, Samuel - 12/17/45
STUART, W. P. - 5/29/44
STYLES, John - 2/12/48
SUBLEN, Capt G.A.- 4/15/47
SUBLETT, Valentine M.-
8/21/44
SUBR[L?] ETT, V. M. -
3/16/43
SULIVA[N?}S, Adam -
4/15/47
SULLES, John B. - 7/6/43
SULLIVAN, Adam -1/14/43
SULLIVAN, Michael -
10/17/46
SULY, J.- 10/2/44
SURE, William - 4/15/48
SUTHERLAND, N.T.- 8/8/46;
4/15/47
SUTHERLAND Dr. - 6/24/46
SUTTLE, M.G. - 10/9/47
SUTTON, J. Edgar - 7/3/47
SUTTON, Thomas. - 7/15/48
SUTTON, Capt. -7/1/48
SWANSON, J. - 2/6/45
SWIGLEY, Joseph - 11/28/46
SYMS, Charles- 10/9/47
SYMS, Reddick J.- 10/16/47

T

TABIN, Anson -7/3/47
TABOR, Dr.- 4/17/44
TAGGLE, Jackson - 3/2/43
TALBOT, A.G.- 4/15/47
TALBOTT, Miss A. E.-
4/8/48
TALBOTT, Mrs Isabel -
10/17/46
TALBOTT, John A. - 4/6/43;
6/2/47;-11/13/47
TALLBOT, Rev. N.M.-
10/17/46
TALTON, John F..- 7/15/48
TANKEARSLY, Elizabeth, -
2/6/47
TANKERSLEY, Richard -
11/19/45; 1/14/46; 4/15/47
TANNER, J. R. - 10/15/42
TANNER, (first name not
given) - 1/30/47
TANSOR, E. S.- 6/24/48
TARRANT, Gen. E .H. -
8/20/42; 10/29/42; 1/14/43;
2/23/43; 3/9/43; 6/8/43;

7/20/43; 2/3/44; 9/11/44;
4/3/44; 12/12/44; 1/16/45;
5/13/45; 6/7/45; 8/8/46;
7/10/47; 7/17/47; 10/16/47
TATE, James M. 7/15/48
TAYLOR, Anderson - 4/6/43
TAYLOR, Claxson, J.-
2/13/47
TAYLOR, E.-
7/15/46;10/17/46
TAYLOR, James F - 8/7/47
TAYLOR, John - 3/13/45
TAYLOR, Joseph P.- 1/14/46
TAYLOR, Nancy - 10/2/44
TAYLOR, R. H - 2/13/47
TAYLOR, R. M.- 10/17/46
TAYLOR, Samuel - 12/5/44
TAYLOR, William . -
1/28/46; 2/11/46
TEAGUE, William - 10/17/46;
7/3/47
TELARK, William - 10/17/46
TENSEY, Posey - 7/15/48
TERREL, John - 6/3/48
TERRY, John - 10/17/46;
7/3/47; 7/15/48
THOM, Rev. David K. (see
also Thomas, David and
D.K.) - 7/6/43; 1/13/ 44
THOM, James - 7/17/47
THOM, John -1/8/48
THOM, Josiah - 10/9/47
THOM, Willson - 12/3/45
THOMAS, Andrew -12/10/42
THOMAS, D. K.- 5/29/44
THOMAS, David - 11/11/43;
2/13/47
THOMAS, Elijah - 4/15/47
THOMAS, F.M..- 7/15/48

THOMAS, Henry - 7/3/47
THOMAS, J. D. -
4/17/44;2/27/47
THOMAS, J. F.- 5/29/44
THOMAS, J. H.- 12/26/44
THOMAS, Jesse E. - 2/13/47
THOMAS, John - 1/21/43;
2/13/47; 2/27/47; 7/3/47
THOMAS, Marrion - 7/3/47
THOMAS, Richard -
1/21/43; 2/27/47
THOMAS, T.M.- 4/8/48
THOMAS, Warfield- 4/8/48
THOMAS, Washington -
4/15/47
THOMAS, William, -
4/15/47
THOMAS, Miss - 4/8/48
THOMPSON, Capt E. J -
8/7/47
THOMPSON, E.- 5/29/44
THOMPSON, Edward -
10/2/44
THOMPSON, Ervin - 6/9/47
THOMPSON, Franklin -
4/15/47
THOMPSON, Giles -
10/17/46; 4/22/47
THOMPSON, J. Esq. -
10/17/46
THOMPSON, James A.-
2/13/47
THOMPSON, Miss Jane -
7/3/47
THOMPSON, Lucretia -
5/29/44
THOMPSON, Nancy -
2/13/47
THOMPSON, W.C.-

10/15/42; 1/23/45; 7/26/45
THOMPSON, William -
2/13/47; 4/22/47; 7/17/47
THOMPSON, (first name not given) 4;5
THRESHER, Franklin - 2/13/47
THROCKMORTON John A.- 5/15/44
THROCKMORTON, Malinda 5/15/44
THROCKMORTON, Robert M.- 2/13/47
THROCKMORTON, W. E. - 5/15/44
THRURSTON, A. S.- 6/22/47
THRUSTON A.J.- 6/22/47
TIGERT, William - 2/27/47
TIMMINS (first name not given)- 3/23/43
TIMMS, V. B.- 10/30/47
TIMS, Vincent B.- 10/9/47
TINER, Jesse - 4/22/47
TINNAN [see also Tinnin], L. W.- 1/13/44; 3/20/44; 5/29/44; 7/12/45; 12/24/45
TINNAN,[see also Tinnin] William - 1/13/44; 7/12/45; 12/24/45
TINNAN, Major - 2/4/43
TINNI[A?]N, William - 2/27/47
TINNIN, L. W.(see also Tinnan) - 2/27/47; 4/15/47
TINNIN, W. H.- 4/15/47
TISDALE, John - 9/25/47
TITUS, A.J.-6/15/43; 3/9/44; 11/12/45; 12/17/45; 2/4/46; 6/17/46; 7/1/46; 8/8/46;

7/1/46; 10/17/46; 8/14/47; 8/21/47; 12/11/47; 2/12/48; 6/10/48; 7/1/48; 7/22/48
TITUS, A. Jackson - 6/22/47; 6/30/47
TITUS, Andrew - 8/20/42
TITUS, James Col.- 3/9/44; 12/5/46
Titus, .Rebecca -12/5/46
TITUS, T.F.- 3/9/44
TODD, Elizabeth - 4/9/44; 7/24/44; 1/16/45; 12/17/45; 1/7/46; 1/14/46; 6/17/46; 7/1/46; 12/12/46; 12/25/47; 1/8/48; 7/29/48; endnote 16
TODD, Wm. S. - 7/6/43; 11/27/44; 4/15/47; 6/22/47; 6/30/47; 2/12/48
TOLER, Richard H. - 2/20/45; 5/31/45
TOLER, Judge - 8/7/44
TOLLETT, Wesley - 3/23/43
TOM, slave -7/27/43; 12/16/43; 5/15/44
TOMBERLIN, James - 3/27/47
TOMILSON, J. W – 11/2/43
TOMILSON, Richard - 1/21/43
TOMILSON, Wm.- 7/3/44
TOMILSON, (first name not given) -12/10/42
TOMPSON, William - 10/17/46
TONALISSON. R - 9/21/43
TONE, George N. - 7/3/47
TOPP, William - 8/8/46
TOWERS, Catherine - 1/21/46 TOWERS, George

W.-1/21/46
TOWNEY, John R.-10/9/44
TOWNEY, R. - 1/14/43
TRAVELSTEAD, Anthony.- 7/15/48
TRAVELSTEAD, Lt. E.C. - 7/15/48
TRIGG, Edward S.- 10/9/47
TRIGG, Jas.-1/21/46; 12/11/47
TRIMBLE, Henry -11/ 26/42; 5/8/44; 2/19/48
TRIMBLE, Mrs. Martha- 2/13/47
TRIMBLE, William - 1/21/46;12/11/47
TRUESDALE, J. N.- 5/29/44
TUCKER, Jefferson -10/9/47; 1/8/48;7/15/48
TUGGLE, Jackson - 4/15/47
TUMEY, John R.- 1/13/ 44; 7/3/44; 1/14/46
TUNE, David J.- 4/15/47
TUNE, William - 10/9/47
TUNS, Mrs. Rebecca - 10/17/46
TURGGLE, John H.. 7/15/48
TURGLE, Jackson - 10/9/44
TURLEY, William - 4/15/47; 7/3/47
TURNBULL, Robert - 4/22/47
TURNBULL, Turner B.- 4/22/47
TURNER, George -1/21/46
TURNER, H. J - 12/26/44
TURNER, Henry - 2/13/47
TURNER, Jas.- 1/21/46
TURNER, John - 4/3/44; 2/13/47

TURNER, M.M.- 10/10/46
TURNER, Mariah -1/21/46
TURNER, Mary - 8/20/42
Turner S.S. -12/12/46; - 4/1/47
TURNER, Samuel S.- 9/11/44; 11/12/45; 1/14/46; 1/21/46
TURNER, Sarah - 8/20/42; 3/9/44
TURNER, William.- 5/29/44; 2/13/47
TURNER,(first name not given) - 6/14/45; 11/19/45
TURNEY, Moses - 2/13/47
TUS, Tumaggas - 10/9/47
TUSHKAHIMITAH- 4/22/47
TWEEDY, John - 9/11/44
TWEEDY, Thompson- 10/10/46
TYRES, Elisha - 2/13/47
TYERS, Robert M - 6/24/48
TYSON, J. W.- 7/1/46
TYSON, John - 2/4/46

U

UNDERWOOD, Ann - 2/13/47
UNDERWOOD, Elijah C.- 2/13/47
UPSHAW, A. M. M. - 3/11/48
UPSHAW, E. W.- 8/5/48
URGUHART, Allen - 10/15/42; 2/23/43; 4/17/44; 5/29/44; 5/13/45; 8/29/46; 10/10/46

URSERY, J. E.- 4/15/47
URY, Ennis - 6/7/45; 1/21/46
USRY, James - 7/3/47

V

VADEN, James B. -6/19/44
VAN VAUGHT, John 10/9/47; 12/11/47
VAN POOL, Obed.- 2/13/47
VAN ZANDT, Hon. Isaac - 7/10/47; 10/9/47; 11/6/47
VAN DYKE, Mr. (first name not given)- 11/20/44
VAN DYKE, Mrs. Delia F.- 7/3/44
VAN DYKE, John - 12/19/44; 12/26/44
VAN DYKE , L. D. -12/16/43; 5/29/44;11/27/44; 2/20/45; 5/13/45; 11/19/45; 1/21/46; 8/8/46; 12/5/46; 1/8/48
VAN DYKE , Nancy - 12/19/44; 12/26/44
VANLANDINGHAM, Alfred - 4/15/47
VAUGEY, Andrew - 8/27/42
VAUGHN, Mont - 8/20/42
VAUGHT , J. B.-7/3/47
VEACH, Capt.- 6/3/48; 7/1/48
VERLON, G. W.-1/8/48
VERMILLION, H. F. - 7/17/47
VERNOOT [Vernoy?], C. - 3/13/45
VAN DYKE, John - 12/19/44,
12/26/44; 10/9/47
VERNOY, C. - 4/27/43
VERNOY, G.-7/3/47
VICE, Nathaniel - 4/15/47; 7/3/47
VICKENS, Eli - 10/17/46
VICTOR, Palangue, Mons.- 4/15/47
VIELLIERS, Henri H - 2/13/47
VINCENT, Thomas - 7/26/45; 1/14/46
VINING, J.- 10/10/460
VINING, Will. W.- 3/27/47; 6/22/47; 11/20/47
VINING, W. H.- 8/8/46; 11/28/46;12/19/46
VINING, Thomas. L.- 1/14/46;1/21/46; 2/4/46
VINING, Jephtha . -2/6/47; 1/15/48
VINING, John Jones - 4/17/44, 7/3/44
VINING, Martha - 6/22/47
VINING, Thomas - 3/27/47
VINING, W.H.- 8/7/47; 10/9/47;1/15/48; 4/1/48; 6/24/48
VINING, Wade H. - 12/10/42;12/17/42; 1/14/43; 6/29/43; 7/6/43; 10/14/43; 5/1/44; 7/3/44; 12/5/44; 1/23/45; 2/13/45; 2/6/45; 5/13/45; 12/17/45; 2/4/46; 2/27/47; 6/22/47
VINING, William W - 8/8/46
VINING, Capt. - 6/8/43
VISE Nathaniel - 11/28/46
VISER [see Visor], Peter -

1/14/43
VISOR [See Viser], Peter - 6/3/48
VIVIAN, James - 2/13/47
VON BIBBER, H.- 10/30/47
VOWEL, William -1/8/48; 3/11/48;4/8/48

W

W. P. Dickson & Co.-4
WABB, D.- 2/13/47
WADE, E. B.- 7/17/47
WAFER, Elizabeth - 3/23/43; 6/8/43; 10/2/44
WAGAN, D.A.- 5/29/44
WAGGONER, Daniel - 7/3/47; 10/9/47; 1/8/48
WAGLEY, Joseph - 10/10/46; 4/8/48
WAGLEY, Simeon - 1/14/43
WAIT, Pator - 10/15/42
WAITS, James - 10/7/43; 1/13/ 44; 4/3/44; 10/9/44; 7/26/45; 4/8/48
WALDEMAN, F.- 7/31/47
WALDEMAN, Mrs - 7/31/47
WALDEN, J.- 5/29/44
WALDING, Greenberry - 4/6/43
WALDRIP, Andrew B - 2/13/47
WALDRIP, William - 2/13/47
WALIS, James - 11/19/45
WALKER, Albert G.- 2/13/47
WALKER, Benjamin - 10/15/42
WALKER, Elias F.- 9/11/44

WALKER, Geo. W - 4/22/47
WALKER, J. - 8/19/48
WALKER, J. H.- 7/3/44
WALKER, J. W. 7/15/48
WALKER, James- 10/10/46; 1/8/48
WALKER, Jesse - 2/6/45, 12/17/45
WALKER, Lewis H -6/30/47
WALKER, R.- 5/29/44
WALKER, Richard .- 6/22/47
WALKER, Samuel N. - 10/9/47
WALKER, Miss Sarah - 8/8/46
WALKER, Sussanah - 4/8/47
WALKER, Thomas - 10/17/46; 2/13/47
WALKER, District Attorney. 7/10/47
WALKER, Dr. - 2/4/46, 6/17/46
WALL, D. W.- 10/17/46
WALL, John - 4/15/47
WALL, Leonard -10/9/44
WALL, Preston H.- 2/13/47
WALLACE, Alfred -11/19/45
WALLACE, Andrew M.- 10/10/46
WALLACE, Ernest - endnote 1
WALLACE, Jesse - 10/15/42
WALLACE, Joseph M. - 4/22/47
WALLEN, James - 11/25/43
WALLER, Bowen - 10/16/47

WALLER, (first name not given) - 11/6/47
WALLIS, E. P. - 8/14/47
WALLIS, Miss Mary J. - 10/9/47
WALLIS, William M.- 10/9/47
WALSH, C. M.- 8/8/46
WALTON, Gen. Charles - 5/13/45
WALTS, James - 7/3/44
WARD, A.M.- 4/15/47
WARD, Augustus -7/3/47
WARD, H.- 10/9/47
WARD, Dr. J.- 11/23/45;4/22/47
WARD, J. C.- 2/13/47
WARD, J. J.- vi; 7/6/43
WARD, James J –vi; 1/28/43; 2/4/43; 4/6/43; 5/11/43; 7/6/43; 9/28/43; 5/1/44; 3/13/45; 3/13/45; 5/31/45; 11/19.45; 1/14/46; 4/15/47;10/9/47; 4/22/48 7/15/48; 7/29/48
WARD, Sr., Jas. J.- vi; 6/28/45
WARD, Jr , Jas. J.- vi; 6/28/45
WARD, John - 7/6/43
WARD, Jordan - 10/10/46; 4/8/47
WARD, Mrs. Levion - 7/6/43

WARD, Mathias - 5/13/45; 4/8/48
WARD, Morris -11/11/43; 7/3/44
WARD, Nancy Ann - 5/31/45

WARD, Samuel - 7/17/47
WARD, Sarah - 4/15/47
WARD, T. J. - 1/28/43
WARD, Thomas William - 5/30/45
WARD, W. R .D.-12/10/42
WARD, William - 2/27/45, - 3/6/45;10/9/47;11/20/47;0/30/47
WARD, Dr. (first name not given)- 7/5/45; 11/23/45; 1/9/45
WARD (first name not given)- 9/14/43
WARDLAW ,David. - 3/16/43; 2/6/47
WARDLAW, James - 2/6/47
WARDLAW, John . - 2/6/47
WARDS, W.- 5/29/44
WARE, Andrew - 7/6/43
WARE, J.- 5/29/44
WARE , Dr. John - 12/10/42; 1/14/43; 5/11/43;7/6/43; 11/19/45; 10/17/46; /29/47; 7/22/48
WARE Joseph - 10/17/46
WAREHOOF, James W -11/26/42
WARFIELD, C.A.- 6/7/45
WARFIELD, Charles -7/1/48
WARHOP, Mrs. Elizabeth - 7/3/47
WARHOP, J.- 7/3/44
WARNER, William - 8/8/46'
WARREN, James C. - 2/20/45
WARREN, J H - 10/9/47
WARREN, James F.-7/3/47; 1/8/48

WARREN, Col.-7/3/47
WARRIN, Abel- 10/17/46
WARSON, Jane- 10/10/46
WASHBURN, Thomas S.- 10/17/46
WASSON, A.-7/3/47
WASSON, Hiram -7/3/47
WATERS, Daniel -3/27/47
WATERS, E. Bateman - 3/27/47
WATKINS, R. R.- 1/28/43
WATSON, A.D.- 6/7/45
WATSON, Colman –10/28/43
WATSON, Cookman -2/19/48
WATSON, Evan T. -9/25/47
WATSON, James - 1/14/43
WATSON, John M.- 3/2/43; 4/6/43
WATSON, M.- 10/2/44
WATSON, Ordera - 7/27/43
WATSON, Rhoda - 1/14/43
WATSON, Solomon - 8/7/44
WATSON, Thomas - 10/16/47
WATSON, William A. - 10/17/46
WATSON, first name not legible. - 1/23/47
WAUHOP, James W. - 12/5/44
WEATHERED, Lafayette - 7/24/47
WEATHERED, M. W. - 6/22/47; 8/28/47
WEATHERED, Mrs. Martha (Maum) - 9/10/42; 1/28/43; 6/15/43; 6/22/43; 6/29/43; 2/17/44; 6/5/44; 12/10/45; 3/13/47; 6/30/47; 4/1/48; end note 16

WEATHERED, Robert - 1/14/43; 5/18/43; 11/27/47; 12/4/47; endnote 16
WEATHERSPOON, Martha- 11/ 26/42
WEATHERSPOON, Wiley - 5/13/45
WEAVER, Samuel. - 6/10/46
WEBB, A.W.- 10/10/46; 7/3/47
WEBB, Alexander W.- 10/9/44; 5/13/45; 10/10/46
WEBB, John - 10/9/47
WEBB, S.-7/3/47
WEBB, Samuel- 10/10/46
WEEN David R.- 5/29/44; 10/2/44
WELCH, Daniel -1/8/48
WELCH, John - 6/15/43
WELCH, William. - 3/11/48
WELLBORN, C. C. 3/11/48
WELLBORN, Charles C. - 9/11/44; 6/17/46; 8/15/46; 11/7/46; 5/19/47; 7/15/48
WELLBORN, K. A. - 8/20/42; 8/8/46
WELLBORN, William - 11/26/42; 7/3/44; 5/19/47
WELLS, Isaiah - 8/8/46; 8/7/47;12/11/47; 1/8/48; 4/22/48
WELLS, Oliver - 2/13/47
WELLS, Rev. R.- 2/13/47
WELLS, Rezin - 2/13/47
WELLS, Parson - 2/13/47
WELLS, Maj.- 7/3/44
WELSH, Wm.- 1/14/46
WENNER, Martin - 10/9/47
WESERN, Thomas E.-

6/16/47
WEST, Adelia F. - 5/29/44
WEST, Edward - 10/22/42;
1/14/43; 5/111/43; 6/8/43;
7/27/43; 5/29/44; 11/27/44;
1/23/45; 5/20/45; 1/7/46;
1/14/46; 2/4/46; 2/1/46;
10/24/46; 11/28/46; 2/20/47;
2/27/47;4/22/47; 8/7/47;
10/9/47; 11/20/47; 1/8/48;
1/15/48; 1/29/48; 3/18/48;
4/1/48; 7/22/48; 7/15/48
WEST ,George- 4/22/47
WEST, J. W. -1/8/48
WEST, John - 8/16/45;
4/1/47; 4/8/47; 4/15/47
WEST. Jonathan - 11/19/45
WEST, Terrel- 10/10/46;
4/8/48
WEST, Sheriff (first name not given) - 4/13/43
WEST, (first name not given) - 5; 7/6/43
WESTERMAN, Benjamin - 4/15/47
WESTERMAN, William F. - 4/8/48
WESTERMAN, Wilson -1/8/48

WETMORE Alex - endnote 3
WETMORE George - endnote 3
WEVER, John W.- 2/3/44
WHEAT, Josiah P. -11/ 26/42
WHEAT, Joshua - 7/3/44
WHEAT, Wm.- 7/3/44
WHEAT, (first name not given) -4/8/48
WHEELER, Richard C.-

10/9/47
WHEELER, Thomas - 2/13/47
WHITAKER, Robert - 4/15/47; 10/9/47
WHITAKER , Sarah - 10/28/43
WHITAKER , Willis 10/28/43
WHITE, Benjamin - 9/25/47
WHITE, Harvey - 2/23/43; 7/31/44
WHITE, Jefferson - 11/19/45
WHITE, Joseph - 10/9/44
WHITE, Lewis L - 10/9/47
WHITE, Robert. - 1/23/47
WHITE, Sam'l D.- 7/6/43; 2/17/44; 5/1/44; 12/24/45; 10/10/46; 7/3/47
WHITE, Thomas J.- 5/29/44; 7/26/45; 8/8/46
WHITE, Mrs. V.P.-1/8/48
WHITE, W. W.- 4/8/47; 7/3/47
WHITE, William T. - 10/9/47; 2/13/47
WHITEMAN, David W.- 10/10/46; 10/9/47
WHITEMAN, J - 4/8/48
WHITESIDE, W. H - 4/15/47
WHITESIDES, Mrs. Florinde 4/15/47
WHITESIDES, John M.- 7/26/45
WHITESIDES, Wm. N. - 1/14/46; 4/15/47
WHITFIELD, Green W. - 4/24/44

WHITFIELD, Wright W. - 4/24/44
WHITING, Samuel C.- 6/3/48
WHITINGTON, William T.- 7/3/47
WHITNEY A.H.- 10/17/46; 4/22/47; 4/22/47
WHITLEY, Alex - 2/13/47
WHITLEY, Mills - 5/4/43
WHITNEY, Jason - 5/4/43
WHITSON, Mrs. Esther.- 7/15/48
WHITTAKER, Robert -7/3/47
WHITTENBERG, Iraneus - 2/13/47
WHITTINGTON, William T. - 1/8/48
WHITTLESEY, J. A. - 1/14/46
WHORTON, Margaret - 4/6/43

WICKS William P., Jr.- 10/17/46
WIDEMAN, Edward - 9/10/42; 2/23/43; 5/29/44
WIDEMAN, T.- 5/29/44
WIGGONS, Mrs. Mary,- 4/8/48
WILDER, Capt E. M - 8/7/47
WILEY, A.P. - 8/12/48
WILEY, Malvina - 1/14/43
WILEY, William E. - 12/10/42
WILKINS, George - 4/15/47; 10/9/47
WILKINS, John O.-10/7/43; 10/9/44; 1/23/47
WILKINS, Mrs. Mary -1/8/48
WILKINS, Sarah C.- 2/3/44
WILKINS, William - 10/9/47

WILKINSON John; - 4/3/44; 5/13/45; 5/26/47; 7/3/47
WILKINSON, Mrs. Mary- 7/15/48
WILLIAMS, A.A.- 2/6/45
WILLIAMS, A.G.-5/29/44
WILLIAMS, A.N.- 4/15/47; 7/3/47
WILLIAMS, Alex - 7/26/45
WILLIAMS, David - 6/9/47; 4/8/48
WILLIAMS, Rev. E. B.- 7/3/47
WILLIAMS, Mrs. Elizabeth - 7/3/47
WILLIAMS, Ephraim - 11/26/42
WILLIAMS, George 2/13/47
WILLIAMS, H. L.-3/9/44; 3/20/44; 5/29/44
WILLIAMS, J. J. - 10/29/42; 10/16/47; 12/18/47; 4/8/48
WILLIAMS,, J. M.- 2/13/47
WILLIAMS, J. R.-7/3/47
WILLIAMS, James- 1/23/47; 2/13/47
WILLIAMS, Jesse - 2/13/47
WILLIAMS, John. - 7/26/45; 11/19/45; 1/23/47; 2/13/47
WILLIAMS, Jonas W. - 10/24/46; 11/28/46
WILLIAMS, Joseph - 4/15/47
WILLIAMS, Larena - 3/9/44
WILLIAMS, M.G.- 10/17/46
WILLIAMS, Philip - 2/13/47
WILLIAMS, Philip G.-7/3/47
WILLIAMS, Reuben W.- 10/2/44; 7/17/47

WILLIAMS, Robert - 8/20/42; 11/18/43; 7/1/46; 10/10/46
WILLIAMS, S.A.- 4/22/47
WILLIAMS, Stirling E. - 4/3/44; 5/29/44
WILLIAMS, Thomas - 10/9/47
WILLIAMS, V.- 10/10/46
WILLIAMS, W. M - 2/27/47
WILLIAMS, W. S. H.- 1/14/46
WILLIAMS, Warner - 1/15/47
WILLIAMS, Warren C.- 5/29/44
WILLIAMS, William - 10/10/46;2/13/47; 4/8/47; 4/22/47; 8/7/47; 2/19/48; 8/5/48
WILLIAMS, William M. - 12/31/42; 1/14/43; 7/6/43; 3/2/44; 3/9/44; 3/20/44; 2/6/45; 3/13/45; 6/7/45; 12/24/45
WILLIAMS, (first name not given) - 2/23/43
WILLIAMSON, Clark - 4/15/47; 4/22/47; 7/3/47; 10/9/47
WILLIAMSON, Isaac C.- 2/6/45; 2/27/47
WILLIAMSON, J.P. - 1/28/43
WILLIAMSON, John - 2/13/47
WILLIAMSON, Joseph - 4/8/47
WILLIAMSON, Matilda - 7/26/45
WILLIAMSON, William M - 4/8/47
WILLIAMSON & BOWERMAN 3/23/43; 10/9/44; 2/6/45
WILLISON [Willson], Thomas

-11/26/42; 5/11/43; 7/27/43; 12/9/43; 2/3/44; 6/26/44; 1/23/45; 11/23/45; 11/12/45; 7/3/47
WILLOW, Louisa - 8/27/42
WILLS, J. W.- 10/10/46
WILLS, HAMP - 4/22/47
WILLS, Maj - 4/3/44
WILLSON, Thomas, - 1/5/47
WILSON, David - 10/17/46; 2/13/47; 4/22/47
WILSON, F. - 4/22/47
WILSON, George - 6/8/43; 1/13/ 44; 5/15/44; 10/2/44; 5/31/45; 11/19/45; 8/5/48
WILSON, H. W.- 5/29/44
WILSON, Hurly - 4/22/47
WILSON, Isaac - 8/20/42; 7/20/43; 1/13/44
WILSON, J. - 5/29/44
WILSON, James - 7/6/43; 3/6/45; 3/13/45; 8/8/46
WILSON, Jason - 11/25/43; 3/2/44; 3/20/44; 5/29/44; 5/31/45; 8/5/48
WILSON, Col. John - 7/26/45; 8/7/47
WILSON, K. - 4/22/47
WILSON, Gen. M.G. - 1/23/45; 7/8/46; 10/17/46
WILSON, Mary -1/21/46; 2/13/47
WILSON, Richard,- 4/15/47
WILSON, Robert - 10/17/46
WILSON, Thomas R. - 4/22/47;4/15/48; 7/1/48
WILSON, William - 2/13/47
WILSON (first name not given), - 4/17/44 6/7/45

354

WILSON, Mrs.(first name not given) - 7/24/44
WILT, Eli W - 2/13/47
WIMS, W. - 7/15/48
WINDEL, Johnson P.-1/8/48
WING, Carrol -1/14/43
WINGATE, Truit -10/9/44
WINLOCK, William H.-1/8/48

WINSLOW, John - 10/9/47
WINSTON, William C. - 4/8/48
WINTER, James - 4/8/48
WINTER, Minerva - 4/8/48
WISE, James - 9/25/47
WITHER John W - 4/3/44
WITHINGTON, William T. - 7/15/48
WITIN, R. M.- 5/29/44
WITT, William - 7/17/47
WOOD, David L.- 2/13/47
WOOD, Col. G.T. - 10/29/42
WOOD, George T. - 6/22/47; 7/17/47; 9/25/47; 10/9/47; 7/1/48
WOOD, James A.- 1/14/46; 2/13/47
WOOD, - 11/6/47
WOOD, DR.- 5/29/44; 1/23/45
WOODARD, (first name not given)- 10/17/46
WOODLAND, James W. - 11/19/45
WOODLEY, John - 10/24/46
WOODROE, N. K. - 1/21/43; 12/3/45
WOODROE, Nancy [see Woodward, Nancy K].-

1/9/45; 11/12/45; 1/5/47;
WOODRO[W]E, Simeon K. - 1/21/43; 1/9/45; 11/12/45; 12/3/45; 1/5/47;
WOODS, Elisha - 2/13/47
WOODS, J. W. - 4/3/44
WOODS, John - 10/10/46; 10/9/47
WOODS, Thomas -10/9/44; 1/23/45; 5/13/45
WOODSWORTH, D.-5/19/47
WOODSWORTH, H.D. - 10/2/47
WOODSWORTH, Henry D. - 6/10/46
WOODSWORTH, M[H?] D.- 7/3/47
WOODWARD, H.G. - 7/17/47
WOOLDRIDGE, Master - 6/15/43; 6/22/43
WOOLERTON, William - 10/28/43
WOOLLIN, Rev. J. C.- 7/3/47
WOOLRIDGE, John R - 3/23/43
WOOLRIDGE, Wm. - 4/29/48
WOOTEN, J.B.- 7/17/47
WOOTEN, James Benj.- 1/14/43; 7/6/43; 7/20/43; 1/13/ 44; 7/31/44; 9/11/44; 12/17/45; 2/21/46;10/23/47
WOOTEN, James - 8/8/46; 8/15/46; 2/6/47; 6/22/47; 2/12/48
WOOTEN, Dr. G. W. - 12/19/46; 2/27/47

WOOTEN, John - 8/12/48
WOOTEN, William - 8/8/46; 1/8/48
WOOTEN, (first name not given)- 11/6/47
WORCESTER, N. - 5/29/44
WORCESTER, S.- 5/29/44
WORKMAN, Mrs. L.F.- 10/2/44
WORTHINGTON, C.- 5/29/44; 10/17/46
WORTHINGTON, Chessly - 4/22/47
WORTHINGTON, Christy - 10/15/42
WORTHMAN, Henry - 2/20/45
WORTHAM, Thomas - 5/29/44
WRAY, L.- 7/31/44
WREN, J.D.- 3/27/47
WREN, Johnson - 11/6/47
WREN, Nicholas - 1/23/45
WREN, W. W.- 1/28/43
WRIGHT, Claiborne - end notes 3; 7
WRIGHT, Fisher - 2/13/47
WRIGHT, G. W. - 3/4/48; 6/3/48
WRIGHT, Geo. W.- 4/6/43; 6/15/43; 6/22/43; 7/6/43; 9/14/43; 12/9/43; 1/13/ 44; 3/9/44; 5/15/44; 12/12/44; 6/7/45; 12/24/45; 12/12/46; 2/27/47; 3/20/47; 12/18/47
WRIGHT, Hardy –endnote 3
WRIGHT, Maj. J.P.- 4/8/48
WRIGHT, James G - 9/10/42; 1/14/43; 5/8/44; 11/27/44; 12/12/44

WRIGHT, Jill –endnote 3
WRIGHT, John M.-11/19/45
WRIGHT, John W - 2/13/47
WRIGHT, T. G. - 8/20/42; 10/29/42; 12/24/42; 2/4/43; 5/11/43; 7/20/43; 12/9/43; 1/13/ 44; 3/20/44; 5/1/44; 6/26/44; 7/3/44; 7/24/44; 7/31/44; 5/30/45; 6/28/45; 7/12/45; 12/24/45; 1/14/46; 6/17/46; 7/1/46; 10/16/47; 12/11/47; 6/3/48
WRIGHT, Thomas - 10/7/43; 1/13/44, 1/23/45; 7/26/45; 11/19/45
WRIGHT Travis G. - 2/27/47
WRIGHT, William - 10/9/47
WRIGHT, Wilson - 6/30/47
WRIGHT, (first name not given) - 6/7/45
WRIGHT & MONTGOMERY - 8/20/42; 1/14/43; 6/26/44; 7/24/44
WRIGHT, Ragsdale & - 4/8/47; 6/3/48
WYATT, Col. P. S - 8/8/46
WYCKUM, Samuel - 1/13/44
WYMAN, Mrs. Martha - 4/15/47
WYNNE, Dr. Robert H. - 2/4/46
WYNN, Capt. William - 12/11/47
WYNNE, W. H. - 4/29/48
WYNNE, William H.- 7/17/47

Y

YARBOROUGH, Jno. O.- 2/13/47

YARBOROUGH, Stephen - 10/9/47
YATES, William - 2/27/47
YEARY, John -3/2/44;, 3/20/44; 5/29/44; 5/31/45
YOUNG, C..S - 8/20/42
YOUNG, Charles -10/28/43
YOUNG, David - 5/13/45
YOUNG, E.- 12/8/43
YOUNG, Mrs. Electa Angelina - 1/16/45
YOUNG, Elijah - 5/29/44; 10/17/46; 4/8/47
YOUNG, F.- 12/17/45; 2/4/46
YOUNG, H.P.- 2/23/43; 7/3/44
YOUNG, Henry . -2/6/47
YOUNG, Col. Hugh F.- 1/14/43; 10/14/43; 1/13/ 44; 3/16/44; 1/16/45; 3/13/47; 4/1/47; 5/19/47; 6/9/47; 7/17/47;10/16/47; 10/23/47; 10/30/47
YOUNG, R - 7/3/44
YOUNG, W.C.- 10/24/46
YOUNG, Wesley. - 2/6/47
YOUNG, William C.- 8/20/42; 3/23/43; 1/28/43; 5/11/43; 5/18/43; 10/14/43; 2/24/44; 4/3/44; 5/1/44; 2/6/45; 5/13/45; 5/30/45; 6/7/45; 7/5/45; 7/26/45; 12/24/45; 1/14/46; 7/1/46; 8/8/46; 11/28/46; 2/27/47; - 6/22/47; 2/12/48; 3/11/48
YOUNG & MORGAN - 3/6/47
YOUNGER, James - 7/24/44

Z

ZACHARY, Alexander - 1/21/46
ZAGAN, James - 5/29/44
ZIMMERMAN, James M.- 2/13/47

Other Heritage Books by Richard B. Marrin:

Abstracts from The Clarksville Standard
(Formerly The Northern Standard*)*
Volume 7: August 6, 1859–May 25, 1861

Abstracts from the New London Gazette*:*
Covering Southeastern Connecticut, 1763–1769

Abstracts from the New London Gazette*:*
Covering Southeastern Connecticut, 1770–1773

Abstracts from The Connecticut Gazette
(Formerly The New London Gazette*):*
Covering Southeastern Connecticut, 1774–1776

Abstracts from The Connecticut Gazette
(Formerly The New London Gazette*):*
Covering Southeastern Connecticut, 1777–1779

Abstracts from The Connecticut Gazette
(Formerly The New London Gazette*):*
Covering Southeastern Connecticut, 1780–July 25, 1782

*A Glance Back in Time: Life in Colonial New Jersey (1704–1770)
as Depicted in News Accounts of the Day*

Going to Court in Texas: Riding the Circuit, 1842–1861

New Jersey During the Revolution, as Related in the News Items of the Day

Passage Point: An Amateur's Dig into New Jersey's Colonial Past

*Runaways of Colonial New Jersey: Indentured Servants,
Slaves, Deserters, and Prisoners, 1720–1781*

Other Heritage Books by Richard B. Marrin and Lorna Geer Sheppard:

Abstracts from The Northern Standard *and the Red River District [Texas]:*
Volume 1: August 20, 1842–August 19, 1848

Abstracts from The Northern Standard *and the Red River District [Texas]*
Volume 2: August 26, 1848–December 20, 1851

Abstracts from The Clarksville Standard
(Formerly The Northern Standard*)*
Volume 4: 1854–1855

Abstracts from The Clarksville Standard
(Formerly The Northern Standard*)*
Volume 5: 1856–1857

Abstracts from The Clarksville Standard
(Formerly The Northern Standard*)*
Volume 6: 1858–1859

*The Paradise of Texas: Clarksville and
Red River County, 1846–1860
Volumes 1 and 2*

Other Fireside Fiction by Richard B. Marrin:

The Retaking of America

www.ingramcontent.com/pod-product-compliance
Lightning Source LLC
Chambersburg PA
CBHW060551230426
43670CB00011B/1774